Policy Change under New Democratic Capitalism

Democratic capitalism in developed countries has been facing an unprecedented crisis since 2008. Its political manageability is declining sharply. Both democracy and capitalism now involve crucial risks that are significantly more serious than those observed in earlier periods. The notion of policy regimes has gained new significance in analysing the possibilities for a post-neoliberal alternative. Policy innovations directed towards an economic breakthrough require both political leadership and a new economic theory. The processes of political decision making have become quite distant from the public realm, and a limited number of economic and political elites exert influence on public policy.

This book examines, from a policy regime perspective, how developed countries attempt to achieve such a breakthrough at critical junctures triggered by economic crises. It initially assesses the nature of the present crisis and identifies the actors involved. Thereafter, it provides an analytical definition of a crisis, stressing that most crises contain within them the potential to be turned into an opportunity. Finally, it presents a new analytical design in which we can incorporate today's more globalized and fluid context.

Hideko Magara is Professor in the Graduate School of Political Science, Waseda University, Japan.

Routledge Research in Comparative Politics

58 Government Accountability and Legislative Oversight
Riccardo Pelizzo and Frederick Stapenhurst

59 Corruption and Legislatures
Riccardo Pelizzo and Frederick Stapenhurst

60 Global Perspectives on the Politics of Multiculturalism in the 21st Century
A case study analysis
Edited by Fethi Mansouri and Boulou Ebanda de B'béri

61 Party Organization and Electoral Volatility in Central and Eastern Europe
Enhancing voter loyalty
Sergiu Gherghina

62 Politics of Religion and Nationalism
Federalism, Consociationalism and Seccession
Edited by Ferran Requejo and Klaus-Jürgen Nagel

63 Deficits and Debt in Industrialized Democracies
Edited by Gene Park and Eisaku Ide

64 Citizenship and Democracy in an Era of Crisis
Edited by Thomas Poguntke, Sigrid Roßteutscher, Rüdiger Schmitt-Beck and Sonja Zmerli

65 Drivers of Integration and Regionalism in Europe and Asia
Comparative perspectives
Edited by Louis Brennan and Philomena Murray

66 Generations, Political Participation and Social Change in Western Europe
Maria T. Grasso

67 The Politics of Think Tanks in Europe
Jesper Dahl Kelstrup

68 The Statecraft of Consensus Democracies in a Turbulent World
A comparative study of Austria, Belgium, Luxembourg, the Netherlands and Switzerland
José M. Magone

69 Policy Change under New Democratic Capitalism
Edited by Hideko Magara

Policy Change under New Democratic Capitalism

Edited by Hideko Magara

Routledge
Taylor & Francis Group
LONDON AND NEW YORK

First published 2017 by Routledge

2 Park Square, Milton Park, Abingdon, Oxfordshire OX14 4RN
711 Third Avenue, New York, NY 10017

Routledge is an imprint of the Taylor & Francis Group, an informa business

First issued in paperback 2018

British Library Cataloguing in Publication Data
A catalogue record for this book is available from the British Library

Library of Congress Cataloging in Publication Data
A catalog record for this book has been requested

ISBN: 978-1-138-20440-9 (hbk)
ISBN: 978-1-138-36599-5 (pbk)

Typeset in Times New Roman
by Wearset Ltd, Boldon, Tyne and Wear

Contents

Notes on contributors vii
Foreword x
Acknowledgements xi

PART I
Introduction 1

1 New models of democratic capitalism and policy regime change 3
HIDEKO MAGARA

PART II
Models of new democratic capitalism 17

2 Crisis, opportunity and democracy in contemporary Europe 19
PHILIPPE C. SCHMITTER

3 The rise of the European consolidation state 27
WOLFGANG STREECK

4 Cost of democracy: changing aspects of modern democracy 47
HIROSHI SHIRATORI

5 Institutional change and regime crisis: a critical viewpoint on neoliberalism 70
TOSHIO YAMADA

PART III
Comparative analyses 89

6 The political-economic implications of de-industrialization with varieties of capitalism: an EU–Japan comparative analysis 91
HIROYASU UEMURA AND SHINJI TAHARA

7 Growth, employment, and social security governance in the EU and Japan 121
KOJI FUKUDA

8 The diversity of the "neoliberal policy regime" and income distribution 139
YUJI HARADA

PART IV
Regime competition in international rivalry and cooperation 169

9 Using neo-functionalism to understand the disintegration of Europe 171
PHILIPPE C. SCHMITTER AND ZOE LEFKOFRIDI

10 From the variety of socioeconomic regimes to contemporary international relations 202
ROBERT BOYER

11 Balance-of-payments constraints, change in income distribution, and economic growth in the era of globalization 223
HIROSHI NISHI

Index 248

Contributors

Robert Boyer is an Economist, former Director at the French National Centre for Scientific Research (CNRS) and former Director at the École des Hautes Etudes en Sciences Sociales (EHESS-Paris). He is currently Research Associate at the Institut des Amériques in Paris. He has been co-developing *régulation* theory since the 1970s, i.e. an analysis of the long run transformations of capitalist economies. He is also Honorary Fellow of the Society for the Advancement of Socio-Economics and President of the association Recherche et Régulation. For more information and a full list of publications, see www.robertboyer.org.

Koji Fukuda is Professor of International Public Administration at the School of Political Science and Economics, Waseda University. He is President of the European Union Studies Association Japan (EUSA Japan); Vice-President of the Japan Association of Global Governance. He received his PhD in Political Science from Doshisha University. He served as Research Fellow at the College of Europe in Brugge (1992–1993). He co-edited *European Governance after Nice* (RoutledgeCurzon, 2003, with Hiroya Akiba). He is co-author of *Economic Crises and Policy Regimes* (E & E, 2014, Hideko Magara, ed.) and *The European Union and Japan* (Ashgate, 2015, Paul Bacon *et al.*, eds).

Yuji Harada is Associate Professor at Fukuyama City University, Hiroshima, Japan. He was educated at Nagoya University (PhD). His research focuses on diversity of capitalisms, industry structural change, and theory of institutions. His publications include 'Asian capitalisms: institutional configurations and firm heterogeneity' (co-authored with H. Tohyama) in Boyer *et al. Diversity and Transformations of Asian Capitalisms* (Routledge, 2012).

Zoe Lefkofridi is Assistant Professor of Comparative Politics at the University of Salzburg and Joint Jean Monnet–Max Weber Postdoctoral Fellow at the Robert Schuman Centre for Advanced Studies (RSCAS) at the European University Institute (EUI), Florence. Her teaching and research focus on democracy and representation in Europe and beyond, with a focus on political inequalities and extremism. Her work appears in *European Political Science Review*, *European Union Politics*, *West European Politics* and *Comparative European Politics*, among others.

Hideko Magara is Professor of Political Science at Waseda University. Her research focuses on the mutual impacts between party politics and economic policies in capitalist democracies. She is the author of various books and articles, including *Economic Crises and Policy Regimes* (2014), *Politics of Structural Reforms: Social and Industrial Policy Change in Italy and Japan* (co-edited with S. Sacchi, 2013). She is an associate member of the Science Council of Japan, and former President of Japan Association for Comparative Politics.

Hiroshi Nishi is Associate Professor at Hannan University, Osaka. His research interests include Keynesian macroeconomics, institutional economics, and the Japanese economy. His recent publications include: 'A multi-sectoral balance-of-payments-constrained growth model with sectoral heterogeneity', in *Structural Change and Economic Dynamics* (2016), 'Structural change and transformation of growth regime in the Japanese economy', in *Evolutionary and Institutional Economics Review* (2016) and 'Comparative evaluation of post-Keynesian interest rate rules, income distribution, and firms' debts for macroeconomic performance', in *Cambridge Journal of Economics* (2015). He holds a PhD in Economics from Kyushu University.

Philippe C. Schmitter is the 2009 recipient of the Johan Skytte Prize, the 'Nobel in Political Science', 'for his path-breaking work on the role of corporatism in modern democracies, and for his stimulating and innovative analysis of democratization'. He was Professor of Political Science at the European University Institute in Florence, Department of Political and Social Sciences until September 2004. He was then nominated Professorial Fellow and later also Professor Emeritus at the same institution. Previously he was Professor in the Politics Department of the University of Chicago (1967–1984), at the European University Institute (1982–1986) and at Stanford (1986–1996). He has published books and articles on comparative politics, on regional integration in Western Europe and Latin America, on the transition from authoritarian rule in Southern Europe and Latin America, and on the intermediation of class, sectoral and professional interests. His current work is on the political characteristics of the emerging Euro-polity, on the consolidation of democracy in Southern and Eastern countries, and on the possibility of post-liberal democracy in Western Europe and North America.

Hiroshi Shiratori is Professor in Political Science and International Relations at the Graduate School of Public Policy, Hosei University. He spent the academic year 2015–2016 as Visiting Fellow at Pembroke College and Nissan Institute of Japanese Studies, St. Antony's College, University of Oxford. In the academic year 1998 he was Visiting Professor at Mannheimer Zentrum für Europäische Sozialforschung, Universität Mannheim, and in the academic year 1994–1995 as NAVF Stipendiat (Research Fellow of the Norwegian Research Council), Universitet i Oslo. One of his publications is *Citizens, Elections, Parties and Nation States* (Tokai University Press, 2003).

Wolfgang Streeck is Director Emeritus and Professor at the Max Planck Institute for the Study of Societies in Cologne, Germany. From 1988 to 1995 he was Professor of Sociology and Industrial Relations at the University of Wisconsin-Madison. His latest publications include: *How Will Capitalism End? Essays on a Failing System* (Verso Books, 2016); *Buying Time: The Delayed Crisis of Democratic Capitalism* (Verso Books, 2014); *Politics in the Age of Austerity* (ed., with Armin Schäfer; Polity Press, 2013); *Re-Forming Capitalism: Institutional Change in the German Political Economy* (Oxford University Press, 2009); and *Beyond Continuity: Institutional Change in Advanced Political Economies* (ed., with Kathleen Thelen; Oxford University Press, 2005). His current research interests are crises and institutional change in the political economy of contemporary capitalism.

Shinji Tahara is Researcher at the Economic and Social Research Institute (ESRI) in Cabinet Office of Japan. He received a PhD in Economics from Yokohama National University in 2011. He has participated in annual estimates of the SNA (National Accounts of Japan) as Unit Chief of Commodity Flow Method and compilation of the Input–Output Table in Japan. He has also researched adoption of the 2008 SNA in Japan. His main research themes in economics are de-industrialization and structural change in industries. His work appears in *Revue de la régulation*, among others.

Hiroyasu Uemura is Professor of Economics at Yokohama National University, Japan. He graduated from the Graduate School of Hitotsubashi University. He is a contributor to *régulation* theory, i.e. a research programme which analyses how economic institutions evolve in the long run and defines diverse contemporary brands of capitalism. He has published books and articles widely in the field of institutional economics and macroeconomic analysis. These include Boyer, Uemura and Isogai (eds) *Diversity and Transformations of Asian Capitalisms* (Routledge, 2012) and Yokokawa, Yagi, Uemura and Westra, R. (eds) *The Rejuvenation of Political Economy* (Routledge, 2016).

Toshio Yamada is Emeritus Professor at Nagoya University, having previously served as Professor of Economic Theories at Osaka City University and Nagoya University, Japan. His research interests focus on French *régulation* theory, Japanese civil society thought, and contemporary capitalism. His works in English include *Japanese Capitalism in Crisis* (2000, co-edited with R. Boyer), and 'Economic crises and growth regimes' (in H. Magara ed., *Economic Crises and Policy Regimes*, 2014).

Foreword

It gives us great pleasure to announce that Hideko Magara has recently completed editing the fifth volume of the book *Studies*, a Waseda Institute of Political Economy research series published in English.

Waseda Institute of Political Economy was founded in April 1978. We have several research groups dealing with current trends and issues in the fields of political science and economics. Our aim is to continually promote and provide financial support to the research studies published as part of the series.

We sincerely hope that our research activities will contribute towards enhancing research in political science and economics.

Kazumi Shimizu, Director
Waseda Institute of Political Economy
Waseda University, Tokyo
March 2016

Acknowledgements

This volume is the first research outcome of the international project *Growth, Crisis, Democracy: The Political Economy of Social Coalitions and Policy Regime Change*, which is supported by the Japan Society for the Promotion of Science through their programme Grant-in-Aid for Scientific Research (A) (25245023) during the academic years 2013–2016.

Since 2013, we have organized a series of international meetings every year at Waseda University, Tokyo, and/or International House of Japan. We also had two overseas meetings, one in November 2014 at European University Institute, Fiesole, Italy, which was hosted by Philippe Schmitter, and the other in November 2015 at Pembroke College, Oxford University, UK, which was hosted by Hiroshi Shiratori and Stephen Whitefield.

I gratefully acknowledge Masao Abiko, Ronald Dore, Jeffrey Frieden, Takeshi Hieda, Machiko Osawa, Andrea Revelant and Petra Schleiter, who presented their latest research in various international meetings either in Tokyo or in Europe. We were deeply inspired by their works, which were closely related to our project.

I also thank Koichi Suga, Kazumi Shimizu and Hidetoshi Nakamura, my colleagues at Waseda University, for their institutional support. Tatsuhiko Yamabe, Marc Brazzill and Yuiko Imamura helped me greatly in organizing and managing the international meetings in Tokyo and abroad. Publication of the book is partially supported by Waseda Institute of Political Economy.

Hideko Magara
Tokyo
July 2016

Part I

Introduction

1 New models of democratic capitalism and policy regime change

Hideko Magara

Introduction: policy regime change

Democratic capitalism in developed countries has been facing an unprecedented crisis since 2008. Its political manageability is declining sharply. Both democracy and capitalism now involve crucial risks that are significantly more serious than those observed in earlier periods (Crouch 2013; Schmitter 2013; Streeck 2013). In this context, the notion of *policy regimes* has gained new significance in analysing the possibilities for a post-neoliberal paradigmatic alternative. Policy innovations directed towards an economic breakthrough require both political leadership and a new economic theory (Magara 2014; Przeworski 2001, 2014).

This volume examines, from a policy regime perspective, how developed countries attempt to achieve such a breakthrough at critical junctures triggered by historic economic crises. Under the neoliberal policy regime, a serious challenge to democracy currently exists, in that the processes of political decision making have become quite distant from the public realm, and a limited number of economic and political elites exert influence on public policy (Crouch 2013). By and large, the more neoliberal an economy becomes, the less democratic its politics tends to be. In this project, we first observe main reasons why the social-democratic policy regime, the regime that preceded neoliberalism, came to an end. We then show the nature of the present crisis and identify the actors involved. Thereafter, we provide an analytical definition of a crisis, stressing that most crises contain within them the potential to be turned into an opportunity. We then develop a new analytical design in which we can incorporate today's more globalized and fluid context.

Presently, the legitimacy of the neoliberal policy regime is seriously questioned. Its economic performance has been incomparably abysmal. While some political elites attempt to move to a new policy regime, others prefer maintaining the status quo. In whose hand does the key to a new period of economic growth rest?

The central problem of political management in advanced societies today is related to forms of economic transformation. The economy is in the midst of transition from an old order to a new order, and this transformation is often said to be nonlinear. In this chapter, I first go back to the 1980s and 1990s to show why and how the old regime, which had been based on corporatist coalitions, collapsed. I will then provide an analytical framework by which we can explore possibility and difficulty of transitions to new policy regimes.

1 River of no return: limits of the social-democratic policy regime

Faced with growing inequality and low economic growth under the ongoing neo-liberal policy regime, some may embrace nostalgic feeling for the social-democratic policy regime. However, they at the same time know that they cannot go back to the golden decades after the Second World War. If the social-democratic policy regime was based on coalitions between managers and workers, the most important player whose positional changes need to be highlighted should be unions.

Already in the 1980s, the post-Fordist trends such as technological renovation and flexible specialization were observed in almost every industry. Such industrial arrangements tended to be problematic particularly for the Left, because these processes thrust a dilemma before the leftist parties, namely the trade-off between ideological loyalty and capitalist efficiency (Smith 1995: 2).

By the early 1970s, West European labour, as a political actor, had become so influential as to establish the welfare state. Yet the labour movement had already passed its heyday in the period between 1965 and 1975 (Therborn 1984: 5–38). Each economy's internationalization was inevitable and the states were losing their traditional power. Highly interdependent relationships in the international economy were emerging, and each government was forced to make its own economic policies fit the world economy. The autonomy of governments radically declined.

These waves of internationalization damaged social democracy, the welfare state and neo-corporatism, and labour all too soon lost its role as each country's political-economic protagonist. The social-democratic government in each nation failed to redefine the meaning of labour in response to internationalization. At the same time, the centralized nature of corporatism retarded the appropriate response to internationalization on labour's side. The intensifying international competition triggered by European integration sent the one-nation complete welfare state into a crisis. High wages increased labour costs. The provision of high levels of welfare was said to be connected with declining productivity. Without resolving the problems of weakening international competitivity, the welfare state was unable to survive.

Ironically, it was the managers who promptly reacted to internationalization, who were successful in redefining labour and provided workers with labour incentives. In order to survive in international competition, managers promoted high-technologization and reduced excesses in the labour force, while providing the highly educated, powerful, intellectual specialists with sufficient autonomy, job responsibility and job motivation (Jacobi *et al.* 1986; Piore and Sabel 1983). Contrary to the corporatists' expectations, in Western Europe during the 1980s, capital became more internationally dispersed rather than concentrated within domestic markets, the density of organized labour declined, and the neo-conservative governments made every effort to remove the privileges of labour unions. Moreover, professionals in the new service sector were indifferent to collective action based along class lines. Faced with this reality, the West European specialists argued that organized capitalism was ending (Lash and Urry 1987) and that the decentralization of European industrial relations (Ferner and Hyman 1992) and the challenge of flexibility (Baglioni and Crouch 1990) were beginning.

There have been various explanations for the breakdown of corporatism. Corporatism was originally domestic coalitions (Streeck and Schmitter 1991), and the contents of compromises tended to bear on the distribution of domestic resources. When the internationalization of the economy began, however, each economy's dependence on exports grew drastically, and it became increasingly difficult to evaluate what was sacrificed through the process of domestic compromises between the managers and the unions. While overseas production grew, the service sector was also enlarged, which lowered the importance of the mass production sector which was once the corporate base. At the same time, the weakening leadership of labour in the mass production sector, the deepening cleavages between the private and the public sectors, the increase of the female workforce, and the domestic sector triggered by the intensifying international competition are all factors that interacted in a complex manner, and workers' identity based on being the working class gradually eroded to become a thing of the past (Lash and Urry 1987: 123–124). The present day's capitalist transformation tends to collide with the interests of labour (Schmitter 1990).

1.1 The limits of two growth models: the social-democratic model and the Japanese model

Already in the early 1990s pessimism regarding West European labour politics was expressed in the misgivings over the idea that three economic patterns could dominate advanced societies (Esping-Andersen 1992). The first was the high-tech, low-employment pattern. In an export-oriented economy the competitive firms which pursue high-tech manufacturing try to maintain their global status by promoting labour restructuring. While they focus on the technology of capital-intensive production, they at the same time execute mass layoffs. The managers, who attach particular importance to R&D, abandon unskilled workers and choose only employees with high and flexible technological skills. The added value grows, but labour costs also increase. Due to the rigidly structured centralized unions, the service sector cannot absorb the unemployment. The service sector may become informal and cannot achieve growth.

The second is the pattern of internal corporate welfare. Collective bargaining is conducted at the local or company levels, and micro-regulation becomes dominant. Labour diversifies. Each employee's welfare depends on the performance of the individual company for which she/he works. The difference in fringe benefits increases, and the dualism in the labour market becomes more serious.

The third pattern is related to the low-wage service economy. The service sector, in which even full-time workers cannot afford decent lives, is formed. The low wages and unstable employment are institutionalized and structured.

Not all advanced societies followed exactly these paths. It should be noted, however, that already in the 1980s advanced countries had some common characteristics (Regini 1992), although their political-economic patterns up until the 1970s had demonstrated a variety of features – corporatism, dualism and pluralism – and their economic performances varied by country (Goldthorpe 1984). While the managers regained both the economic and political initiative to localize industrial relations, the fragmentation of labour and a drastic increase of unemployment became visible.

There once was an argument insisting that the most important factor that brought about changes in the international economy and the unions' decline in advanced societies since the 1980s was the rise of Japan in the world markets and the impact of the Japanese management style (Turner 1991). According to this view, not only did Japan push its low-cost, high-quality products into the world markets, and rapidly enlarge its share of the international market, but also the Japanese corporations' production model, capable of responding quickly to changes in the market, had a decisive impact on the renovation of the production pattern in each advanced country.

Each country's companies dispersed their production sites all over the world. High-technologization accelerated. The world markets became more interdependent and more competitive. The restructuring of production and technological innovation became a life-or-death problem. The necessity for companies to reorganize their internal labour markets increased. The managers/capitalists, who believed it to be essential to terminate the old pattern of collective bargaining with the unions and to restructure the work system in order to maintain and strengthen their international competitivity, began to seek flexibility in the workplace and more responsibility on the part of their workers. They were eager to establish a new paradigm of production. Since all these changes happened in the factories, i.e. the production sites, the employees' concerns centred on their own companies only. The national identity of unions was lost. The restructuring of the workforce could bring high productivity, yet at the same time it could lead to the reduction of the workforce.

These phenomena were apt to be lumped together as 'Japanization'. Nonetheless, the so-called Japanese style of management was different from the new management style the European corporations were trying to establish. In order to make this difference clearer, I will briefly compare labour incentives and employment, income distribution and the performance of labour markets of Europe with those of Japan under the old policy regime.

1.2 Labour incentive and employment: 'non-free full employment' vs. 'inactive full employment'

In the social-democratic model the existence of the centralized and comprehensive unions had almost the same meaning as worker control. The means of production were privately held, but it was possible for workers to obtain substantial concessions from the managers either by their strategies over specific issues or by their strong negotiating power. Yet the unions had some limits. There was no guarantee that they could always obtain the outcomes they had expected. For instance, unions were able to exert a strong influence on wages, but their power was relatively limited in determining the levels of employment and investment.

The vulnerability of social democracy was revealed especially when faced with the problem of declining productivity under the welfare state. In competitive labour markets, companies pay higher wages than the standard wages in order to prevent their workers from initiating a slowdown. If one company pays out for wage hikes, every company pays out for wage hikes. When every company raises wages, workers lose the incentive not to be lazy in their work. Yet the demand for labour will decrease and unemployment will occur, because all companies raise wages. Under unemployment, workers never start a slowdown, even though all companies are paying the same wages. If they are fired, it will be difficult to find new jobs (Elster and Moene 1989: 6).

With the Japanese model, in which life-time employment was institutionalized and the labour markets were dualist, the cost of changing jobs was extremely high, even though unemployment was held at low levels. Since a change of job could mean being demoted to a lower class, workers maintained a certain level of productivity even with the low rates of unemployment, without strongly demanding higher wages and without being lazy at work.

Workers do not start a slowdown either when the cost of changing jobs is set by the managers to be high, as in the Japanese model, or when the unemployment rate is high. Workers can be lazy when they can easily find the same kinds of jobs elsewhere. While managers took the initiative in choosing the Japanese style of 'non-free full employment', for quite a long time the European social-democratic forces were forced to choose bitterly between either unemployment or 'inactive full employment'.

1.3 Income distribution/redistribution: public solution vs. private solution

Compared with other advanced countries, the Japanese provision of welfare to its citizens has been kept at the lowest levels since 1955 under conservative governments. The Japanese citizens could not expect the state to provide them with quotidian public benefits, but Japanese firms selectively provided their workers with private benefits through their own company welfare facilities. In this situation, working people withdrew from politics and devoted themselves to being loyal to the companies for which they work. The income differential between the privileged sector (large firms) and other sectors (small firms) was never negligible, and the difference in fringe benefits, which hardly appeared in statistical figures, was always large.

The latter employees, however, did not choose to correct these problems politically – that is, through the welfare state. Rather, they have given an implicit consensus to the Japanese pattern of political-economic management by affiliating themselves with the former, by seeking private benefits, and thus by enlarging the national economy, while neglecting the income difference. The interests of the weaker sector were not always the same as those of the strong sector. Nonetheless, they thought the game was positive-sum. The employers and the employees, also, did not always share common interests, but they considered that both of them wanted to promote economic growth by cooperating with each other in managing the economy. In this context, not only the managers and the employees in the privileged sector, but also the workers in the weak sector, did not understand the role of the welfare state. They believed they could obtain their own benefits only though corporate activities in the marketplace. The public sphere and the political sphere became stunted. Voters' political apathy was determined when they perceived that politics could do nothing to help resolve their everyday problems. This structure, however, collapsed due to intensifying international competition and the pressures of globalization.

The West European coalition was quite different. In order to enhance the status of the low-income strata, the West European governments carried out income policies and solidaristic macroeconomic policies. The employees in the weaker sectors, unlike their Japanese counterparts who chose a private solution, tried to reduce via the public sector the income difference by utilizing the welfare state. In times of economic boom the middle class accepted these policies. As a matter of fact, they even gained some benefits from this cooperation. With the event of a recession, however, this turned from a positive-sum game among the working people into a negative-sum game. The economic crises and subsequent waves of restructuring did not hit all sectors evenly. The stronger sectors no longer agreed to policies that aimed at mitigating the negative impacts of recession on the weaker sectors; they became more selfish.

1.4 The performance of labour markets

How did the Japanese and European labour markets perform? In the first half of the 1980s, it was thought that unemployment was caused by excessively high wages compared to productivity. According to this view, the market mechanism needed to be enhanced in order to remove unemployment. It was also argued that the best adjustment for perfect employment was to reform industrial relations. The existence of strong unions as well as state regulations became the targets of criticism in the sense that the rigid labour markets had caused poor economic performances in Europe.

In the late 1980s, however, it was recognized that the relationship among the competitive wage determination, the density of the unions, and the unemployment rates was much more complicated than neoliberals had once thought. From the late 1970s to the 1980s, decentralization of industrial relations spread in advanced societies. Nonetheless, unemployment grew. It was argued again that the high level of employment could be achieved not by flexibility in labour markets but by the appropriate macro-institutions (Bruno and Sacks 1985;

Tarantelli 1986). The competitive market without any adjustment may possibly be connected to high unemployment rates. According to this argument, the combination of two factors – (1) market mechanisms, and (2) consensus building through macro-institutions – was the best formula to resolve unemployment problems (Bowles and Boyer 1990).

Yet it was also pointed out that unemployment rates could not be a sufficient indicator to assess the performance of labour markets. One of the problems in advanced societies was that the number of poorly paid jobs was increasing. The statistically low unemployment rates, thus, did not always mean a good performance in the labour market, especially when the wage differences by sector or by gender were perceptible (Rowthorn 1992). The number of poorly paid people with unstable jobs was gradually growing. The 'working poor' strata sustained the economy of advanced societies from the bottom. Rowthorn's study demonstrated that in Austria, which had been thought to be a typical corporatist country with centralized unions and 'good' economic performance, the wage differences both by sector and by gender were much larger than those of other West European countries. It also revealed that Japan, a typical non-corporatist nation with an 'exceptionally good' labour market performance, had larger wage differences in the 1980s than those of the USA. Japan was categorized as a typical working-poor society (see Table 1.1).

There have been various arguments about the decline of social democracy. According to those who try to explain the social-democratic parties' retreat with economic factors, the post-Fordist transformation of industry, particularly two

Table 1.1 Dispersion of hourly earnings in the late 1980s

	Coefficient of variation (%)		*F/M ratio (%)*
	Industry	*Industry + service*	*(ILO data)*
Austria	18	27	70
Norway	12	15	82
Sweden	9	10	87
Denmark	13	14	85
Finland			76
Germany			73
Netherlands	11	17	77
Belgium			77
New Zealand			72
Australia	17	18	74
France	19	18	82
UK	18	21	73
Italy			86
Japan	34	35	49
Switzerland	17	18	70
USA	20	30	68
Canada	21	28	64

Source: Rowthorn (1992: 91).

structural changes in the economy – (1) the shift to small-scale production and (2) the increase in private non-industrial sector employment – brought about the decline of European social-democratic parties. The industrial restructuring certainly rendered two problems among social-democratic parties: first, traditional unions were no longer able to create organized votes of members as they once did, and second the ties between the unions and social-democratic parties turned into a burden because non-union voters increasingly recognized the unions as selfish and particularistic interest groups (Pontusson 1995: 495–533).

On the contrary, there is another argument which stressed the inappropriateness in explaining post-Fordist transformation only by economic factors. According to this view, it is true that the post-industrial international economic order brought an impasse to social-democratic parties. Yet, it argues there was a great deal of variation in parties' responses in each country, reflecting the parties' own infrastructure, programmes, and ideology. The post-Fordist shift can be characterized by the decrease of the number of workers in heavy industry and the weakening of the labour unions, as well as by the increase of other employment and low-waged services. It should not be overlooked, however, that labour politics in each country has varied considerably. The difference in the leftist parties in each country significantly influenced not only the nature of politics but also the patterns of post-Fordist economic restructuring. The outcomes varied according to the extent that leftist parties were wounded (Piven 1991: 6–9), but many of them alleviated the costs of post-Fordist transformation and managed to react to the world economy in terms of growth as well as market share (Piven 1991: 11–12).

The seriousness of the blows that the unions have suffered since the 1980s differs by country. The workers' shift from the manufacturing industry to the service industry, the changes in workers' consciousness from collectivism to individualism, and the rise of post-industrial values were the common phenomena in advanced societies, which did not explain why some countries' unions suffered more serious losses than their counterparts in other countries. Here, the boundary between individualism and collectivism was rather a subtle matter. It was more realistic to think that even in the heyday of labour movements, most members participated in the unions not for the collectivism itself but for their intention to achieve their individualistic goals.

In extreme cases, indeed, rank-and-file members may have adhered passively to their union as merely one among the many other bureaucratic institutions associated with the employment relationship. Indeed, if the meaning of 'new individualism' is actually a greater concern with broader aspects of the quality of life than the old economistic priorities of collective bargaining, this might be seen not simply as a challenge but also as an opportunity for trade unions (Hyman 1992: 160–161).

Nonetheless, it is also true that the restructuring of employment provides the unions with an utterly new opportunity. Women, part-time workers, professions in non-manufacturing sectors – the growing importance of these people demonstrates that renovating labour unionism is a pressing need and that new organizations, new activities, and new forms of democracy are keenly awaited. In retrospect, after the heyday of craft unionism, there came massive waves of labour movements based on wide-ranging workers' interests (Regini 1992: 13).

2 In search of a new policy regime

In the midst of a world-wide political-economic impasse and an ever-increasing wealth inequality, social scientists often revert to the classics for guidance, only to realize, painfully, that the world has changed drastically and – no matter how relevant they were in the twentieth century – the past prescriptions, including Keynesian policies, cannot be applied exactly to the present disorder.

The world has changed indeed. While the interests of working people are diverging even at the domestic level, the interests of a small number of economic elites are converging globally. Collective action among workers is becoming increasingly difficult to implement in the domestic arena, but it is easier than ever for economic elites to achieve collective action in both the domestic and the global dimension. Why is the numerically far larger popular class unable to outdo an ultra-minority comprising global financiers and multinational entrepreneurs? This is one of the biggest puzzles facing political scientists. Simple electoral analyses do not provide satisfactory answers. Because the multilayered interest structures in advanced countries have become heavily nested, no analysis can solve the puzzle without examining various aspects of the domestic and global political economies simultaneously.

2.1 Crisis and opportunity

Big crises often require visible changes in the rules of the game, which face great resistance from those actors who have an investment in the present institutions. Our project has three basic analytical dimensions: international system, capitalism and democracy. Democracy inevitably contains vulnerable characteristics in the sense that it can easily degenerate into oligarchy. For instance, today a tiny proportion of the total population, a handful of financial and political elites, possess a large portion of the political control in most democracies. Compared with capitalism, which can adapt relatively easily within itself, democracy does not have a self-adjustment mechanism and the international system appears to be in crisis.

Within this tripartite structure (Figure 1.1), various actors with different expectations interact. In analysing policy regimes, we observe the nature of polities, believing that the type of democracy matters. Does a country have a presidential or parliamentarian polity? Institutional differences, such as the degree of centralization, also play a crucial role. The international dimension is significant as well. The nature of the international system, including the European Union (EU), the International Monetary Fund (IMF), and other international organizations, constrains the domestic decision-making process, as can be observed in the diffusion phenomenon at the EU regional level. The analysis of how

Figure 1.1 The tripartite structure.

domestic leaders react to international constraints is one of the most significant parts of our project.

At the same time, we clarify the nature of a crisis. Is the crisis endogenous or exogenous? Is it generic or specific? What is its origin? How large is its magnitude and how wide is its scope? In what ways does the crisis affect different actors? A crisis can often have a particularly strategic impact on certain actors. Some actors, such as veto players, tend to be less affected or may maintain their advantage throughout a crisis.

One of the most common phenomena that typify a crisis is that the actors are aware of the situation but cannot solve the problems within the established rules (Amable 2003; Boyer 2014; Kahler and Lake 2013; Magara 2014). However, when the actors do ultimately recognize the need to change the rules, it may be possible to turn the crisis into an opportunity. In this sense, awareness is key in analysing how such transformation from crisis to opportunity can occur.

2.2 Three models of capitalist democracy

Does a more liberal economy lead to less democratic politics? What does a more social economy bring about? While the autonomy of property is firmly protected under capitalism, normative dimensions, including economic and social equality, are often postponed (Bartels 2008; Hacker and Pierson 2011).

We assume that there exist three models of capitalist democracy within the present far-reaching trend of globalization: (1) liberal democracy; (2) technocratic rational-based democracy; and (3) Weberian political entrepreneurship. The first model, liberal democracy, is obviously a classic one. It presumes that a crisis will provoke a response from the public. This model in particular makes much of the political response from below (citizens), as people have freedom to organize, political parties attempt to respond to voters through elections, and movements such as those organized by environmentalists often play a significant role. This model, however, seems unlikely to be effective today because in recent years no government formed following democratic election, including those of Barack Obama in the USA and François Hollande in France, has been successful in implementing policies responsive to the demands of citizens.

In the technocratic rational model, which stresses the importance of elite decision makers rather than mass politics (Heclo 2010), awareness of an economic crisis is channelled through the elites (the epistemic community). Under this model, certain guardian institutions, such as a central bank, play a definitive role in exerting the regulatory power of modern democracy. Compared with the liberal democratic model, the technocratic rational model currently seems to have a more significant impact.

Sweden is an example of a successful technocratic rational model, in which the decision-making system is highly centralized and governing is viewed as an issue related to technical 'engineering'. Sweden's renewed success in reducing huge deficits has been the result of a return to traditional technocratic policy making that departs considerably from the methods of more populist governments. In Sweden, a very limited number of elites examine the technical aspects of reforms and formulate policies in a single package that is not subject to legislative or electoral pressures. The Swedish system has been successful because there was a high degree of agreement between the governing political parties and because there were few or no veto players. Additionally, decisive government action was vital in achieving results (Steinmo 2013).

This model, however, also contains some basic problems. For example, apart from the Swedish case, which appears to be rather exceptional, are elites really sufficiently democratic to pursue the best interests of their fellow citizens? This question becomes particularly difficult in a context full of vested interests and where corruption has historically been substantial.

Third, the Weberian model is based on political entrepreneurship and entails a quite visible invasion of charismatic leaders into the realm of political administration. In this model, the charismatic leaders are not bound by any association with political parties. They sometimes attempt to implement 'necessary' policies that are not fully democratic in nature through 'institutionally democratic' methods. The model reminds us of the colourful, populist new leaders of various countries. When limited social interests form a coalition of the '*bloc bourgeois*' type (Amable and Palombarini 2014), unarticulated interests of the popular class can easily create fanatical supporters of the charismatic leaders.

This volume clarifies both the strengths and the weaknesses of these models of democracy. If the liberal democratic model were working well, political realignment through elections would follow. However, the liberal democratic model does not currently function effectively. In many cases, there is very little change and no action. We will investigate the permanent changes that occur in ruling coalitions. Any policy regime shift can be understood as a Kuhnian paradigm shift (Kuhn 2012) in the sense that there is a change in the political rules of the game.

2.3 Aims of the book

One possible alternative to the neoliberal policy regime may be to establish a new form of flexible and decentralized bargaining in response to the variety of citizens' professions and their positions in the markets. Yet even in this case, a mechanism of macro-political bargaining, both domestically and internationally, will be necessary to secure basic social equity (Regini 1992; Teague and Grahl 1992). This requires working people to overcome a difficult problem concerning how to build macro-institutions by mitigating the confrontation among various sectors, including women, youth, and the unemployed.

The main theme of today's democracy is to turn one's eyes to the so-called 'outside of politics' such as families, workplaces, schools, and communities (Bobbio 1987; Bowles and Gintis 1987). The present-day workers' representative, likewise, cannot maintain their legitimacy without facing seriously the 'outside of the labour' – that is, the entirety of democracy which contains culture, new values, environmental protection, and human rights.

This volume consists of a set of comparative studies that will be conducted jointly by international researchers and will integrate theories and approaches in political science with economics and sociology. It will examine various institutional and strategic aspects of capitalist democracy so as to construct a general and dynamic analytical framework, offering new models of democratic capitalism and policy regime change. Our project examines how changes in growth models affect societal changes by focusing on the role of politics. This relationship can be expressed as a political-economic cycle (cf. Franzese 2002) in which capitalism influences democracy and vice versa while both interact with the international dimension. We will also explore some difficult (but not infeasible) alternatives to the neoliberal model.

The authors in this volume wish to make a significant contribution to the study of political economy by constructing a new interdisciplinary approach, analysing critical junctures of the paradigmatic change in world politics and the economy, and seeking ways to overcome the most urgent global issues related to economic crises. We believe that this volume provides various implications for both developed countries and developing ones newly making the transition to democracy.

References

Amable, B. (2003) *The Diversity of Modern Capitalism*, Oxford: Oxford University Press.

Amable, B. and S. Palombarini (2014) 'The *bloc bourgeois* in France and Italy', in Magara, H. (ed.), *Economic Crises and Policy Regimes: The Dynamics of Policy Innovation and Paradigmatic Change*, Cheltenham: Edward Elgar.

Baglioni, Guido and Colin Crouch (eds) (1990) *European Industrial Relations: The Challenge of Flexibility*, London: Sage.

Bartels, L. (2008) *Unequal Democracy: The Political Economy of the New Gilded Age*, Princeton, NJ: Princeton University Press.

Bobbio, Norberto (1987) *The Future of Democracy: A Defense of the Rules of the Game*, Cambridge: Polity.

Bowles, Samuel and Robert Boyer (1990) 'Labour market flexibility and decentralization as barriers to high employment? Notes on employer collusion, centralized wage bargaining and aggregate employment', in Renato Brunetta and Carlo Dell'Aringa (eds), *Labour Relations and Economic Performance*, London: Macmillan.

Bowles, Samuel and Herbert Gintis (1987) *Democracy and Capitalism: Property, Community, and the Contradictions of Modern Social Thought*, New York: Basic Books.

Boyer, R. (2014) 'How do polity and economy interact within Régulation Theory? Consequences for policy regimes and reform strategies', in Magara, H. (ed.), *Economic Crises and Policy Regimes: The Dynamics of Policy Innovation and Paradigmatic Change*, Cheltenham: Edward Elgar.

Bruno, M. and Jeffrey Sacks (1985) *Economics of Worldwide Stagflation*, Oxford: Blackwell.

Crouch, C. (2013) 'From markets versus states to corporations versus civil society?', in A. Schafer and W. Streeck (eds), *Politics in the Age of Austerity*, Cambridge: Polity.

Elster, Jon and Kark Ove Moene (1989) 'Introduction', in Jon Elster and Karl Ove Moene (eds), *Alternatives to Capitalism*, Cambridge: Cambridge University Press.

Esping-Andersen, Gosta (1992) 'The emerging realignment between labour movements and welfare states', in Mario Regini (ed.), *The Future of Labour Movements*, London: Sage.

Ferner, A. and R. Hyman (eds) *Industrial Relations in the New Europe*. Oxford: Blackwell.

Franzese, R. (2002) *Macroeconomic Policies of Developed Democracies*, New York: Cambridge University Press.

Goldthorpe, John H. (ed.) (1984) *Order and Conflicts in Contemporary Capitalism: Studies in the Political Economy of Western European Nations*, Oxford: Oxford University Press.

Hacker, J.S. and P. Pierson (2011) *Winner-Take-All Politics: How Washington Made the Rich Richer and Turned Its Back on the Middle Class*, New York: Simon & Schuster.

Heclo, H. (2010) *Modern Social Politics in Britain and Sweden*, Colchester: ECPR Press.

Hyman, Richard (1992) 'Trade unions and the disaggregation of the working class', in M. Regini (ed.), *The Future of Labour Movements*, London: Sage.

Jacobi, Otto, Bob Jessop, Hans Kastendiek and Marino Regini (eds) (1986) *Technological Change, Rationalization and Industrial Relations*, London: Croom Helm.

Kahler, M. and D.A. Lake (2013) 'Anatomy of crisis: the Great Recession and political change', in M. Kahler and D.A. Lake (eds), *Politics in the New Hard Times: The Great Recession in Comparative Perspective*, Ithaca, NY: Cornell University Press.

Kuhn, T. (2012) *The Structure of Scientific Revolutions*, 50th anniversary edition, Chicago, IL: University of Chicago Press.

Lash, Scott and John Urry (1987) *The End of Oranized Capitalism*, Madison, WI: University of Wisconsin Press.

Magara, H. (2014) 'Growth, crisis, regime change', in H. Magara (ed.), *Economic Crises and Policy Regimes: The Dynamics of Policy Innovation and Paradigmatic Change*, Cheltenham: Edward Elgar.

Piore, Michael and Charles Sabel (1983) *The Second Industrial Divide*. New York: Basic Books.

Piven, Frances Fox (1991) 'The decline of labor parties: An overview', in F.F. Piven (ed.), *Labor Parties in Postindustrial Societies*, Cambridge: Polity.

Pontusson, Jonas (1995) 'Explaining the decline of European social democracy: the role of structural economic change', *World Politics* 47: 495–533.

Przeworski, A. (2001) 'How many ways can be third?', in Andrew Glyn (ed.), *Social Democracy in Neoliberal Times: The Left and Economic Policy since 1980*, Oxford: Oxford University Press.

Przeworski, A. (2014) 'Choices and echoes: stability and change of policy regimes', in H. Magara (ed.), *Economic Crises and Policy Regimes: The Dynamics of Policy Innovation and Paradigmatic Change*, Cheltenham: Edward Elgar.

Regini, Marino (1992) 'Introduction: the past and future of social studies of labour movement', in Marino Regini (ed.), *The Future of Labour Movements*, London: Sage.

Rowthorn, Bob (1992) 'Corporatism and labour market performance', in Jukka Pekkarinen, Matti Pohjola and Bob Rowthorn (eds), *Social Corporatism: A Superior Economic System?*, Oxford: Clarendon.

Schmitter, P.C. (1990) 'Sectors in modern capitalism: Modes of governance and variations in performance', in Renato Brunetta and Carlo Dell'Aringa (eds), *Labour Relations and Economic Performance*, London: Macmillan.

Schmitter, P.C. (2013) 'The crisis of the euro, the crisis of the European Union and the crisis of democracy in Europe', prepared for the 1st International Symposium, Growth, Crises, Democracy, Waseda University, 17 December 2013.

Smith, W. Rand (1995) 'Industrial crisis and the Left: Adjustment strategies in socialist France and Spain', *Comparative Politics* 28 (1): 2.

Steinmo, S. (2013) 'Governing as an engineering problem: the political economy of Swedish success', in A. Schafer and W. Streeck (eds), *Politics in the Age of Austerity*, Cambridge: Polity Press.

Streeck, W. (2013) 'The crisis in context: democratic capitalism and its contradictions', in A. Schafer and W. Streeck (eds), *Politics in the Age of Austerity*, Cambridge: Polity.

Streeck, Wolfgang and Philippe Schmitter (1991) 'From national corporatism to transnational pluralism: organized interests in the single European market', *Politics and Society* 19 (2): 133–164.

Tarantelli, Ezio (1986) *Economia politica del lavoro*, Torino: UTET.

Teague, Paul and John Grahl (1992) *Industrial Relations and European Integration*, London: Lawrence & Wishart.

Therborn, Goran (1984) 'The prospects of labour and the transformation of advanced capitalism', *New Left Review* 145: 5–38.

Turner, Lowell (1991) *Democracy at Work: Changing World Markets and the Future of Labor Unions*, Ithaca, NY: Cornell University Press.

Part II

Models of new democratic capitalism

2 Crisis, opportunity and democracy in contemporary Europe

Philippe C. Schmitter

In the Chinese language, the ideograph for crisis and for opportunity is the same.[1] In the languages of Europe, they are not the same – although they may be connected through a complex set of political processes. Moreover, it is by no means assured whether, if the connection exists, it will be positive or negative, i.e. that it leads to a better or a worse outcome.

Nothing could be more apposite than this connection today in Europe, which is suffering from not one but three concurrent crises: (1) its common currency, the euro; (2) its common institution, the European Union (EU) and (3) its common political regime, liberal democracy. Needless to say, the simultaneity of these crises – the likelihood that they will affect each other – makes it much more difficult to predict the outcome.

In this chapter, I will focus primarily on the potential impact of these crises and their effect on the process of European integration – with the understanding that this could eventually have a significant impact on the practice of democracy within the EU member states. We begin with the observation that there is nothing new about crises in this process, from its very beginning in the early 1950s with the European Coal and Steel Community. One could even say that crises have been an integral part of it and, moreover, they have tended to have a positive effect. The usual reaction by member governments has been to respond by increasing the authority and expanding the tasks of the institutions of the EU and its predecessors (ECSC, EEC, EC) in order to resolve the crises.

The underlying reason for this seems obvious. It begins with the unprecedented nature of the process of integrating sovereign national states peacefully into an encompassing regional organization. The actors involved have an intrinsic difficulty in acting rationally because it is so difficult to assess the costs and benefits of possible courses of action: first, because the range of alternatives (especially given the presumption of peaceful negotiation among relative equals rather than violent imposition by the strongest) is so different from analogous choices made during their respective processes of national integration; second, because however well-considered their policies and well-intentioned their implementation, they are bound to generate unexpected and, often, undesired consequences; and third, if these were not enough, the ECSC/EEC/EC/EU has repeatedly changed its overriding goal from integrating the market for coal and steel, to providing regional security, to promoting trade in industrial goods, to subsidizing agriculture, to encouraging cross-national investment, to liberalizing financial flows, to coping with the competitive pressures of globalization – not to mention the more recent ones of coordinating police cooperation, controlling borders, standardizing visa and asylum requirements, regulating energy networks, improving regional transport systems and producing a common foreign and security policy. Each time the process has expanded its *compétences*, the stakes in the game have involved ever more complex packages of policies whose interactive effects and emergent properties have proven more difficult to predict. And, if all this were not enough, one of the greatest successes of European integration has been the incorporation of new member states – 22 in addition to the original six. Each time this has occurred, the effects on existing policy commitments and the likelihood of agreeing upon new ones has become less predictable.

The present crisis of the euro and the 'sovereign debt' of several of its member states is a near perfect example of how causal complexity, unanticipated consequences and decisional uncertainty can have a significant and cumulative impact on regional integration. Some 41 years ago, in an article revising the neo-functionalist approach, I imagined four successive 'good' crises that the EU might face in the future and that might drive the process further.[2] What each was supposed to do was to build upon frustrated or disappointed member expectations in the pursuit of some common objective. This would compel actors to redefine either the tasks or the level of authority (or both) of regional organizations by reaching a collective agreement that would 'spill-over' into previously unsatisfactory or ignored policy areas. What has (heretofore) made the EU unique is precisely this capacity to exploit successive crises positively by repeatedly breaking out of its momentary zone of organizational indifference. At least until now, no other regional organization has acquired this dynamic characteristic.

My fourth 'transcending' crisis was virtually identical to what is presently occurring with regard to the euro (Figure 2.1). *In theory*, I argued it should compel actors in member states: (1) to engage in more comprehensive policy coordination across sectors and policy arenas, thereby institutionalizing at the supra-national level the mechanisms of policy harmonization, budgeting and taxation characteristic of a federal government; and (2) to break out of predominantly national political alliances and form more salient supra-national ones, thereby laying the foundation for the establishment of the most important missing element in the Euro-polity, namely a distinctively European party system. *In short, this was supposed to be the crisis that would drive the EU from economic to political integration.*

Unfortunately, *in practice*, the outcome – at least so far – has been the opposite. Member governments seem to be retreating to more restrictive and nationalistic calculations of interest. Led by overt German recalcitrance (but supported quietly by other 'Northern' states), there has been little sign of the sort of cross-national partisan solidarity or the need for comprehensive policy coordination that I had anticipated. Some members have even experienced the revival of extreme right-wing

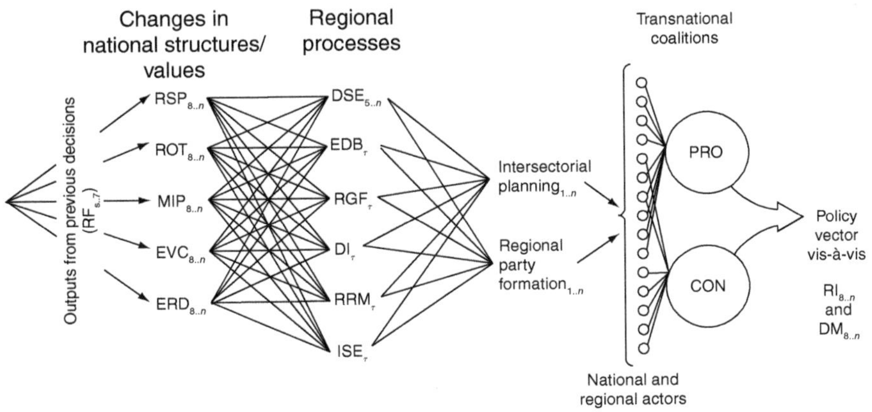

Figure 2.1 The 'fourth' or 'transcending' cycle of crisis decision making.

Source: author.

nationalist parties and movements that are overtly contrary to any further 'spill-overs'. A few of them even advocate outright withdrawal, not just from the euro, but from the EU as such. The emerging Euro-polity seems further than ever from acquiring its distinctive party system. Moreover, mass publics – rather than favouring more integration in gratitude for the benefits it has given them – have by and large expressed hostility to the prospect.

Could it just be that the 'good' crisis that I imagined some 40 years ago has turned out to be a very 'bad' one? For not only is the crisis of greater magnitude at the supra-national level than expected, but it also seems to have penetrated much deeper and more negatively into national political institutions and public opinion. *It is even plausible to imagine a vicious triangle emerging: first, the collapse of the euro; then the collapse of the European Union; and finally, the collapse of democracy in its member states.*

Let us look at these three crises to assess how serious are their implications and how closely they may be related to each other.

1 The euro crisis

If it were just a matter of sustaining the existence and value of the euro as the common currency of 17 EU member states, the solution seems to be falling (slowly and painfully) into place. Europeans have discovered that they may not yet have a common identity, but they do already share a common fate – and the euro binds them to it. The cost of unravelling these ties is simply too uncertain and threatening. If this implies accepting a range of previously unthinkable policies – from issuing euro-bonds, to creating a Europe-wide system of deposit insurance and banking supervision, to allowing unlimited purchases of sovereign debt by the European Central Bank, to empowering the Commission to monitor and supervise national budgetary and fiscal policies, to granting to the European Court of Justice extensive powers to review compliance and punish infractions by member states, even to mutualizing a fixed proportion of the debts of member countries by means of which, the Eurozone members would agree to pool the risk in order to reduce the spread in interest rates among them and to protect the value of the euro vis-à-vis other currencies. To make these commitments credible, they will have to have a firm legal foundation and probably some source of EU 'own' resources – perhaps in the form of an earmarked tax on financial transactions. This may sound like an enormous transfer of national sovereignty to a remote and complex set of supra-national institutions. And it is.

What just might tip the balance is if one EU member were to defect or be expelled from the club. Greece seemed a likely candidate for the latter; Great Britain is currently contemplating the former. If the result of either type of 'spill-back' were economically catastrophic, then it might serve to convince even the most reluctant of its other members to accept the mega-package deal outlined above. One hopes that this will not happen, but accepting 'the Mother of All Spill-Overs' just may take such a shock.

But what if the real problem were not the euro? What if the crisis runs deeper and long precedes the decision to establish a common currency? Economic growth and real wages in Europe began to decline already in the 1980s. The accelerated expansion of both public and private credit also pre-dates the introduction of the euro. Something fundamental seems to have changed in the nature of capitalism during the last quarter of the twentieth century – at the end of the so-called '*Trente Glorieuses*' years of uninterrupted economic growth, greater income equality and enhanced social protection. How much the integration of Europe contributed to this unprecedented prosperity is debatable, but one cannot question the fact that the EEC/EC/EU was credited, not only with maintaining a security community among the states of the region, but also with creating a climate for superior economic performance and social justice.

For the last 20–30 years, the EU has become associated with gradually declining to negative outcomes. Ever since the Single European Act in 1986 and the Maastricht Treaty in 1992, its policies have conformed closer and closer to neoliberal doctrinal principles of financial liberalization and market deregulation. And in the last 2–3 years, the euro and the policies of the ECB have been specifically (and accurately) perceived as mechanisms for enforcing austerity and accused of fostering not just lower growth and greater inequality, but also decline in real incomes, as well as massive increases in unemployment. If this were not enough, international capital markets discovered that the government bonds rapidly accumulated by those member states that could no longer devalue their currencies to enhance competitiveness had reached such a magnitude that they might not be repaid – and these speculators started treating them as equivalent to private or corporate debt by demanding a premium for the greater risk involved. Much of this might have occurred without the common currency, but it has been blamed for it.

If this scenario is correct, it suggests a fundamental and irreversible rupture of the social contract – whether the explicit result of corporatist concertation or the outcome of pluralist pressures – that has characterized the European political economy in the postwar period. Globalized finance capitalism has made it impossible for states to raise sufficient revenues to cover the expenses of such a contract – so they have to borrow and borrow more to meet the expectations of their citizens. The level of taxation on middle and lower classes has reached the saturation point and it has become impossible to tax the rich since they have so many means of hiding income or shifting it to foreign sites. If that were not enough, the implacable demography of an ageing population is raising the costs of retirement and health policies – and these older people continue to vote at a time when younger ones are abstaining more and more. In other words, saving the euro might be futile if this deeper contradiction is not addressed.

2 The EU crisis

In principle, the EU could survive without a common currency. It did so rather well for four decades. Admittedly, the failure of monetary integration would probably signal an end to aspirations for eventual political integration – but this would not be regretted by many of its citizens (especially those living in Great Britain and Denmark).

Obviously, a great deal would depend on how the euro went under. A gradual negotiated retreat or one that left it the common currency of some subset of member states would be more tolerable. However, this seems highly unlikely and a chaotic *sauve-qui-peut* would trigger enduring political and legal recriminations that would make policy making in other areas virtually impossible. If nothing else, the euro crisis has exposed a highly salient and deep cleavage between Northern creditor and Southern debtor countries that will be hard to overcome – especially since it has been accompanied by a revival of stereotypes about national character and historical resentments about German domination. Prior to this, the underlying cleavage structure was basically pluralist with different sets of winners and losers across changing policy arenas – held together by the Franco-German duopoly with the former providing the ideas and the latter the money. This time there is a clear and cumulative pattern of conflict, and France and Germany are not in sufficient agreement to overcome the gap.

But the most serious threat to the EU may emerge precisely because its members are successful in saving the euro. The only way of accomplishing this seems to be via the devolution of extraordinary *compétences* upon its institutions, especially the Commission and the ECB. Not only would they have to substantially increase the number of their functionaries and experts, but – in order to be credible – these additional commitments would also have to be funded through 'own resources' that would not depend on periodic member approval – something that has heretofore been denied it on such a scale. Whether through a fee on financial transactions, an increment to the VAT tax or a flat Euro-levy, it would definitely raise the sensitive issue of the EU's democracy deficit. Up to now, this issue has been finessed on the grounds that the EU was either just another intergovernmental organization or a supra-national regulatory agency.

But such a massive transfer of sovereign authority and financial resources would definitely raise the eternal issue of 'no taxation without representation' and require the introduction of new mechanisms of democratic participation and accountability, or the legitimacy of the whole operation would be constantly challenged. The classic formula of increasing the powers of the European Parliament has failed in the past and would be even more insufficient under such circumstances. So far, the various packages of proposed fiscal, budgetary and regulatory measures to save the euro have completely ignored the imperative of political legitimation. Presumably, the dominant approach rests on the assumption by technocrats that the rescue of the euro will be 'self-legitimating'. Europeans will be so grateful for what has *not* happened to them that they will not ask how it was done and what it cost.

3 The crisis of European democracy

Democracy in Europe at the national or sub-national level emerged quite independently of the process of European integration and, therefore, the collapse of the EU would not seem to threaten its viability. Elsewhere, I have even argued that its multilayered and polycentric system of 'supra-national governance' has had some negative effects on the practice of domestic democracy.[3] *Ergo*, getting rid of it might even help to improve the quality of democracy at the national and sub-national levels.

For the EU has long had an ambiguous relation to democracy. It requires something like a liberal, representative, constitutional version of it (along with respect for human rights, rule of law and capacity for administering EU directives and regulations) as a condition for membership, but it does not itself practice this type of democracy. As some wag once put it, 'If the EU were to apply to join itself, it would be rejected.' By applying strict conditionality to the post-Communist Central and Eastern European candidates, it undoubtedly contributed to the relatively rapid and successful consolidation of democracy there and its subsequent role with regard to pending candidates from South-Eastern Europe seems also to have been positive. But its feeble efforts to democratize itself, mainly by directly electing European deputies and increasing their parliamentary powers, have been insufficient to overcome the basic impediment that its government, the Commission, does not reflect the partisan preferences expressed by European voters and its Commissioners are chosen by opaque negotiations among member governments.

With or without the EU, however, European national democracies have been in trouble for several decades. The paradox of these times is that, precisely when so many aspiring *neo*-democracies emerged to the East, the *archeo*-democracies of the West were entering into crisis. Their citizens started questioning the very same 'normal' institutions and practices that new democratizers were trying so hard to imitate. And they tended to find them deficient, if not to say, outright defective. The list of morbidity symptoms is well known (if not well understood): citizens have become more likely to abstain from voting, less likely to join or even identify with political parties, trade unions or professional associations, more likely not to trust their elected officials or politicians in general and much less likely to be satisfied with the way in which they are being governed and the benefits they receive from public agencies.[4]

None of these symptoms can be attributed directly to the EU, but that does not mean they could not get worse in its absence. Again, a great deal depends on how the EU goes into demise and what consequences this triggers. A 'soft landing' that leaves intact many of its treaty-based obligations, does not threaten the established security community and protects much of the basic structure of regional trade and investment might have little impact. Again, this seems unlikely. A 'hard landing' will involve many unfulfilled contracts, multiple law suits, considerable disruption in trade and capital flows and, of course, lots of resentment – not just between individuals and firms but between nation states. And these are very likely to be polarized along geographic, cultural and political lines – with the Northern 'hard-working and abstemious' creditors pitted against the Southern 'lazy and spendthrift' debtors.

One clear signal has already emerged. Voters in national elections during the past three years have demonstrated an unprecedented propensity for throwing incumbents out of office. Historically, European democracies were built upon hegemonic parties that ruled for long and consistent periods of time. Now, there are no more ruling parties, only governing ones. Whether of the centre-right (e.g. France, Italy, the Netherlands, Denmark, the Czech Republic) or of the centre-left (e.g. Portugal, Spain, Hungary, Ireland, Slovenia, the United Kingdom, Finland), the tenure of virtually all European governments has become precarious. Moreover, citizens have shifted an increasing proportion of their votes to fringe populist parties of either the Right or Left. Such populisms are an intrinsic, if periodic, temptation in all democracies.[5] They are the side product of systems of sclerotic and oligarchic political parties that have become incapable of representing existing citizen preferences or articulating credible future projects for the polity as a whole. They are not so much anti-democratic as they are less politically liberal, sometimes 'supra'-constitutional and often economically imprudent. Even when they do not succeed in occupying governing positions, they can push more established, centrist parties into adopting items from their platforms, thereby, making it increasingly difficult for them to form coalition governments.

Democracy in Europe was already changing before the euro crisis and the EU crisis emerged. It will survive both of them, but in so doing it will have to become even more different from the one that Social Democrats and Christian Democrats built after the Second World War. It will have to find (and institutionalize) a new social contract and a more regulated political economy – not to mention novel channels of democratic participation and mechanisms for accountability to citizens.

4 Conclusion

The crisis is not over and its consequences will be felt for some time to come. Which means that there still exists an opportunity to turn an apparently bad crisis into a good one. Moreover, the instrument for doing so already exists in the form of that unprecedented (but still not accomplished) delegation of *compétences* to the Commission, the European Central Bank and the European Court of Justice. What will make the difference will be the purpose for which these supra-national institutions will exercise those powers.

What if the EU, instead of promoting orthodox neoliberal policies of fiscal balance, budgetary austerity, lower welfare provisions and greater labour market flexibility at the national level, switched direction and became an aggressive supra-national agent of growth and job creation via the issuing of euro-bonds guaranteed by all member states and the launching of a programme of European-scale public works in energy and transport – even in research and development – financed by the European Investment Bank? There does seem to be a critical mass of dissident economists (and plenty of social scientists) in favour of this, as well as an emerging coalition of national governments (of the Right in Spain and Portugal, of the Left in France and of Technocrats in Greece and Italy). Even the centrist Dutch government recently made similar noises by questioning the sacrosanct status of the 3 per cent barrier on budget deficits. Whether this will prove sufficient to nudge the German government, and with it the Board of the ECB, and, eventually, the European Council in such a new direction remains to be seen. But if it is sufficient and (even more problematic) if it is successful, then the EU would re-acquire and greatly strengthen its association with economic prosperity and social justice – that famous European Model of Society that Jacques Delors was so fond of invoking. Seen from this (admitted improbable) perspective, the current euro crisis could just be the detonator of that 'Transcending Cycle' that I imagined 40 years ago.

Notes

1 I have been informed that this is not the case in Japanese and Korean, but wonder whether this is a matter of substance or just form.

2 P.C. Schmitter, 'A revised theory of regional integration', *International Organization*, Vol. 24, No. 4 (1970), 836–868. Also published in L. Lindberg and S. Scheingold (eds), *Regional Integration: Theory and Research* (Cambridge, MA: Harvard University Press, 1971), 232–265.

3 P.C. Schmitter, 'Will EMU make it easier or more difficult to democratize the EU', in F. Torres, A. Verdun, C. Zilioli and H. Zimmermann (eds), *Governing the EMU* (Florence: EUI, 2004), 99–110; also published in F. Torres, A. Verdun, C. Zilioli and H. Zimmermann (eds), *EMU Rules: The Political and Economic Consequences of European Monetary Integration* (Baden Baden: Nomos, 2006), 101–110.

4 P.C. Schmitter and Alexandre Trechsel (eds), *The Future of Democracy in Europe: Trends, Analyses and Reforms* (Strasbourg: Council of Europe Publishing, 2004).

5 P.C. Schmitter, 'The vices and virtues of populism', *Aspenia*, Vol. 12, No. 35–36 (2007), 42–48; also published as 'I populismi: vizi e virtù', *Aspenia*, Vol. 12, No. 36 (2007), 71–78; also published as 'Los vicios y virtudes de los "populismos": un balance general', *El Debate Político: Revista Iberoamericana de Análisis Político*, Vol. 3, No. 4/5 (2006), 208–214.

3 The rise of the European consolidation state

Wolfgang Streeck

The rise of the *consolidation state* follows the displacement of the classical *tax state*, or *Steuerstaat* (Schumpeter 1991 [1918]), by what I have called the *debt state* (Streeck 2014a), a process that began in the 1980s in all rich capitalist democracies. Consolidation is the contemporary response to the 'fiscal crisis of the state' envisaged as early as the late 1960s (O'Connor 1970a, 1970b, 1973) when postwar growth had come to an end. Both the long-term increase in public debt and the current global attempts to bring it under control were intertwined with the 'financialization' of advanced capitalism and its complex functions and dysfunctions (Krippner 2005; Magdoff and Sweezy 1987; Strange 1998; van der Zwaan 2014), which occurred alongside and as part of the neoliberal transformation of the capitalist political economy. As I will show, the ongoing shift towards a consolidation state involves a deep rebuilding of the political institutions of postwar democratic capitalism and its international order, in particular in Europe where consolidation coincides with an unprecedented increase in the scale of political rule under European Monetary Union (EMU) and the transformation of the latter into an asymmetric fiscal stabilization regime.

1 From the fiscal crisis of the state to the Great Recession

By the mid-1970s, the accumulated debt of states in the OECD world began to increase steeply and steadily (Figure 3.1). Indebtedness rose by and large regardless of country, national economic performance, and the political complexion of the government of the day. North Sea oil made a difference for Britain, unification for Germany, the rise and fall of defence spending for the USA, but always only temporarily. Indebtedness increased for two decades until the mid-1990s, when debt levels seemed to stabilize. After 2008, however, they rapidly returned to the long-term trend.

A growing level of public debt is the result of cumulative, non-Keynesian[1] deficits in public budgets: of an enduring inadequacy of government revenue compared to government spending. A popular explanation for this is offered by the 'public choice' school of institutional economics, which considers public finance as a poorly managed 'common pool' from which democratic-electoral majorities and office-seeking politicians may satisfy ever more extravagant

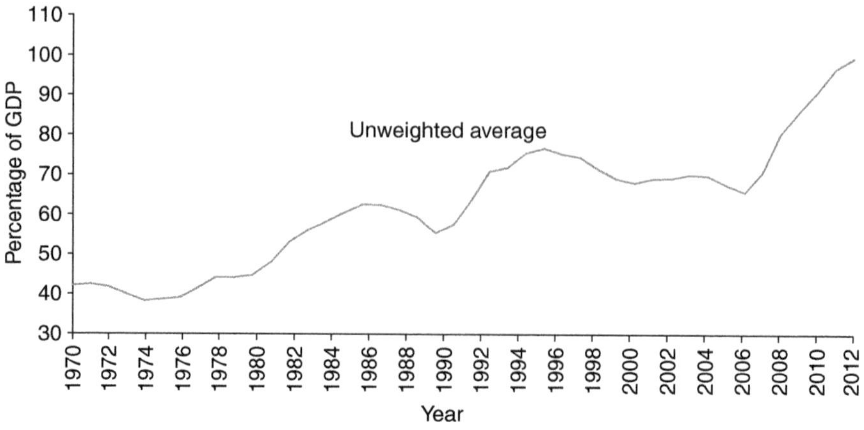

Figure 3.1 Government debt as a percentage of GDP, 1970–2013.

Source: OECD Economic Outlook No. 95, own calculations.

Notes

Countries included: Australia, Austria, Belgium, Canada, Denmark, Finland, France, Germany, Greece, Ireland, Italy, Japan, Netherlands, Norway, Portugal, Spain, Sweden, Switzerland, UK, USA.

collective demands without having to assume responsibility for the costs (Buchanan and Tullock 1962). As I have shown (Streeck 2014c), however, the secular rise of public debt in OECD countries coincided with a general, equally secular decline in the political power of organized labour and social-democratic politics, as indicated by long-term declining rates of unionization, falling participation in national elections, an almost complete disappearance of strikes, high and steady rates of unemployment, stagnant wages and rising economic inequality (Schäfer and Streeck 2013).

If redistributive democracy didn't do it, what did? As mentioned above, the Marxist theorist James O'Connor, writing in the tradition of authors such as Schumpeter and Goldscheid (Goldscheid 1926, 1976 [1917]), predicted already in the late 1960s a widening gap between the fiscal means governments could mobilize under capitalist relations of production and ownership, and the demands on state support made by an advancing capitalist economy. States under capitalism, according to O'Connor, had to provide for the legitimacy as well as the efficiency of capital accumulation – the former through all sorts of social consumption, the latter through investment in a public infrastructure. O'Connor also expected mounting pressure on state finances by public sector trade unions claiming the same wages and benefits as workers in private industry and thereby exposing the state to the 'cost disease' of the service sector (Baumol 1967). It is interesting that Daniel Bell, almost at the opposite end of the political spectrum, found much to endorse in O'Connor's analysis, although he seems to have placed the emphasis, somewhat like the public choice school, less on functional needs and structural contradictions than on cultural change away from Protestant values towards materialistic consumerism, or 'bourgeois hedonism' (Bell 1976: 250).[2]

In hindsight, the route from the tax state to the debt state looks less straightforward than one might have expected. Empirically, deficits became endemic and debt started to accumulate after the end of inflation in the early 1980s. Before then, high inflation had substituted for real growth by wiping out parts of the public debt, thus slowing down its accumulation. For a while it had also kept up employment.[3] With monetary stabilization, unemployment became high and chronic, causing social spending to increase until, with a delay of a decade or so, it was brought under control by neoliberal 'reforms'. Up to this point, public debt was basically a matter of the inertia of social security systems functioning as 'automatic stabilizers'.[4] In addition, however, the end of inflation ended what is called 'bracket creep': the movement of tax payers into higher income tax rates with rising nominal incomes. In fact, it reinforced tax resistance in particular among the middle class and lent momentum to calls for 'tax reform', meaning tax cuts that primarily benefited the payers of high taxes – like the Reagan tax cuts of the early 1980s.

Overall, the 'fiscal crisis of the state' turned out to be caused less by an increase in citizen entitlements than by a decline in the taxability of democratic-capitalist societies (Figure 3.2).

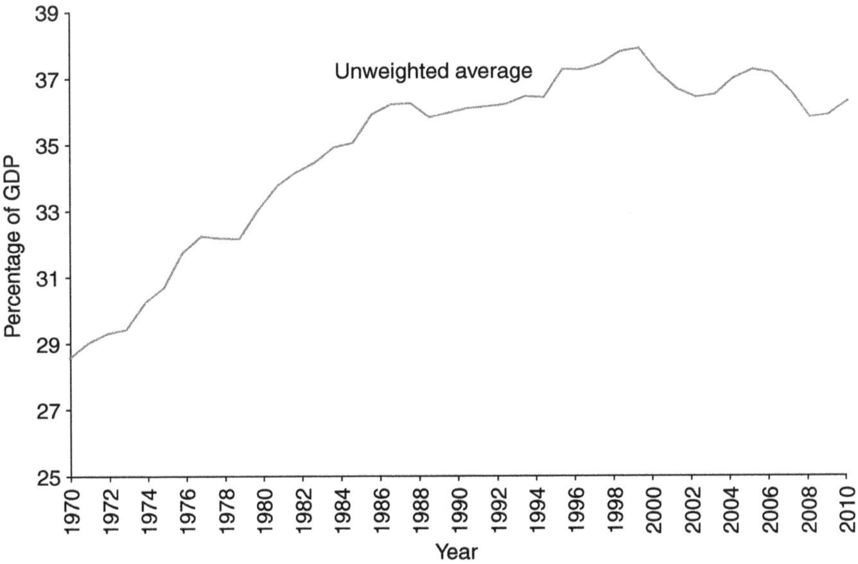

Figure 3.2 Total tax revenue as a percentage of GDP, 1970–2011.

Source: OECD Revenue Statistics, own calculations.

Notes

Countries included: Australia, Austria, Belgium, Canada, Denmark, Finland, France, Germany, Greece, Ireland, Italy, Japan, Netherlands, Norway, Portugal, Spain, Sweden, Switzerland, UK, USA.

While tax revenue had kept pace with public spending by and large until the mid-1980s, later it began to stagnate until, after a short recovery, it started declining at the end of the century. In 2008, taxation levels were back where they had been two decades earlier. A contributing factor was the 'globalization' of the capitalist economy, which led to increased tax competition among countries (Piketty 2014), resulting in tax cuts for corporations and earners of high incomes (Genschel and Schwarz 2013). It also extended the opportunities for owners of capital to evade taxation by moving assets between countries or into international tax havens (OECD 2013; Zucman 2015). If, in other words, the increasing fiscal problems of the rich capitalist democracies after the 1970s were due to a revolution of rising expectations, that revolution occurred not among ordinary citizens but among capital and those in command of it.

Another respect in which early theories of fiscal crisis had failed to anticipate what was coming was that they underestimated the possibilities of capitalist states to finance deficits for a protracted period of time by borrowing. Actually the rise of public debt in the final third of the twentieth century and beyond was linked to the financialization of the capitalist economy, which included an explosive growth of its financial sector and of the amount of credit money it produces (Krippner 2005; van der Zwaan 2014). Credit enabled states under capitalism to live with a widening gap between citizen demands and capitalist needs for infrastructural support on the one hand and, on the other, the increasingly powerful resistance by tax payers – individual as well as corporate – against paying the bill. Financialization made it possible for governments to push back the moment when they had to do something about the increasing inadequacy of their fiscal means. Low nominal interest rates, brought about by the return to 'sound money' after 1980, helped as they made rising debt levels more manageable; in fact, they soon began luring governments into substituting credit for taxes as the latter became more difficult to collect. There also was an international dimension to the debt state as the USA began to sell its public debt abroad to sovereign investors, especially to the governments of oil-producing countries looking for opportunities to 'recycle' their surpluses and in return gain military protection against regional adversaries and their own peoples.[5]

In subsequent years 'financial services' became the most important growth industry by far in both the USA and the UK (Krippner 2011). After the end of the Bretton Woods monetary regime, with the dollar continuing to be the leading global reserve currency, the USA enjoyed the 'exorbitant privilege' (Giscard d'Estaing) of being able to indebt itself internationally in its own currency and service its debt by printing basically unlimited amounts of it. The rich supply of fiat dollars that ensued nourished an expanding financial industry in the USA which was soon to turn into the financial sector of capitalism world-wide. Aggressive deregulation of financial institutions allowed for unprecedented 'financial innovations' that attracted capital from all over the world and became a major instrument for governments not only looking for new economic growth but also desperately seeking access to credit. Indeed, as the overall credit supply expanded, it was not just states that became increasingly leveraged but also corporations and, later, private households. Thus the rise of the debt state became embedded in a movement of advanced capitalism as a whole towards higher and higher indebtedness across the board – with public debt in fact amounting to no more than a small share of overall debt (for the USA, see Figure 3.3).[6]

How closely the management of the debt state came to be connected to the leveraging of capitalism in general became particularly visible in the 1990s when first attempts were made at fiscal consolidation. In the USA, Clinton had won the presidency in 1992 by promising to do something about 'the double deficit' in the federal budget and the balance of trade. The 'peace dividend' after 1989 seemed to open a window of opportunity for spending cuts, and the experience in a country like Sweden of two successive fiscal crises (1977 onwards and 1991 onwards) was seen as a general warning signal.[7] Orchestrated by the USA through international organizations like the OECD and the IMF, capitalist democracies made an effort to break the upward trend in their indebtedness by returning to balanced budgets through spending cuts and reforms of their budgeting institutions (Poterba and von Hagen 1999). Indeed, countries succeeded in the 1990s in bringing down public expenditure to levels that more closely matched their stagnant revenue (see Figure 3.2). In the USA, this went as far as producing a budget surplus by the end of Clinton's second term. It should be noted, however, that this was due to a large extent to low interest rates made possible by monetary expansion, to savings on defence spending in the wake of 1989 (soon to prove short-lived), to economic growth (especially in the financial sector) inflating the denominator of the debt equation, and to savings on social security (as a result of both low unemployment and cuts in entitlements).[8]

The consolidation attempts of the 1990s responded to, perhaps misinformed, concerns among American voters about high public debt. But one can also

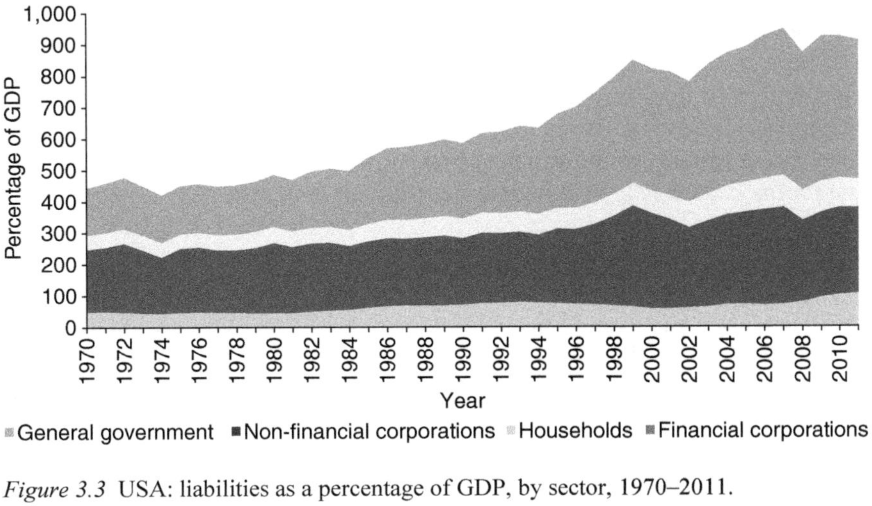

Figure 3.3 USA: liabilities as a percentage of GDP, by sector, 1970–2011.

Source: OECD National Accounts Statistics (Database): financial balance sheets – non-consolidated stocks.

assume that creditors were concerned about the long-term solvency of sovereign borrowers. In any case, pressure for fiscal consolidation presented an opportunity for cutting back the state in favour of the private sector, by referring citizens to private credit as a substitute for previously free public services. Thus, financialization not only *required* fiscal retrenchment – to ensure the further creditworthiness of sovereign borrowers – but it also contributed to it, and with it to the retrenchment of the state in the course of the neoliberal revolution that began in the 1980s. As households indebted themselves to compensate for cuts in public provision, aided by deregulation of credit and low interest rates furnished by obliging central banks, they opened the door for the private sector to move into fields that had previously been the domain of government. They also filled the gap in aggregate demand caused by cuts in public spending – an effect referred to as 'privatized Keynesianism' (Crouch 2009, 2011).[9]

Far from being unsuccessful, the first wave of consolidation managed to bring down public debt during the decade from the mid-1990s to the eve of the Great Recession (see Figure 3.1). This was helped in Europe by the Maastricht Treaty on European Monetary Union and its debt limits, while it was ended for the time being in the USA after 2001 by the Bush tax cuts and rapidly rising defence spending. However, all gains from consolidation were undone when the pyramid of private debt that had grown alongside public debt, and all the more after the increase of the latter had temporarily been halted, collapsed in the financial crisis of 2008. Here again, the close interconnection between the debt state and the financialization of modern capitalism became apparent as states found themselves forced to absorb the bad debt created by the private sector under financial deregulation. States also had to take up additional debt for stimulus spending to prevent a complete breakdown of their national economies (for the rise in public debt at the global level after 2008, see Figure 3.4).

Ironically, it was the debt that states incurred to protect societies from the fallout of speculative lending and borrowing – encouraged by government policies of deregulation and cheap money – that made 'financial markets' even more suspicious than they already were about states' capacity to live up to their obligations as debtors. When declining creditor confidence showed itself in rising risk premiums on government bonds from a number of countries, it was time for the *debt state* to be rebuilt into a *consolidation state*.[10]

2 Consolidation in hard times

Understanding the politics of the consolidation state requires a look at the political economy of the debt state. The rise of the debt state took place simultaneously with a general increase in economic inequality and was closely linked to it. Overall it was deeply intertwined with the neoliberal transformation of advanced Western capitalism. The declining taxability of capitalist economies in the course of 'globalization' produced a rising demand for credit on the part of governments, while tax cuts for the increasingly rich provided for the corresponding supply. As a result, the debt state found it convenient to substitute

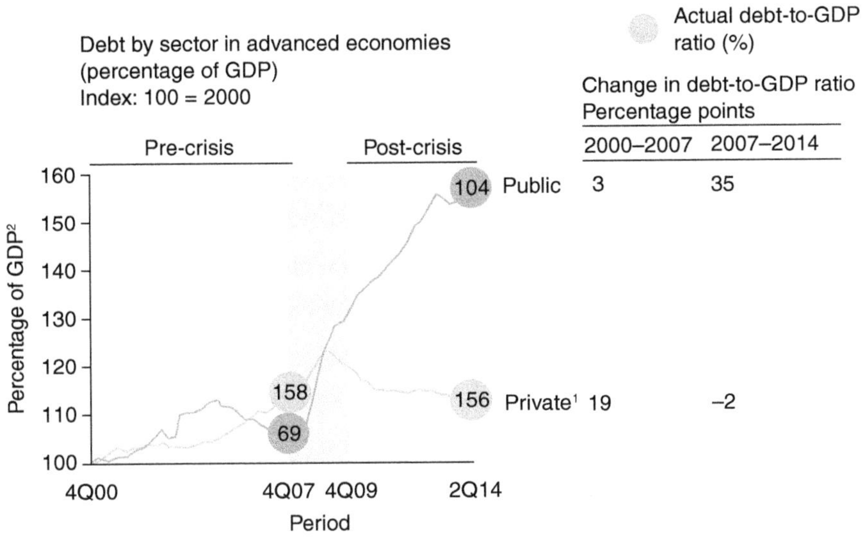

Figure 3.4 From private to public debt in advanced economies, 2000 to 2014.

Source: 'Debt and (not much) deleveraging', February 2015, McKinsey Global Institute, www.mckinsey.com.

Notes
1 Includes households and non-financial corporate sector debt.
2 Debt as a percentage of GDP is indexed to 100 in 2000; numbers are not actual figures.

credit for ever more difficult-to-collect taxes, to the extent that citizens acting as financial investors continued to consider government bonds safe. States going into debt allow citizens with high incomes to keep their money instead of having it confiscated, invest it safely, collect interest on it, and pass it on to their children. Unlike what is sometimes suggested in the literature (Wagschal 1996), the rich in rich democracies are not necessarily opposed to government debt if the alternative is higher taxes, especially for them. What they must be concerned about, however, is too much debt compromising the capacity of governments to service it.

How much is too much cannot be answered generally. Indebted states default if they cannot repay old debt by taking up new debt. At what level of indebtedness financial markets will cease to extend credit to states differs, because it depends not on the magnitude of the existing debt as such, but on the confidence of the markets in it being repaid. As debt levels rise, therefore, debt states must intensify their efforts to secure that confidence to avoid rising risk premiums curtailing their ability to borrow. Normally states can be expected to do their utmost *not* to default, as this may for a long time exclude them from borrowing. One advantage they have is that they may use legal force – on their citizens – to raise the funds they need to pay their creditors. Governments may also oblige some of their subjects, especially financial firms under prudential supervision, to invest part of their capital in government bonds, on the premise that these are particularly safe. On the other hand, a sovereign government cannot be forced to pay back its debt and can in principle unilaterally cancel it. In particular, there is no legal way today for creditors to take possession of a defaulting debtor state's assets; in the past this was sometimes done by war. Attempts to establish an international bankruptcy regime for states that would regulate the rights and obligations of debtors and creditors and establish some form of international jurisdiction have so far been unsuccessful.

Fiscal consolidation, then, is essentially a confidence-building measure. Its objective is to make a state safe for financial investment by making it clear to the financial markets that the state will be in a position to service its debt. Consolidation is rarely about states ceasing to borrow altogether. Even after a state's accumulated debt has begun to shrink, there will long remain old debt that has to be refinanced on a revolving basis. Regardless of whether their debt is growing or declining, states thus continue to have a vital interest in low risk premiums on government bonds, since even a minor increase in the average rate of interest they have to pay may wreak havoc on their finances.[11]

Today's emerging consolidation state is a political-institutional response to financial market demands for a break in the trend towards ever higher public indebtedness, at a time when debt levels are rising dramatically, annihilating all gains from the first wave of consolidation that began in the 1990s. To continue lending, financial markets want to be assured that public debt is under political control, certified by a demonstrated capacity of governments to halt and indeed reverse its long-term growth. Creditors' calls for consolidation reflect the experience of the last four decades that the Keynesian promise of governments deleveraging in good times to be able to incur new debt in bad times had not been kept: that fiscal reflation had a ratchet effect producing ever higher debt levels, in effect continuously expanding public expenditure. Consolidation is to reverse what had increasingly seemed like a one-way street towards insolvency, and to make governments return once and for all to fiscal solidity and sustainability.

Debt containment or reduction may be achieved by not replacing paid-back debt or, failing that, by 'financial repression': a combination of low interest rates with higher rates of inflation, or nominal growth, over a longer period of time, by which existing debt is slowly devalued. Lowering or at least stabilizing public debt by financial repression may be an acceptable way of restoring financial credibility, as long as the resulting 'haircut' remains moderate and big investors are given early enough warning. Consolidation as a confidence-building measure proceeds, almost as a matter of course, *not by raising revenue but by cutting expenditure*. Exceptions may be higher sales taxes, user fees, and social security contributions, making tax regimes more regressive. Much-publicized efforts to close tax loopholes and prevent international base shifting have yet to produce results; in any case, they would seem capable at most of slowing down the decline of tax revenue, not of ending or reversing it. A budget surplus, including one owed to lower interest rates or unexpected increases in tax revenue, is preferably used to pay off debt or cut taxes, to suppress political temptations to restore previous spending cuts and maintain the pressure to consolidate by cutting public spending (Haffert 2015).

An established consolidation state is one that has managed to institutionalize a political commitment and build a political capacity never to default on its debt, projecting an uncompromising determination to place its obligations to its creditors above all other obligations. It features a general configuration of political forces – a regime, as defined by Pierson (2001)[12] – that makes spending increases difficult while making spending cuts, on everything except debt service, easy. Countries with a small state, like the USA and Japan, are more likely to be recognized as consolidation states since a small government share in the economy can be taken to indicate both an entrenched aversion to state spending and the possibility for tax increases as *ultima ratio* in financial emergencies.[13]

A country that comes close to the ideal is the USA, which combines powerful anti-taxation politics with a sacrosanct constitutional commitment never to compromise its 'full faith and credit'.[14] In fact, in the USA, as in no other country, it is understood across the political board that properly servicing the public debt must take precedence over everything else, including public pensions. Even the Tea Party movement contributed – unintentionally – to the perception of the USA as a solid debtor when it was defeated in 2011 and 2013 over the national debt ceiling by a coalition between the president and the Republican leadership – who at the time could not agree on anything except that the USA must in all circumstances service its debt, including by incurring more debt.

I have described the debt state elsewhere (Streeck 2014a: 80ff.) as having two constituencies, citizens and creditors – or two peoples, a *Staatsvolk* and a *Marktvolk.* Debt states have to be loyal to both, with the two struggling over who is to be the principal stakeholder and who, in a fiscal crunch, has to give. The consolidation state settles that struggle in favour of its second constituency, its *Marktvolk*, by firmly internalizing the primacy of the state's commercial-contractual commitments to its lenders over its public-political commitments to its citizenry. In a consolidation state, citizens lose out to investors, rights of citizenship are trumped by rights out of commercial contracts, voters range below creditors, the results of elections are less important than those of bond auctions, public opinion matters less than interest rates and citizen loyalties less than investor confidence, and debt service crowds out public services (for an ideal-typical representation of the relations between debt states and their two constituencies, see Table 3.1). One could also speak of two kinds of public debt: *explicit* in relation to 'the markets' and *implicit* in relation to citizens, the latter to be served after the former – or of two classes of property rights or entitlements: *capitalist* and *civic*, the former rising above the latter. In short, a consolidation state may be described as one whose *commercial market obligations* take precedence over its *political citizenship obligations*, with citizens lacking access to political or ideological resources with which to contest this.

Converting a popular democracy into a consolidation state takes time since it requires disempowering democratic-egalitarian politics in favour of solid

Table 3.1 The debt state and its two peoples

Staatsvolk	*Marktvolk*
National	International
Citizens	Investors
Civil rights	Claims
Voters	Creditors
Elections (periodic)	Auctions (continual)
Public opinion	Interest rates
Loyalty	'Confidence'
Public services	Debt service

Source: Streeck (2014b: 81).

customership in financial markets. The goal is to resolve the basic *ambivalence of democracy* as a depersonalized and therefore less capricious, longer-lived and more reliable debtor, on the one hand, and a sovereign agent of wealth allocation and redistribution, on the other. This involves tying the hands of the state by redefining its sovereignty into a guarantee of its ability to repay its debt, for example by making balanced budgets an enforceable constitutional requirement. While a balanced budget or a budget surplus may be presented by governments to citizens as a step on the way to governmental independence from financial investors,[15] the immediate purpose is to reassure lenders that their investment is safe and that they can at any time be paid and repaid. Lower risk premiums may also be achieved by other institutional reforms, to the extent that these credibly prevent future governments from once again mitigating capitalist distributional conflicts by public spending and thereby jeopardizing the state's reliability as a debtor.

Preventing the debt state from predating on its lenders may also be done by international means. States have a collective interest to ensure that the reputation of sovereign debtors in general is not jeopardized by wayward governments using their sovereignty to expropriate their lenders. International institutions like the IMF, the World Bank, and the EU help potentially insolvent states with loans, on the condition they reform themselves so that they can credibly promise not again to overdraw their accounts. Discipline may also be exercised by hegemonic countries aligned with global financial markets, such as the USA. The latest case here is Argentina. Having borrowed in New York, the country unexpectedly found itself under the jurisdiction of an American court, which declared the restructuring in 2002 of part of its debt to be illegal.[16] As all major banks have, by necessity, subsidiaries in the USA, any government using the banking system to handle its financial transactions may be exposed to American legal action defending the property rights of investors in public debt.

The turning of the debt state of the late twentieth century into a consolidation state takes place in hard economic times. With economic inequality growing everywhere, debt-financed social expenditure helped states maintain an appearance of egalitarian even-handedness. Budget balancing by cutting social benefits and social services risks a democratic backlash unless political institutions are rebuilt to insulate economic policies from popular-electoral pressures, in a Hayekian (Streeck 2014a) or post-democratic (Crouch 2004) way. Moving towards a consolidation state is also made difficult by the fact that it is taking place at a time of low growth, if not secular stagnation,[17] with austerity likely to cause further economic contraction (Blyth 2013). (It is at the same time made more urgent by the additional debt accumulated as a result of the financial crisis of 2008.) To investors in public finance seeking reassurance that their investment is safe, economic growth is as important as balanced budgets; both are, however, difficult if not impossible to achieve at the same time. Politically, neoliberal institutional reforms and fiscal austerity are hard to impose under conditions of low growth and rising inequality on a society that still has recourse to democratic elections, while economically the two may further impair aggregate demand and produce a deflationary downward spiral. Although the reigning neoliberal political-economic doctrine promises growth as a future reward for present austerity, for investors waiting to be paid that promise may be too uncertain, and the future too far away, to make them feel better.

The transformation of the debt state into a consolidation state is under way, but it is far from smooth. While interrelated through global financial markets, its local manifestations differ, although the logic governing them is the same. Some institutional reforms have been implemented, but many are still work in progress. In Europe especially, consolidation is politically contested, in particular in countries like France and Italy. As creditors worry about consolidation subverting economic growth, and governments about austerity undercutting political stability, public debt has further increased in most countries and is still rising – even though nobody believes present levels to be sustainable. Currently much of the refinancing of debt states is provided by central banks, in the USA and Japan directly, in Europe indirectly by the European Central Bank (ECB) lending to national banking systems which, in turn, lend to their national states.[18] But although the balance sheets of the leading central banks have rapidly expanded since 2008 (Figure 3.5), historically low interest rates and unprecedented infusions of liquidity into the world economy have as yet failed to stimulate economic growth and thereby make market-conforming reforms more palatable, not to mention help states pay their lenders. Like public debt, there is agreement among economic elites that the policy of cheap money cannot be continued forever. What is being debated is how long it can still be relied upon and how it can be ended without causing a new political-economic megacrisis.

3 The European consolidation state

The emerging consolidation state in Europe differs in several respects from the US model. Western European countries do not have command of a hegemonic currency, and redistributive democracy has not yet lost its popular support. Nor is the primacy of states' explicit debt to capital markets over their implicit debt to their citizens as well established as in the USA, and the same applies to austerity as a

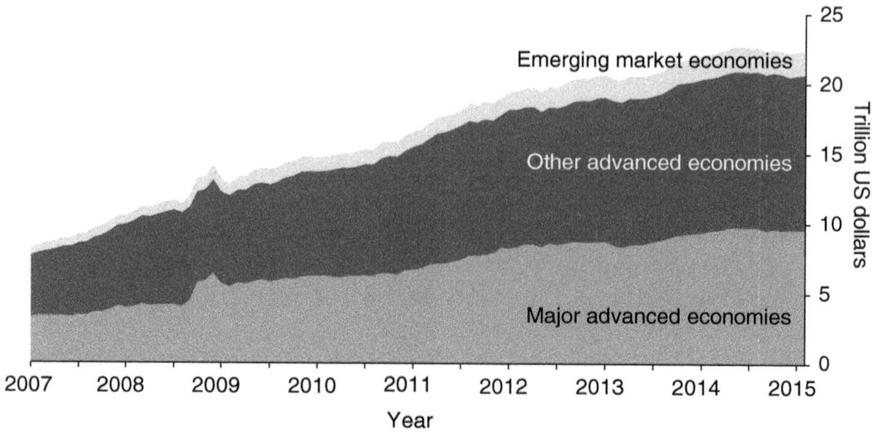

Figure 3.5 Total central bank assets.

Source: Bank for International Settlements, 85th Annual Report (2014/2015), statistical data.

Notes

Major advanced economies: The euro area, Japan and the USA. Other advanced economies: Australia, Canada, Denmark, New Zealand, Norway, Sweden, Switzerland and the UK. EMEs: Argentina, Brazil, Chile, China, Chinese Taipei, Colombia, the Czech Republic, Hong Kong SAR, Hungary, India, Indonesia, Korea, Malaysia, Mexico, Peru, the Philippines, Poland, Russia, Saudi Arabia, Singapore, South Africa, Thailand and Turkey.

principle governing domestic state activity, except perhaps in Britain and post-communist Eastern Europe (which did, however, not have enough time since 1989 to build up potentially critical amounts of public debt). Also, in the Europe of the EMU, consolidation takes on a peculiar form as it proceeds under an international regime governing the fiscal and financial policies of a collection of formally sovereign nation states, so as to secure their compatibility with a common supra-national monetary policy. Unless otherwise indicated, the following discussion will focus only on the eurozone, or *Euroland*, and its member states.

The construction of the euro monetary regime betrays its origin in the first global consolidation wave in the 1990s. Member states were not allowed to run budget deficits above 3 percent of GDP, and accumulated debt was not to exceed 60 percent. The sole mission of the ECB was to defend monetary stability, and extending credit to member states was explicitly forbidden. Like the German Bundesbank, the ECB is independent from elected government and insulated from electoral pressures; in fact, it is even more independent as it does not have a unified (supra-national) government as a political counterpart; instead it faces a council of heads of national governments. Member state compliance with the rules of Euroland is to be enforced by another non-political supra-national authority, the European Commission. Soon this regime, fashioned after the German model, proved unable to enforce fiscal discipline even on Germany. It also failed to prevent the post-2008 euro crisis, when public and private debtors in a number of EMU member countries suddenly turned out to be over-indebted and lost the confidence of their creditors, especially as their national economies became locked into stagnation, with a possibility of debt deflation. As a consequence, risk premiums on public debt in several EMU member countries began to rise; in countries like Italy, Greece, Spain and Ireland they reached previously unmanageable levels.

As indicated, there are no general economic limits to public debt, which requires strictly individualized, case-by-case risk assessment on the part of creditors. Under EMU, financial markets had freely lent to weaker member countries at historically low interest rates, apparently on the assumption that, regardless of the treaty, their debt would somehow be mutualized, in the sense of Europeanized, should they become insolvent. After 2008 this turned out to be an illusion, probably inspired by integrationist forces in the Commission, and lending to Mediterranean countries turned out to have been an international equivalent to subprime lending in the US housing market. Since servicing the accumulated debt remained a national responsibility, it became apparent that the decoupling of fiscal and financial policy from national democracy, as demanded by financial markets, had not gone far enough. Democratic resistance to austerity in the South and to a 'transfer union' in the North stood in the way of restoring investor confidence in Southern member states. Hopes that growth would return as a result of neoliberal 'reform' of fiscal policies and institutions, as well as of labour markets and social security systems, were either disappointed or remained untested, as reform got stuck in domestic politics. In the resulting stalemate, the ECB is buying time for the euro by flooding the markets with money, as a functional equivalent to debt mutualization, to keep interest rates low and member states solvent, while continuing to insist that national governments have in return to push through institutional and economic reforms, so as to make European capitalism, as organized in the EMU, more 'market-conforming' (Angela Merkel).

The rebuilding of the EMU state system into a *multinational European consolidation state* proceeds slowly and fitfully, punctuated by national and European elections that force governments to make themselves appear responsive to citizen concerns, including those they otherwise discredit as 'populist'. While the emerging European consolidation state amounts to a novel kind of political-economic regime, it is being developed out of the EMU in a path-dependent process of gradual institutional reform. Its outstanding characteristic is a unique amalgam of national, international and supra-national rules and institutions, of constitutions and treaties, and of national politics and international relations. What results is *a state consisting of states*, with a domestic politics that combines diverse national polities, foreign relations between nation states, and supra-national authority wielded over them in their collective name by bureaucratic agencies. As a fiscal consolidation regime, the EMU in its evolving form as an international consolidation state may be characterized as follows:

1 In a first approximation, the emerging European consolidation state is a mutual surveillance and control arrangement among what are still formally

sovereign nation states. It is founded on a shared interest in states' collective reputation in financial markets and on the recognition that the default of one state may have adverse effects on all others; for example, in the form of higher interest rates or of repercussions on national banking systems. The transformation of the EMU into an international consolidation state on top of a set of national welfare states is to secure an ever tighter coupling of member states' economic behaviour through mutual observation, supervision, and discipline. Institutional development starts from the original structure of the EMU as established in the 1990s, which is being expanded and strengthened in the course and the aftermath of the post-2008 fiscal crisis, among other things through new regulations, in particular the so-called Six-pack, and new treaties like the Fiscal Compact passed in late 2011 and early 2012, respectively.[19]

2 As an international regime not directly exposed to traditional class politics and popular democracy, the European consolidation state is in a better position than a nation state to impose on unreliable electorates a market-conforming fiscal policy, a policy of austerity, and the primacy of debt service over public services. Disempowering the *Staatsvolk* in favour of the *Marktvolk* (Table 3.1) by institutionally decoupling popular democracy from the management of the economy[20] is more easily done by means of international than national politics. As the community of states gains power over its members, through both horizontal international agreements and vertical supra-national institutions, it can even recall elected heads of national governments and install in their positions representatives of the international financial industry, as was done by the European Council in Greece and Italy in November 2011.[21] The objective is to wrest what is left of national sovereignty over economic policy from notoriously difficult national electorates through aggressive institutional reform at international as well as national level.

3 More than in any nation state, the EMU's central bank, the ECB, can act as an independent external force in relation to democratic governments. Administering the monetary policy of 18 nation states, it is sufficiently far away from the domestic politics of each of them to be able to make monetary policy support for national governments conditional on their cooperation on fiscal policy and institutional reform. Together with other international organizations, in particular the IMF and the European Commission, the ECB has on several occasions deeply intervened into the domestic politics of formally still sovereign states, among other things prescribing to the Greek government how many civil servants it had to dismiss and when. Since the ECB must be concerned above all about the confidence of financial markets in the currency that it administers, the reforms it demands from member states can only be of a market-conforming kind. In particular, the ECB cannot be supportive of any egalitarian-redistributive ambitions of national governments. The ECB's unprecedented political independence translates into an unprecedented capacity to cater to the interests of financial markets and firms and into unprecedented dependence on their good will.

4 The international relations embedded in the EMU consolidation state are highly asymmetrical. Economically weak countries, while in the majority, face a small number of economically strong countries in a position effectively to dictate to them, by threatening to withhold financial support. Germany, on account of its regained economic power after 2008 and as the main beneficiary of the EMU due to its export strength and to currently low European interest rates,[22] de facto governs the EMU as a German economic empire. In the form of the euro, it imposes on the rest of Europe a hard currency of the kind Germany has become used to since the war, including on countries like France and Italy that have long relied on a soft currency as a means of managing domestic distributional conflict while intermittently relying on devaluation to restore temporarily their international competitiveness.[23] There is no provision in the treaties for turning the EMU into an arrangement for international redistribution, also known as a ‘transfer union’. In any case, even Germany and France together are far too small to provide the weaker Mediterranean countries with more than symbolic economic assistance (Streeck and Elsässer 2014). To the extent that some redistribution from the strong to the weak is required for keeping over-indebted states solvent and monetary union together, it must be accomplished through covert channels, also because of voter resistance in the European North. Serving as an invisible conduit for money transfusions is another function today performed by the ECB.

5 The institutional reforms imposed under the EMU on its over-indebted member states would, if carried out to their end, result in a deep restructuring of national political economies, especially in the Mediterranean countries. Based on the ‘German model’ as it is understood today,[24] such reforms would in particular undo the historical class compromise in countries like Italy and France which accepted high rates of inflation and high public spending, including frequent public deficits, as a price for social peace (Blankart 2013; Hall 2012). High inflation made high public debt bearable because it devalued the debt on a current basis; low interest rates and high state subsidies provided for stable employment; and negative effects on external competitiveness were compensated from time to time by devaluation. To the extent that this system supported ‘rigid’ labour markets, short working hours, costly public services, high and early pensions, and high and regular nominal wage increases, it was a thorn in the eye of a growing middle class, as well as of technocratic-nationalist elites bent on ‘modernizing’ their countries. To them, the EMU promised to break institutionally entrenched resistance to capitalist modernization by undoing the various economic fixes on which their national class compromise depended. By having the bitter medicine of austerity and flexibility forced on their countries from the outside, they hoped these would ultimately become able to ‘stand on their own feet’, get ready for ‘globalization’, and compete successfully with Germany, in particular.

EMU and the international consolidation state growing out of it represent a unique opportunity for the capitalist penetration and rationalization of resistant economies, states and societies. Still, as long as there is a danger of democratic obstruction, change towards market-conforming democracy – i.e. democracy de-coupled from the management of the market economy – can be administered only slowly. Both national and international politics around fiscal consolidation are complex and convoluted; see the agonies of the Hollande government in France, originally elected to replace *Merkozy*, in the face of German pressures to join German–European international consolidation policies. See also the rise in Germany of the anti-euro party, AfD, which expresses and indeed cements German resistance to a 'transfer union', not to speak of the growing tensions between France and Italy on the one hand and Germany on the other. Since the end of 2014, the discussion was about a managed devaluation of the common currency as a substitute for national devaluation; about extending the consolidation deadlines of the Fiscal Compact; and about 'growth programmes' for the South and for France, to be funded by new debt even though debt is already at a historical high and adding to it has not produced growth for at least a decade now; in fact, it has coincided with declining growth. Given the unsustainability of further debt accumulation, these are rearguard battles on a collective march towards balanced budgets and smaller states, enforced by pressures from financial markets on the one hand, and by German hegemony on the other.

Notes

1 Non-Keynesian, because Keynesian debt is supposed to be paid off as the economy returns to an adequate level of growth and public budgets generate a surplus of revenues over expenditure. Anti-Keynesian economists, in particular in the USA, tried early on to blur this difference by accusing Keynes of having provided spendthrift governments with a good conscience when they overdrew the public accounts (Buchanan and Wagner 1977, 1978).
2 On Bell in this context, see Krippner (2011).
3 On the political functions of inflation and the way they were taken over, in part, by public debt in the 1980s, see Streeck (2011, 2014a).
4 That is, it was *not* a matter of growing demands for public handouts by spoiled citizens. However, unemployment insurance has undoubtedly become essential for the legitimation of the capitalist economic system, and citizen entitlements for support in times of economic stress can be curtailed only at high political risk, at least outside the USA.
5 Later, China became one of the leading creditors of the American state, mostly in order to finance the US trade deficit and keep the country's domestic market open for its exports.
6 The same general development is observed at the global level (McKinsey Global Institute 2015).
7 On Sweden, see Mehrtens (2014) and Haffert and Mehrtens (2015).
8 Between 1993 and 2000, public expenditure in the USA declined by 4 per cent of GDP while tax revenue increased by 2 per cent. The 1993 federal deficit of 4 per cent of GDP turned into a surplus of 2 per cent in 2000. See Pierson (1998, 2001).
9 See, in addition, among others, Prasad (2012), Rajan (2010) and Trumbull (2012).

10 Obviously there is no one-to-one relationship between a country's level of indebtedness and the risk premium it has to pay in capital markets – Japan, for example, refinances its huge national debt at record low interest rates. At the same time, sudden jumps in interest rates for just a few countries (e.g. Greece, Ireland and Portugal in the post-2009 period) are apparently capable of setting in motion a general effort at regaining market confidence by 'reform', as in the EU.

11 In a country with a total debt of 100 per cent of GDP and a government share of 40 per cent of GDP, an increase in the average interest rate on a state's accumulated debt by two percentage points would mean an increase in public spending by five percentage points. To indicate the order of magnitude, total defence spending for most NATO countries is far below 2 per cent of GDP.

12 According to whom a regime is a 'configuration of political interests, institutions, and policy arrangements that structure conflicts over taxes and spending ... a particular political context of institutions, powerful organizations, public policies, and dominant ideas' (Pierson 2001: 56–57).

13 Thus, Japan could in principle resolve its huge public debt problem by introducing a higher sales tax, and the USA could do the same with a federal gasoline tax, even one remaining clearly below European levels.

14 Article IV, Section 1 of the US Constitution, which has come to be interpreted as applying to US treasury bonds and similar financial commitments.

15 See, for example, the various interview statements by the former Swedish Prime Minister, Göran Persson, reported by Mehrtens (2013).

16 This followed years of inventive attempts by American 'vulture funds' to mobilize the civil law of several countries to make the Argentine state deliver on the original conditions of the loan. Essentially what this was about was substituting national commercial law for the still non-existent international sovereign bankruptcy law. See the *New York Times*, 'Vulture fund news', http://topics.nytimes.com/top/reference/timestopics/subjects/v/vulture_funds/index.html, accessed 24 September 2014.

17 As suggested by none other than Lawrence ('Larry') Summers, in a now legendary presentation at the IMF Economic Forum on 8 November 2013. See also his essay a few weeks later in the *Financial Times*, where he proposes that even before the crisis of 2008, 'bubbles and loose credit were only sufficient to drive moderate growth'. Lawrence Summers, 'Why stagnation might prove the new normal', *Financial Times*, 15 December 2013, http://larrysummers.com/commentary/financial-times-columns/why-stagnation-might-prove-to-be-the-new-normal, accessed 27 March 2016.

18 The ECB is not allowed under the Maastricht Treaty to lend to member countries, which is why it had to devise ways to circumvent the treaty.

19 Details of rules and procedures are, as always in the EU, extremely complex and fully comprehensible only for experts. In essence, the updated macroeconomic regime of the EMU involves binding obligations for member states to commit themselves constitutionally to balanced budgets. It also institutes comprehensive current surveillance of member states' fiscal policies by the European Commission. Under the so-called Excessive Deficit Procedure, states may be subject to heavy automatic fines if they fail to keep their public deficits below specified limits. Moreover, under the Excessive Imbalance Procedure, countries may be specifically ordered by the Commission to revise their macroeconomic policies and change relevant institutions, such as their national collective bargaining regimes and their social policies, so as to make them compatible with supra-national coordination. Individual policy directives may extend to a wide range of issues not hitherto under EU jurisdiction. For more, see Höpner and Rödl (2012), Scharpf (2013: 134–136) and Streeck (2014a: 107–109).

20 I have described this as the imposition of a Hayekian regime on the European political economy (Streeck 2014a).

21 When the prime minister of Greece, Andreas Papandreou, was replaced with the central banker Lukas Papademos, and the Italian prime minister, Berlusconi, had to

resign in favour of the former European Commissioner and Goldman Sachs functionary, Mario Monti.

22 This was different in the early 2000s when euro interest rates, set to combat inflation in the South, were too high for low-inflation Germany (Scharpf 2013).

23 There is now a large body of literature on the frictions caused by differently organized national political economies being forced under a common monetary regime. See, for example, Armingeon and Baccaro (2012), Blankart (2013), Feldstein (2011), Hall (2012), and Johnston and Regan (2014).

24 Some two decades ago, the 'German model' was known for relatively low inequality and high social protection under a negotiated social compact between capital and labour. Today, Germany is identified with rapidly rising inequality, stagnant wages, zero inflation, budget balancing and 'welfare reform'.

References

Armingeon, Klaus and Lucio Baccaro, 2012: Political Economy of the Sovereign Debt Crisis: The Limits of Internal Devaluation. *Industrial Law Journal*. Vol. 41, No. 3, 254–275.

Baumol, William J., 1967: Macroeconomics of Unbalanced Growth: The Anatomy of Urban Crisis. *American Economic Review*. Vol. 57, No. 3, 415–426.

Bell, Daniel, 1976: The Public Household: On 'Fiscal Sociology' and the Liberal Society. In D. Bell, *The Cultural Contradictions of Capitalism*. New York: Basic Books.

Blankart, Charles B., 2013: Oil and Vinegar: A Positive Fiscal Theory of the Euro Crisis. *Kyklos*. Vol. 66, No. 3, 497–528.

Blyth, Mark, 2013: *Austerity: The History of a Dangerous Idea*. Oxford: Oxford University Press.

Buchanan, James M. and Gordon Tullock, 1962: *The Calculus of Consent: Logical Foundations of Constitutional Democracy*. Ann Arbor, MI: University of Michigan Press.

Buchanan, James M. and Richard E. Wagner, 1977: *Democracy in Deficit: The Political Legacy of Lord Keynes*. New York: Academic Press.

Buchanan, James M. and Richard E. Wagner, 1978: The Political Biases of Keynesian Economics. In: Buchanan, James M. and Richard E. Wagner, eds, *Fiscal Responsibility in Constitutional Democracy*. Leiden: Martinus Nijhoff.

Crouch, Colin, 2004: *Post-Democracy*. Cambridge: Polity Press.

Crouch, Colin, 2009: Privatised Keynesianism: An Unacknowledged Policy Regime. *British Journal of Politics and International Relations*. Vol. 11, No. 3, 382–399.

Crouch, Colin, 2011: *The Strange Non-Death of Neoliberalism*. Cambridge: Polity Press.

Feldstein, Martin S., 2011: The Euro and European Economic Conditions. Working Paper 17617, National Bureau of Economic Research.

Genschel, Philip and Peter Schwarz, 2013: Tax Competition and Fiscal Democracy. In: Schäfer, Armin and Wolfgang Streeck, eds, *Politics in the Age of Austerity*. Cambridge: Polity.

Goldscheid, Rudolf, 1926: Staat, öffentlicher Haushalt und Gesellschaft. In: Gerloff, Wilhelm and Fritz Neumark, eds, *Handbuch der Finanzwissenschaft*. Tübingen: C.F. Osiander.

Goldscheid, Rudolf, 1976 [1917]: Finanzwissenschaft und Soziologie. In: Hickel, Rudolf, ed., *Die Finanzkrise des Steuerstaats. Beiträge zur politischen Ökonomie der Staatsfinanzen*. Frankfurt am Main: Campus.

Haffert, Lukas, 2015: *Freiheit von Schulden – Freiheit zum Gestalten? Die Politische Ökonomie von Haushaltsüberschüssen*. Frankfurt am Main: Campus.

Haffert, Lukas and Philip Mehrtens, 2015: From Austerity to Expansion? Consolidation, Budget Surpluses, and the Decline of Fiscal Capacity. *Politics and Society*. Vol. 43, No. 1, 119–148.

Hall, Peter, 2012: The Economics and Politics of the Euro Crisis. *German Politics*. Vol. 21, No. 4, 355–371.

Höpner, Martin and Florian Rödl, 2012: Illegitim und rechtswidrig: Das neue makroökonomische Regime im Euroraum. *Wirtschaftsdienst – Zeitschrift für Wirtschaftspolitik*. Vol. 92, No. 4, 219–222.

Johnston, Alison and Aidan Regan, 2014: European Integration and the Incompatibility of Different Varieties of Capitalism: Problems with Institutional Divergence in a Monetary Union. MPIfG Discussion Paper 14/15, Max Planck Institute for the Study of Societies.

Krippner, Greta R., 2005: The Financialization of the American Economy. *Socio-Economic Review*. Vol. 3, No. 2, 173–208.

Krippner, Greta R., 2011: *Capitalizing on Crisis: The Political Origins of the Rise of Finance*. Cambridge, MA: Harvard University Press.

McKinsey Global Institute, 2015: *Debt and (Not Much) Deleveraging*. London: McKinsey & Company.

Magdoff, Harry and Paul M. Sweezy, 1987: *Stagnation and the Financial Explosion*. New York: Monthly Review Press.

Mehrtens, Philip, 2013: Staatsentschuldung und Staatstätigkeit: Zur Transformation der schwedischen politischen Ökonomie. Doctoral Dissertation, Max-Planck-Institut für Gesellschaftsforschung und Wirtschafts- und sozialwissenschaftliche Fakultät der Universität Köln.

Mehrtens, Philip, 2014: *Staatsschulden und Staatstätigkeit: Zur Transformation der politischen Ökonomie Schwedens*. Frankfurt am Main: Campus.

O'Connor, James, 1970a: The Fiscal Crisis of the State: Part I. *Socialist Revolution*. Vol. 1, No. 1, 13–54.

O'Connor, James, 1970b: The Fiscal Crisis of the State: Part II. *Socialist Revolution*. Vol. 1, No. 2, 34–94.

O'Connor, James, 1973: *The Fiscal Crisis of the State*. New York: St. Martin's Press.

OECD, 2013: *Addressing Base Erosion and Profit Shifting*. Paris: OECD.

Pierson, Paul, 1998: The Deficit and the Politics of Domestic Reform. In: Weir, Margaret, ed., *The Social Divide: Political Parties and the Future of Activist Government*. Washington, DC: Brookings Institution Press and Russell Sage Foundation.

Pierson, Paul, 2001: From Expansion to Austerity: The New Politics of Taxing and Spending. In: Levin, Martin A., M.K. Landy and M. Shapiro, eds., *Seeking the Center: Politics and Policymaking at the New Century*. Washington, DC: Georgetown University Press.

Piketty, Thomas, 2014: *Capital in the Twenty-First Century*. Cambridge, MA: Harvard University Press.

Poterba, James M. and Jürgen von Hagen, eds, 1999: *Institutions, Politics and Fiscal Policy*. Chicago, IL: University of Chicago Press.

Prasad, Monica, 2012: *The Land of Too Much: American Abundance and the Paradox of Poverty*. Cambridge, MA: Harvard University Press.

Rajan, Raghuram J., 2010: *Fault Lines: How Hidden Fractures Still Threaten the World Economy*. Princeton, NJ: Princeton University Press.

Schäfer, Armin and Wolfgang Streeck, 2013: Introduction. In: Schäfer, Armin and Wolfgang Streeck, eds, *Politics in the Age of Austerity*. Cambridge: Polity.

Scharpf, Fritz W., 2013: Monetary Union, Fiscal Crisis, and the Disabling of Democratic Accountability. In: Schäfer, Armin and Wolfgang Streeck, eds, *Politics in the Age of Austerity*. Cambridge: Polity, 108–142.

Schumpeter, Joseph A., 1991 [1918]: The Crisis of the Tax State. In: Swedberg, Richard, ed., *The Economics and Sociology of Capitalism*. Princeton, NJ: Princeton University Press, 99–141.

Strange, Susan, 1998: *Mad Money: When Markets Outgrow Government*. Ann Arbor, MI: University of Michigan Press.

Streeck, Wolfgang, 2011: The Crises of Democratic Capitalism. *New Left Review*. Vol. 71: 5–29.

Streeck, Wolfgang, 2014a: *Buying Time: The Delayed Crisis of Democratic Capitalism*. London: Verso Books.

Streeck, Wolfgang, 2014b: Has Capitalism Seen Its Day? Anglo-German Foundation Lecture, the British Academy, London, 23 January 2014.

Streeck, Wolfgang, 2014c: The Politics of Public Debt: Neoliberalism, Capitalist Development, and the Restructuring of the State. *German Economic Review*. Vol. 15, No. 1, 143–165.

Streeck, Wolfgang and Lea Elsässer, 2014: Monetary Disunion: The Domestic Politics of Euroland. MPIfG Discussion Paper 14–17, Max Planck Institute for the Study of Societies.

Trumbull, Gunnar, 2012: Credit Access and Social Welfare: The Rise of Consumer Lending in the United States and France. *Politics and Society*. Vol. 40, No. 1, 9–34.

van der Zwaan, Natascha, 2014: Making Sense of Financialization. *Socio-Economic Review*. Vol. 12, No. 1, 99–129.

Wagschal, Uwe, 1996: *Staatsverschuldung: Ursachen im internationalen Vergleich*. Opladen: Leske + Budrich.

Zucman, Gabriel, 2015: *The Hidden Wealth of Nations: The Scourge of Tax Havens*. Chicago, IL: The University of Chicago Press.

4 Cost of democracy

Changing aspects of modern democracy[1]

Hiroshi Shiratori

Introduction: the cost of democracy and the rise of the New Right parties

Where are the modern democracies heading these days? What is the most recent change in the advanced democracies? To review these questions in full, we need to look at the recent electoral outcomes that raise relevant evidence for further speculation.

One of the changes in the attitude toward social policy in modern democracies is that the role of the state has been reviewed and changed from the generously spending welfare state to the stingily saving welfare state, so as to cope with the globalization of the world economy. It has been argued that the state should not intervene in the economy to set regulations or to impose duties and taxes on the market, for it hinders the freedom of action of enterprises and individuals. In most of the advanced countries that are influenced by the globalization of their economies, the state has become something that restrains the economy's liberty.

With the coming of the age of the neoliberal policy regime at the global level in the 1980s, the era of Thatcherism and Reaganomics, the deregulation of state interventions prevailed in most advanced countries. Too much regulation and too much tax cause stagnation of the country's economy and weaken its presence in the global economy. These policy changes do not come as a matter of course. Some might say the change in the outcome of the policy of government is insufficient. There was a thrust from political groups that were ardently pursuing the reduction of the "cost of democracies" in the 1990s, for the advanced democracies could not maintain the stance of generous welfare state spending. These groups are the New Right parties. The New Right parties are eager to attack the unnecessary welfare costs of government. They see the over-encompassing welfare scheme of modern democracies to be too much. They feel self-help is important to overcome crises, not to resort to and wait for the state to assist because the state is not liable to assist people who do not strive to help themselves. The state has a lack of financial resources to maintain and enhance its welfare schemes. Not only could it not pay for its own welfare schemes, it could not afford the other aspects of democracy imposed by the international system.

The more democracy is absorbed from the global economy, the more the deregulation and the reduction of duties and taxes became salient. This is one of the reasons we saw another rise of the New Right parties after the economic crisis of the 2010s.

1 Changing aspects of modern democracies

1.1 "The cost of democracy" and the New Right party

The "cost of democracy" is in focus in the present political debate on the European Union (EU). In Europe, there is a question of the cost of the EU democracies (Hix and Lord 1997). In May 2014, the European Parliamentary elections were held. There are several important aspects. First, this election was the first election to be held with 28 member states of the present EU. Second, the result of the election was astonishing. Although they did not enjoy the majority of seats, the EU-skeptic political groups have assembled remarkably high proportions of the votes. To name some of the political parties which belong to these groups: the *Front National* (FN, the National Front) of France (Rydgren 2004b), *Dansk Folkeparti* (DF, the Danish Peoples Party) of Denmark, and *Sverigedemocraterna* (SD, the Swedish Democratic Party) of Sweden (Rydgren and Ruth 2011). These parties' ideology is not only called "EU-skepticism," but also the New Right ideal. It was the 2014 European Parliament election that marked the rise of the New Right parties. This election was the first Europe-wide election since the euro crisis of 2010. It can be said that the euro crisis is itself an outcome of the globalization of the economy. What is more, the rise of the New Right parties can be seen as a reaction to the economic crisis.

It is important to review the outcome of the election. In France, the FN won 23 seats out of the 74 seats allocated to the country. The FN became the largest political group to represent France. In the UK, the UK Independent Party (UKIP) became the largest political group to represent the country; it gained 24 seats out of the 73 seats allocated to the country. In Denmark, DF, a split-away faction from *Fremskridtspartiet* (Progressive Party), became the largest political group to represent the country, holding four out of 13 seats.

These right-wing tides were apparent in many European countries. In Austria, the *Freiheits Partei Österreich* (FPÖ, Austrian Liberal Party) hold four out of 18 seats allocated. In Finland, *Perussuomalaiset* (PS, True Finns) received two out of 13. In Germany, the newly founded *Alternative für Deutschland* (AfD, Alternative for Germany) won seven seats out of 96. In Italy, *MoVimento 5 Stelle* (M5S, 5 Star Movement) enjoyed 17 seats out of 73. In the Netherlands, *Partij voor de Vrijheid* (PVV, Liberal Party) received four out of 26.

These parties can be classified as Euro-skeptics, as well as New Right parties. They tend to have a strong populist party leader who is photogenic and can attract people's attention. Most of them are against immigration. They sometimes claim withdrawing from the EU will reduce immigration. For them, to stay in the EU is harmful to their nation because it requires the unnecessary "cost of democracy." They think it is too much for them to pay their tax to save the bankrupted economies of other EU member states, such as Greece. They want to protect their people's lives from the burden of paying for other nations, to enhance individual economic endeavor in the private sector of their modern democracies. In sum, they are not only dealing with the cultural aspect of the country but the economic aspect of the nation. It can be said that they are concerned with "the cost of democracy."

Klaus von Beyme was one of the scholars aware of the rise of these New Right parties after World War II. Beyme identified three phases of the New Right parties since 1945. The first phase was the "postwar neo-fascism" of Italy; the second phase was the "new waves of social deprivation" in Scandinavia; and the third phase was the "unemployment and xenophobia" in France (Beyme 1988: 8–12). It can be said that the first phase suggests the emergence of the Old Right parties after World War II; the second and third phases are the emergence of the New Right parties. For the latter phases, Beyme explains the second phase to be the Poujardist one which handles "the tax revolt and the anti-welfare state movement" and the third phase as "caused by the unemployment and xenophobia." From the outset these New Right parties are dealing with the "cost of democracy" in relation to government revenue and expenditure.

We shall not evaluate the New Right parties as mere racist, xenophobic and neo-Nazi parties.

1.2 What is the meaning of "the cost of democracy" and who are the New Right parties?

There is a parallel tide in the modern democracies in the East. Toru Hashimoto, mayor of Osaka as well as the head of the Japan Restoration Party at that time, commented on the cost of democracy on February 3, 2014. He argued that "the expenditure of the election can be said the cost of democracy." People who support the Japan Restoration Party often criticize the inefficiency of bureaucracy and raise the question of the cost of democracy. What, then, do we mean by "the cost of democracy?"

The cost of democracy includes various aspects of modern democracies. It entails total expenditure of "the democratic government," whether presidential or parliamentary style, majoritarian or consensus. Often, it focuses around the debate of choosing big government or small government, i.e., the balance of taxation and the social services offered by the government. It is a matter and an aspect of the cost of public demand and party supply of the democracies (Norris 2005).

This chapter aims at a theoretical and systematic understanding of the global development of parties that pursue the reduction of the cost of democracies. The main focus will be the changing nature of the party system of the modern democracy in the East and West, from "the party freezing" (the advent of a stable state in the party system) to the emergence of the new parties in the political landscape. My analysis is based on cleavages which stem from sub-cultures in each democracy.

The question of "the cost of democracies" has been raised by the New Right parties for two decades. It seems they have gained in power ever since the economic crises, such as the bankruptcy of Lehman Brothers in 2008 or the euro crisis from 2010. These crises are impacted by, and impact on, international society. The economic crisis focuses governments' policies on fiscal aspects. In order to cope with the crisis, the New Right parties pursued review of revenues and expenditure of the government; they aimed to cut back in both areas.

Who are the New Right parties? According to Hans-Georg Betz, the New Right parties are: *Lega Nord* (Northern League) of Italy, *Autopartei* (Auto Party) of Switzerland, FN of France, *Republikaner* (Republicans) of Germany, *Ny Demokrati* (New Democracy) of Sweden, *Fremskridtpartiet* of Denmark, *Fremskrittspartiet* (Progressive Party) of Norway, FPÖ of Austria, *Vlaams Blok* (Flemish Block) of Belgium (Betz 1994: 3). Herbert P. Kitschelt followed Betz and broadened some of the scope to include other parties – FN of Britain, France and Wallonia; not only Republicans but also *Deutsche Volksunion* (DVU, German People's Union) in Germany; *Centrumpartij* (Centre Party) in the Netherlands; among others (Kitschelt and McGann 1995: 1). There are several differences between these parties. Some are founded on their cultural identities to a certain degree; however, they all deal with the defense of their own economic interests and the "cost of democracy."

They exercise populist policies – e.g., cutting off tax revenues of the government – and nationalistic appeals against immigrants. According to their political position, sometimes they are called "radical right" (Kitschelt and McGann 1995; Mudde 2007; Norris 2005), "right wing extremism" (Merkl and Weinberg, 1997), "extreme right" (Eatwell and Mudde 2004; Hainsworth 2008; Ignazi, 2003; Mudde 1996, 2000; von Beyme 1988), "radical right wing populist" (Rydgren 2004a; Zaslove 2009), "the right-wing populist parties" (Betz 1993, 1994; Betz and Immerfall 1998). In this chapter we shall be confined to the term "New Right parties" to refer to these political parties, for it is not clear to what degree these political parties are extreme or radical. The term shall be treated as neutral, only to identify new parties that hold right-wing ideologies.

It is important to note that they are populists. In order to gain seats in the assembly of the parties, they might express themselves strongly to draw many people's attention. In some cases they are quite successful. In the Norwegian case, *Fremskrittspartiet* became the major political party in Storting. In 1997, 2005 and 2009 Storting elections they became the second largest party; they became the third largest party in the 1989 and 2013 elections. They formed a coalition government together with *Høyre* (Conservatives) after the 2013 election. It was the first ever New Right party to enter Norwegian government.

This Norwegian *Fremskrittspartiet* was established in 1973. However, their success started in the late 1990s. It was inspired by Mogens Gilstrop's Danish *Fremskridtspartiet* (Keman and Müller-Rommel 2012). The founder of the party, Anders Lange, named the party "The Anders Lange's Party for a Strong Reduction in Taxes, Duties and Public Intervention" (*Anders Langes Parti til sterk nedsettelse av skatter, avgifter og offentlige inngrepp*). Lange died in 1974. After

Lange's death, Carl I. Hagen took over leadership of the party. It changed its name to *Fremskrittspartiet* in 1977. Their basic aim was reduction of taxes; however, they gradually took on xenophobic policies (Art 2011; Rydgren 2006).

1.3 Rise of the New Right parties in East and West: a global phenomenon?

These New Right parties can be seen as the reaction to the internationalization of the economy from the 1980s, which was triggered by the neoliberal policy regime at the global level and enhanced by the globalization of the economy after the end of the Cold War from the 1990s. The market-centered policy regime of the neoliberals triggered the review of the unnecessary expenditure of the government, for the central ideal of the neoliberal policy regime at the global level was the efficiency of the system. Based on this anti-taxation policy, they can pretend to support popular issues in relation to the global economy. Anti-immigration policy is definitely one of these popular issues (Mair *et al.* 2004).

The result of the 2014 EU Parliament election can be seen as a reaction to the global economy. In particular, EU democracies have experienced the so-called "euro crisis." Their confidence in the internationalization of the European nation state and the belief in the global economy have been threatened by the euro crisis. EU-skepticism has gained support; however, the Group of the European Peoples Party (EPP), mainly Christian Democrats, and the Group of the Progressive Alliance of Socialists and Democrats in the European Parliament (S&D), mainly Social Democrats, have won the majority of seats. European integration was imperiled by the New Right parties at the election, but it seems EU democracies have succeeded in sticking to the integration process. Although the European integration process has survived, the presence of the EU-skeptic groups, including the New Right parties, cannot be overlooked.

This rise of the right wing ("*høyre vind*" in Norwegian) is not only a European issue. There is a parallel change in Asian democracies. For example, there is the rise of the New Right parties in Japan. The Japan Innovation Party, formerly the Japan Restoration Party, and Tax Reduction Japan can be seen as the New Right parties of Japan.

In order to review long-term party system change in modern democracies, it is necessary to compare a democracy that has a long, uninterrupted history, and also in order to test the party system change to the global one, it is necessary to scrutinize democracies in the East and West. It is for this reason that in this chapter it is appropriate to compare the change in the Japanese party system with the European changes.

My analysis is based on Rokkan's political theory of sub-culture-based politics (Shiratori 1994). Using his theories, I shall present in this chapter a reconsideration of the modern democracies in a broader perspective. Theoretically, subcultures are the expression of cleavages. Often, cleavages are spoken of in relation to political parties. It is important to note that the "party systems do not simply reflect cleavages in a social structure" (Lane and Ersson 1994: 12). Following the argument of Jan-Erik Lane and Svante O. Ersson, we assume that "political parties may be approached as intermediators between social cleavages and political decision-making in government political structures" (Lane and Ersson 1994: 102). In that respect, if there is a change in a party system of a modern democracy, theoretically, there could be a possible change in cleavages which arise from social structures. What is more, if this party system change has occurred not only in Europe but also in Japan in a parallel manner, then it can be said that there is a possibility that similar changes in modern democracies are going on at a global level.

What might be the incident that triggered these global changes in the party systems of each modern democracy? It is too early to name the cause, but only to suggest that the coming of the global economic era of the neoliberal policy regime at the global level and one of its outcomes, the economic crisis, could have possibly triggered the change in people's views on revenues and expenditures of the state. In the end, the party system reacts to these changes.

In "the cost of democracies" debate, on what kind of services does the government spend the most? What might be the target of the cost-cutting New Right parties?

The greatest expenditure is that on welfare in the social-democratic welfare regime. However, it is inevitable, in the end, that all democracies have to attain a welfare state, whether it is social-democratic, liberal or conservative.

Next, we review and scrutinize the development of the party system in modern democracies.

2 Stability and change in party systems

2.1 Political parties as the expression of the cleavages: the East and the West

Rokkan and Lipset have explained party systems and four cleavages in Western Europe (Lipset and Rokkan 1967). In a similar way, the development of a party system in a democracy in the East, Japan, can be analyzed following World War II. The famous freezing hypothesis, that "the party systems of the 1960s reflect, with few but significant exceptions, the cleavage structures of the 1920s" (Lipset and Rokkan 1967) was confirmed in 1970s by Richard Rose and Derek W. Urwin (Rose and Urwin 1970). This line of argument was re-confirmed by Stefano Bartolini and Peter Mair in the 1990s (Bartolini and Mair 1990). It has been argued that West European party systems are remarkably stable, with few exceptions. These cleavages can be found in the newly democratized countries of the former Communist regime in the 2000s (Whitefield 2002). There is an attempt to broaden its scope (Schmitter 2006). It is needless to argue that this notion of cleavage can be applied to non-West European areas.

It was under "the 1955 set up" era that the sub-culture-based democracy was formed that characterizes Japanese politics. The long-lasting one-party dominance of the LDP in Japan was backed by the coalition of the agricultural interest of *Nokyo* (the farmer's organization) in rural and suburban areas and the interest of *Keidanren* (the entrepreneur and the big business organization) in urban areas. Thus, the LDP enjoyed the only "catch-all party" position in both rural and urban areas. It can be said that "the 1955 set up" is "the party freezing era" of modern Japan.

Let us turn to the evaluation of cleavages in modern democracies. In his original concept of cleavages, Rokkan formulated four cleavages: they are center–periphery cleavage, state–church cleavage, land–industry cleavage and owner–worker cleavage. There may be some modifications in order to clarify the notion of cleavages and the applied Parsonian a-g-i-l scheme.

2.2 Four cleavages in a global perspective: the party freezing era until the 1980s

We can relate these four cleavages to the parties from the viewpoint of party ideologies. They are as follows.

2.2.1 Center–periphery cleavage: pre-modern cleavage

In Europe there are abundant examples of regional and ethnic parties. These parties might fall into this category. In Britain there are regional parties: the Scottish Nationalist Party for Scotland, founded 1934; and Plaid Cymru, 1925, for Wales. In Finland there is an ethnic party, *Svenska folkpartiet i Finland* (SFP) or in Finnish, *Suomen ruotsalainen kansanpuolue* (RKP) (the Swedish Peoples' Party) of Finland, founded 1906.

In Japan no political party clearly represents this cleavage under the 1955 set up. However, there could be a latent source of conflict in Japan. The ruling party, the LDP, itself originally had strongholds in the peripheral countryside. But it does not mean there is no such cleavage in Japan. For example, Okinawa Prefecture was once an independent Ryukyu kingdom, and there is a certain number of *Ainu*, or in their usage *Utari*, in Hokkaido. If we use Rokkan's cleavage theory, we can shed light on these potential sources of cleavage.

2.2.2 State–church cleavage: pre-modern cleavage

Many European countries have Christian Parties. For example, there are *Kristelig Folkeparti* (KrF, the Christian People's Party) in Norway, *Democrazia Cristiana* (DC, Christian Democracy) of Italy and *Christlich Demokratische Union Deutschlands* (CDU, the Christian Democratic Union) in Germany. They are the party expression of the church–state cleavage. These parties reflect the longstanding conflict concerning the legitimacy of secular power and religious authority.

In Japan there is no church-based political party. However, if we take the function of the churches, e.g., Christians as a religious group, we may find some equivalent in the Komei Party.

2.2.3 *Land–industry cleavage: early modern cleavage*

In the first phase of the Industrial Revolution there was a conflict between landowners' interests and the factory entrepreneur's interests. This conflict was backed by the geographical constellation of rural areas and urban areas. Landowners' interests were represented by conservative parties and the factory entrepreneur's interests by liberal parties. The most famous example might be the Conservative Party, founded in 1834, and the Liberal Democratic Party, founded in 1988 – its predecessor Liberal Party was founded in 1834 – in Britain. These parties appear not only in Britain but also in other European countries. In Scandinavia, in Norway, there are *Høyre* (the Conservative Party, founded in 1859), *Senterpartiet* (the Center Party, former *Bondepartiet*, the Farmers Party, founded in 1920) and *Venstre* (the Liberal Party, founded in 1884).

In Japan only the Liberal Democratic Party (LDP), founded in 1955, represented both agricultural and industrial interests. Originally, the LDP had its stronghold in provincial areas, and it has often been characterized as a party of farmers that has been able to remain in power by over-representing rural constituencies in the Diet. In 1955 almost half (43 percent) of the supporters of the LDP were farmers (Curtis 1988: 120). It is true that until the end of the 1960s the LDP was primarily concerned with people in rural areas of Japan. However, the demographic change that was caused by rapid industrialization and urbanization has somewhat changed its character. The LDP in the 1970s became less a party of the primary sector because demographic changes forced the party to secure the support of other constituencies to remain in power. This meant a transformation to a "catch-all" party. Curtis further explained the behavior of the LDP: "The LDP's success in retaining power owes a great deal to its ability to closely track changes in its social and economic environment and to adjust its policies accordingly" (Curtis 1988: 45).

2.2.4 *Owner–worker cleavage: old Left–Right cleavage in modern democracies*

Almost all democracies have cleavages concerning the owner and worker. According to Bartolini and Mair, it is the most important source of the cleavage which generates the Left–Right divergence (Bartolini and Mair 1990). This owner–worker cleavage was triggered by the growing number of industrial workers and the penetration of the ideas of Karl Marx. There are socialist parties, communist parties and social-democratic parties in Western Europe. In Britain there is the Labour Party, which was founded in 1900 and is backed by trade unions. In Britain the Labour Party took over from the Liberal Party the position of one part of the two-party system. There is a long tradition of a communist party in Italy. It was originally founded in 1921 as *Partito Comunista d'Italia* (PCd'I, the Communist Party of Italy). It had been outlawed under Benito Mussolini's fascist regime and changed its name to *Partito Comunista Italiano* (PCI, Italian Communist Party) in 1943. This *Partito Comunista Italiano* was the largest communist party in Western Europe. It changed its name to *Partito Democratico della Sinistra* (PDS, Democratic Party of the Left) in 1991 to become a moderate socialist party. In Scandinavian countries there are strong social-democratic parties which retain their position as the ruling parties. In Norway there is *Arbeiderpartiet* (A/Ap, the Labour Party), founded in 1887; and in Sweden there is *Sveriges socialdemokratiska arbetareparti* (SAP, Swedish Social Democratic Party), founded in 1889. There is *Parti socialiste* (PS, the Socialist Party), founded in 1969 in France, and *Sozialdemokratische Partei Deutschlands* (SPD, the Social Democratic Party of Germany), founded in 1875 in Germany, with the preceding party founded in 1863.

There is a parallel development in Japan with the Japan Socialist Party (JSP), which was reunited in 1955.

2.3 The realignment and dealignment in the era of internationalization and globalization of national economies

The above-mentioned "party freezing" in modern democracies and its stability were backed by the growing economy and the formation of welfare states. The rise of affluent societies in every advanced democracy has created the atmosphere of "value-change" in voters' minds (Inglehart 1977, 1990). Based on these "party freezing" statuses as an original position, there occurred gradual change in the party systems of modern democracies. New Left parties appeared in the 1980s. Ronald Inglehart saw the decline of the old cleavage politics and a marked increase in issue voting. The formation of Green parties, with their post-materialist environmental appeal, saw an attempt to depart from the established party politics of old Left–Right issues.

It can be said that the 1980s was the age of the New Left parties. Hans-Georg Betz said that the conflict which arose in the 1980s

> saw a significant fragmentation of the Left. Distancing themselves from what they considered the growth-oriented "old politics" of socialists and social democrats, Green, left-socialist, and similar left-libertarian parties succeeded in establishing themselves in the party systems of a number of advanced West European democracies.
>
> (Betz 1994: 2)

It was Kitschelt who named these New Left parties as "the left-libertarian parties" (Kitschelt 1988). Countries where the modernization process was slower than in Western democracies, e.g., Japan and other Asian countries, did not see the development of the New Left parties. It can be explained by the fact that they pay much more attention to materialist and/or developmentalist values than post-materialist values.

At the same time, modern democracies experienced the rise of the neoliberal policy regime at the global level in the 1980s. The too-broad expansion of the welfare system and the excessive intervention of the state in the societies of each modern democracy paved the way to questioning the current politics of the time. Ronald Reagan and Margaret Thatcher were ardent advocates of a market-oriented small-state ideal. In Japan, the prime minister, Yasuhiro Nakasone followed. They pursued "the cost of democracy" aspect. In order to reduce "the cost of democracy," they reviewed the expenditure of the state and reduced state interference in society. The deregulation policies of the market-binding regulatory schemes was remarkable. These policies were followed in most advanced democracies in reaction to the internationalization of their economies. After the Cold War, in the 1990s, this internationalization of economies was enhanced and deepened, taking the form of a "global economy."

There is a parallel argument. Betz saw that advanced Western societies had confronted "a fundamental restructuring of their economies, dramatic changes in their social structure and value system, and a major transformation of their culture" during the 1970s and 1980s (Betz 1994: 27). According to his argument, this was a result of two revolutions; first, "the final breakthrough of capitalism on a world-wide scale," and second, "the advent of a global economy, where capital and labor, production and markets, information and technology are organized across national boundaries." I see these changes under the heading of "the global revolution." My usage of the term "the global revolution" is similar to Betz's; however, there is a slight difference. I would like to emphasize the importance of the transfer and the diffusion of policy over the border, whether it is sub-national or national. The policy of the New Right parties on the cost of democracies is not only due to the cultural aspect (maintaining their uniqueness), but also to cope with the globalization of their economies and to hinder unnecessary expenditure in modern democracies so as to maintain people's economic status. These are the questions raised by the New Right parties. Thus, the New Right parties have emerged in most modern democracies at the same time (see Table 4.1).

In other words, it can be said that the rise of the New Right parties from the 1990s onward has been a reaction to the coming of the global economy after the Cold War. It is not only the internationalization of nation states but the globalization of the national economy. In the age of globalization, capitalistic ideals and market-centered policy have been triumphant all over modern democracies, as was apparent in European democracies. The internationalization of the nation state and the interdependence of the state economy were very much apparent in that region, and can be seen in the creation of the European common market and the invention of a common currency, the euro, in the 1990s. They are absorbed in the global economy through the EU. It is no wonder that the New Right parties first gained power in Europe.

As mentioned above, it has been considered that *Lega Nord*, *Vlaams Block* and *Autopartei* are examples of New Right parties. *Lega Nord* was founded in 1991 as a federation of several regional parties of northern and central Italy. *Vlaams Block* was founded in 1978. *Autopartei* was founded in 1984; it later changed its name to *Freiheits Partei der Schweiz* in 1994. These parties gained power after the 1980s. Betz also recognized that the presence of the New Right

Table 4.1 Development of party systems in a global perspective

Era	*Policy regime in global level*	*Voter alignment*	*Party system and social movement*	*Europe*	*Japan*
Second World War and Cold War	Social Democratic	Stability of Voter alignment	Party freezing	1920–1960s	1955–1993
Vietnam War	Social Democratic	Dealignment and realignment	Protest movement	1960–1970s	1960–1970s
End of the Cold War	Neoliberal	Dealignment and realignment	New Left parties	1980s	NA
Globalization	Neoliberal	Dealignment and realignment	New Right parties	1990s onwards	2010s

Source: created by author.

Parties is not only a European phenomenon, but a global trend backed by the globalization of the economy. This market-oriented trend was strengthened by the coming of neoliberal policy regimes at the global level (Shiratori 2014). Betz traces examples in a broader context; in the USA from the nationalist populism of Pat Buchanan to the anti-establishment populism of Ross Perot; in India The Bharatiya Janata Party's blend of free-market liberalism and (anti-Islamism) Hindu fundamentalism; in Canada, Preston Manning's Reform Party; and in Russia Vladimir Zhirinovsky's Liberal Democratic Party. Betz concluded "that the wave of contemporary radical right-wing populism, unlike other right-wing radical or extremist movements in the postwar period, is a response to developments shared by all or at least most Western-style democracies" (Betz 1994: 23).

Kitschelt sees this change in line with Betz. "Societal change in contemporary capitalism has increased the salience of political partisan appeals to economy rightist positions favoring market allocation over political redistribution of economic resources" (Kitschelt and McGann 1995: 1). He saw the rise of new parties, especially, the rise of New Right parties as due to "the transition to a postindustrial economy in which citizen's political preferences and salient demands differ from those that prevailed in the Keynesian Welfare State of the post-World War II era, peaking in the 1960s."

There are clear-cut distinctions between the New Left parties and the New Right parties. Kitschelt argues that the New Left parties "stand for 'leftist' income distribution by way of encompassing social policies in the economic sphere and 'libertarian' democratic participation and maximum individual autonomy in politics and cultural sphere," while the New Right parties "advocates rightist free-market economics and 'authoritarian' hierarchical arrangements in politics, together with a limitation of diversity and individual autonomy in cultural expressions" (Kitschelt and McGann 1995: 1). In his use of the word "the Left-Libertarian" and "the New Right Extremists," he sees the post-industrial politics of modern democracies as "characterized by a main ideological cleavage dividing left-libertarians from right-authoritarians."

Kitschelt sees the rise of the New Right parties as a reaction to the New Left parties. According to Kitschelt, "in a structural perspective, the New Right constitutes the mirror image and opposite political pole of a New Left that began to mobilize in the 1960s." It is somewhat questionable to see the New Right party as a mere reaction to the New Left party, for the New Right party appears in the modern democracy that does not have the winning record or clear presence of a New Left party, such as Japan. It must be better to evaluate the rise of the New Right parties as endogenous parties that have reacted to the changes in social conditions of modern democracies. Their main focus is not to attack the New Left parties, but rather to cope with the new conditions of modern democracy – the internationalization and globalization aspects.

It can be said that the internationalization and globalization of the nation state and its economy create the crisis of cultural identity and stable employment of each modern democracy. The more the level of internationalization and globalization rises, the more the level of the crisis follows. In this respect, it is misleading to understand New Right parties as mere racist, cultural xenophobic parties. The core of the battle cry of the New Right parties in modern democracies is the question concerning the expenditure of the government that arises from the internationalization and globalization of the nation states, i.e., the question concerning the "cost of democracies."

In West European democracies, the New Right parties experienced a massive breakthrough in the 1980s and early 1990s. This was in line with the coming of the global economy and it can be seen as one of the most significant signals of a fundamental transformation of politics in advanced modern democracies. They are distant both "from the backward-looking, reactionary politics of the traditional extremist (i.e., neo-fascist and neo-Nazi) Right as well as its proclivity for violence." According to Betz, "these parties are posing the most significant challenge to the established structure and politics of West European democracy today" (Betz 1994: 3).

Betz pointed out the character of the New Right parties:

> Generally, the majority of radical right-wing populist parties are radical in their rejection of the established socio-cultural and sociopolitical system and their advocacy of individual achievement, a free market, and a drastic reduction of the role of the state without, however, openly questioning the legitimacy of democracy in general.
>
> (Betz 1994: 4)

It can be said that originally most of the New Right parties assembled their strength by promoting a radical neoliberal program. After that, if this programmatic appeal loses its power, then they might adopt anti-immigrant positions.

3 The rise of the New Right parties in a global perspective

3.1 The New Right party in a comparative perspective

3.1.1 Welfare states and New Right parties

Let us start from the reevaluation of Rokkan's cleavage theory. Before we go further down to comparative inspection of a democracy, we must reconfirm the historical aspect of the four-cleavages theory. Rokkan and Lipset argue: "Parties do not simply present themselves de novo to the citizen at each election; they each have a history and so have the constellations of alternatives they present to the electorate" (Lipset and Rokkan 1967: 1–2).

Let us look at the historical development of the notion of cleavages. In his interpretation of the Parsonian scheme, Rokkan assumes a model of the process of nation building which he later develops into four phases: (1) penetration (state formation in a narrow sense); (2) standardization (nation building); (3) participation (democracy, foundation of political rights); and (4) distribution (welfare states, foundation of social rights) (Lipset and Rokkan 1967: 9).

According to the Rokkanian four phases of nation building, it is inevitable for the government to construct some certain scheme of a welfare system (Iversen 2005). However, there are several questions raised by the New Right parties. Is it necessary to pay so much money to the government? How can we afford to support such a high welfare standard? Is there anywhere we can find unnecessary governmental expenditure? Is there any way to reduce the tax? Why do we need to follow global ordinance?

The above-mentioned Hashimoto was the head of the Japan Restoration Party together with Shintaro Ishihara from 2012. In 2014 it was split into Hashimoto's Japan Innovation Party and Ishihara's Party for Future Generation. These parties can be categorized as New Right parties together with Takashi Kawamura's Tax Reduction Japan. Furthermore, Yoshimi Watanabe's Your Party, which disbanded in 2014, also fell into that category. The origin of the Japan Innovation Party was the Osaka Restoration Association, which was one of the so-called "local parties." The local parties in Japan mostly pursued self-rule by residents and the cutting of unnecessary expenditure of bureaucracies. At first, one of the battle cries of the party at the local level was "to abolish unnecessary expenditure of the bureaucracy of Osaka." This policy has been consistent since its foundation. Along with other modern democracies, Japan has experienced the rise of the New Right parties: not only the Japan Restoration Party, but also Tax Reduction Japan.

In the European political landscape there is an abundance of examples of New Right parties. Following Betz and Kitschelt, as mentioned above, *Fremskridtspartiet* of Denmark can be seen as one of the predecessors of this category. *Fremskrittspartiet* of Norway, FPÖ of Austria, and FN of France all fall into this category in contemporary European politics. Japanese New Right parties have somewhat similar policies in some respects.

3.1.2 Decline of the old Left–Right politics: dealignment and realignment in the East

What are the common features of the New Right parties? They have a populist leader. They usually criticize the unnecessary expenditure of the government. Sometimes they even pursue reducing taxes. They appeal to the cultural identity whether it is national or local. Sometimes – not in every case however – they have a xenophobic character.

In general, they are against leftist parties. Leftist parties are eager to construct social security schemes. In order to build up a sufficient social security scheme, they tend to raise taxes. This line of argument was triumphant during the period of the social-democratic policy regime at the global level after 1945, before the coming of the neoliberal policy regime in the 1980s.

Why do these parties emerge into modern democracies? After the 1980s, the policy regime at the global level changed from social-democratic to neoliberal. The neoliberal policy regime was characterized by the fundamental market orientation of the neoliberal government. The New Right parties are on one hand in line with this neoliberal government; on the other hand they are a reaction to this trend. This neoliberal policy regime prevailed with the coming of the globalization era after the end of the Cold War.

It is important to note that the New Right parties are different from the neoliberal parties. For the neoliberals, it is inevitable to join the global market; however, the New Right party supporters are sometimes against this global trend. They have the character of conservative ideologies. They can be seen as splitting from conservatives to a certain degree.

Thus, the approaches of the Right and the Left are totally different. According to Amable, they are different in the following ways: the Right follows "supply-side" policy (Giscard d'Estaing, Chirac, Sarkozy); the Left follows "demand-supporting" policy (Mitterrand, Hollande). In the end, governmental expenditure tends to rise under leftist governments (Amable 2014).

Along with other modern democracies, democracy in Japan has experienced a drastic political change based on the above-mentioned sub-cultures and, consequently, it experienced party system change in the 1990s. It is necessary to review the recent change in Japanese politics.

The political turmoil of the 1990s has deeply influenced Japanese politics, which had been characterized by a one-party dominant system for many years. It can be said that one of the biggest changes is the waning and disappearance of the former opposition parties. The Socialist Democratic Party of Japan (the SDPJ) had lost power and most of the other smaller opposition parties under the 1955 setup ceased to exist.

The disappearance and waning of some of the major parties before the post-Cold War era and drastic changes in its policies and platforms concealed the existing conflicting structural cleavages in Japan. The *seikaisaihen* (the reformulation of the political landscape) of the center and the frequent changes of party members and parties created political distrust among Japanese people. Most of the governments of Japan from 1993 have consisted of coalition governments. This can be seen as the beginning of a new era, the 1993 setup.

The election after 1993 has clearly impressed upon Japanese voters that the political system of Japan is in a phase of "realignment." The waning of the SDP and gains of the DPJ clearly showed change in the party system in Japan. This marks the beginning of the new era, the 1993 set up of Japanese politics (Shiratori 2000, 2003).

It seems that Japanese politics is experiencing a new era. However, the existing cleavages and sub-cultures in modern democracies remain. This development is parallel with other modern democracies.

3.2 The formation of new parties under the globalizing world: finding party expression in reaction to the neoliberal policy regime

The political turmoil of modern democracies that started in the 1990s went on into the twenty-first century. Along with this political turmoil, in Japan there appeared new parties in reaction to the coming of the global economy. Although they are small, they clearly show the existence of latent cleavages in Japanese politics (Müller-Rommel and Pridham 1991). The globalization of the economy and the coming of the neoliberal policy regime at the global level have revitalized latent cleavages that have been hidden under the old Left–Right politics. It caused the eruption of the New Right parties.

After the eruption of the new parties under the LDP–Komei-led government, there was the "Regime Change Lower House Election" of 2009. The LDP and Komei lost the election and the DPJ became the ruling party. In this flux there appeared several New Right parties. Osaka Restoration Association and Tax Reduction Japan were formed in 2010. They can be seen as reactionary parties toward the socialist democratic oriented DPJ policy. The two parties can be evaluated as the subject vs. dominant culture cleavage, representing local parties of Osaka and Nagoya, respectively. Gradually, they took the form of New Right parties. Next, I shall review the original profiles of these parties in comparison with European parties.

3.2.1 Subject vs. dominant culture cleavage

Osaka Restoration Association and Tax Reduction Japan were both founded by leaders of local politics in 2010. Toru Hashimoto, the governor of Osaka Prefecture, created the former party; Takashi Kawamura, the mayor of Nagoya city, created the latter. They have some sense of being "anti-Tokyo oriented" political cultures. These two parties represent their respective regions politically.

There is a parallel move in the European political landscape. In the regional reaction to the globalization of the economy, the Scottish National Party has gained seats in the 2015 UK General Election. It can be seen that the globalization of the economy has made the latent cleavages more clear. Originally, *Lega Nord* of Italy and *Vlaams Blok* of Belgium were also defenders of their regional interests against the globalizing economy. UKIP can be seen as the protector of the UK as a region in Europe.

3.2.2 The New Right parties

Based on these cleavages that have been revitalized by the globalization of the world economy, there emerged the New Right parties. In Japan, Osaka Restoration Association turned into the Japan Restoration Party in 2012; it has now split and merged with some dissenters from Your Party in 2014 to form Japan Innovation Party. Together with local parties, Tax Reduction Japan and the Japan Innovation Party support the reduction of the "cost of democracy." They have a populist leader and right-wing ideals. It became the third largest party in the Lower House of the Japanese Diet in 2014. The right wing is apparent in modern democracy in the East.

At a glance over the political landscape of modern democracies, the New Right parties are well represented in most cases. Especially, they were welcomed by voters who are skeptical of the globalizing economy after the economic crisis in the 2010s (Table 4.2).

Table 4.2 Critical junctures and cleavages from a global perspective

Critical juncture	*Cleavages*	*Political parties*
National revolution	Dominant culture vs. Subject culture State vs. religious group	Regional parties, conservative parties, religious parties
Industrial Revolution	Secondary Sector vs. primary sector Owners vs. workers	Agricultural parties, liberal parties, socialist, communist and social democratic parties
Global revolution (1980s on)	Value change and more expenditure of government Question of welfare and less expenditure of government	New Left parties, ecological parties, New Right parties, populist parties

Source: created by author.

It is not by chance that the New Right parties appeared and hold seats in modern democracies. They have some similar policies toward "the cost of democracy" that fits with people's skepticism toward the neoliberal market-oriented policy regime, as well as the generously spending welfare state. It is no wonder they share somewhat similar policies. It is because they face the same problem of globalization and how to cope with it, so policies have been transferred across borders.

3.3 Waning populist appeal and the end of the New Right parties? 2015 UK General Election and 2015 Osaka Referendum

Ever since the 1990s, it has been said that one of the common symptoms of advanced modern democracies was the rise of the New Right parties. They became quite salient at the 2014 European Parliament election. Quite recently, however, in 2015, there appeared several examples that go against this trend.

First, the 2015 UK General Election on May 7 was one of the most interesting British elections of the twenty-first century. Against all the electoral forecasts, the Conservatives, headed by David Cameron, held the majority of the Parliament. On the right wing of the political spectrum, UKIP, which showed remarkable success in the European Parliamentary elections in 2014, won 12.4 percent of the votes cast on the polls and gained approximately 10 percent more votes than in the 2010 election. However, they can only enjoy one seat this time.

A similar phenomenon has appeared in another democracy in the East, Japan. The Japan Innovation Party, the former Japan Renaissance Party, which has a populist leader and was a newly established national party in the 2010s, tried to change the local ruling system of Osaka. In order to pass its appeal to the Diet, they dared to launch a referendum on May 17, 2015. Based on the popularity of the party leader, Toru Hashimoto, they believed they could win the support of the majority of Osaka's voters.

The result of the referendum, deciding whether to merge Osaka Prefecture and Osaka City, was not in line with the ideas of Hashimoto and the Japan Innovation Party. The voters of Osaka rejected the idea of abolishing Osaka City and merging it into Osaka Prefecture by a slight majority. The difference between the Yes vote (49.6 percent) and No vote (50.4 percent) was less than 1 percent of the votes cast for that referendum. After the referendum, Hashimoto announced that he would resign the party leadership.

Are these incidents showing the end of the tide of the New Right? It seems premature to declare the doom of the New Right at this moment; rather, these events seem just a disturbance to this trend. We can say we are still in the era of the New Right. FN of France will exercise its power on French politics as well as the European Parliament. In some countries, the New Right party, for example *Fremskrittspartiet* in Norway, might play an important role in the government for some time. It is not the end of the New Right parties.

Hashimoto's original reason for the formation of the Japan Innovation Party, originally the Japan Renaissance Party, was "the cost of democracy." He criticized the ruling system of local government of Osaka as wasting the budget as there are similar facilities both for Osaka Prefecture and Osaka City; he sees it as an example of "an unnecessary dualism" of the local government. He said that if Osaka Prefecture and Osaka City merged into one, they could utilize the resources much better. In order to avoid unnecessary public expenditure, he argued that the inefficient dualistic system of Osaka Prefecture and Osaka City had to be abolished and merged into one. It is for this reason that Osaka's local branch of his Japan Innovation Party, Osaka Restoration Association, has a home page named "One Osaka!"

This "cost of democracy" argument is an important part of the New Right parties. UKIP is famous for its party constitution:

> The Party believes that the United Kingdom of Great Britain and Northern Ireland (hereinafter "The United Kingdom") should only be governed by her own citizens and that its governance shall at all times be conducted first and foremost in the interests of the United Kingdom and its peoples and that the only laws that should apply within the jurisdiction of the United Kingdom are those wholly made by the Parliament of the United Kingdom. To that end it shall be the policy of the Party that the United Kingdom shall cease to be a member of the European Union and shall not thereafter make any Treaty or join any international organization which involves in any way the surrender of any part of the United Kingdom's sovereignty.
>
> (www.ukip.org/the_constitution)

In order to accomplish these objectives, UKIP clarified its policy. According to the party constitution, it defines itself as "a democratic, libertarian Party." The party espouses policies that "seek to diminish the role of the State," "lower the burden of taxation on individuals and businesses" and "ensure proper control over the United Kingdom's borders." It is important to note that the issue concerning immigration and the control of borders comes after the issue of the "cost of democracy," i.e., the deregulation of the state and the cutting of the tax burden.

In that respect, we can say that the main objectives of the New Right parties are not always xenophobically oriented, but "cost of democracy" oriented. It is the starting point of almost all New Right parties. That is the basic difference which we discern from the Old Right parties to the New Right parties. The Old Right parties, or in more familiar terms the neo-Nazis, are intrinsically xenophobic in their policies and tend to pay much attention to the culturally nationalistic ideal. However, the New Right parties' concerns are essentially the economic aspects of modern democracies. They are basically in line with the neoliberal economic ideals of Reaganomics or Thatcherism. In order to pursue economic freedom, they tend to reduce the role of the state and insist on the reduction of taxes and other forms of economic burden. In short, the difference between the Old Right parties and the New Right parties are their orientation toward the main policies. The Old Right is prone to speak xenophobically in a cultural and racial way; the New Right parties begin from the deregulation of the state and are inclined to speak of tax reduction. This cultural and racial inclination and the economic tendency show a difference in the basic attitude toward policies.

Following emergence as a marginal political party in the party family in each democracy in the 1980s, every New Right party strived to attract voters' attention to survive elections. In order to win the election, they have to use the media to send an image of the party because of their lack of organizational support compared to the established parties of the day. It is no wonder that these New Right parties have populist characters from the outset. This lack of supportive organizations has paved the way for these New Right parties to become populist parties of the modern age. They are free from trade unions, religious groups and big businesses. The only possible way to gain support among the constituencies is to rely on the personal charm of the party leader. The leaders of the New Right parties pretend to be charismatic. First, to create this charismatic figure the party leaders of the New Right tend to present a somewhat strong image. Second, as a populist party, they are eager to offer new policy aspects – one of the important new fields would be issues concerning immigration. The xenophobic character of the New Right parties is not essential; rather, it can be said to be an additional aspect used to gather votes. Most New Right parties start out from "the cost of democracy" questions and still question the unnecessary expenditure of the government.

4 Conclusion: policy transfer at the party level?

I aimed to apply Rokkan's theory with reference to the possible application of his general theory to the twenty-first-century world, as well as to the non-Western European area from a standpoint of sub-culture-based politics.

Japan is just another modern democracy that experienced a history of authoritative regimes and being a late-comer to modernization. Along with globalization of its economy, Japan might have experienced policy transfer at the party level. As the Norwegian Progressive Party has transferred the New Right policies from the Danish Progressive Party, this line of policy transfer at the international level might shed new light on the analysis of comparative political party research (Shiratori 2014).

From that perspective, the 2014 European Parliament election can be analyzed in the same way. The 2014 European Parliament election was an important election in two senses. First, it was the first election held after the euro crisis. Second, the outcome of the election marks the rise of the New Right party.

Although the EPP and S&D hold a majority in Parliament, we can see the reaction toward the Europeanization and the globalization of nation states, i.e., the neoliberal policy regime at the international and the global level.

This trend of the right wing was apparent in European countries. However, it is not only a European phenomenon, but is also apparent in another democracy in the East, Japan.

We can see that the New Right parties in Japan, the Japan Reformation Party and Tax Reduction Japan, together with other new parties that emerged in reaction to the neoliberal policy regime of Japanese politics, are parallel parties to those of Europe: *Fremskrittspartiet*, DF and FN.

It seems that the right wing is rising after the economic crisis. They pursue the small state and self-determination of the nation state against globalization. If we can see this battle cry of the cutting of "the cost of democracy" as another example of policy transfer at the party level, there is a chance that we are moving from the neoliberal policy regime to the new conservative policy regime at the global level. It can be seen that the rise of the New Right parties shows clear symptoms of possible change in the party system of modern democracy.

Each democracy has its own policy regime at the national level – say, Japan as a conservative policy regime state and Norway as a socialist democratic policy regime state. Even in a socialist democratic policy regime like Norway, the New Right parties are in power at the moment. It can be said that the coming of the age of the neoliberal policy regime triggered the question of the efficiency of democracy, and this question has allowed the New Right parties to gain popularity and support. In most modern democracies the New Right political parties appeared, pursuing the cutting of taxes. One of the most eminent examples would be the Progressive Parties in the Nordic countries. They form their support in reaction to the socialist democratic policy regime at the national level. In Japan, there appeared the Japan Innovation Party in 2014 and Tax Reduction Japan of Nagoya in 2010. They can be evaluated as the reaction to the socialist democratic ideal of the DPJ under economic recession. Along with its predecessors, which appeared as a reaction to the neoliberal policy orientation of the Koizumi administration, these new parties represent structural changes of a modern democracy, Japan. It has been said that Japan was free from structural cleavages; however, I see a promising breakthrough in applying the cleavage model. I have started from theoretical clarification of the cleavages that appeared in the party system under the party freezing era and its change in the dealignment and realignment era. It can be said that the new party system in modern democracies, after the rise of the New Right parties, might be analyzed from the point of view of uncovering the latent cleavages and finding new expressions in parties in reaction to policy regime change at the global level.

Acknowledgments

I am indebted to comments from Philippe Schmitter and Hideko Magara on the earlier version of this chapter. I am also indebted to comments from Stephen Whitefield on the New Right conception during my stay in Oxford, 2015–2016, and to comments from Peter Flora on the Rokkan framework during my stay in Mannheim, 1998. I have also benefited from comments by Henry Valen, Oddbjørn Knutsen, Erik Allardt, Jan-Erik Lane, Derek W. Urwin, Lars Svåsand and Stein Kuhnle during my stay in Oslo, 1994–1995.

Note

1 This chapter was partly written on the basis of an article written in French and published in a French academic journal. Hiroshi Shiratori, "Le mouvement référendairen au Japon après la Guerre froide: Une analyse comparative inspirée de Rokkan," *Revue Française de Science Politique*, Volume 51, Numéro 4, August 2001.

References

Amable, Bruno, *The Unsolved Contradictions of the Modernists: Economic Policy Expectations and Political Crisis in France 1978–2012*. Working Papers of the Centre d'Économie de la Sorbonne, 23, 2014.

Art, David, *Inside the Radical Right: The Development of Anti-Immigrant Parties in Western Europe*, New York: Cambridge University Press, 2011.

Bartolini, Stefano and Peter Mair, *Identity, Competition, and Electoral Availability: The Stabilization of European Electorates 1885–1985*, Cambridge: Cambridge University Press, 1990.

Beyme, Klaus von, "Right-Wing Extremism in Post-War Europe," *West European Politics*, Vol. 11, No. 2, 1988, pp. 1–18.

Betz, Hans-Georg, "The New Politics of Resentment: Radical Right-Wing Populist Parties in Western Europe," *Comparative Politics*, Vol. 25, No. 4, 1993, pp. 413–427.

Betz, Hans-Georg, *Radical Right-Wing Populism in Western Europe*, Basingstoke: Macmillan, 1994.

Betz, Hans-Georg and Stefan Immerfall, eds., *The New Politics of the Right: Neo-Populist Parties and Movements in Established Democracies*, Basingstoke: Palgrave Macmillan, 1998.

Curtis, Gerald L., *Japanese Way of Politics*, Washington, DC: Columbia University Press, 1988.

Eatwell, Roger and Cas Mudde, eds., *Western Democracies and the New Extreme Right Challenge*, London: Routledge, 2004.

Hainsworth, Paul, *The Extreme Right in Western Europe*, London: Routledge, 2008.
Hix, Simon and Christopher Lord, *Political Parties in the European Union*, Basingstoke: Macmillan, 1997.
Ignazi, Piero, *Extreme Right Parties in Western Europe*, Oxford: Oxford University Press, 2003.
Inglehart, Ronald, *Silent Revolution: Changing Values and Political Styles among Western Publics*, Princeton, NJ: Princeton University Press, 1977.
Inglehart, Ronald, *Culture Shift in Advanced Industrial Societies*, Princeton, NJ: Princeton University Press, 1990.
Iversen, Torben, *Capitalism, Democracy and Welfare*, Cambridge: Cambridge University Press, 2005.
Keman, Hans and Ferdinand Müller-Rommel, eds., *Party Government in the New Europe*, London and New York: Routledge, 2012.
Kitschelt, Herbert, "Left-Libertarian Parties: Explaining Innovation in Competitive Party Systems," *World Politics*, Vol. 40, No. 2, 1988, pp. 194–234.
Kitschelt, Herbert and Andrew McGann, *The Radical Right in Western Europe: A Comparative Analysis*, Ann Arbour, MI: University of Michigan Press, 1995.
Lane, Jan-Erik and Svante O. Ersson, *Politics and Society in Western Europe*, 3rd edition, London: Sage, 1994.
Lipset, Seymour M. and Stein Rokkan, eds., *Party Systems and Voter Alignments; Cross National Perspectives*, New York: The Free Press, 1967.
Mair, Peter, Wolfgang C. Müller and Fritz Plasser, eds., *Political Parties and Electoral Change: Party Responses to Electoral Markets*, London: Sage, 2004.
Merkl, Peter H. and Leonard Weinberg, eds., *The Revival of Right Wing Extremism in the Nineties*, London: Routledge, 1997.
Mudde, Cas, "The War of Words: Defining the Extreme Right Party," *West European Politics*, Vol. 19, No. 2, 1996, pp. 225–248.
Mudde, Cas, *The Ideology of the Extreme Right*, Manchester and New York: Manchester University Press, 2000.
Mudde, Cas, *Populist Radical Right Parties in Europe*, Cambridge: Cambridge University Press, 2007.
Müller-Rommel, Ferdinand and Geoffrey Pridham, eds., *Small Parties in Western Europe: Comparative and National Perspectives*, London: Sage, 1991.
Norris, Pippa, *Radical Right: Voters and Parties in the Electoral Market*, Cambridge: Cambridge University Press, 2005.
Rose, Richard and Derek W. Urwin, "Persistence and Change in Western Party Systems Since 1945," *Political Studies*, Vol. 18, No. 3, 1970, pp. 287–319.
Rydgren, Jens, "Explaining the Emergence of Radical Right-Wing Populist Parties: The Case of Denmark," West *European Politics*, Vol. 27, No. 3, 2004a, pp. 474–502.
Rydgren, Jens, *The Populist Challenge: Political Protest and Ethno-Nationalist Mobilization in France*, New York: Berghahn Books, 2004b.
Rydgren, Jens, *From Tax Populism to Ethnic Nationalism: Radical Right-Wing Populism in Sweden*, New York: Berghahn Books, 2006.
Rydgren, Jens and Patrick Ruth, "Voting for the Radical Right in Swedish Municipalities: Social Marginality and Ethnic Competition?," *Scandinavian Political Studies*, Vol. 33, No. 4, 2011, pp. 202–225.
Schmitter, Philippe, "Just What Might an Eventual Euro-Party System Look Like (With Apologies to Stein Rokkan and His Many Followers)," European University Institute, mimeo, 2006.

Shiratori, Hiroshi, "Theoretical Foundation of Sub-Culture-Based Politics: Reconsidering Early Works of Stein Rokkan," *Journal of Behavioral and Social Sciences*, Vol. 3, 1994, pp. 78–79.

Shiratori, Hiroshi, "Touketsukasetsu no Nihon ni okeru kento" (Examining "Freezing Hypothesis" in Japan), *Houseikenkyu (Journal of Law and Politics)*, Vol. 4, No. 1, 2000.

Shiratori, Hiroshi, *Toshi tai Chihou no Seijigaku (Politics of Urban and Rural Confrontation in Contemporary Japan)*, Tokyo: Ashi-Shobo, 2003.

Shiratori, Hiroshi, "Multilevel Policy Regimes, Political Cleavages and Party Systems: Horizontal and Vertical Transfer of Policies and its Effects," in Hideko Magara ed., *Economic Crises and Policy Regimes: The Dynamics of Policy Innovation and Paradigmatic Change*, Cheltenham: Edward Elgar, 2014.

Whitefield, Stephen, "Political Cleavages and Post-Communist Politics," *Annual Review of Political Science*, Vol. 5, 2002, pp. 181–200.

Zaslove, Andrej, "The Populist Radical Right: Ideology, Party Families and Core Principles," *Political Studies Review*, Vol. 3, No. 3, 2009, pp. 309–318.

5 Institutional change and regime crisis

A critical viewpoint on neoliberalism

Toshio Yamada

1 The world financial crisis and neoliberalism

The Lehman shock of 2008 and the following world financial crisis attracted public attention as a once-in-a-century crisis. Many political economies found some limits of neoliberalism and market fundamentalism in this crisis or confirmed a crisis of finance-led capitalism. At the same time, some political economies anticipated a historical turning point or epochal refraction in the crisis.

However, eight years after the Lehman shock, neoliberal ideas and policies seem to be as dominant as ever, in spite of serious failures, including political control by Wall Street in the USA. It also does not seem that the form of capitalism dominated by finance has disappeared. Or are we witnessing a sprouting of new and strong politico-economic systems or ideas that have to substitute those of neoliberalism? Further, even if so, will the new ones really pave the way for a democracy that meets contemporary requirements?

It is true that, in the midst of the crisis, not only were economic emergency measures taken, but various institutional reforms were also carried out at the level of central government and central banks. Reforms were also carried out in regional banks and individual companies. But are these measures and reforms as a whole constituting a new socioeconomic regime going forward? Eight years after the shock, frankly speaking, it seems difficult for us to be sure about the direction in which the regime is evolving. We must, therefore, consider both the tenaciousness and variability of institutions and regimes. This leads us to the question of what determines institutional change and how it occurs.

This chapter, keeping problems of today's neoliberalism in mind, proposes some basic theoretical elements concerning the crisis of the neoliberal regime. The word "regime" refers to a political, economic, and ideological system with some coherence, domestically or internationally. A regime consists of institutions that, as a whole, are complementary and hierarchical to one another.

Two concepts of regime are relevant to us. The first is the concept of a "policy regime," proposed by Przeworski (2001, 2014). According to him, in modern democratic politics, major political parties, regardless of their partisan stripes, tend to propose similar policies. That is, once a party comes to office by making a major successful policy innovation, those policies will be followed by the opposition party, if elected. The difference between the two parties thus becomes so small that one can identify a movement of convergence toward a new state of policy equilibrium, referred to as a "policy regime." A policy regime lasts for decades and changes infrequently. A successful policy innovation in a country may be followed by the other countries, thus spreading internationally. Przeworski identifies two policy regimes over nearly the past 100 years: (1) the Keynesian one from the 1930s through the high economic growth following World War II, and (2) the neoliberal one from the 1970s/1980s to the present.

This concept of a "policy regime" is attractive because it describes a main trend in world history, especially concerning the current trend of the international spread of neoliberal policies and ideologies. However, its shortcoming is that it understands contemporary world history as a mere paradigmatic change from Keynesian to neoliberal policy regime. Countries under the same policy regime do not necessarily converge to the same socioeconomic system. Diversity and specificity of capitalist countries matter. We therefore need a second concept of regime, a "growth regime." This originates from the French *régulation* theory, and generally implies a set of overall regularities in macroeconomic variables of a particular country at a particular time. A growth regime may generate a vigorous "mode of development" when supported by proper institutions and "mode of *régulation*," but, if not, the regime will decline and fall into crisis.[1] In this chapter, however, we use the term "growth regime" expansively, that is, almost in the connotation of a "mode of development." See Table 5.1 for the

Table 5.1 Growth regime and policy regime

	1950s–1960s	*1970s/1980s*
Policy regime	Keynesian	Neoliberal
Growth regime		
Hegemonic growth regime	Fordist or industry-led	Finance-led
Spatial diversity of growth regime/socioeconomic model		
Hall and Soskice (2001) on main OECD countries		LMEs CMEs
Amable (2003) on main OECD countries		Market-based Asian Continental European Social-democratic Mediterranean
Boyer (2011) on the world as a whole		Dominant financier Innovative industrialist Developmentalist Rentier Dependent financier Disarticulated Pre-industrial

Source: author.

existing growth regimes or socioeconomic types; the table has been created based on the studies of Hall and Soskice (2001), Amable (2003), and Boyer (2011).[2] In this chapter we will mainly cover the finance-led growth regime, focusing on the USA, the hegemonic country.

In short, "regime" here designates either the concept of a "policy regime" that grasps trends in world history, or a "growth regime" that covers the spatial varieties of capitalism. As was mentioned above, a regime, be it policy regime or growth regime, consists of a coherent body of institutions. Regime changes therefore presuppose changes in the regime's core institutions, and regime crises involve crises of core institutions as well. After some theoretical discussion on institutional changes (Sections 2 to 4), this chapter proposes a critical viewpoint on the current neoliberal policy regime and on the finance-led growth regime (Section 5), before ending with concluding remarks (Section 6).

2 Path dependence and regime crisis

Path dependence theory has greatly influenced discussions on institutional change in recent years. In effect, when we extract an essential historical recognition undergirding theories of policy regimes and growth regimes, we can find in them a kind of theoretical configuration of path dependence. For example, Przeworski's policy regime theory examines historical evolutions in the following framework: policy innovation (that is considered to occur in a period of crisis) → state of policy equilibrium (policy regime) → new policy innovation. In the case of growth regime theory for regulationists, at least in its origin, a similar historical trajectory is supposed: structural crisis → durable growth (growth regime) → new structural crisis.

We can define a pattern of historical perspective in the following way. At first, conventional institutions are reexamined and signs of new institutions emerge at a critical epoch (period of crisis); then comes the forging of proper institutions and policies supporting economic development and political stability (period of durable growth or political equilibrium). At last, with the passage of time, these measures reach a deadlock, resulting in a new epoch of regime crisis and institutional innovation (new period of crisis).

As shown, intentionally or not, the historical perspective of policy and growth regime theories stands, to some extent, on the model of path dependence theory. In this sense, the latter is situated as a starting point for understanding changes in institutions and regimes. There is already an extensive literature covering various opinions in many academic disciplines on path dependence theory.[3] In this chapter we focus on the development of this theory only with respect to the study of institutions, especially in an academic tradition of "historical institutionalism," which has greatly extended path dependence theory.

The characteristics of path dependence theory from a historical perspective are, *grosso modo*, summarized as follows. A historical path begins with an epoch called a "critical juncture" where many possibilities for the future push and jostle amidst chaos and disorder. However, over time, one or few possible paths, often resulting from relatively small events, will be taken by the society. What institution or path will be chosen is, in many cases, dependent on "contingent" or "exogenous" shocks. However, once a path is chosen, it creates "positive feedback" or "increasing returns," reproducing itself for a considerably longer period, and thus institutions and paths lock-in particular patterns. This is the stable period for institutions. Eventually, however, the path becomes unstable owing to the emergence of a new situation, leading to a period of abrupt path collapse and new groping: a new period of critical juncture (Deeg 2001; Mahoney 2000; Pierson 2000).

Path dependence theory, thus, still understands history in an original framework: critical juncture → developmental trajectory (reproduction of path) → critical juncture. Its historical perspective is well summed up as "long continuities" periodically interrupted by "radical shifts" (Pempel 1998: 3; Thelen 2004: 28). The merits of path dependence theory in the field of institutional studies include the following: (1) it facilitates a dynamic, historical understanding of institutions (i.e., theory of institutional change) by moving away from a static, unchangeable view of institutions often presupposed in the comparative statics of institutions (Figure 5.1a); (2) it discusses changes in history, including qualitative transformations of economic societies, instead of providing an uninterrupted view of history that is monotonous and simply involves consecutive, quantitative, and often linear variations (Figure 5.1b); (3) it distinguishes between the generating and existing causes of institutions by clearly distinguishing between periods of critical juncture and reproduction (Figure 5.1c), leading to a rejection of a functionalist explanation of institutions, which insists that the existence of institution *A* is due to its function *A'*; and (4) it allows for a discussion on different types of capitalism by its emphasis on concrete historical events and their path-founding roles.

Although path dependence theory has facilitated a discussion on institutional change, its understanding of institutional change is not necessarily persuasive. Among the many critiques of the theory, the following are most relevant: (1) it identifies causes of institutional changes solely in exogenous or contingent

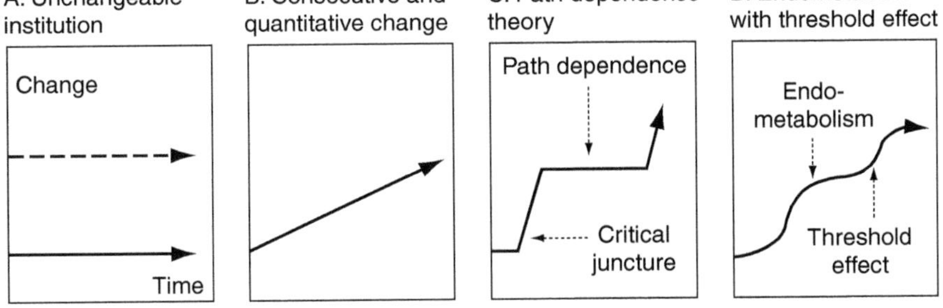

Figure 5.1 Various views on institutional change.

Source: author.

shocks; (2) it does not focus on the importance of big events early in a sequence, but emphasizes only small events (Deeg 2001; Schwartz 2001); (3) it detects moments of institutional change, not "gradual" and "endogenous" change, but "radical" change, at a critical juncture; and (4) as Thelen (2003, 2004) points out, it involves a mechanical dichotomy that divides history into periods of institutional change (critical juncture) and institutional stability (reproduction) (Figure 5.1c).

These four points must be overcome by a more developed discussion of institutional change (e.g., Figure 5.1d). The path dependence theory, in spite of its cultivation of a historical view that is punctuated by regime crisis, does not suggest how a regime crisis occurs. Thus, in the next section, we provide some consideration to the essence of institutional change by examining discussions on the types of institutional changes.

3 Endometabolism of institutions and types of institutional change

One could obtain many classifications of institutional change from various criteria. The most well-known typology was principally proposed by Kathleen Thelen. This typology classifies institutional change into four types from a viewpoint of its "process" (incremental or abrupt) and "result" (continuity and discontinuity): (a) "reproduction by adaptation" (*incremental* process of change with *continuous* result of change); (b) "survival and return" (*abrupt* process with *continuous* result); (c) "gradual transformation" (*incremental* process with *discontinuous* result); and (d) "breakdown and replacement" (*abrupt* process with *discontinuous* result) (Streeck and Thelen 2005: 9; Thelen 2009: 475).

"Reproduction by adaptation" (a) describes a state in which established institutions, while adapting themselves to the evolutions of times, maintain, reproduce, and endure themselves. "Survival and return" (b) represents the case in which, although there might happen to be a transitory institutional change owing to an attempt at abrupt institutional transformations, the attempt would soon go wrong and the original institutions would return. However, in reality, these two are not cases of institutional change, but of institutional endurance, so long as the "result" is ever "continuous." Thus, in Thelen's classification, we find only two types of actual institutional changes: "gradual transformation" (c) and "breakdown and replacement" (d). Gradual transformation refers to a situation where, notwithstanding a partial and gradual process of changes, the accumulation of changes for a long time may result in a discontinuous breaking up in comparison to the initial institutions. This is the situation to which Thelen attaches particularly great importance. The "breakdown and replacement" designates a type of change in which institutions suffer sudden transformations leading to results that are disconnected from previous ones. This is a type of change in which previous institutions are replaced almost at a stroke in a critical moment, similar to a war, the Great Recession, or a revolution. Besides, in Thelen's classification as a whole, institutional changes are essentially distinguished only by whether they are "incremental" or "abrupt," a typology too simple to be effective.

We therefore intend to construct a slightly more detailed typology. Keeping Thelen's viewpoint that classifies the "process" of institutional change into "gradual" and "abrupt (radical)" categories, we must pay attention also to the "causes" of institutional change. Although there may be many causes of institutional change, here we categorize them into "endogenous" and "exogenous" from a much wider point of view. As one may not simply distinguish between "gradual" and "radical" concerning the actual process of institutional change, so one may not easily tell "endogenous" from "exogenous" with respect to the causes of institutional change, because causes normally arise in complicated relations. However, we dare to propose our typology in the simplest way, as shown in the Table 5.2.[4]

The most important and core cause of institutional change is "endometabolism" (a), that is, a gradual institutional change with endogenous cause. Endometabolism is a concept to which the *régulation* school has been more or less attached, and is in general defined as "the process by which the functioning of the structure alters the structure itself" (Boyer and Saillard 1995: 337). In the field of political economy, it is defined as "the transformation of a mode of development under the impact of its proper internal dynamics" (Boyer 2004: 197).[5] In short, as a living thing alters, through everyday metabolic functions, its biological structure, passing from infancy to youth to prime-of-life to old-age in the medium to long run, an institution gradually changes itself based on its own dynamics. This is the endometabolism of an institution.

When we understand the "institution" broadly in the framework of "institutional structure," the whole configuration of endometabolism becomes clearer.

Table 5.2 Types of institutional changes: process and causes

		Causes of change	
		Endogenous	*Exogenous*
Process of change	Gradual	*Endometabolism*: gradual transformation of institution by means of its own functioning (a)	*Hybridization*: gradual penetration and mixture of foreign and international impacts (c)
		Modes of change: layering, drift, conversion	
	Radical	*Threshold effect*: internal collapse of institution through reaching threshold of endometabolism (b)	*Big events*: international shocks, wars, revolutions, etc. (d)
		Mode of change: displacement	

Source: author.

By functioning, the institution alters not only (1) itself, but also (2) the external environment surrounding it, and (3) the various strategies of agents who act under given institutions. An institution modifies its institutional structure by way of its endometabolism. By way of the institutional environment, the process moves to the institution itself, and finally, to the strategy of actors. The strategy of actors indicates a will and behavior that is adopted by various socioeconomic groups interested in the institution concerned and is often fortified by the formation of a political coalition. Such a political factor becomes very important in institutional change or endometabolism.

The endometabolism of an institution, however, often opens to a drastic collapse of an institution or leads to a regime crisis once it reaches a certain threshold. Having kept overall stability in spite of its endometabolism, an institution may at last plunge into an area of instability, that is, radical and nonlinear institutional change with endogenous cause. This is called the "threshold effect" (b) in Table 5.2 and Figure 5.1d. It is also discussed using terms such as "cut points, or tipping points" (Pierson 2004: 84). Arriving at a threshold effect, one often witnesses not only an economic crisis but also a political crisis, including a split in the hitherto dominant political coalition.[6] For example, the stagflation crisis in the 1970s was an episode of radical change that was brought about by exceeding a certain threshold of the endometabolic alteration of the Fordist growth regime (Boyer 2004: 195–196), resulting in a breakdown of the Fordist capital–labor alliance. Endometabolic alterations in contemporary socioeconomics can be illustrated, for instance, by urbanization, globalization, de-industrialization, financialization, and an aging society. Some advanced capitalist countries have gone beyond a kind of tipping point, leading to drastic nonlinear transformations.

The third type of institutional change is "hybridization" (c): a gradual institutional change with exogenous cause. When the endometabolism has its origin inside the same space, hybridization designates an institutional change caused by an interaction with another space, i.e., a foreign country or international environment. Here we would like to limit the usage of the word "hybridization" only to the case of exogenous and *gradual* change.[7] For example, although a country may make an effort to imitate, import, and transplant a foreign institution, it often becomes impossible to establish the same institution. Rather, as time goes by, we find a mixture of a traditional institution and a foreign one, giving rise to an original institution. This is well illustrated in postwar Japan by the birth of the Toyota production system. This was an original system, notwithstanding Toyota's initial intention to learn and introduce the Ford system from the USA.

As the last type of change, we can point to "big events" (d), such as a war, a revolution, the Great Recession, grand political conversions in foreign countries, natural disasters, and various international or non-economic shocks. These can result in a radical institutional change with an exogenous cause.[8] As an illustration, we can count the Great Depression of the 1930s, World War II, the Nixon shock, the oil shocks, the Asian currency crisis, the Lehman shock, etc. However, in reality, it is impossible to mechanically discern exogenous (big events) and endogenous (threshold effect) events, because the matter depends on the point of view or time horizon of the observers. For example, the Nixon shock may be categorized, on the one hand, as a "big event" if it is taken as an unexpected surprise, but on the other as a "threshold effect" if one considers this event in the medium to long period of the continuous decrease of gold reserves in the USA and the gradual devaluation of the dollar. The same is true of the other examples. What should also not be forgotten is that the threshold effect and big events often join a regime crisis.

4 Gradual change of institutions and political elements

From the discussion mentioned above, we placed our starting point of understanding institutional change on the *gradual* change of institutions: "endometabolism" (a) and "hybridization" (c) in Table 5.2. However, this does not mean that radical changes or critical junctures emphasized by path dependence theory do not matter. Critical junctures often correspond to a tipping point where gradual changes reach a certain critical mass, apart from exceptional accidental big events.

The gradual nature of institutional change was already emphasized by North (1990). Defining the institution as "the rules of the game," North at the same time paid attention to a tenaciousness of "informal constraints" (routines, customs, traditions, conventions, and cultures) vis-à-vis "formal rules" (constitutions, statutes, common laws, specific bylaws, and individual contracts), and emphasized the adhesiveness or non-variability of informal constraints. In consequence, even if formal rules are changed, or radical institutional changes are put into effect through revolution, conquest, and so on, the changes eventually become incremental because of the tenacious nature of informal constraints (North 1990: ch. 10). Here, we find also a matter of discrepancy between the institution itself and its interpretation or enforcement by actors.

One of the points made by Thelen[9] that contributes the most to this discussion resides in her typology of the modes of gradual institutional change. Regarding gradual institutional changes, she first proposed two modes: "layering" and "conversion" (Thelen 2003: 225–230; 2004: 35–36). Institutional layering means adding or superposing new institutions over old ones without dismantling the latter. As for institutional conversion, this term designates a situation in which, even when the environments around conventional institutions have changed, the institutions are rather reinterpreted and differently enforced without formal or legal changes. In this case, the role and function of the institution concerned naturally changes from the initial role and function.

Thereafter, she classifies various modes of gradual change by adding some new types. These include "drift" and "displacement" of institutions, which are important among new supplemented modes in Streeck and Thelen (2005: 31). Institutional displacement indicates an abolition of the old institution and introduction of the new, that is, a substitution of the new for the old institution. However, this mode might rather be classified into radical change, not gradual change. In contrast, institutional drift refers to a situation in which, although the environments have changed, the institution remains invariable and constant, resulting in an unsuitable institution. In this case, the institution loses its enforcement power and becomes ineffective. This is also a kind of gradual and substantial change of an institution.

Based on the above understanding, Thelen classifies various modes of gradual institutional change from the standpoint of characteristics of the political context, that is, strong or weak veto possibilities, and of the targeted institution, such as high or low levels of discretion in interpretation and enforcement (Mahoney and Thelen 2010: 19; Thelen 2009: 489). This is well known.

Here, however, having proposed a standpoint that put the essence of gradual institutional change on "endometabolism" and "hybridization," we would like to analyze the modes of institutional change differently from the Thelen typology. On what differences in the endometabolism of institutions are the three modes of incremental change (layering, conversion, and drift) based? As shown in the previous section, the endometabolism of institutions includes, through the functioning of an institution, an alteration of the (1) surrounding environments of the institution, that is, contexts that the institution is embedded in, (2) institution itself, and (3) strategies of various actors, that is, their interpretation, enforcement, and approval/disapproval of the institution. When we grasp the institution more broadly as an institutional structure that consists of three aspects – "environment" (context surrounding the institution), "institution" (institution as a text), and "application" (interpretation and application of text by actors, or, a kind of textual criticism of institution) – the modes of gradual institutional change can be conceptualized as differences or discrepancies among the three aspects. This is described in Table 5.3.

Suppose that at an initial period (period 1), an institutional structure I_1 has an institution a under its environment A and that institution a is interpreted and enforced in a form of α. Here, α is supposed to be the most authentic and suitable form of application for institution a. This is expressed as $I_1\ (A, a, \alpha)$. In this state, there is no discrepancy among the three aspects, and the institution is reproduced steadily. However, the institution is always in its process of endometabolism. In the second period (period 2), where the endometabolic process has reached a certain extent, the institutional environment will change from A to B.

Table 5.3 Modes of institutional change viewed from a framework of institutional structure

	Period 1	*Period 2*	*Modes of change*	*Speed of change*
Environment	A	B		
Institution	a	b	Displacement: $I\ (B, b)$, $I\ (B, b, \beta)$	Radical
	a	$a+b$	Layering: $I\ (B, a+b)$	Gradual
	a	a	Drift: $I\ (B, a)$	
Enforcement	a	a	Conversion: $I\ (B, a, \beta)$	
	α	β		

Source: author.

In this period, the environmental change includes a great transformation of the context as a whole, as well as an emergence of new situations around individual institutions. One may otherwise consider not only a change on the part of the environment, but also a gap between an institution and the environment due to alterations of the institution itself. In any case, some change in the institutional context is expressed in B.

If, then, a new institution b is promptly established coping with a new environment, leading to an emergence of a new institutional structure, expressed $I_2(B,b)$ or $I_2(B,b,\beta)$, it is a "displacement" of an institution. As we have already pointed out, institutional displacement would be rather a radical than gradual change; so, this is not our main object here. It is in the case that the old institution a is not substituted by a new one such as b that gradual changes matter. This is also the case when the conventional institution a shows some tenaciousness.

At first, one can imagine a situation in which, under a new environment B, a new institution b is added to the old one a, such that b is superposed on a. In short, this is the case in which a new institution b is established corresponding to a new environment B, but in which the traditional institution a also survives. Thus, institutions a and b often coexist in confrontation or complementarity in such situations. This situation of $I(B,a+b)$ is institutional "layering."

Second, when, without such coexistence, the old institution a still survives under changed environment B, we see an institutional "drift," which can be expressed $I(B,a)$. This case may arise due to the ignorance and incompetence of policy makers or by the rejection of institutional reforms by social groups that benefited from the conventional institution. Institutional drift naturally brings a substantial dysfunction.

However, even in this situation, if there is some room for discretion regarding the enforcement of the institution or if there are strong interested groups that can impose their own interpretation of an institution on politics and society, then the old institution a would be changed by interpreting institution a as β, which involves adapting to environment B. This is the third case of gradual institutional change, that is, institutional "conversion" formulated by $I(B,a,\beta)$.

We can therefore understand the gradual change of an institution as intermediate forms between the two ideal configurations of an institutional structure: $I_1(A,a,\alpha)$ and $I_2(B,b,\beta)$. The tenacious character of an institution produces these forms. What is important is that it is rather these intermediate forms that are the normal states of an institution, and also that each intermediate form, although keeping a medium- or short-term stability, will gradually but steadily proceed to an endometabolic change. The normal essence of an institution or regime lies in its gradual change, notwithstanding its apparent stability.

As shown, an institution changes gradually through endometabolism and hybridization. When the gradual changes arrive at a tipping point or encounter abrupt big events, the change may become radical. Whether it is gradual or radical, the agents or actors who are active under the institutions ultimately define institutional change. It is through the activities of the actors under the institutions that institutions themselves are partially revised and that the environments surrounding the institutions change. In turn, the strategies of actors change to correspond to environmental changes, and through this process a new and different enforcement or interpretation of institutions emerges. Thus, institutions that have been stably reproduced as a whole in spite of partial revisions may eventually become unstable and break down.

At this point, political moments matter decisively. At least with respect to institutions that are economically important, the political role is crucial. That is, actors reexamine and revise their strategies under new environmental conditions. They then organize or reorganize a new "social coalition" or "political coalition," aiming at the realization of institutions conforming to their new strategies or at removal of institutions unfavorable to them.[10] Of course, the degree and forms of organization would be quite various, from a solid collusion to an implicit and transitory coordination, or from sharing of the same philosophy to a connection of bribery. In any case, actors aim at organizing the majority or dominant social group in order to accomplish their own interests. In the process reorganization of group members or recombination of coalitions naturally occur.

5 Economic backgrounds and political powers of neoliberalism

We have above reviewed theories regarding the elements and modes determining changes of institutions and regimes. Based on our discussions, in this section we intend to propose a critical angle on the current neoliberal regime, focusing on its economic backgrounds and political moments.

The neoliberal policy regime was established on the grave of the previous Keynesian one, and especially in hegemonic countries the finance-led growth regime was established on the grave of the Fordist one. Of course, this reestablishment was never an automatic and necessary course of things, but a consequence of clear and particular wills of dominant social groups as well as of a recomposition of a political coalition to realize their wills, on the one hand. However, on the other, at the same time, we cannot miss the objective changes of institutional structure that, due to the endometabolic process of Keynesian–Fordian regime, greatly altered the conventional institutional contexts in the advanced capitalist countries. Fordism has undermined its own foundational environments exactly because of its success.

Let's start with the latter aspect before examining the former. As a result of the development of Fordist institutions and growth regimes, the advanced countries initially experienced industrialization. This resulted, on the one hand, in an intensification of international competition propelled by overcapacity in production and, on the other, in the slowdown of productivity gains and the acceleration of wage increases and inflation. Influential international events like the Nixon shock and oil shocks in the 1970s prompted these tendencies. Before long, out of fierce international competition emerged a multi-nationalization of the firms and a *globalization* of the economy. Advanced countries conducted *de-industrialization* with the slowdown of industrial productivity and the rise of newly industrialized economies. As a result of both, *financialization* of the economy arose, mainly in the hegemonic countries. Globalization, de-industrialization, and financialization imply a great transformation of the economic context. This transformation is also a consequence of reaching a threshold of endometabolic changes of the Fordist growth regime.

De-industrialization produced a drop in the number of organized workers in large manufacturing firms and also a drop in the unionization rate, resulting in a sharp decline in the power of the working class (Crouch 2004: ch. 3; Glyn 2006: ch. 5). Employment shifted to the service sector. Along with the tertialization of employment, the interests of employees diversified and split, on account of the smaller size and uncertainness of management characteristics of the service sector, and the diversification of employment forms, including non-regularization. The so-called "unity" of laborers disappeared.

In addition, engineers and civil servants formerly also joined laborers in a narrow sense. Moreover, there existed a broad "capitalist–citizen accord" (Bowles *et al.* 1990: 57) or "state–citizen accord," which involved not only wage earners but also, through the welfare state, the non-active population. The "Fordist coalition" or "Keynesian coalition" in the postwar period consisted of such a wide alliance by workers, citizens, and capitalist managers. This coalition has collapsed, however, with the decline of laborers' power due to the de-industrialization of the economy and the non-regularization of employment. Here we see that people became losers as workers.

The intensification of international competition and the *globalization* of the economy have also drastically changed institutional environments. Here, it must be noted that imported consumption goods at cheap prices, as a result of more openness to foreign trade, merely made up for wage stagnation because of the decline of labor's power. These goods were principally provided by the newly industrialized countries, headed by China. Nations in the advanced countries, as "consumers" that enjoy cheap imported goods, have thus regained what they lost as "laborers" (Boyer 2011: 25; Reich 2009: ch. 2). People became, as it were, winners as consumers. At the same time, there has appeared, beyond a simple trade relationship between the advanced and emerging countries, a new political and economic context – the multi-nationalization and fortification of giant firms in the advanced countries.

Multinational firms, together with financial businesses that have rapidly extended thanks to the development of new financial technologies and instruments, substantially pushed the globalization of the economy. The development of global financial business and the *financialization* of the economy involved many workers. Higher rates of aging in societies increased the number of people who live on pensions; thus, a mass of retired workers became, so to speak, rentiers. Here we see an increase in the influence of pension funds. For their part, active workers compensated the stagnation of wage incomes by gaining various financial incomes, especially in good times. People, in this way, have begun to appear as "investors" on behalf of "workers" (Reich 2009: ch. 2). People are now (temporary) winners as investors.

Now, people become defined as "consumers" and "investors" more than "workers." This also implies that people assume a role of "debtor."[11] The emergence of the mass having these new aspects has supported the neoliberal or finance-led regime from the remote side.

Thus, the endometabolism of the Fordist regime ultimately resulted in an emergence of preconditions for de-industrialization, globalization, and financialization. However, as suggested at the beginning of this section, these preconditions have been realized in a particular and solid direction only by getting support of neoliberal policies and ideas instead of Keynesian ones. Above all, they have been realized by establishing a new political coalition that promotes these policies and ideas, a "neoliberal coalition." The neoliberal coalition carried out its own interests powerfully and strategically by not only founding new institutions favorable to it, but also gradually changing conventional institutions

Contrary to its superficial discourses of "free competition," "efficiency of the market" (deregulation), and "retreat of the state" (privatization, tax reduction), the core substance of neoliberalism firmly resides in a movement of power restoration of the upper classes (Harvey 2005: 19, 38, 156). Their restoration of powers is above all founded on establishing a system in which financial returns increase explosively: a finance-led growth regime. In effect, neoliberalism, although having achieved only a poor performance in productivity gains and economic growth, attained a great deal with respect to the distribution of wealth for the upper classes. As is very well-known, the consequences of this regime are currently a huge concern around the world, with the issue of "increasing inequalities" being central (Piketty 2014). The upper classes have undoubtedly restored their economic power.

At the center of the upper classes are situated the super-rich, including the top managers of global financial businesses and giant multinational firms. The alliance of these two makes the core of the neoliberal coalition. Around them exist the middle-class executives, the bureaucracy, the accountants, the lawyers, the consultants, the economists, the journalists, the self-employed, and so on (Harvey 2005: 33–34). Despite including this second file, the neoliberal coalition remains a minority when contrasted with the Fordist one. The range of this coalition is very narrow.[12] However, one of the advantages of the neoliberal coalition lies in that it has successfully attracted many consumers and investors as members of the most external circle in the coalition's concentric structure (Martinelli 2014: 295).

The interests of the involved consumers and amateur investors do not necessarily correspond with those of the core players. Rather, the former often become victims of neoliberal policies. But those who work in manufacturing, as well as in various jobs and professions that have been created mainly in the service sector, are obliged to have an intense contact with the giant global enterprises that supply cheap consumption goods. They are also obliged to deal with the financial markets that offer apparently attractive chances of financial incomes. The neoliberal coalition has thus succeeded in establishing a wide coalition, so long as it can draw the ambiguous strata of consumers and investors that support the core of the coalition.

Though the neoliberal coalition is very fragile in its wideness, its core part is very strong because of its political power. This is the decisive advantage of the coalition. Big enterprises have now obtained not only an economic power but also a political power (Crouch 2004: 105, 2011: 94–95; Reich 2009: ch. 4). That is, big firms, to gain economic advantages over their rivals, have strengthened their influence in the field of political decision making, thus entering a political competition. This is mediated by money in the hands of firms and by strong lobbying funded with this money, leading to institutional changes including layering, drift, and conversion. With respect to the role of politics, politicians become more and more reliant on political funds offered by firms, particularly in a context of ever-growing campaign funds (Martinelli 2014: 297). Naturally, it becomes impossible for politicians to implement policies that are contrary to big firms' interests. Here, we witness the establishment of a finance–manager–politician complex. In short, money dominates politics, and politics becomes an instrument serving the privileged classes. This is the reason why, even after the recent world financial crisis, the politico-economic regime of neoliberalism can survive today.

6 Conclusion

Neoliberalism, behind its appearance of "free competition" and "retreat of the state," has survived by means of hidden strategies such as "political monopoly" and "takeover of the state." Neoliberalism results therefore in not merely increasing inequalities economically, but also a dysfunction or breaking up of democracy politically. This is already often pointed out by many. For example, Robert B. Reich, detecting "the triumph of capitalism and the decline of democracy" under neoliberalism, criticizes this trend as follows: "We in our capacities as consumers and investors have done significantly better. In our capacities as citizens seeking the common good, however, we have lost ground" (Reich 2009: 7, 50). Moreover, as Colin Crouch warns: "If the wealthy interests are able to convert wealth into political power – as is very often the case – they are able to distort both the market economy and democracy" (Crouch 2013: vii).

Thus, the neoliberal regime is fundamentally incompatible with democracy. Rather, the neoliberal regime appears as a destructive moment of democracy. In addition, the finance-led regime is always in economic instability, so long as it is driven by financial bubbles. The existing neoliberal coalition is constantly exposed to the risk of a split due to its unstable dynamics. However, from a more fundamental point of view, an authentic regime crisis of neoliberalism, if it may be, would be realized only when the power of citizens who claim the democracy becomes greatly revived.

Neoliberalism, after having experienced the economic crisis of 2008, is now producing a greater and greater decline of political democracy. When a movement of "*revendication*" by citizens reaches a certain level against increases in inequality that are too large and democracy that is too dysfunctional, then the regime crisis would become not only "economic" but also "political." The requisite conditions for this regime crisis include the formation of a new political coalition for a new civil society. In any case, the contradiction of neoliberalism and democracy may lead to a deep structural crisis of the regime.

Notes

1 The concept of "mode of *régulation*" must be understood not only from an economic viewpoint, but also from a political one:

> For the theory of *régulation*, institutions are a product of "political compromises" or "institutionalized compromises"; this has prevented the adoption of the functionalist hypothesis characterizing almost all economic theories. The analysis of institutional change would thus impose an explanation of the social and political impact of an economic trajectory.
>
> (Amable and Palombarini 2005: 249)

2 See also Yamada (2014).

3 The beginning of path dependence theory in recent years has been credited to David (1985) and his discussion on technological trajectory, and to Arthur (1994) in the field of economics, considering his research on complex systems.

4 In Table 5.2, some rubrics are inserted as "mode of change" because we anticipate the discussions in the next section.

5 According to Boyer (2005: 70), "Endometabolism is the inner development of tensions within a given architecture." From the *régulation* school, Frédéric Lordon was the first to focus on "endometabolism" in 1993. Later, he wrote:

> In order to represent the regulationist insight completely, a means of formalising endogenous processes of structural change is needed. This type of change, given the distinctive term endometabolism [...], where structural deformations are gradually generated from a repetition of conjuncture over a long period, is especially resistant to formalisation.
>
> (Lordon 1995: 178)

By incorporating the concept of endometabolism, the *régulation* theory attained to a more effective view on history that surpasses a somewhat mechanical view (à la theory of punctuated equilibrium) in the path dependence theory.

6 Considering this threshold effect, path dependence theory, which presupposes that a critical juncture (radical change) occurs only exogenously, must be criticized in that it misses major aspects of change. Cf.:

> In formal path dependence, critical junctures cannot emerge from the normal processes of change inside a path.... The new critical juncture arose endogenously (and dialectically) from the path's own internal logics, rather than arising exogenously.
>
> (Schwartz 2001: 11–12)

> Contrary to the theory of path dependence which asserts that only exogenous change can move actors off a current path, an exogenous shock is *not* the only way a path gets disrupted, i.e., a process of fundamental institutional change is initiated.... Ultimately, a mixture of endogenous and exogenous pressures led to a series of path-changing initiatives.
>
> (Deeg 2001: 10–11)

7 Restricting "hybridization" within something exogenous may raise some questions. This is because, by definition, hybridization is a hybrid of something endogenous and exogenous. However, we categorize it into something exogenous on the grounds that it includes contacts with an external space.

8 Concerning the main causes of transformation of the mode of *régulation*, the *régulation* school, showing some shifts of emphasis over time, attaches importance to both the endogenous threshold effect and the exogenous big events. Cf.:

> After having privileged the initial conception – necessity of a radical change to explain a transformation of the mode of *régulation* – the studies have progressively explored the possibilities of endometabolism, that is, brutal alteration of the mode of *régulation* under the effect of the accumulation of a series of marginal changes.
>
> (Boyer 2004: 205)

Nevertheless, the next sentences clearly show that the regulationists have never abandoned the crucial role of big and radical events on the transformation of the growth regime or mode of *régulation*:

> When the *régulationist* scholars did their groundbreaking research, first on the United States, then on France, they were surprised to find that the war and major crises had been crucial episodes in the changes of regimes of accumulation and modes of *régulation*. These episodes were seen to have been nothing less than social laboratories.
>
> (Boyer 2013: 13)

9 Thelen (2004: 30–31) indicates her methodological viewpoints on institutional change as follows: (1) criticizing discussions that draw a sharp line between the analysis of institutional stability and institutional innovation and that regard all changes as exogenous, she exhibits a pattern of incremental change; (2) disagreeing with the functionalist theories of institutional origins and the punctuated equilibrium theories of institutional change, as well as with the tendency of "automaticity" of institutional reproduction sometimes implied in the logic of path dependence (especially of increasing returns), she shows how elements of stability and change are often inextricably intertwined; and (3) together with the power-distributional theories, she underscores the contested nature of institutional development and the important role of changes in the political coalitions.

10 Concerning the formation and change of institutions, Amable (2003: ch. 2) already referred, as the definitive moment, to "political coalition" on the basis of "dominant social bloc." Thelen (2014: 10) also emphasizes "the political coalitions on which [...] institutions rest."

11 Crouch makes an ironic expression of "privatized Keynesianism," stating: "Instead of governments taking on debt to stimulate the economy, individuals and families did so, including poor ones" (Crouch 2011: 114).

12 "The new neoliberal class coalition that had become hegemonic in the 1980s was a narrow one, comprising the rentier capitalists, the highly paid financiers and traders that managed their wealth, and the top executives of the major multinational enterprise" (Bresser-Pereira 2014: 60).

References

Amable, Bruno (2003), *The Diversity of Modern Capitalism*, Oxford: Oxford University Press.

Amable, Bruno and Stefano Palombarini (2005), *L'Economie politique n'est pas une science morale*, Paris: Raisons d'Agir.

Arthur, W. Brian (1994), *Increasing Returns and Path Dependence in the Economy*, Ann Arbor, MI: University of Michigan Press.

Bowles, Samuel, David. M. Gordon, and Thomas. H. Weisskopf (1990), *After the Waste Land: A Democratic Economics for the Year 2000*, New York: M.E. Sharpe, Inc.

Boyer, Robert (2004), *Une théorie du capitalisme est-elle possible?* Paris: Odile Jacob.

Boyer, Robert (2005), "Coherence, Diversity, and the Evolution of Capitalisms: The Institutional Complementarity Hypothesis," *Evolutionary and Institutional Economics Review* 2(1), pp. 43–80.

Boyer, Robert (2011), *Les financiers détruiront-ils le capitalisme?* Paris: Economica.

Boyer, Robert (2013), "Capital in the Twenty-First Century: A Regulationist View," *Revue de la Régulation* 14, http://regulation.revues.org/10618, accessed June 23, 2014.

Boyer, Robert and Yves Saillard (eds.) (1995), *Régulation Theory and the State of the Art*, London: Routledge.

Bresser-Pereira, Luiz Carlos (2014), "The Hegemony Constraints in the Neoliberal Years of Capitalism," in: Magara, Hideko (ed.), *Economic Crises and Policy Regimes: The Dynamics of Policy Innovation and Paradigmatic Change*, Cheltenham: Edward Elgar, pp. 56–78.

Crouch, Colin (2004), *Post-Democracy*, Cambridge: Polity.

Crouch, Colin (2011), *The Strange Non-death of Neoliberalism*, Cambridge: Polity.

Crouch, Colin (2013), *Making Capitalism Fit for Society*, Cambridge: Polity.

David, Paul (1985), "Clio and the Economics of QWERTY," *American Economic Review*, 75(2), pp. 332–337.

Deeg, Richard (2001), "Institutional Change and the Uses and Limits of Path Dependency: The Case of German Finance," Max-Planck-Institut für Gesellschaftsforschung Discussion Paper 01/6, November.

Glyn, Andrew (2006), *Capitalism Unleashed: Finance, Globalization, and Welfare*, Oxford: Oxford University Press.

Hall, Peter and David Soskice (eds.) (2001), *Varieties of Capitalism: The Institutional Foundations of Comparative Advantages*, Oxford: Oxford University Press.

Harvey, David (2005), *A Brief History of Neoliberalism*, Oxford: Oxford University Press.

Lordon, Frédéric (1995), "Formalising Regulationist Dynamics and Crises," in Boyer, Robert and Yves Saillard (eds.) (1995), *Régulation Theory and the State of the Art*, London: Routledge pp. 174–180.

Mahoney, James (2000), "Path Dependence in Historical Sociology," *Theory and Society* 29(4), pp. 507–548.

Mahoney, James and Kathleen Thelen (eds.) (2010), *Explaining Institutional Change: Ambiguity, Agency, and Change*, New York: Cambridge University Press.

Martinelli, Alberto (2014), "A Political Analysis of the Global Financial Crisis: Implications for Crisis Governance," in: Magara, Hideko (ed.), *Economic Crises and Policy Regimes: The Dynamics of Policy Innovation and Paradigmatic Change*, Cheltenham: Edward Elgar, pp. 283–313.

North, Douglass C. (1990), *Institutions, Institutional Change and Economic Performance*, Cambridge: Cambridge University Press.

Pempel, T.J. (1998), *Regime Shift: Comparative Dynamics of the Japanese Political Economy*, Ithaca, NY: Cornell University Press.

Pierson, Paul (2000), "Increasing Return, Path Dependence, and the Study of Politics," *American Political Science Review* 94(2), pp. 251–267.

Pierson, Paul (2004), *Politics in Time: History, Institutions, and Social Analysis*, Princeton, NJ: Princeton University Press.

Piketty, Thomas (2014), *Capital in the Twenty-First Century*, Cambridge, MA: The Belknap Press of Harvard University Press.

Przeworski, Adam (2001), "How Many Ways Can Be Third?" in Andrew Glyn (ed.),

Social Democracy in Neoliberal Times: The Left and Economic Policy since 1980, Oxford: Oxford University Press, pp. 312–333.

Przeworski, Adam (2014), "Choices and Echoes: Stability and Change of Policy Regimes," in: Magara, Hideko (ed.), *Economic Crises and Policy Regimes: The Dynamics of Policy Innovation and Paradigmatic Change*, Cheltenham: Edward Elgar, pp. 33–55.

Reich, Robert B. (2009), *Supercapitalism: The Battle for Democracy in an Age of Big Business*, London: Icon Books.

Schwartz, Herman (2001), "Down the Wrong Path: Path Dependence, Markets, and Increasing Returns," unpublished manuscript, University of Virginia.

Streeck, Wolfgang and Kathleen Thelen (2005), "Introduction: Institutional Change in Advanced Political Economies," in: Streeck, W. and Thelen, K. (eds.), *Beyond Continuity: Institutional Change in Advanced Political Economies*, Oxford: Oxford University Press, pp. 1–39.

Thelen, Kathleen (2003), "How Institutions Evolve: Insights from Comparative Historical Analysis," in: Mahoney, James and Rueschemyer, Dietrich (eds.), *Comparative Historical Analysis in the Social Sciences*, Cambridge: Cambridge University Press, pp. 208–240.

Thelen, Kathleen (2004), *How Institutions Evolve: The Political Economy of Skills in Germany, Britain, the United States, and Japan*, Cambridge: Cambridge University Press.

Thelen, Kathleen (2009), "Institutional Change in Advanced Political Economies," *British Journal of Industrial Relations* 47(3), pp. 471–498.

Thelen, Kathleen (2014), *Varieties of Liberalization and the New Policies of Social Solidarity*, New York: Cambridge University Press.

Yamada, Toshio (2014), "Economic Crisis and Growth Regimes," in: Magara, Hideko (ed.) *Economic Crises and Policy Regimes: The Dynamics of Policy Innovation and Paradigmatic Change*, Cheltenham: Edward Elgar, pp. 79–100.

Part III

Comparative analyses

6 The political-economic implications of de-industrialization with varieties of capitalism

An EU–Japan comparative analysis

Hiroyasu Uemura and Shinji Tahara

Introduction

De-industrialization, defined as the relative decline in output and employment in the manufacturing industry, has occurred not only in European economies but in all advanced economies since the 1970s. In the Japanese case, in particular, de-industrialization has accelerated very rapidly, faced with institutional changes in the domestic economy and changes in international economic relations. Furthermore, de-industrialization has exhibited different patterns with different varieties of European capitalism.

In this study we analyze the transformations of growth regimes and changes in industrial and employment structures to understand the structural characteristics of de-industrialization in Japan and the following European countries: Germany, France, Italy, and the UK. We attempt to extend the theoretical framework of the growth regime in *régulation* theory, taking account of long-term industrial structural changes. In particular, changes in macroeconomic patterns and industrial structures are analyzed with the World Input–Output Database (WIOD).[1] Furthermore, we discuss the political-economic implication of de-industrialization in each country, investigating the transformation of dualistic social structures.

In our analysis, we follow three specific themes. First, we analyze the growth processes and de-industrialization in Germany, France, Italy, the UK, and Japan, focusing especially on changes in institutional forms and the transformations of growth regime from the viewpoint of *régulation* theory (Boyer 1988; Petit 1986).[2] Second, we analyze structural linkages between the manufacturing industry and the service industry to understand the characteristics of de-industrialization in each economy. In this regard, we extend the method of the analysis of de-industrialization based on input–output analysis that was developed by Franke and Kalmbach (2005) to analyze the German economy. In particular, we use the WIOD in our structural analysis of de-industrialization. Third, we consider the political-economic implication of de-industrialization and the increase in various service activities with the varieties of capitalism. In addition, we investigate shifts in income distribution and the transformations of dualistic structures and fragmentation in each society (Emmenegger *et al.* 2012).

1 Theoretical framework of de-industrialization

1.1 Dynamics of the growth regime and de-industrialization

De-industrialization should be analyzed in the framework of economic growth and industrial structural change. In the process of economic growth, the dynamic interaction of demand and supply factors plays a key role, and the interaction of real and financial factors influences the dynamics of the economy. Furthermore, industrial structural change should be integrated in the analysis of economic growth, especially when we consider the process of de-industrialization.

Based on this theoretical framework, we explain the dynamics of the growth regime and de-industrialization from the perspective of *régulation* theory (Boyer 1988; Petit 1986). First of all, the cumulative effect of productivity growth and output growth determines the dynamism of a growth regime. This effect operates more strongly in the manufacturing industry (Kaldor 1978). The framework of cumulative growth and de-industrialization is depicted in Figure 6.1.

The main logic of demand formation is as follows. Productivity gains are distributed into wages and profits, and an increase in profits has a positive effect on the expected profit rate and investment. Then, an increase in investment realizes more profits. Therefore, there is cumulative causality between the profit rate and the accumulation rate. Furthermore, investment leads to an increase in intermediate inputs from either manufacturing sectors or the service sectors. At the same time, an increase in wages leads to more consumption demand (Rowthorn

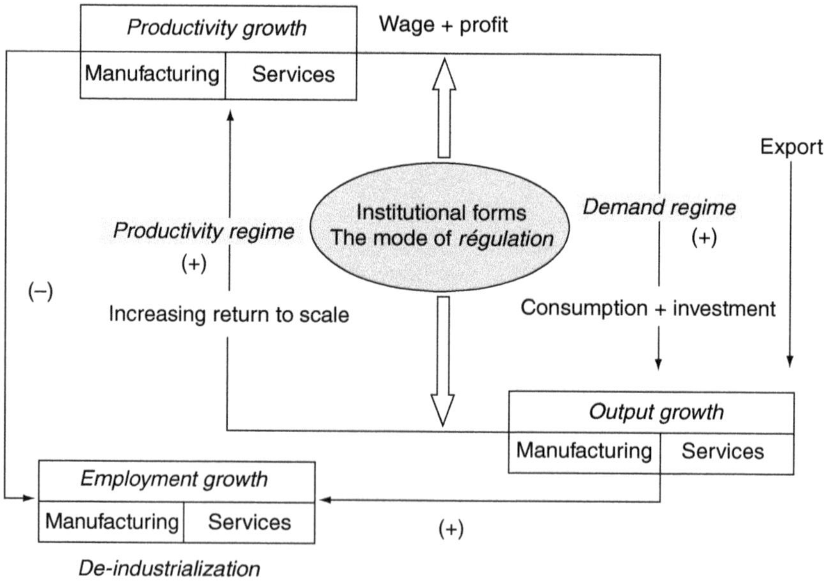

Figure 6.1 The growth regime and de-industrialization.

Source: Uemura and Tahara (2014).

1982; Taylor 1991). The markets of consumer durable goods and consumer services expand accordingly.

Next, there is a linkage effect from consumption to investment. This consists of both short-period and long-period effects. For the former effect, changes in demand influence investment through the adjustment of capacity utilization in the manufacturing industry. For the latter effect, a continuous expansion of consumption influences the expected return of investment, leading to a continuous increase in investment. In the actual process of investment decisions, these effects are integrated in the decision to invest. The accumulation rates are not uniform across the industries as profitability differentials exist. In this context there exist two patterns of demand formation, depending on the patterns of coordination in the financial system and the wage–labor nexus. If investment is highly sensitive to profits, the causal chain is called "profit-led growth." On the contrary, if investment is very sensitive to demand expansion, the causal chain is called "wage-led growth." Furthermore, the causal chain productivity–unit labor costs–export also plays a crucial role in the growth of the manufacturing industry, which is the basic logic of "export-led growth."

In summary, all of these linkages, from productivity gain to demand formation, are called the "demand regime" in *régulation* theory (Boyer 1988).[3] The demand regime can be expressed in the following way:

$$(\textit{growth rate of real output}) = f(\textit{growth rate of labor productivity}) \qquad (6.1)$$

Final demand is divided into three components: domestic final demand, export and import, as follows:

$$(\textit{growth rate of final demand}) = (\textit{contribution of domestic final demand}) + (\textit{contribution of export}) - (\textit{contribution of import}) \qquad (6.2)$$

Each of the components can be regarded as a function of productivity growth. Furthermore, final demand induces intermediate demand, which can be studied by input–output analysis. In our framework of input–output analysis, the input coefficient matrix is divided into the matrix of domestic input ratios and technology coefficient matrix by following the framework by Franke and Kalmbach (2005) and Uemura and Tahara (2014), and we obtain the following relations:

$$(\textit{growth rate of real output}) = (\textit{contribution of domestic final demand}) + (\textit{contribution of export}) - (\textit{contribution of import}) + (\textit{contribution of technological coefficient}) + (\textit{contribution of domestic input}) + (\textit{residual}) \qquad (6.3)$$

Next, the linkage from demand growth to productivity growth is another major causal chain in the economy. An increase in investment leads to an increase in productivity by replacing capital equipment. This effect is more remarkable in the manufacturing industry than the service industry, with the dynamics of introducing new capital equipment and scrapping old capital equipment. Furthermore, an increase in demand leads to productivity growth through increasing return to scale, especially in the manufacturing industry. This is often called the "Kaldor–Verdoorn Law." In addition, innovation contributes to productivity growth depending on the social system of innovation in each national and regional economy. In summary, these linkages from demand growth to productivity growth are called "the productivity regime" (Boyer 1988).

$$(\textit{growth rate of labor productivity}) = g(\textit{growth rate of real output}) \qquad (6.4)$$

For the linkages between the manufacturing and the service industries, the following points are noted in the study of de-industrialization (Petit 1986). First, cumulative causation between output growth and productivity growth operates strongly in the manufacturing industry. Second, the manufacturing industry has its own "subsystem dynamics" (Landesmann and Scazzieri 1996) and causes changes in the linkage between the manufacturing industry and the business-related service industry with the externalization of business activities, which are reflected by the technology coefficient. The spill-over effect of intermediate demand between the manufacturing and service industries contributes to output growth and productivity growth in both industries.

The dynamism of output growth and productivity growth determines the dynamics of employment growth, which provides a basic framework of de-industrialization in terms of employment.

$$(\textit{growth rate of employment}) = (\textit{growth rate of real output}) - (\textit{growth rate of labor productivity}) \qquad (6.5)$$

Therefore, in a mature economy in which the percentage of agricultural employment has become very small, de-industrialization occurs in terms of the relative share of employment when the growth rate of real output minus the growth rate of productivity in the service industry is bigger than that in the manufacturing industry. This dynamic was formalized originally by Baumol, and was applied to the process of de-industrialization in Rowthorn's model (Baumol 1967; Rowthorn and Wells 1987). De-industrialization brings about an increase in service employment with a skill bifurcation, depending on institutional characteristics in the labor market, and this shift of employment influences the transformation of the social welfare system in each country (Emmenegger *et al.* 2012; Iversen and Cusack 2000).

Furthermore, foreign trade and foreign direct investment have the following important effects on the de-industrialization process. Trade specialization between manufactured goods and services influences the dynamism of the national economy, influenced by the exchange-rate system. For example, the export goods manufacturing industry could be a starting point of "cumulative causation," producing tradable products with increasing returns to scale. On the contrary, if the national economy depends significantly on export of natural resources, this could exacerbate long-term economic stagnation. The pattern of trade specialization causes a "virtuous circle" or "vicious circle" with the conflict of interests among different industrial sectors. Foreign direct investment sometimes has both the positive effect of promoting the international division of labor and the negative effect of accelerating de-industrialization.

1.2 Four types of de-industrialization

The condition for de-industrialization in terms of employment is usually explained by focusing on the difference between the growth rate of real output and that of labor productivity (Baumol 1967; Rowthorn and Wells 1987). In this study, by focusing on interdependent industrial structures between the manufacturing service sectors, we define four types of de-industrialization. The first type is "positive de-industrialization," in which the growth differentials of labor productivity between the manufacturing sector and the service sector bring about a shift in employment from the manufacturing to the service sector. The second type is "negative de-industrialization," which is caused by decreasing demand and stagnant output in the manufacturing sector. These two types were formalized originally by Rowthorn and Wells (1987). Moreover, the third type is "de-industrialization through manufacturing–service linkages," which is brought about by an increase in intermediate inputs from the business-related service industry to the manufacturing industry, inducing an increase in employment in the business-related service industry. The fourth type is "de-industrialization by the shift of final demand to the service sector," which is included in the long-term changes in final demand structures. These four types of de-industrialization are summarized in Table 6.1.

2 Comparative analysis of de-industrialization in Germany, France, Italy, the UK and Japan

2.1 Overview of de-industrialization patterns

De-industrialization has proceeded in most of the advanced countries since the 1970s, and especially after the 1990s it accelerated in some countries owing to financial globalization and increasing international production linkages. Thus, de-industrialization has shown different features with different types of capitalism, depending on the institutional arrangements of the economy. However, there are few studies that develop the analysis of the relationship between the varieties of capitalism and the different patterns of de-industrialization.

According to the study by Amable (2003), five types of capitalism can be identified: "market-based capitalism," "social-democratic capitalism," "Asian capitalism," "continental European capitalism" and "Mediterranean capitalism." These different types of capitalism have different institutional arrangements and institutional complementarity in product markets, wage–labor nexus, the financial sector, social protection and education. Taking account of Amable's typology, our comparative analysis of de-industrialization focuses mainly on countries with different types of advanced capitalism, as follows: Germany and France (continental European

Table 6.1 Four types of de-industrialization

	Output		*Labor productivity*		*Employment*	
	Manufacturing	*Service*	*Manufacturing*	*Service*	*Manufacturing*	*Service*
Positive de-industrialization	Increase or constant	–	Considerably increase	–	Constant or decrease	Increase
Negative de-industrialization	Decrease	–	–	–	Decrease	Increase
De-industrialization through manufacturing-service linkages	Increase	Increase	–	–	–	Increase
De-industrialization by the shift of final demand to the service sector	–	Increase	–	–	Decrease	Decrease

Source: Uemura and Tahara (2014).

Note
(–) shows that the direction cannot be determined.

capitalism), Italy (Mediterranean capitalism), the UK (market-based capitalism) and Japan (Asian capitalism).[4] We investigate how different varieties of capitalism with different institutional arrangements show different patterns of de-industrialization and have different political-economic consequences.

We provide an overview of the patterns of these advanced economies. Figures 6.2 and 6.3 show real growth rates and unemployment in Germany, France, Italy,

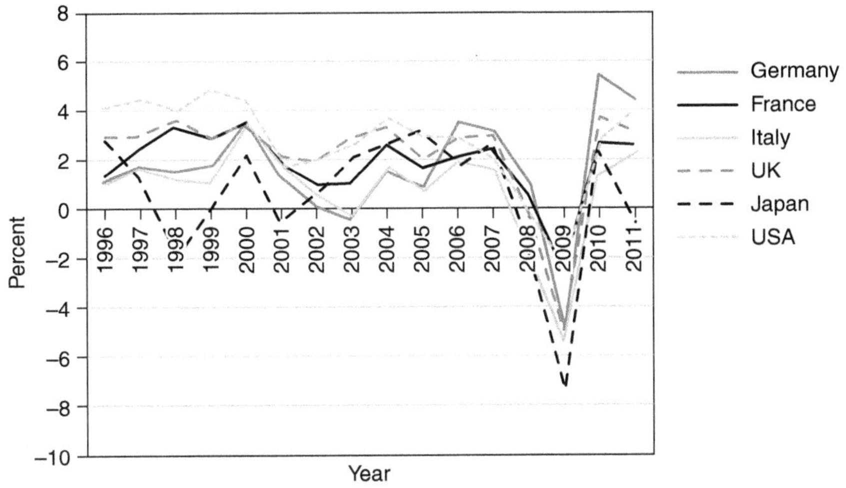

Figure 6.2 Growth rates of real output.

Source: WIOD 2014.

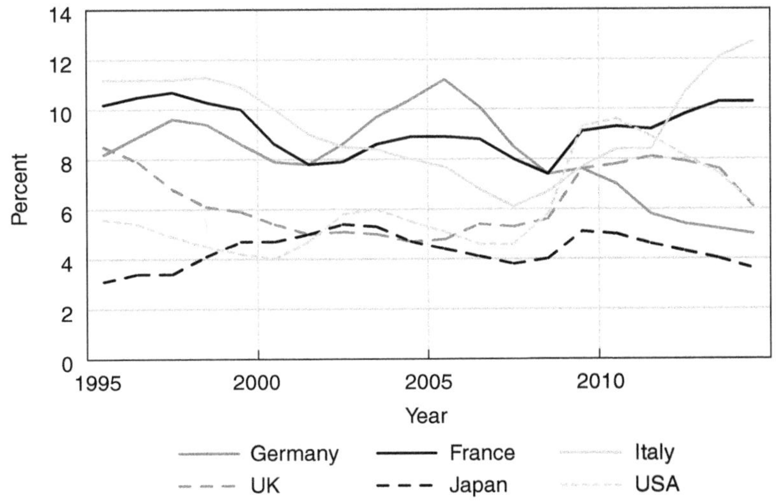

Figure 6.3 Unemployment rate.

Source: Eurostat.

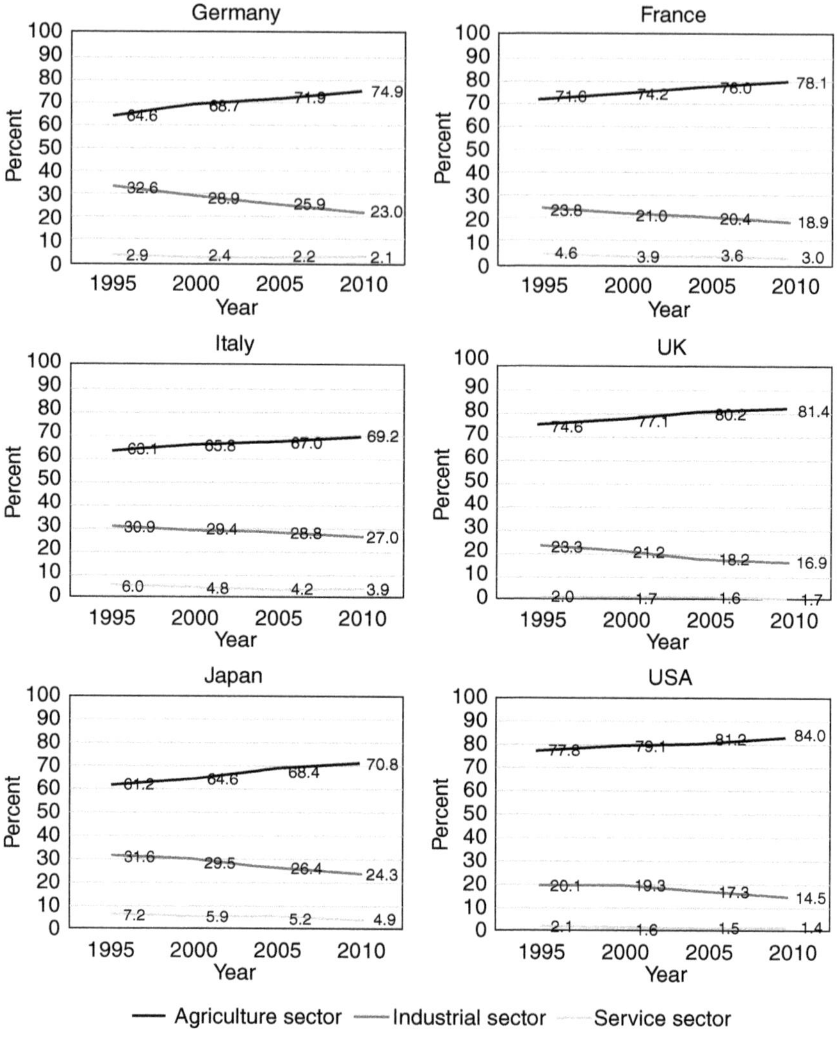

Figure 6.4 Industrial structural changes: Germany, France, Italy, the UK and Japan.

Source: WIOD 2014.

the UK, Japan and the USA; Figure 6.4 identifies industrial structural changes in terms of employment in these countries. De-industrialization has occurred universally in all of these advanced countries. In particular, the ratios of service employment are very high in the USA, the UK and France, and de-industrialization has accelerated recently in Germany and Japan.

In order to investigate the pattern of de-industrialization, we use a more detailed classification of industrial sectors, shown in Table 6.2, in which "the

Table 6.2 Industrial classification for the analysis of de-industrialization

1	Agriculture	Agriculture, forestry, fisheries, livestock and sericulture farming
2	Export core manufacturing	Transportation equipment, general machinery, electronic and electrical equipment, etc. (Export/output ratio is more than 20 percent in each country)
3	Other manufacturing	Other manufacturing industries than the export core
4	Other industries	Construction, electricity, gas, water supply, mining
5	Financial services	Financial intermediary services
6	Business-related services	Rental of office equipments and goods, advertisement, information services and internet-based services, wholesale, research, telegraph and telephone, mail, transportation
7	Consumer services	Retail, insurance, real estate, transportation, broadcasting, entertainment, eating and drinking places, accommodation
8	Public services	Education, medical, hygiene

Source: author.

export core manufacturing" industry is defined as that showing more than 20 percent of exports per unit of output in each country.

Based on the industrial classification in Table 6.2, the employment shares of "export core manufacturing," "financial services," "business-related services," "consumer services" and "public services" are seen for Germany, France, Italy, the UK, Japan and the USA in Figure 6.4. Different structural patterns are observed among these countries. The ratio of "export core manufacturing" is very high in Germany, which is a core exporter in the EU. On the contrary, the ratio of "financial services" is relatively high in the UK and the USA, which are typical "market-based capitalism" countries where financialization has proceeded very rapidly. In this regard, the growth pattern in each country is reflected by types of capitalism and the pattern of de-industrialization. As for "business-related services," the ratio has been high in the UK and France, and it has been increasing in Germany and Japan. According to research by Franke and Kalmbach (2005) and Uemura and Tahara (2014), "export core manufacturing" and "business-related services" have very strong linkages in Germany and Japan. Both countries are "coordinated market economies" (Hall and Soskice 2001; Schröder 2013). When analyzed more closely, however, they have different institutional arrangements as different types of capitalism, even though they show rather similar patterns of de-industrialization. Furthermore, the ratio of "public services" is relatively high in the USA and France, and also has been increasing very rapidly in Japan. The "public services" industry plays the role of employment absorber in the process of de-industrialization (Iversen and Cusack 2000). Especially, "negative de-industrialization" is often compensated by the expansion of "public services," which causes the political problem of increasing public debt.

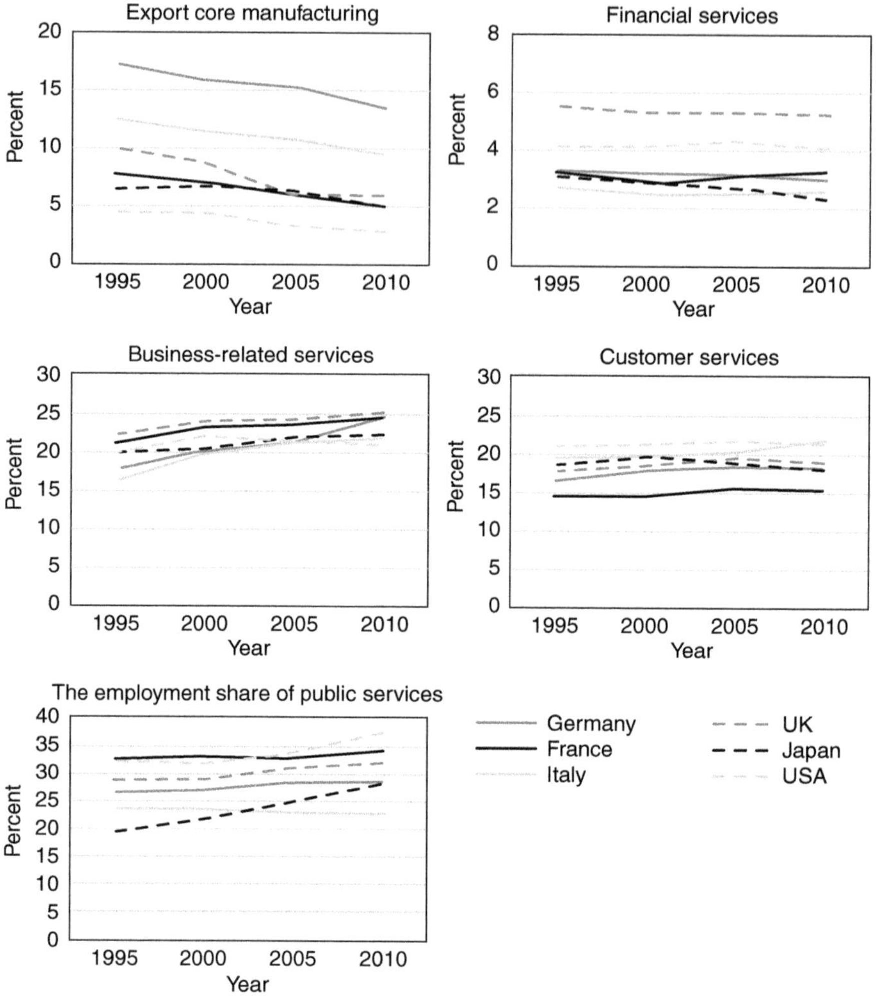

Figure 6.5 Share of employment.

Source: WIOD 2014.

2.2 Comparative analysis of growth regime and de-industrialization

Based on equations (6.3) and (6.5), a comparative analysis of de-industrialization is conducted for the UK, Germany, France, Italy, the UK and Japan. The period of analysis is from 1995 to 2009 owing to the data limitations of the WIOD.[5] During this period, the euro was established as a single currency for most EU countries in 1999, and resulted in a large trade imbalance between Germany ("continental capitalism") and Italy ("Mediterranean capitalism"), amplifying the heterogeneity of the eurozone economies. In 2008 the subprime crisis hit all

European economies, followed by the euro crisis in 2011. The euro crisis exacerbated sovereign debt crisis in the Southern European economies, causing governance problems in European integration (Boyer 2013; Majone 2014). The subprime crisis also influenced the Japanese economy, which was, moreover, damaged by the Great East Japan Earthquake in 2011 (see Figure 6.2). In this situation, Japanese firms are shifting their productive activities to East Asian countries.

The results of the input–output analysis of de-industrialization are summarized in Table 6.3, which shows the components of real output growth, the growth rate of labor productivity and the growth rate of employment. We can identify the transformations of the growth regime and the different patterns of de-industrialization in each country.

In the following part of this section, the results of the analysis of the growth regime and the pattern of de-industrialization are explained for Germany, France, Italy, the UK and Japan with reference to their specific industrial structures and institutional arrangements that have experienced economic fluctuations and crises since the mid-1990s.

2.2.1 Germany (continental European capitalism)

Germany has large competitive firms with an institutionally coordinated system of employment and an effective skill formation and qualification system with corporatism arrangements in a strong manufacturing sector. These firms have exported final and intermediate goods to other EU member countries and the rest of the world, and Germany has gained more trade surplus since the euro was established.

1995–2000. Led by a large increase in export demand, "the export core manufacturing" industry realized high rates of output growth and productivity growth, exhibiting cumulative growth. As a result, employment decreased only slightly, and very weak "positive de-industrialization" occurred. Furthermore, the growth of "business-related services" occurred mainly by the technological coefficient effect, leading to an increase in employment. Therefore, the German economy remarkably exhibited "de-industrialization through manufacturing–service linkages," which corresponds to the analysis of Franke and Kalmbach (2005).

2000–2005. After the euro was established as a single currency in 1999, export demand increased continuously, even though it was counterbalanced by imports of final and intermediate goods in Germany. Therefore, "export core manufacturing" showed high growth rates, and "positive de-industrialization" proceeded in the German economy. Moreover, the growth of "consumer services" was weak and "public services" absorbed employment, putting pressure on the German welfare state (Martine and Thelen 2007; Thelen, 2014).

2005–2009. Germany's "export core manufacturing" industry, hit by the subprime crisis, showed negative growth, which is very exceptional in the German economy. At the same time, outputs fell in "other manufacturing" industry. Therefore, "negative de-industrialization" occurred in Germany in this period.

Table 6.3 Decomposition of real output growth (%)

1995–2000 (annual rate)

		Real output	*Final demand*	*Export*	*Import*	*Technology*	*Domestic input*	*Residual*	*Employment*	*Labor productivity*
Germany	1 Agriculture	1.8	2.3	3.0	–3.4	1.5	–1.5	–0.2	–2.8	4.6
	2 Export core manufacturing	4.4	2.1	6.3	–5.0	3.0	–1.7	–0.2	–0.8	5.2
	3 Other manufacturing	0.5	1.4	2.6	–2.6	0.7	–1.3	–0.2	–0.5	1.1
	4 Other industries	–1.0	–0.2	1.2	–2.1	2.2	–1.1	–0.9	–3.3	2.4
	5 Financial services	6.3	5.9	2.8	–2.3	0.7	–0.8	0.0	0.3	5.9
	6 Business-related services	4.3	1.2	2.7	–2.7	3.7	–1.0	0.3	3.2	1.1
	7 Consumer services	1.9	1.8	1.0	–1.2	0.9	–0.5	0.0	2.3	–0.4
	8 Public services	2.1	1.7	0.2	–0.3	0.6	–0.1	0.0	1.3	0.8
France	1 Agriculture	2.9	3.0	2.6	–2.3	0.2	–0.1	–0.5	–1.8	4.7
	2 Export core manufacturing	8.7	5.8	9.0	–8.0	3.9	–1.8	–0.2	–0.7	9.5
	3 Other manufacturing	7.1	4.7	3.7	–3.7	2.8	–0.2	0.0	0.1	7.1
	4 Other Industries	–3.3	0.4	1.4	–2.6	0.0	–1.5	–1.1	–0.2	–3.1
	5 Financial services	3.7	1.6	1.3	–1.0	1.3	0.4	0.1	–0.2	3.9
	6 Business-related services	4.6	4.3	3.0	–2.8	1.2	–0.7	–0.4	3.8	0.7
	7 Consumer services	3.4	3.3	1.0	–1.0	0.4	–0.2	–0.1	1.5	1.9
	8 Public services	1.9	2.1	0.2	–0.4	0.1	–0.1	–0.1	1.5	0.4

Italy	1 Agriculture	1.3	3.6	1.3	−1.7	−0.9	−0.6	−0.3	−3.5	4.8
	2 Export core manufacturing	3.2	3.3	2.6	−3.6	1.4	−0.6	0.0	−0.5	3.7
	3 Other manufacturing	2.7	2.8	1.7	−2.1	0.9	−0.4	−0.1	0.2	2.5
	4 Other Industries	2.1	2.0	0.7	−2.1	2.9	−1.0	−0.4	0.4	1.7
	5 Financial services	4.9	0.8	0.7	−0.7	3.0	0.3	0.7	−0.4	5.3
	6 Business-related services	4.9	2.9	1.1	−1.8	2.9	−0.4	0.3	5.0	−0.1
	7 Consumer services	2.4	2.3	0.6	−0.8	0.5	−0.2	0.0	0.5	1.9
	8 Public services	1.6	1.2	0.1	−0.1	0.4	0.0	0.0	0.8	0.8
UK	1 Agriculture	−1.3	6.4	0.6	−2.1	−5.0	−1.0	−0.1	−3.0	1.7
	2 Export core manufacturing	2.5	4.6	4.1	−6.0	2.7	−2.4	−0.5	−1.4	3.9
	3 Other manufacturing	0.7	3.8	0.7	−1.6	−1.6	−0.3	−0.4	−1.0	1.7
	4 Other industries	2.3	2.5	0.8	−1.2	0.5	−0.3	0.0	0.3	2.1
	5 Financial services	7.6	5.4	2.9	−1.4	1.3	−0.5	−0.1	0.5	7.1
	6 Business-related services	8.9	4.9	1.9	−1.8	3.3	−0.3	0.9	2.6	6.3
	7 Consumer services	4.3	4.2	0.5	−0.7	0.6	−0.2	0.0	2.2	2.1
	8 Public services	2.7	2.0	0.2	−0.1	0.5	0.0	0.1	1.3	1.4
Japan	1 Agriculture	−0.3	0.2	0.5	−0.1	−0.7	−0.1	−0.1	−4.2	3.9
	2 Export core manufacturing	2.7	1.4	2.2	−1.4	1.1	−0.5	0.0	−1.0	3.8
	3 Other manufacturing	−1.3	−0.2	0.6	−0.4	−0.8	−0.4	−0.1	−2.6	1.3

continued

Table 6.3 Continued

		Real output	*Final demand*	*Export*	*Import*	*Technology*	*Domestic input*	*Residual*	*Employment*	*Labor productivity*
	4 Other industries	–1.6	–1.8	0.2	0.0	0.8	–0.6	–0.1	–1.5	–0.1
	5 Financial services	0.3	–0.1	0.3	0.0	0.3	–0.1	–0.1	–1.9	2.2
	6 Business-related services	2.4	1.0	0.8	–0.5	1.3	–0.3	0.0	0.4	2.0
	7 Consumer services	0.7	1.0	0.1	–0.1	–0.3	–0.1	0.0	0.4	0.3
	8 Public services	2.3	2.2	0.0	0.0	0.1	0.0	0.0	1.0	0.6

2000–2005 (annual rate)

		Real output	*Final demand*	*Export*	*Import*	*Technology*	*Domestic input*	*Residual*	*Employment*	*Labor productivity*
Germany	1 Agriculture	0.0	0.3	2.6	–1.6	–0.2	–1.0	–0.1	–1.8	1.8
	2 Export core manufacturing	1.7	–1.1	5.1	–1.9	1.9	–1.8	–0.3	–1.4	3.1
	3 Other manufacturing	0.7	–0.8	2.5	–0.8	0.3	–0.6	–0.1	–1.6	2.2
	4 Other industries	–2.0	–1.9	1.3	–1.8	2.5	–1.3	–0.6	–4.3	2.3
	5 Financial services	0.9	0.7	0.5	–0.8	1.2	–0.4	–0.1	–0.6	1.5
	6 Business-related services	1.6	0.2	2.8	–1.2	1.1	–0.9	–0.2	1.1	0.5
	7 Consumer services	0.9	0.5	0.9	–0.4	0.3	–0.3	–0.1	0.4	0.5
	8 Public services	0.8	0.4	0.3	–0.1	0.2	0.0	0.0	0.8	–0.1

France	1 Agriculture	1.0	2.3	0.8	–1.4	–0.5	–0.2	–0.1	–1.3	2.3
	2 Export core manufacturing	3.1	3.9	4.8	–5.4	1.9	–0.9	–0.1	–2.5	5.6
	3 Other manufacturing	0.8	2.2	1.8	–2.5	0.4	–0.8	–0.1	–1.2	2.1
	4 Other industries	2.0	1.4	0.5	–0.5	0.5	0.1	0.0	1.3	0.8
	5 Financial services	3.4	2.3	0.9	–0.3	0.5	0.5	0.1	1.3	2.1
	6 Business-related services	3.8	3.5	1.2	–1.8	1.9	–0.3	0.1	1.4	2.4
	7 Consumer services	1.6	2.2	0.5	–0.6	–0.1	–0.1	–0.1	1.6	0.0
	8 Public services	1.2	1.4	0.1	–0.1	0.0	0.0	0.0	0.7	0.5
Italy	1 Agriculture	–0.4	1.2	0.7	–0.7	–1.4	–0.2	–0.1	–1.6	1.2
	2 Export core manufacturing	–0.2	0.2	0.6	–0.9	0.3	–0.5	0.0	–0.4	0.2
	3 Other manufacturing	0.9	0.7	1.0	–0.8	0.5	–0.3	0.0	0.4	0.6
	4 Other industries	1.7	1.7	–0.1	–1.3	2.1	–0.6	0.0	2.8	–1.1
	5 Financial services	2.2	1.2	0.4	–0.8	2.1	–0.4	0.1	0.6	1.6
	6 Business-related services	2.5	1.5	0.6	–0.9	2.1	–0.3	0.1	2.4	0.1
	7 Consumer services	1.1	1.1	0.1	–0.1	0.0	0.1	0.0	2.1	–1.0
	8 Public services	1.3	1.8	0.0	0.0	–0.4	0.0	0.0	0.6	0.6
UK	1 Agriculture	1.1	1.8	0.4	–2.3	0.2	–0.4	–0.1	0.4	0.7
	2 Export core manufacturing	–2.4	0.6	–1.2	–0.7	–0.3	–0.7	–0.1	–5.4	3.1
	3 Other manufacturing	–0.6	1.4	0.3	–1.7	–0.2	–0.4	–0.1	–3.0	2.4

continued

Table 6.3 Continued

		Real output	*Final demand*	*Export*	*Import*	*Technology*	*Domestic input*	*Residual*	*Employment*	*Labor productivity*
	4 Other industries	1.2	3.2	–0.2	–1.0	0.1	–0.6	–0.2	1.7	–0.5
	5 Financial services	4.7	7.0	1.6	–1.4	0.0	–0.8	0.1	0.8	3.9
	6 Business-related services	4.1	4.3	1.5	–1.4	1.4	–0.3	0.2	1.2	2.9
	7 Consumer services	3.9	4.0	0.6	–1.1	1.8	–0.5	0.0	1.8	2.1
	8 Public services	5.2	4.1	0.2	–0.3	1.8	0.0	0.5	2.4	2.8
Japan	1 Agriculture	–1.5	0.1	0.8	–0.3	–1.1	–0.9	–0.1	–2.9	1.4
	2 Export core manufacturing	4.0	3.4	3.6	–2.4	0.8	–0.5	–0.1	–1.3	5.3
	3 Other manufacturing	–1.4	0.5	1.2	–0.9	–1.3	–0.7	–0.1	–3.3	1.9
	4 Other industries	–1.8	–1.2	0.3	–0.3	0.5	–0.7	–0.2	–2.6	0.9
	5 Financial services	2.0	2.2	0.7	–0.4	0.1	–0.3	–0.2	–1.8	3.8
	6 Business-related services	2.2	1.9	0.9	–0.4	0.6	–0.3	–0.1	0.9	1.4
	7 Consumer services	0.3	0.9	0.2	–0.1	–0.6	–0.1	–0.1	–0.5	0.8
	8 Public services	2.5	2.8	0.0	0.0	0.0	0.0	0.0	2.7	–0.2

2005–2009 (annual rate) *2005–2010 for Japan

		Real output	Final demand	Export	Import	Technology	Domestic input	Residual	Employment	Labor productivity
Germany	1 Agriculture	1.4	0.5	0.9	–2.0	5.1	–2.3	–1.0	0.2	1.2
	2 Export core manufacturing	–1.6	–0.2	–0.9	–0.5	0.6	–0.5	–0.1	–1.0	–0.6
	3 Other manufacturing	–4.3	–2.2	0.2	–0.2	–0.5	–0.7	0.0	–5.1	0.8
	4 Other industries	0.8	–0.4	0.2	1.1	–1.1	0.9	–0.2	0.9	1.8
	5 Financial services	2.9	3.0	1.3	–0.4	–0.5	–0.3	–0.1	0.1	2.8
	6 Business-related services	1.7	0.7	0.7	–0.3	1.0	–0.2	–0.1	4.9	–3.2
	7 Consumer services	0.6	0.4	0.0	0.0	0.3	0.0	–0.1	1.3	–0.7
	8 Public services	2.2	2.0	0.0	0.0	0.0	0.0	0.0	1.7	0.5
France	1 Agriculture	6.7	3.1	1.9	–1.8	2.7	0.4	0.4	–4.0	10.6
	2 Export core manufacturing	1.0	2.1	–0.9	–1.1	–0.4	1.6	–0.1	–3.4	4.4
	3 Other manufacturing	5.4	4.2	0.7	–1.9	1.6	1.2	0.1	–4.2	9.7
	4 Other industries	–0.7	0.0	–0.3	0.5	–1.4	1.2	–0.5	1.6	–2.4
	5 Financial services	1.7	3.7	–0.3	–0.1	–1.8	0.5	–0.1	1.5	0.2
	6 Business-related services	2.5	2.6	–0.1	–0.7	0.6	0.5	0.0	1.4	1.2
	7 Consumer services	–0.4	0.7	0.0	–0.2	–1.0	0.2	–0.1	–0.1	–0.3
	8 Public services	–0.7	0.0	0.0	0.0	–0.6	0.0	0.0	1.3	–2.0

continued

Table 6.3 Continued

		Real output	*Final demand*	*Export*	*Import*	*Technology*	*Domestic input*	*Residual*	*Employment*	*Labor productivity*
Italy	1 Agriculture	–2.1	–2.1	–0.6	1.3	–0.2	0.2	–0.2	–1.5	–0.7
	2 Export core manufacturing	–4.3	–2.3	–1.9	1.9	–1.3	0.0	0.0	–2.3	–2.0
	3 Other manufacturing	–5.1	–2.1	–1.4	1.8	–2.7	0.0	0.1	–1.9	–3.2
	4 Other industries	–2.1	–1.8	–0.7	–0.4	3.4	–1.4	–0.9	0.5	–2.6
	5 Financial services	2.3	2.3	0.0	0.4	0.3	–0.3	–0.2	1.4	0.9
	6 Business-related services	–0.7	–1.1	–1.0	0.6	1.3	–0.3	–0.3	1.3	–2.0
	7 Consumer services	–0.2	–0.1	–0.4	0.4	0.1	0.0	–0.1	2.1	–2.3
	8 Public services	1.2	1.0	–0.1	0.0	0.2	0.0	0.0	0.4	0.8
UK	1 Agriculture	–1.5	–0.2	0.3	–0.3	0.3	–1.3	0.0	2.4	–3.9
	2 Export core manufacturing	–3.4	–1.9	0.4	–0.5	5.2	–4.0	–1.8	–1.3	–2.1
	3 Other manufacturing	–3.5	–1.2	0.5	–1.0	0.5	–1.4	–0.2	–3.2	–0.3
	4 Other industries	–2.7	–1.5	0.0	–0.3	0.6	–1.0	–0.2	0.1	–2.9
	5 Financial services	1.2	–1.2	3.6	–0.5	0.9	–0.9	–0.2	0.8	0.5
	6 Business-related services	1.5	–0.2	1.0	–0.7	3.3	–1.1	–0.3	1.3	0.2
	7 Consumer services	0.4	0.2	0.2	–0.2	0.9	–0.5	–0.2	0.5	–0.2
	8 Public services	0.9	1.9	0.0	–0.1	–0.5	–0.2	–0.1	1.4	–0.5

Japan	1 Agriculture	–1.1	–0.9	0.3	0.6	–1.2	0.2	–0.1	–1.8	0.7
	2 Export core manufacturing	1.2	1.5	–1.0	0.5	0.9	–0.3	–0.1	–0.5	1.6
	3 Other manufacturing	–1.9	–0.6	0.5	0.1	–1.7	0.1	0.0	–2.4	0.5
	4 Other industries	–3.0	–2.2	0.1	–0.3	–0.2	0.2	–0.1	–2.3	–0.7
	5 Financial services	–3.3	–0.5	0.0	–0.2	–2.7	–0.1	0.0	1.1	–4.4
	6 Business-related services	–1.8	–1.1	0.4	0.0	–1.4	0.0	–0.1	0.7	–2.6
	7 Consumer services	0.5	0.7	0.0	0.2	–0.3	0.0	0.0	0.1	0.5
	8 Public services	1.4	1.7	0.0	0.0	0.1	0.0	0.0	0.4	1.1

Source: WIOD 2014.

Even in this situation, "business-related services" retained sufficient employment-absorption capacity by absorbing workers who were released from the manufacturing sector. This caused a decrease in the unemployment rate even in the recession (see Figures 6.2 and 6.3).

2.2.2 France (continental European capitalism)

France has various manufacturing and consumer service industries as well as a relatively competitive agricultural sector. As institutional characteristics, the French economy has strong institutional regulations for minimum wages, unemployment assistance and the public skill formation system in the labor market, but individualization has proceeded in the French employment system.

1995–2000. In the French case, export demand was very strong for "the export core manufacturing" industry and "the other manufacturing" industry, which realized high rates of output growth and productivity growth, and thus cumulative growth. As a result, employment decreased only slightly, and very weak "positive de-industrialization" proceeded. Furthermore, the growth of "business-related services" occurred mainly by an increase in final demand rather than technological coefficient effects, which led to an increase in employment. In other words, "de-industrialization through manufacturing–service linkages" was relatively weaker in France than in Germany. Furthermore, the "public services" also absorbed employees on the basis of the French welfare state.

2000–2005. Even after the establishment of the euro in 1999, export demand was continuously high, although it was counterbalanced strongly by large amounts of imports of final and intermediate goods. Therefore, "export core manufacturing" showed high growth rates and "positive de-industrialization" occurred. All the service industries, "financial services," "business-related services," "consumer services" and "public services" continued to absorb employment in France.

2005–2009. The effect of the subprime crisis was relatively mild in France, and "export core manufacturing" industry and "the other manufacturing" industry maintained positive growth rates. Therefore, in those industries, "positive de-industrialization" continued with a slightly increased unemployment rate (see Figure 6.3). At the same time, "agriculture" maintained competitiveness, showing relatively higher growth rates of output and labor productivity, which is a typical feature in France.

2.2.3 Italy (Mediterranean capitalism)

Italy traditionally has a large number of heterogeneous small and medium-sized firms in the manufacturing and consumer service industries. The labor market is segmented and less flexible, with workers having different skills, and the manufacturing and service industries with low productivity play the role of absorbing employment in the labor market. The Italian economy has had a trade deficit since the euro was established.

1995–2000. Output growth was maintained firmly in "export core manufacturing" industry, "other manufacturing" industry and "other industry," while productivity growth was not as high in these industries. Therefore, de-industrialization was mitigated to a relative extent in the Italian economy. A very remarkable feature of the Italian economy is the fact that productivity growth was relatively low in the manufacturing industry. While "financial services" and "business-related services" were expanding, productivity growth remained very low, especially in "business-related services."

2000–2005. After the euro was established as a single currency in 1999, "export core manufacturing" industry lost its international competitiveness and exhibited negative growth rates. The main cause of the sharp fall was very stagnant export demand and sharply increased imports. In this period, the transformation of the growth regime occurred alongside an increasing trade deficit in Italy. Under this condition, productivity growth was very low even in "export core manufacturing," and thus mildly "negative de-industrialization" occurred in the Italian economy.[6]

2005–2009. "Export core manufacturing" and "other manufacturing" industries showed negative growth rates in output as well as labor productivity, and thus, strongly "negative de-industrialization" occurred in the Italian economy. In this situation, workers were absorbed by "consumer services" and other private services, which are traditionally an employment sponge in the Italian economy. Generally, the private service industries play an important role in absorbing employment in Italy, even while causing a very sharp increase in the unemployment rate (see Figure 6.3).

2.2.4 The UK (market-based capitalism)

De-industrialization started in the UK early in the 1950s, and has accelerated since the long-term structural crisis of the 1970s. In the 1980s there was a lot of debate about the nature of de-industrialization in the UK (Rowthorn and Wells 1987). "Financial services" and "business-related services" have expanded rapidly in tandem with financial liberalization and deregulation, which were brought about by neoliberalist policies in the UK since the 1980s.

1995–2000. While "export core manufacturing" industry, "other manufacturing" industry and "other industry" grew firmly owing to the increase in final demand, productivity growth was higher than output growth. Therefore, "positive de-industrialization" occurred in this period. Moreover, output and employment grew in "financial services," "business-related services" and "consumer services." However, productivity growth was so high in "financial services" and "business-related services" that employment growth in these sectors was rather modest in the British economy.

2000–2005. This includes a time of recession in the British economy, and output and employment fell considerably in "export core manufacturing" due to a fall in exports. Therefore, "negative de-industrialization" occurred in "export core manufacturing" and "other manufacturing." In this period, "financial services" did not grow sufficiently, so employment was absorbed by only "public services."

2005–2009. The subprime crisis hit the British economy and "financial intermediary services" and "business-related services" showed negative growth rates owing to a sharp fall in final demand and export demand. Furthermore, productivity growth was negative in many industries, so the British economy exhibited very strong "negative de-industrialization" in this period. This shows that the British economy is relatively vulnerable to a financial crisis.

2.2.5 *Japan (Asian/innovation-led capitalism)*

Large firms in "export core manufacturing" industry have played a very crucial role in the Japanese economy, and are supported by efficient subcontracting networks. The externalization of business activities and workers from the manufacturing sector to the service sector was remarkable, with increasing non-regular workers after the structural crisis in the 1990s (Boyer and Yamada 2000; Boyer *et al.* 2012; Uemura 2012). This has caused increasing inequality in income and wealth in the Japanese economy.

1995–2000. Even in the long-lasting recession of the 1990s, output increased in "export core manufacturing" industry, which was a sharp contrast to the negative growth of output in "other manufacturing" and "other industry." Accordingly, "positive de-industrialization" was sustained in "export core manufacturing" industry, while "negative de-industrialization" occurred in "other manufacturing" and "other industry." Furthermore, "business-related services" and "public services" grew steadily in terms of output and employment. Strong linkages between the "export core manufacturing" sector and "business-related service" sector showed a similar pattern to that in the German economy (see Uemura and Tahara 2014).

2000–2005. This period includes a recovery process from the long-lasting recession; "export core manufacturing" industry exhibited very high output growth and productivity growth, leading to "positive de-industrialization." The growth of labor productivity was enhanced by the externalization of business activities and workers to "business-related services." Furthermore, both output and employment increased in "financial services," "business-related services" and "public services." In this regard, a new growth pattern emerged in the first half of the 2000s, but this did not realize a new and stable growth regime as new rules and mechanisms to coordinate overseas activities of Japanese firms and domestic structural changes were not established.

2005–2010. When the subprime crisis hit the Japanese economy in 2008, the growth of "export core manufacturing" industry became stagnant, and "other manufacturing" and "other industry" showed negative growth rates. Accordingly, the Japanese economy exhibited overall "negative de-industrialization." In this situation, "financial services" and "business-related services" also showed negative growth rates, and their labor productivity fell sharply. As a result, employment was relatively maintained via intrinsic institutional mechanisms in the Japanese labor market, even though many non-regular workers were fired. In this situation, "public services" absorbed employees, which kept the unemployment rate relatively low (as seen in Figure 6.3), but caused severe problems for public finances.

In summary, we can point out three important aspects for studying de-industrialization in advanced economies from our findings in the international comparative analysis. First, it is important for political-economic studies to identify what types of de-industrialization have proceeded in certain industries, and in particular whether the patterns are "positive" or "negative." This depends on the varieties of growth regime at different times and places in the development of capitalism. Second, the strength of manufacturing–service linkages determines the pattern of output–employment dynamics in both sectors and the nature of conflict among sociopolitical groups. Very strong linkages are observed in Germany and Japan, where large manufacturing firms dominate the economies and have some common interests with firms in the business-related service industry. Third, we should carefully investigate which service sectors absorb workers who have been released from the manufacturing sector. Are they private services or public services; large firms or small and medium-sized firms? As mentioned in the country-specific analyses above, different service sectors absorb workers in Germany, France, Italy, the UK and Japan. In general, "public services" absorbed workers who are released by the manufacturing industry in the process of de-industrialization, but this process has been influenced by the recent transformation of the welfare state, which causes more dualistic structures in these countries (Schäfer and Streeck 2013; Thelen 2014).

3 Political-economic influences of de-industrialization with varieties of capitalism

3.1 De-industrialization and labor market segmentation

Increased employment in the service sector that proceeds in tandem with de-industrialization may cause unemployment problems and social inequality. Rowthorn and Glyn pointed out that changes in employment were not uniform across sectors after the 1970s as they included shifts in employment from the manufacturing sector to the service sector, with consequently rising unemployment (Rowthorn and Glyn 1990). Moreover, they argued that the employment problems should be analyzed not only at the macroeconomic level but also from the viewpoint of interactions between structural changes and labor market segmentation. By doing so, it becomes evident that an increase in employment in the service sector may cause the risk of structural unemployment problems and more social inequality in the process of de-industrialization in advanced countries.

Analyzing the changing patterns of inequality and dualism in advanced countries, Emmenegger *et al.* (2012) pointed out the political-economic problems which are caused by de-industrialization in European countries. In particular,

Häusermann and Schwander (2012) argued that new patterns of inequality appear due to strengthened insider–outsider relations with increasing unstable employment in the de-industrialization process in advanced capitalism. Furthermore, some studies have pointed out that in Germany and Japan, "business-related services" have expanded to maintain the export core manufacturing industry, and this is called "the strategy of saving industry" (Palier and Thelen 2012; Peng 2012). This shift has been accompanied by an increase in part-time and low-skilled workers and the increasing instability of employment in the service sector. In particular, in Japan "positive de-industrialization" in the "export core manufacturing" industry has accelerated in tandem with the externalization of service activities and the increase in non-regular workers in "business-related services" (Uemura and Tahara 2014). This transformation has changed institutional structures in the segmented labor market in Japan (Lechevalier 2014), which has been weakening company-based trade unions.

3.2 Patterns of fragmentation and income distribution

De-industrialization influences the patterns of dualization and fragmentation as well as income distribution among different groups of workers in political-economic processes with varieties of capitalism. By using socioeconomic accounts (SEA) in the WIOD, we can identify the effect of the expanding service economy on income distribution among workers with different levels of skills in different industries.[7] Table 6.4 shows different structures of income distribution among workers in different industries in Germany, France, Italy, the UK and Japan.

Investigating the relative shares of workers with different skills, we can identify the effects of de-industrialization and the expansion of the service economy on the patterns of income distribution among workers in these industries. In particular, we focus on the following typical industries:

1. Transport equipment (export core manufacturing). The share of income of medium-skilled workers is relatively high in Germany and Japan, even though this does not necessarily exclude high-skilled workers who are educated by on-the-job training in the Japanese case. These workers are employed by large car-manufacturing firms, and are usually members of trade unions which use their political voice.
2. Financial intermediation (financial services). The share of incomes of high-skilled workers is high in the UK and Japan. In these countries, financial intermediation firms usually hire university graduates and pay higher salaries. This has caused greater income inequality in the economy (Piketty 2014). These professional workers in the financial service sector are more individualistic and neoliberal in their political behaviors, and may have dominant influences with their higher incomes and wealth in the economy.
3. Renting of machines and equipment and other business activities (business-related services). The share of income of high-skilled workers is generally high in all the countries, especially in France and the UK. However, this

Table 6.4 Income distribution among workers with different levels of skills: international comparison (2009) (%)

		Germany	*France*	*Italy*	*UK*	*Japan*
Transport equipment	High skill	37.9	37.3	11.7	38.2	24.1
	Medium skill	53.2	43.5	48.3	44.9	64.1
	Low skill	8.9	19.2	40.0	16.8	11.8
Financial intermediation	High skill	37.4	60.7	33.8	53.7	65.1
	Medium skill	59.9	29.8	60.4	39.5	34.2
	Low skill	2.6	9.5	5.8	6.8	0.7
Renting of machines and equipment and other business activities	High skill	53.7	62.4	41.4	60.7	50.5
	Medium skill	40.5	25.2	44.7	28.4	47.3
	Low skill	5.8	12.5	13.9	10.9	2.2
Retail trade, except for motor vehicles and motorcycles; repair of household goods	High skill	25.9	34.2	9.4	24.8	31.6
	Medium skill	63.6	46.8	48.8	52.1	65.0
	Low skill	10.5	19.0	41.8	23.1	3.5
Public administration and defense; compulsory social security	High skill	42.8	35.6	23.8	51.6	49.7
	Medium skill	51.7	42.8	55.9	40.9	47.5
	Low skill	5.5	21.6	20.3	7.6	2.8

Source: WIOD 2014.

does not necessarily mean the employment of these workers, often including non-regular workers, is stable, especially in the Japanese case.

4 Retail trade, except motor vehicles and motorcycles, and repair of household goods (consumer services). The patterns are almost the same in Germany, France, the UK and Japan, but in Italy the income share of low-skilled workers is very high in the retail trade industry. This suggests that retail trade firms, possibly small and medium-sized firms, absorb low-skilled workers in the consumer service industry in Italy, and these workers are not organized by trade unions. This shows the specific characteristics of the Italian labor market and political conditions.

5 Public administration and defense; compulsory social security (public services). Public administration provides stable employment in all of the countries. However, Italy shows institutional specificities in public administration services, in which the income shares of medium-skilled and low-skilled workers are very high. On the contrary, in the UK and Japan, more high-skilled workers are employed with job security in the public sector, mitigating inequality among workers. Those workers often have a political voice regarding public policies.

According to this analysis, we can state that the effect of de-industrialization on income distribution among workers with different skills in an economy can be explained by two factors. These are employment growth differentials among different service sectors, and the income levels of workers with different levels of skills within the service industry with the varieties of capitalism. This structural effect may influence the political-economic situation in terms of conflict and compromise among different social groups in politics.

4 Conclusion

The theoretical framework of de-industrialization was explained from the viewpoint of *régulation* theory, and the comparative analysis of de-industrialization was conducted for Germany, France, Italy, the UK and Japan. Referring to the political-economic implication of de-industrialization, the results of our analysis can be summarized as follows.

First, de-industrialization in terms of employment is seen universally in all the advanced economies, but each economy has different features, depending on its pattern of capital accumulation, institutional arrangements and international economic relations. In particular, the employment dynamics at the industrial level are produced in the "growth regime" which is determined by interactions between the "demand regime" and the "productivity regime" as suggested by *régulation* theory.

Second, four types of de-industrialization are formalized theoretically. These are "positive de-industrialization," which occurs via productivity growth differentials between the manufacturing and the service sectors; "negative de-industrialization," which is caused by stagnant output in the manufacturing sector; "de-industrialization through manufacturing–service linkages," in which services are increasing intermediate inputs to the manufacturing sector; and "de-industrialization caused by the shift in final demand to services." The different logic of de-industrialization is often dominant with different varieties of capitalism in different periods.

Third, the employment ratios of "financial services" and "consumer services" are very high in the UK and the USA, which are usually characterized as "market-based capitalism." Especially, de-industrialization proceeds in tandem with financialization in these countries. The employment ratio of "export core manufacturing" is relatively high in Germany and Japan, even though it has been falling continuously in the process of de-industrialization. "Public services" are relatively large in the USA and France, and they have been increasing rapidly in Japan since the 1990s.

Fourth, based on input–output analysis, different patterns of de-industrialization are identified in different countries. In Germany, the "export core manufacturing" industry has grown with a high growth rate of labor productivity, which causes "positive de-industrialization" with strong linkages between "export core manufacturing" and "business-related services." In France, manufacturing industry has shown steady growth, which has brought about "positive de-industrialization." In Italy, especially after the euro was established as a single currency, "export core manufacturing" and "other manufacturing" industries showed negative growth rates with increasing imports, but the growth of labor productivity was also very low. Therefore, this caused only slightly "negative de-industrialization" in Italy. In the UK, "financial services" and "business-related services" grew with high productivity in the boom period, while the "export core manufacturing" industry often showed negative growth, exhibiting "negative de-industrialization." The Japanese pattern is somewhat similar to the German one, with strong linkages between "export core manufacturing" and "business-related services." Furthermore, the externalization of business activities and workers from the manufacturing industry to the "business-related services" industry becomes a remarkable feature of the Japanese economy, which causes more instability and inequality in the labor market.

Fifth, concerning the effects of de-industrialization on the labor market and socioeconomic structures, the interactions between the expansion of the service industries and labor market segmentation with social fragmentation play a very crucial role in each economy. In this regard, we should pay more attention to the fact that standard workers in the manufacturing industry decrease rapidly and that diversified workers are absorbed in the various service industries, such as financial services, bushiness-related services, consumer services and public services, which need different levels of skills with different types of employment contract. Accordingly, collective bargaining has been weakened in most countries. Furthermore, this also influences the structures of income distribution in an economy, which implies political effects on social conflict and compromise among fragmented social groups. Moreover, this political-economic influence shows diversifying patterns, depending on the institutional characteristics of the labor market and workers of different skill-levels and political power in different industries with varieties of capitalism.

De-industrialization is a universal and inevitable phenomenon in all advanced economies, but its patterns and structural characteristics differ from country to country, depending on economic structures, institutional coordinating mechanisms, growth regimes and international economic relations. The serious socioeconomic effects of de-industrialization may include dualization and fragmentation in an economy and society, but this can be de-escalated, depending on institutional rules in the labor market and the social policies in each country.

Appendix: method to convert WIOD to real-term data

The WIOD used in the analysis comprises nominal data in dollars. In order to conduct a time-series analysis of industrial structural change, we convert the WIOD data to real-term data by utilizing the exchange rate of each country and output deflator in each industrial sector.

The data of the exchange rates are shown in WIOD (2012 data set), and the deflators of output and intermediate inputs in each industry are provided by socioeconomic accounts (SEA) of WIOD. The SEA deflators are compiled for the values in each column, which causes a discrepancy in the values in each row. Therefore, we use the "double inflation method" to adjust for this gap in values.

Notes

1 For the user guide for WIOD, see Timmer *et al.* (2015).
2 "De-industrialization" has been studied in many European countries since the 1980s (Petit 1986; Rowthorn and Ramaswamy 1999; Rowthorn and Wells 1987). Furthermore, "de-industrialization" has been studied in the framework of *régulation* theory in Japan. For example, see Uemura (1991), Harada (1997, 2007), Tahara (2011), Uemura and Tahara (2014). Furthermore, in political science recently, "de-industrialization" has been a very important topic for political-economic studies (Iversen and Cusack 2000; Emmenegger *et al.* 2012).
3 The growth pattern is different from country to country, depending on the specific institutional arrangements. In the Japanese case, "profit-led growth" played a leading role in the high economic growth of the 1960s, and "export-led growth" became dominant after the 1980s (Uemura 2000, 2012).
4 According to recent studies, there are varieties of Asian capitalism, too. Harada and Tohyama (2012) classified five types of Asian capitalism: "innovation-led capitalism" (Japan, Korea and Taiwan), "city capitalism" (Singapore, Hong Kong), "trade-led industrializing capitalism" (Thailand, Malaysia), "insular semi-agrarian capitalism" (Indonesia, the Philippines) and "continental mixed capitalism" (China). Among these types of Asian capitalism, de-industrialization has started in "innovation-led capitalism" (Japan, Korea and Taiwan).
5 The data from WIOD are calculated in dollars, so we must convert the data into real terms. The conversion procedure is explained in the Appendix.
6 After the euro was established in 1999, the trade imbalance expanded between Germany and Southern European countries very rapidly. In this situation, the euro system caused de-industrialization to accelerate, causing severe unemployment problems in the Southern European economies (see Boyer 2013). De-industrialization has been influenced strongly by the currency system in Europe.
7 "Skill level" in the SEA in WIOD is defined on the basis of education as follows. "Low skill" corresponds to "primary education or first stage of basic education" and "lower secondary or second stage of basic education"; "medium skill" corresponds to "(upper) secondary education" and "post-secondary education"; "high skill" corresponds to "first stage of tertiary education" and "second state of tertiary education." In this definition of skills, however, we should be careful about high-school graduates who develop their skills in on-the-job training in the manufacturing industry in Japan.

References

Amable, M. (2003) *The Diversity of Modern Capitalism*, Oxford: Oxford University Press.

Baumol, W.A. (1967) "Macroeconomics of Unbalanced Growth: The Anatomy of Urban Crisis," *American Economic Review*, Vol. 57, No. 3.

Boyer, R. (1988) "Formalising Growth Regimes," in Dosi, G. *et al.* (eds.) *Technical Change and Industrial Transformation*, London: Pinter Publishers.

Boyer, R. (2013) *The Euro Crisis: History and Policies of the European Integration*, Tokyo: Fujiwara-shoten.

Boyer, R. and Yamada, T. (eds.) (2000) *Japanese Capitalism in Crisis: A Regulationist Interpretation*, London: Routledge.

Boyer, R., Uemura, H. and Isogai, A. (eds.) (2012) *Diversity and Transformations of Asian Capitalisms*, London: Routledge.

Emmenegger, P., Häusermann, S., Palier, B. and Seeleib-Kaiser, M. (eds.) (2012) *The Age of Dualization: The Changing Face of Inequality in Deindustrializing Societies*, Oxford: Oxford University Press.

Franke, R. and Kalmbach, P. (2005) "Structural Change in the Manufacturing Sector and its Input on Business Related Services: an Input–Output Study for Germany," *Structural Change and Economic Dynamics*, Vol. 16, pp. 467–468.

Hall, P. and Soskice, D. (eds.) (2001) *Varieties of Capitalism: The Institutional Foundations of Comparative Advantage*, Oxford: Oxford University Press.

Harada, Y. (1997) "A Study of Theoretical Model of De-industrialization: Focusing on Uneven Development and Cumulative Causation," *Economic Science*, Vol. 45, No. 3.

Harada, Y. (2007) Varieties of Industrial Structural Change: An Attempt of Typology Based on a Multivariate Analysis," in Yamada, T., Uni, H. and Nabashima, N. (eds.) *A New Aspect of Contemporary Capitalism*, Kyoto: Showado.

Harada, Y. and Tohyama, H. (2012) "Asian Capitalisms: Institutional Configuration and Firm Heterogeneity," in Boyer, R., Uemura, H. and Isogai, A. (eds.), *Diversity and Transformations of Asian Capitalisms*, London: Routledge.

Häusermann, S. and Schwander, H. (2012) "Varieties of Dualization? Labor Market Segmentation and Insider–Outsider Divided Across Regimes," in Emmenegger, P., Häusermann, S., Palier, B. and Seeleib-Kaiser, M. (eds.) (2012) *The Age of Dualization: The Changing Face of Inequality in Deindustrializing Societies*, Oxford: Oxford University Press.

Iversen, T. and Cusack, T.R. (2000) "The Cause of Welfare State Expansion: De-Industrialization or Globalization?" *World Politics*, Vol. 52, No. 3, pp. 313–349.

Kaldor, N. (1978) *Further Essays on Economic Theory*, London: Gerald Duckworth.

Landesmann, M.A. and Scazzieri, R. (eds.) (1996) *Production and Economic Dynamics*, Cambridge: Cambridge University Press.

Lechevalier, S. (ed.) (2014) *The Great Transformation of Japanese Capitalism*, London: Routledge.

Majone, G. (2014) *Rethinking the Union of Europe Post-Crisis: Has Integration Gone Too Far?*, Cambridge: Cambridge University Press.

Martine, C.J. and Thelen, K. (2007) "The State and Coordinated Capitalism: Contributions of the Public Sector to Social Solidarity in Postindustrial Society," *World Politics*, Vol. 60, No. 1, pp. 1–36.

Palier, B. and Thelen, K. (2012) "Dualization and Institutional Complementarities: Industrial Relations, Labor Market, and Welfare State Changes in France and Germany," in Emmenegger, P., Häusermann, S., Palier, B. and Seeleib-Kaiser, M. (eds.) (2012) *The Age of Dualization: The Changing Face of Inequality in Deindustrializing Societies*, Oxford: Oxford University Press.

Peng, I. (2012) "Economic Dualization in Japan and South Korea," in Emmenegger, P., Häusermann, S., Palier, B. and Seeleib-Kaiser, M. (eds.) *The Age of Dualization: The Changing Face of Inequality in Deindustrializing Societies*, Oxford: Oxford University Press.

Petit, P. (1986) *Slow Growth and the Service Economy*, London: Frances Printer.

Petit, P. (2005) *Croissance et richesse des nations*, Paris: La Découverte.

Piketty, T. (2014) *Capital in the Twenty-First Century*, Cambridge, MA: Harvard University Press.

Rowthorn, R. (1982) "Demand, Real Wages and Economic Growth," *Studi Economici*, No. 18.

Rowthorn, R. and Glyn, A. (1990) "The Diversity of Unemployment Experiences since 1973," in Marglin, S. and Schor, J. (eds.) *The Golden Age of Capitalism: Reinterpreting the Postwar Experience*, Oxford: Clarendon.

Rowthorn, R. and Ramaswamy, R. (1999) "Growth, Trade, and Deindustrialization," *IMF Staff Papers*, Vol. 46, No. 1.

Rowthorn, R. and Wells, J. (1987) *Deindustrialization and Foreign Trade*, Cambridge: Cambridge University Press.

Schäfer, A. and Streeck, W. (eds.) (2013) *Politics in the Age of Austerity*, Cambridge: Polity Press.

Schröder, M. (2013) *Integrating Varieties of Capitalism and Welfare State Research: A Unified Typology of Capitalism*, Basingstoke: Palgrave Macmillan.

Tahara, S. (2011) "Structural Changes in the Manufacturing Industry and the Service Economy: An Input–Output Analysis of the Japanese Economy," PhD thesis, Yokohama National University.

Taylor, L. (1991) *Income Distribution, Inflation, and Growth: Lectures on Structuralist Macroeconomic Theory*, Cambridge, MA: MIT Press.

Thelen, K. (2014) *Varieties of Liberalization and the New Politics of Social Solidarity*, Cambridge: Cambridge University Press.

Timmer, M.P., Dietzenbacher, E., Los, B., Stehrer, R. and de Vries, G.J. (2015) "An Illustrated User Guide to the World Input–Output Database: The Case of Global Automotive Production," *Review of International Economics*, Vol. 23, pp. 575–605.

Uemura, H. (1991) "De-industrialization and Structural Changes in Capital Accumulation," *Keizaihoron*, Vol. 40, No. 11.

Uemura, H. (2000) "Growth, Distribution, and Structural Change in the Post-War Japanese Economy," in Boyer, R. and Yamada, T. (eds.) *Japanese Capitalism in Crisis: A Regulationist Interpretation*, London: Routledge.

Uemura, H. (2012) "Institutional Changes and the Transformation of the Growth Regime in the Japanese Economy: Facing the Impact of the World Economic Crisis and Asian Integration," in Boyer, R., Uemura, H. and Isogai, A. (eds.) *Diversity and Transformations of Asian Capitalisms*, London: Routledge.

Uemura, H. and Tahara, S. (2014) "The Transformation of Growth Regime and De-industrialization in Japan," *Revue de la régulation*, Vol. 15.

7 Growth, employment, and social security governance in the EU and Japan

Koji Fukuda

Introduction

Globalization and demographic change significantly affect employment, the labor environment, social security, and other social systems. After the financial crisis started in 2008, various social problems arose, such as social exclusion and income disparity, and increasing poverty, especially intergenerational poverty, demonstrating that the crisis was having a serious effect on democracy. We need to consider what types of regime change have taken place in society and on which sectors of the population the burdens have fallen most heavily following the neoliberal restructuring and reforms in the labor market and social security fields that governments have conducted in Japan and Europe since the crisis began to unfold.[1]

Even when economies grow, the trickle-down effect postulated by neoliberals is somewhat minimal and the benefits of growth do not necessarily reach all parts of society. Rather, it has been recognized that economic growth can increase the gap between the rich and the poor and even raise poverty levels in a country.[2] In Japan, nominal growth in GDP exceeded 5 percent in the second half of the 1980s and expanded for 73 straight months from 2002 to 2007.[3] However, poverty rates and income disparity levels also continued to increase during this time.[4] Inequality in the distribution of wealth and income has worsened in conjunction with neoliberal globalization not only in Japan, but also world-wide. Employment insecurity has grown and social stability is vanishing. As with the Great Depression of the 1930s, there has been a trend toward corporations increasing their internal reserves while simultaneously increasing shareholder dividends. This reality diverges in a significant way from the presuppositions of neoclassical economic theory, which hold that corporate profit should be fairly divided among the original factors of production.

In Europe and the USA, Piketty's *Capital in the Twenty-First Century*,[5] which directly addressed these issues, added to the concern about income disparity caused by the return on capital exceeding the rate of economic growth. In Japan it has become clear that the premise that growth brings benefits to the whole of society does not hold true at a time when the safety net of social security is becoming dysfunctional.

Problems like these involve political decision making on whether to prioritize short-term profit for business or to focus on the ethical behavior of business from a long-term perspective. They also involve political choices as to whether it is desirable for society to have an egalitarian economic system that enforces fairness or a system that emphasizes the maintenance of order through stability and growth.

The purpose of this chapter is to analyze changes to governance systems charged with reducing disparity, poverty, and social exclusion, based on a critical approach to the political economy, while also looking at the social and economic characteristics stemming from neoliberal political policies and the functions and responsibilities of families and regional communities.

First, I will give a general outline of the development of policies that are common to Japan and EU member states, as well as the theoretical frameworks necessary for perceiving changes to their social and economic systems.

Second, I will analyze the neoliberal EU internal market integration and growth strategies which date from 1985, as well as currency unification, employment policy, and social protection policy related to social exclusion and poverty in the EU.

Third, I will trace and analyze the background to neoliberal restructuring in Japan, particularly the package of growth strategies and social security reforms known as Abenomics which was launched in December 2012. Based on this evaluation, I will consider issues in governance reform related to economic solidarity, and the construction of systems aimed at expanding the public good.

1 Neoliberal globalization, economic growth, financial crises, and regime changes in socioeconomic systems

Economic bubbles have formed and burst under neoliberalism, and repeated financial crises have occurred and spread throughout the world. After the bankruptcy of Lehman Brothers in September 2008, the possibility emerged that neoliberalism – which encompasses the doctrines of financial capital, market fundamentalism, and shareholder supremacy – could trigger enlarged social disparities and decreased stability. This was demonstrated by changes to systems necessary for the development of neoliberal policy, such as relaxed market regulations, curtailed intervention by nation states in economies, and labor market reform in Japan and Europe. J. Stiglitz strongly criticized neoliberalism of this sort, saying it is a theory with no economic substance which merely expands income gaps and concentrates wealth among the rich and amounts to nothing more than a political slogan.[6] R. Boyer emphasized the necessity of extremely thorough research into political economy projects related to these regime changes.[7] In order to fully understand the academic background to these issues, let us look at some of the existing research.

Soskice focused on production regimes to classify the varieties of capitalism in the world and attempted to describe the mutual, complementary relationships between labor–management relations, work-training systems, inter-enterprise relations, and corporate governance. Regarding production regimes, varied types of capitalist economies are classified into two categories with a focus on labor–management relations: liberal market economies, such as the Anglo-Saxon countries, and coordinated market economies, such as the continental European countries, Nordic countries, and Japan.[8]

Esping-Andersen focused on the concept of "de-commodification" and he further divided Soskice's coordinated market economy into two categories resulting in a total of three.[9] The Nordic countries are classified as "social-democratic welfare states"; continental countries such as Germany, France, and Italy as "conservative welfare states"; and the Anglo-Saxon countries as "liberal welfare states." He broke welfare states down based on the employment policy of each country. In social-democratic regimes, the scale of public expenditure related to social security and welfare is large. These systems attempt to cope with the risks that all people face in life, such as unemployment, poverty, and illness. They are also presupposed on a society with gender equality. In conservative regime systems, which are strongly influenced by Christian democracy, pension, medical insurance, and other social insurance systems are maintained by labor–management agreements in each occupational field. Founded on the stable income of male earners, these systems are upheld by the role of families such as childcare and care for the elderly. Liberal regimes are strongly influenced by market fundamentalism, and the scale of public social security is small. Market-focused systems involve the utilization of private social services within the range that individuals can pay for based on their income and employers' contributions.[10] Esping-Andersen's categories have been criticized for the following reasons: (1) exclusion of social economy and the third sector; (2) exclusion of housing security; (3) "unpaid labor contributed by the caring work of women"; and (4) relying on social models in which men are the earners.[11] Consequently, Esping-Andersen incorporated the gender viewpoint into *Social Foundations of Postindustrial Economies*[12] and created a more advanced "welfare regime" theory.[13] In addition, Lester Salamon recognized the importance of the third sector based on research in the non-profit sector.[14]

Various types of capitalism exist throughout the world; each country has different government structures, business practices, corporate organizations, labor–management relations, and regulatory environments. The regulation school argues, according to research on diverse capitalist models, that coordination via specific formulas in single markets leads in the direction of neoliberal post-Fordism. As R. Boyer and Amable pointed out, there are four separate forms of capitalism operating in Europe. Robert Boyer further divides the conservative welfare state into "state capitalism" (continental European countries) and "quasi-collectivist capitalism" (Japan) for a total of four categories.[15] Moreover, Bruno Amable lists the following five fundamental systems: (1) product markets; (2) paid labor relations; (3) financial intermediation division; (4) social security; and (5) education division. Based on these institutional frameworks, he further classified R. Boyer's "state capitalism" into (1) the continental European model; and (2) the Mediterranean model, for a total of five models including (3) the Asian model; (4) the social-democratic model; and (5) the liberal model.[16] In different types of capitalism such as these, different types of social and political compromise and coordination are performed in each nation in the fields of wage–labor relations and social security.

A common theoretical framework and common classification system are necessary in order to:

- consider how various production methods impact employment, social security, and welfare;
- examine the extent to which the related policy regimes depend on different types of government structures; and
- correlate international comparisons related to employment, and social security regimes under various types of capitalism.

It is necessary to consider employment regimes – made up of connections between labor–management relations, employment security systems, labor market policy, economic policy, industrial policy, and other factors – to compare a wide range of capitalist labor–management relations with social security and welfare systems.

When making comparisons between Japanese and European growth strategies and the Japanese production regime, an essential viewpoint is the perception of the link between the employment and social security regimes as systems that support lives. Employment regimes mean policies and institutional systems for employment stability and expansion, which consist of labor relations, employment security, labor market policy, and economic and industrial policies.

Social security regimes are composed of three elements: (1) public social security systems (social insurance, public assistance, societal allowance, public services, etc.); (2) market systems, including private insurance, corporate welfare, private welfare, and nursing care services; and (3) cooperative body-type systems, such as families and regional volunteer organizations.[17] Japan and Europe are both facing the issues of decreasing birth rates and aging populations; it will be possible to design long-range, effective systems only when viewing taxation systems and financial problems from the perspective of related regime changes in employment and social security.

According to the concepts of neoliberalism and market fundamentalism, because economic activities are determined by the provision side, the relaxing of regulations, provision of tax reductions to the wealthy and high-income earners, reduction of corporate taxes on large enterprises, and increased earnings lead to enlarged investment and consumption. As a result, these ways of thinking emphasize the "trickle-down theory," in which employment grows among the middle class and low-income earners as wealth trickles down, asserting that this leads to economic growth. Neoliberalists also say that, if the government relaxes financial market regulations, limited government intervention can accomplish economic recovery via coordination of the money supply. However, in reality many corporations simply accumulate internal reserves or take action to decrease their interest burden and dispose of bad loans, so labor's share has continually fallen. Corporations, fearing business failure, have enhanced their internal reserves and rapidly increased shareholder dividends to maintain stock prices.

The investor side places importance on the internal rate of return, an index that indicates the annual rate of return on investment. The management side utilizes return on equity (ROE) as an index for the amount of returns given to shareholders, so stock prices have come to be linked with ROE. The aim of managers is to raise the ROE and increase stock prices over the short term, resulting in positive evaluations. There is incentive for chief executive officers, with an average term of office of five years, to work to raise the ROE during their terms and cause stock price rises. The reason for this is that many top managers are given stock option rights as remuneration, so they attempt to make money on financial transactions rather than by producing value through actual economics by developing new products. Corporate value is the aggregate market price, which is determined by ROE, which is calculated by dividing profit per share by net assets per share. Accordingly, top managers attempt to increase stock prices by drastically cutting fixed costs such as personnel expenses and compacting assets. In this way, the manager's interests are the same as fund managers, who wish to increase profit over the short term. Research and development that leads to innovation requires at least seven to ten years, so investment leading to long-term economic growth is difficult. Under neoliberal economics and financial capitalism, the profits of hedge funds, major shareholders, and corporate managers have come to coincide. As a result, there are fewer cases in which overall social profit and the viewpoint of the public good are considered, leading to "social exclusion." This concept arose in France in the mid-1970s and it has been expanded to the dimension of "relative deprivation," which indicates a situation in which people cannot take advantage of social relationships in activities such as employment, work, education, leisure, and family – which are usually available to most members of society – and are estranged because of economic issues related to distribution, such as poverty and unequal earnings.[18]

2 The development of neoliberal policy and social inclusion strategies in EU member states

Economic integration under neoliberalism has taken place in EU countries since the 1980s. Accordingly, laborers have migrated from countries with low wages and little employee protection to countries with high social standards. This has led to the issue of "social dumping" in which overall working conditions deteriorate, wages are suppressed, and employment becomes destabilized in the countries receiving these laborers.

A way of thinking that balances economic growth and social justice can be seen in the 1985 EU Market Integration Plan of Jacques Delors, president of the European Commission. J. Delors stated the necessity of (1) requiring that the relaxing of regulations in labor markets not infringe upon the basic rights of laborers; (2) avoiding social dumping by establishing social standards adopted throughout Europe as a whole; and (3) building a solid foundation for the development of future social policy in the EU.[19]

In March 2000, the European Council in Lisbon set out the Lisbon Declaration,[20] agreeing on a new growth strategy spanning ten years, called the "Lisbon Strategy." Targets included constructing a competitive, sustainable, knowledge-based economic bloc; enhancing the quantity and quality of growth and employment; modernizing the European social model and social protection through a proactive welfare state; eliminating poverty and social rejection; and strengthening social cohesion. This was deemed necessary because "Europeanization" had progressed in several regions in the 2000s due to deepening integration in Europe. Because of European currency unification, the institutional complementarity of various capitalist models had also changed. In particular, as capital moved over borders in the financial market field throughout the eurozone, the various systems in fields related to employment and social security became less stable.

It emerged that the EU market integration plan, issues caused by competition policy and economic and currency unification, and employment issues are all outcomes of neoliberal restructuring. The actual state of free trade and the free movement of capital, labor, objects, and services throughout the EU across national borders is contrary to the philosophy of the European social model. In reality, this has led to suppressed wages for laborers and the abolition of employment security, and increased non-regular employment reduced social protection; alongside was the erosion of various social rights for European citizens.

The concept of the European social model began with the Social Charter: Community Charter of Fundamental Social Rights for Workers adopted at the European Council in Strasbourg in December 1989.[21] The preface of this social charter referred to the concept of social exclusion, the eradication of which was positioned as one principal objective of the EU in the 1997 Amsterdam Treaty.

At the European Council at Laeken in December 2001 held in order to accomplish the goals of the Treaty of Nice, an agreement was formed which would mobilize all stakeholders to (1) encourage participation in employment; (2) facilitate universal access to resources, rights, goods, and services; (3) guard against the risk of social exclusion; and (4) support the most vulnerable people.[22]

The Charter of Fundamental Rights of the European Union, which determined the rights of European citizens, was adopted at the same European Council meeting. In addition, 18 items, called the "Laeken indicators,"[23] were recognized as common indices to combat poverty and social exclusion. These included the ten primary indicators below and eight secondary indices. The secondary indicators focus on the working poor, children, and the elderly, and include systematic gender segmentations:[24]

> (1) At-risk-of-poverty rate, (2) inequality of income distribution, (3) at-persistent-risk-of-poverty rate, (4) relative at-risk-of-poverty gap, (5) regional cohesion, (6) long-term unemployment rate, (7) persons age zero to 65 living in jobless households, (8) early school leavers age 18 to 64 not in

education or training, (9) life expectancy at birth, (10) self-defined health status by income level.[25]

In the EU, "social exclusion"[26] has taken root as a central concept in social policy in addition to the traditional definition of poverty. In contrast to this view of poverty, which simply refers to an insufficiency of income or resources, social exclusion refers to a situation in which individuals' lack of education, health, and social and human networks significantly affect their opportunities for social participation and political expression, ultimately leading to the exclusion of those individuals from society; in turn, this may lead to poverty as well as violations of basic human rights. As opposed to notions of poverty, which focus an individual's financial and social situation, social exclusion focuses on the distancing of an individual from society and the processes by which he or she is denied employment opportunities and the use of social services.

These dynamic indicators focus on the processes that lead to poverty – including the persistence of low income and long-term unemployment – and reflect a pluralistic approach to social exclusion that includes the four dimensions of income and poverty, work, education, and health. The first indicator (low income rate) has been called the "at-risk-of-poverty" rate since 2003. In addition to the various EU organizations and member state governments that take leading roles in combating social exclusion in the EU, the Lisbon Strategy includes socio-economic agents, dialogues between all sorts of public and private organizations and individuals, social partners, coordination with civic sectors such as non-governmental organizations and non-profit organizations, and even the corporate social responsibility of private enterprises.

Ten Central and Eastern European countries joined the EU in May 2004. Accordingly, the Lisbon Strategy was reevaluated in 2005, and the strategy was reorganized with the focus narrowed to growth and employment. The Open Method of Coordination (OMC) between the European Commission and member states was further endorsed for the purposes of social protection and social inclusion. As A.B. Atkinson *et al.* pointed out, the Laeken indicators are indices related to social results; they leave policy measures – in which common objectives are referred to and the indices are improved – to member states. Social coordination via the OMC in the EU is utilized for the processes of (1) poverty and social rejection, (2) pensions, and (3) health preservation, medical care, and nursing care.[27] The integration of these three processes – synchronized with economic policy guidelines and employment strategy cycles – was explored. Plans were made to link public policy related to economic policy, budgetary policy, education and training policy, construction fund programs, and so forth.

A new growth strategy entitled "Europe 2020: A Strategy for Smart, Sustainable and Inclusive Growth,"[28] the successor to the Lisbon Strategy, was formulated by the 2010 European Commission. This new strategy is a fundamental strategy for economic societies over the ten-year period until 2020, based on lessons from the global financial crisis and European debt crisis.

Five principal indices were decided at the June 2010 European Council meeting: (1) improving the employment rate; (2) enhancing research and development investment in the EU; (3) climate change and energy countermeasures; (4) strengthening education and training; and (5) reducing poverty and increasing social inclusion. Number one (employment rate), number four (education), and number five (reducing poverty) are related to social inclusion and exclusion.[29] According to the European Council, the number of people facing the risk of poverty and exclusion can be calculated according to the three indices of risk of poverty, physical deprivation, and jobless households. It says the indices seen as the most suitable by member states can be utilized in setting national goals related to poverty and social inclusion.

The number of people in the EU at risk of poverty or social exclusion comprised roughly 25 percent of the population as of 2012, which may jeopardize the achievement of the Europe 2020 indices.[30] Fiscal reconstruction and the improvement of social protection systems would seem to be required. Also necessary are the promotion of employment for economic growth and restructuring to guarantee appropriate social protection. The role of social protection is to maintain human resources and welfare in Europe and serve as the foundation for future competitive strength and economic recovery. It has been suggested that the poverty reduction targets set forth in the Europe 2020 growth strategy cannot be accomplished by the EU's social policy alone, and that these goals must be reinforced through measures related to the economy, employment, tax systems, and education.

Discourse in the EU surrounding social dialogue, the concept of "social Europe," and solidarity has merely called for EU social policy subordinate to neoliberal principles to cope with actual social problems in each country. The actions of certain member state governments have resulted in some politicians, bureaucrats, and capitalists benefiting by making efforts to appropriate profit through socializing the loss of private enterprises. Accompanied by the rapid increase in budget deficits and public debt, national governments have increased the degree to which financial markets and rating firms are at the mercy of hedge funds. The correction of disparities between member states has not taken place as planned through currency unification; rather, the reality has moved in the direction of enlarged disparities and conflict in societies.

3 Neoliberalism, demographic change, and growth strategies in Japan: employment, the labor market, and social security regime change

Neoliberalism began in Japan in the 1980s and was continued by the Hashimoto, Obuchi, and Koizumi cabinets from 1996 to 2006. The first Abe cabinet continued the neoliberal policy of changes systems via restructuring. During the Nakasone administration, efforts were made to limit government via administrative and fiscal reform. Monetary, fiscal, and labor market regulations were relaxed. In subsequent administrations large-scale privatization, such as Japanese

National Railways, Nippon Telegraph and Telephone Corporation, and the postal service, took place; state-owned land was disposed of; land-use control was relaxed; tax cuts were given to the rich; corporate taxes were cut: the policy interest rate was drastically reduced as a measure against the recession caused by the strong yen; and financial liberalization policy was implemented. Consequently, land and stock prices rose steeply in the latter half of the 1980s, resulting in the bubble economy.

Problems like these involve political decision making on whether to prioritize short-term profit for business or to focus on the ethical behavior of business from a long-term perspective. They also involve political choices as to whether it is desirable for society to have an egalitarian economic system that enforces fairness or a system that emphasizes the maintenance of order through stability and growth. Whether or not the government should intervene to rescue banks in danger of insolvency is an example of the choices to be made. Financial panic is undesirable, because it increases levels of unemployment and poverty and can cause economic contraction and even collapse. If the government intervenes and uses public money to rescue the financial sector, order can be maintained, but those who benefit are the financial elite and the wealthy with massive bank deposits. From the standpoint of fairness, it is undesirable to strengthen the wealthy even more at the expense of the poor. However, being too thorough about fairness might cause economic stagnation or collapse, leaving the poor even worse off.

The composition of families has also changed significantly. As of 2010, the percentage of those 30–34 years old who had never been married in Japan was 47.3 percent of men and 34.5 percent of women.[31] According to the latest census, in 2015, single-person households accounted for 32.4 percent of all households, the largest proportion of any category (Statics Bureau Home, www.stat.go.jp). In 2025, the percentage of unmarried Japanese people is expected to be 28.5 percent of men and 20.8 percent of women, and there are concerns that this will accelerate the aging of society and the low birth rate. Households consisting of a single-income married couple living with two children, which the Japanese social security system has traditionally assumed to be the standard household, accounted for no more than 5.5 percent of the 20–69 age bracket as of 2010.[32] At 32.4 percent there are more single-person households than households consisting of couples with or without children, and all other types in this age group, and the figure is predicted to rise to 39.7 percent by 2035. Against the background of these changes in the structure of the population, there is a strong tendency in Japan for the burden of children's upbringing and caregiving to be primarily the responsibility of women. As a result, despite the desire of many women to work, regular full-time employment is restricted to younger women, with re-employment after childbearing being largely restricted to part-time and low-wage work. Moreover, now that part-time work accounts for nearly half of all employment, re-employment in full-time work after childbearing and after the mandatory retirement age, which is necessary in many cases due to the five-year gap between retiring and receiving a pension as well as the relatively low level of the pension compared to the cost of living, is extremely difficult, making single-income households that need to raise children and care for elderly members at home even more economically vulnerable.

Since the financial crisis the polarization of the Japanese and European labor markets between full-time and part-time work has worsened. Part-time workers in Japan account for 32.3 percent of the total workforce, with women accounting for 57.5 percent of all workers.[33] In Japan the total disposable income of working households has decreased annually since the financial crisis, with the proportion of the working population below the poverty line rising to 8–9 percent. Poverty in Japan is not only the result of unemployment, but also is typically a problem of the working poor (12.9 percent in 2013).[34] This is because wages of workers in non-regular employment are less than half of the wages of workers in regular employment. Many irregularly employed workers have fallen into poverty due to low wages. There are also several problems with working conditions. Long working hours owing to employee overtime for the benefit of companies has become the norm. Many regular employees in the workforce live in fear of being laid off and are forced to work for low wages, to take nominal management positions that are not reflected in their wages, and to work unpaid overtime. This may lead to mental health problems and, in extreme cases, death from overworking.

Since the neoliberal reforms were introduced the "race to the bottom" in the Japanese and European labor markets has intensified because of labor flexibility, the facilitation of dismissal, and the increase in part-time employment. Under the social security system in Japan, where the safety net is particularly inadequate, physical and mental stress for low-income workers, the elderly, and the disabled are considerable, and many have difficulty making their public insurance contributions and therefore cannot access medical services, which results in damage to their health, and economic and social exclusion. Japan's Gini coefficient for income disparity rose from 0.304 in 1985 to 0.488 by 2009.[35] Notwithstanding the period of economic growth from 1985 to 2012, relative poverty levels in Japan actually rose from 12.0 percent to 16.1 percent during that period.[36] This shows that the rise in poverty in recent years is more a result of society's structural problems rather than any economic downturn, indicating a trend toward protracted and persistent poverty. Furthermore, child poverty levels have risen from 10.9 percent in 1985 to 16.3 percent in 2012,[37] giving rise to intergenerational poverty, increasing the risk of low-income employment, poor health, and social exclusion in adulthood.

The Abe administration has amended labor law to further weaken protections for wage laborers, and there is concern about cost-push inflation resulting from the tax increase and rising public utilities charges.

The "third arrow" of "Abenomics" is a growth strategy to strengthen competitive power. To implement this strategy, a prime minister's personal consultative body (chaired by Abe himself) was set up to serve a central role. It is composed only of people who support neoliberalism and market fundamentalism, such as related cabinet ministers, managers from large private enterprises and some start-up companies, as well as Heizō Takenaka, from the Koizumi cabinet. The Abe administration's Industrial Competitiveness Council will implement new growth strategies, such as establishing special economic zones, approving mixed billing to reduce the government's universal health insurance burden, and encouraging migration from stagnant industries to growth industries. To this end, it has introduced policies such as changing the employment coordination system to make it easier to dismiss employees, and it is attempting to abolish regulations that protect laborers and safety nets for citizens to further enforce neoliberalism through market fundamentalism. Policies to encourage demand are necessary for resolving deflation, but the policies of the Industrial Competitiveness Council are only for the supply side and mainly contribute to corporate profit. An FTA (free trade agreement) is an agreement to carry out the trade liberalization of goods and services. An agreement covering fields other than trade, such as the movement of people, investment, government procurement, and protection of intellectual property, can be referred to as an EPA (economic partnership agreement). According to the Ministry of Foreign Affairs of Japan, "the Japan–EU EPA is one of the mega FTAs along with TPP (Trans-Pacific Partnership) and TTIP (Transatlantic Trade and Investment Partnership), aimed at further deepening of the economic relations" between Japan, the EU, and the USA. The Japan–EU EPA will "promote trade and investment" and will "contribute to boosting economic growth, creating employment and strengthening business competitiveness" both in Japan and the EU (www.mofa.go.jp/ files/000013835.pdf, July 30, 2016). The Abe administration is moving toward participating in this EPA, which will make it possible to promote even more widespread liberalization and deregulation in various fields such as agriculture, medical care, finance, and government procurement. The unstable economy reliant on foreign consumption has been normalized; among young people, disparities have become even greater and the employment system is becoming more fragmented. Rapid increases in disparities have been seen in income, assets, health, and education, both when comparing members of the same and different generations.

The progressive tax burden or "tax wedge" (i.e., the net burden after social security benefits are deducted from social security and tax payments) has always been based on the ability to pay. The debate about progressive income taxation comes down to the choice between egalitarian "fairness" or "stability and growth" with an emphasis on maintaining order as a priority. However, according to the OECD's *Taxing Wages* of 2016,[38] Japan ranks in the OECD's lowest category of progressiveness for government efforts to redistribute income. Protection levels from dismissal from part-time or irregular employment for Japanese workers are ranked below the mean for OECD countries, and in an international comparison of wage levels for "the first decile" or those with the lowest incomes, Japan ranked low, below the USA and Canada. Japan also has a low minimum wage, so even people in full-time employment in the first decile fall into poverty. Wages for part-time workers in Japan are 30–40 percent lower than for full-time workers and the casualization of the labor force has advanced without any correction of this disparity. Furthermore, labor costs and employer social security contributions are also low compared with European countries.

Poverty levels in Japan by age group were the second highest after those of the USA in the second half of the first decade of the twenty-first century. Among the population of households with a household head of working age (18–64), poverty reduction rates in Japan are low, but for households in which all adults work, they are actually negative. The government's redistribution of wealth has worsened poverty for households with a dual or single income. Analysis of the Japan Household Panel Survey (which started in 2009) results shows that part-time workers and the self-employed have higher poverty levels in disposable income than in initial income. Because of the regressive social security burden, those on low incomes are at risk of falling into poverty even if they are working. Under Abenomics, reforms to strengthen the rights of businesses to dismiss staff are being pushed through. From the perspective of ensuring labor flexibility, excessively strong restrictions on dismissals may incentivize businesses to respond by hiring more part-timers, agency workers, and contract workers to regulate employee numbers instead of hiring full-time staff. However, if dismissal rights for businesses are strengthened, making it easier to dismiss full-time staff, the workforce will become even more casualized. Flexibility and mobility of labor will increase, but the growing gap between full-time and part-time workers will widen.[39] Abenomics will encourage an increase in the number of part-time workers and add to the destabilization of employment; in particular, we will see increasingly low wages and unstable, part-time employment being shifted onto younger workers. Purchasing power will decrease as household budgets shrink overall, and economic growth and profits will fall with dramatic consequences for tax and social security revenue. In turn, this will further accelerate the development towards an ageing society with a low birth rate. As Dore pointed out, the impacts of neoliberalism have been much greater in Japan than Germany. The percentage of regular employment in Japan as of 2014 is only around 55 percent and the number of young people who are unemployed or non-regular employees is increasing.[40] It seems likely that the increase in the rate of non-regular employment has increased poverty levels in Japan.

4 After Abenomics: what should be done?

From a "stability and growth" standpoint, this means having an income tax within parameters that avoid resistance from the wealthy while being sufficiently progressive to prevent revolt or political conflict among the poor. The optimum solution would seem to be designing a balanced system that does not impede economic growth.

The government, financial circles, and the media in Japan largely agree that the country's social and economic problems cannot be solved solely with increased globalization and business competitiveness. Rather, economic revitalization based on the expansion of domestic demand should be used as an economic strategy that will address the issue of the low birth rate, generate employment, and make enhanced social security sustainable.

Currently a man or a woman whose spouse is in regular or full-time employment pays no income tax and is not required to make any pension or health insurance contributions, so long as he or she earns less than 1.3 million yen each year.

One of the intended reforms of Abenomics is to abolish this situation, a measure intended to encourage full-time home-makers to enter the labor market to maintain economic growth at a time when the working population in Japan is shrinking. However, it will be difficult to reproduce the human resources to generate future economic growth and create the next generation of tax payers without providing incentives to full-time home-makers to care for children at home and without establishing more childcare facilities and other measures to support working women. This is particularly important in Japan due to the high cost of childcare and education. It is necessary to design systems to allow for the provision of more tax incentives and old-age pension waivers for home-makers, depending on how much they work or how many children they have and care for.

Japan's total annual external debt in 2013 was 329 trillion yen, while it had foreign earnings of 582 trillion yen, leaving it with net assets of 253 trillion yen, which is the highest world-wide. In other words, Japan with a GDP one-third that of the USA, has roughly double the latter's net assets. Less than 5 percent (4.83) of Japan's debt is owed to foreign institutions and 95 percent of its 1,000 trillion yen accumulated government debt is owned by the Japanese public. Thus, Japan's financial situation is fundamentally different to that of Greece, where 70 percent of the national debt is foreign-owned (Figure 7.1).

As of 2013, Japan's total income (gross national income, gross domestic product, and income received from abroad less income from Japan payable to

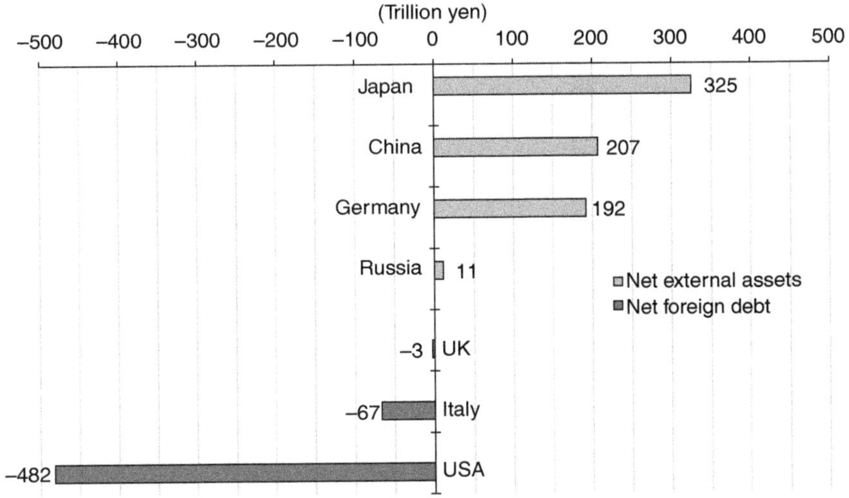

Figure 7.1 Net external assets and net foreign debt 2013.

Source: author, based on statistical data (Table 7.1) from Bank of Japan (www.mof.go.jp/international_policy/reference/iip/2013_g4.pdf (accessed April 30, 2016)) and IMF (IMF (2014), *International Financial Statistics Yearbook 2013*, Washington, DC: IMF.

the rest of the world) still exceeded its GDP by more than 10 trillion yen. As of June 2015, the financial assets of Japanese households exceed 1,717.1 trillion yen, and 51.7 percent of this is in cash or cash equivalents, which is the highest in the world.[41] Japan has already disposed of bad debts worth 0.149 trillion yen, and the groundwork for an expansion of demand is in place despite continuing deflation.[42] However, there are factors that may cause the economy to fail. Japan has a huge domestic market, a high supply capacity, and is neither export- nor import-dependent. Japan depends on exports for 14.6 percent of its GDP, making its export dependency extremely low among major nations.[43]

When countries that have high rates of foreign dependency promote globalization and free trade, they cannot expect growth.

As Table 7.1 and Figure 7.2 show, Japan, with its low rates of import and export dependency, should adopt a very different growth strategy to the highly

Table 7.1 Rates of import and export dependency 2013 (%)

	Japan	*USA*	*Germany*	*France*	*UK*	*China*	*Korea*	*Russia*
Import	17.0	13.9	32.7	24.4	25.5	20.6	42.9	18.0
Export	14.6	9.4	39.9	20.7	18.8	23.3	39.5	25.0

Source: author, based on statistical data from Bank of Japan (www.mof.go.jp/inter national_policy/reference/iip/2013_g4.pdf (accessed April 30, 2016)) and IMF (IMF (2014), *International Financial Statistics Yearbook 2013*, Washington, DC: IMF.

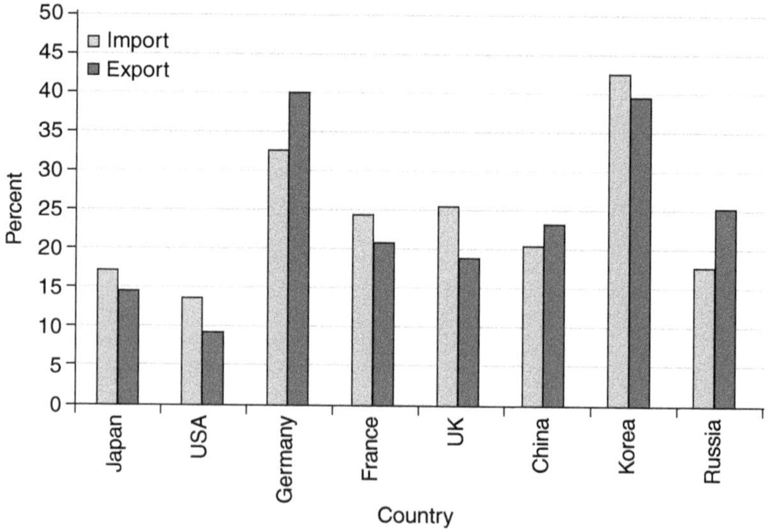

Figure 7.2 Rates of import and export dependency.

Source: This graph was made with Excel by the author, based on the following statistical data. Statistics Japan (2015), Statistics Bureau of Japan(SBJ), www.stat.go.jp/data/sekai/0116.htm#01, (accessed April 30, 2016), IMF(2015), International Financial Statistics Yearbook 2014, UNCTAD (United Nations Conference on Trade and Development).

export-dependent South Korea. There is plenty of room to expand domestic demand to revitalize the economy in Japan as there are many fields in need of public investment: increased budgets for science and technology and public R&D to encourage innovation; childcare provision and maintenance of infrastructure for care facilities for the elderly to cope with Japan's aging population and low birth rate; maintenance of roads and ports; fortifying the country in preparation for earthquakes, typhoons, and other natural disasters; new high-speed rail networks including maglev trains; energy-saving "smart cities"; fields of renewable energy and green innovation; medicine; and life innovation that includes the development of powered exoskeletons (robot suits) to use in home care and daily life assistance for the elderly and the disabled.

Relative to GDP, Japan's rate of energy efficiency is the highest in the world, and the country has a proven track record in achieving economic growth while using less energy. Japan has a huge domestic market and high supply capacity, but the country's current problem is that demand is not keeping pace with supply. It can be said that a "deflation gap" exists when supply outstrips demand and increasing the demand is the best way to fill it. GDP, the sum of personal consumption, government spending, private investment, and net exports, needs to be expanded if the deflation problem is to be solved. Japanese households have the world's largest reserves in terms of both bank deposits and cash holdings, while the Japanese government has no problems securing funding at some of the lowest interest rates in the world. Expanding domestic demand would not therefore appear to be a particularly difficult task, and Japan seems much less likely to default or face a financial collapse than many of the other major countries in the world.

As is clearly shown by the results of an index evaluation in the UK edition of *The Economist* (Table 7.2), a positive working relationship involving industry,

Table 7.2 Global innovation ranking, current and forecast innovation index

	2004–2008		*2009–2013*	
	Index	*Rank*	*Index*	*Rank*
Japan	10.00	1	10.00	1
Switzerland	9.71	2	9.70	2
Finland	9.50	3	9.53	3
USA	9.50	4	9.44	5
Sweden	9.44	5	9.42	7
Germany	9.40	6	9.49	4
Taiwan	9.37	7	9.44	6
Netherlands	9.16	8	9.16	9
Israel	9.13	9	9.20	8
Denmark	9.08	10	9.06	10

Source: author, based on Economist Intelligence Unit (2009), "A New Ranking of the World's Most Innovative Countries," p. 7. http://graphics.eiu.com/PDF/Cisco_Innovation_Complete.pdf (accessed April 30, 2016).

universities, and the government has been achieved in Japan through innovation (starting with Japanese industry's efforts to introduce the best environmental technologies), human resources, sound public security, and high levels of environmental awareness.[44] In addition to innovation, the potential for sustainable development in Japan can be found in areas such as the development of human resources, public regulations, and a policy mix vision that will lead to growth and employment generation.

5 Conclusion

Together with globalization, various neoliberal policies have been implemented in Japan and Europe, and social disparities have expanded in both regions. Although the wealthy, with their unearned income, have become more affluent, the majority of laborers have faced restructuring, salary cuts, and low wages, and their disposable income has declined. The labor market reforms of various countries have only emphasized coordination through "market flexibility" with the priority placed on profit, which has not led to job creation. As of 2014, the percentage of unmarried men in their thirties with regular employment has risen to 37.4 percent.[45] Among those with non-regular employment, 75.6 percent remain unmarried and do not raise a family for economic reasons. Increased growth cannot be expected as social protection is weakening, and growth will probably decline further. Corporations have strengthened their competitive power by depending only on management strategies from a short-range viewpoint, expanding non-regular employment, and suppressing wages. This has certainly not resulted in the strengthening of sustainable, competitive power, and a return to growth.

It is important to decide which areas of public policy be left to the free-market economy with its "law of the jungle" selection system and which areas be protected by the state for the public good in the interest of maintaining a civilized society. Immanuel Kant pointed out that solidarity is important, but so are the rights of individuals. A sustainable international system should be based on this principle in order to find the best possible balance between freedom and public interest.

Notes

1 Koji Fukuda (2014), "The Global Economic Crisis and the Future of Labor Market Policy Regimes: Implications for Economic Governance in the European Union and Japan," Hideko, Magara, ed., *Economic Crises and Policy Regimes: The Dynamics of Policy Innovation and Paradigmatic Change*, Edward Elgar, pp. 327–331.

2 OECD Directorate for Employment, Labour and Social Affairs, "Focus on Inequality and Growth," www.oecd.org/els/soc/Focus-Inequality-and-Growth-2014.pdf, accessed July 1, 2015.

3 IMF (2014), *World Economic Outlook*, www.imf.org/external/index.htm, accessed November 18, 2014, pp. 1–4.

4 The Ministry of Health, Labour and Welfare in Japan announced the relative poverty rate for the first time in October 2009 in order to address the poverty issue. www.mhlw.go.jp/english/wp/wp-hw4/dl/honbun/2_2_3.pdf, accessed November 18, 2014.

5 Piketty, Thomas (2014), *Capital in the Twenty-First Century* (translated by Arthur Goldhammer), Belknap Press.
6 Stiglitz, J.E. (2002), *Globalization and its Discontents*, W.W. Norton & Co.; Stiglitz, J.E. (2006), *Making Globalization Work*, W.W. Norton & Co.; Stiglitz, J.E. (2008), "La fin du nėoliberalisme," *Le Ėchos*, July 21.
7 Boyer, Robert (2014), "How do Policy and Economy Interact within Regulation Theory? Consequences for Policy Regimes and Reform Strategies," Hideko, Magara, ed., *Economic Crises and Policy Regimes*, Edward Elgar, pp. 124–173.
8 Hall, Peter A. and David Soskice (2001), *Varieties of Capitalism: The Institutional Foundations of Comparative Advantage*, Oxford University Press; Schröder, Martin (2013), *Integrating Varieties of Capitalism and Welfare State Research: A United Typology of Capitalisms*, Palgrave Macmillan, pp. 58–59.
9 Esping-Andersen, Gosta (1990), *The Three Worlds of Welfare Capitalism*, Cambridge University Press.
10 Schröder, *Integrating Varieties*, pp. 58–59.
11 Dowd, Rebekah (2013), "Critical Evaluation of Esping-Andersen's The Three Worlds of Welfare Capitalism," Regent's Park Social Policy Tutorial, Michaelmas 2013, p. 2, www.academia.edu/4934406/A_Critical_Evaluation_of_Esping-Andersens_The_Three_Worlds_of_Welfare_Capitalism, accessed November 18, 2014.
12 Esping-Andersen, Gosta (1999), *Social Foundations of Postindustrial Economies*, Oxford University Press.
13 Schröder, *Integrating Varieties*, p. 59.
14 Salamon, Lester M. and Helmut K. Anheier (1998), "Social Origins of Civil Society: Explaining the Nonprofit Sector Cross-nationally," *Voluntas*, 9(3), pp. 213–248.
15 Boyer, Robert, and J. Rogers Hollingsworth (1977), *Contemporary Capitalism, The Embeddedness of Institutions*, Cambridge University Press; Boyer, Roger (2005), "How and Why Capitalisms Differ," *Economy and Society*, 34, pp. 509–557.
16 Amable, Bruno (2003), *The Diversity of Modern Capitalism*, Oxford University Press. Amable, Bruno, Roger Boyer, Colin Crouch, Peter Hall, Gregory Jackson, and Wolfgang Streeck (2005), "Dialogue on Institutional Complementary and Political Economy," *Socio-Economic Review*, 3(2), pp. 359–382.
17 Evers, Adalbert, and Jean-Louis Laville (2004), *The Third Sector in Europe*, Edward Elgar, pp. 15–16.
18 Atkinson, Anthony B. (2009), *The EU and Social Inclusion: Facing the Challenges*, 2nd edn., Policy Press.
19 European Commission (1985), Completing the Internal Market, White Paper from the Commission to the European Council, June 28–29, 1985, COM(85)310 final.
20 European Council in Lisbon March 23–24, 2000, Presidency Conclusions.
21 European Council in Strasbourg December 8–9, 1989.
22 Koji Fukuda and Hiroyi Akiba, eds. (2003), *European Governance after Nice*, RoutledgeCurzon, pp. 173–187.
23 European Commission (2003), Eurostat Directorate E: Social statistics Unit E-2: Living conditions DOC. E2/IPSE/2003, Room Document: Working Group "Statistics on Income, Poverty & Social Exclusion" April 28–29, 2003, www.cso.ie/en/media/csoie/eusilc/documents/Laeken,Indicators,,calculation,algorithm.pdf, accessed April 29, 2016.
24 Atkinson, Anthony B., Eric Marlier, and Brian Nolan (2004), "Indicators and Targets for Social Inclusion in the European Union," *JCMS*, 42, p. 45, pp. 47–75.
25 European Commission, Eurostat Directorate E.
26 European Commission (1992), *Towards a Europe of Solidarity: Intensifying the Fight against Social Exclusion*. COM(92) 542 final, December 23, 1992, http://aei.pitt.edu/4819, accessed April 29, 2016.
27 European Commission (2011), "'Laeken' Indicators-Detailed Calculation METHODOLOGY-E2/IPSE/2003." www.uni-trier.de/fileadmin/fb4/projekte/SurveyStatisticsNet/Ameli_Delivrables/AMELI-WP1-D1.1-20110418.pdf, accessed December 20, 2015.

28 European Commission (2010), *Communication from the Commission EUROPE 2020: A Strategy for Smart, Sustainable and Inclusive Growth*, COM(2010) 2020, http://ec.europa.eu/eu2020/pdf/COMPLET%20EN%20BARROSO%20%20%20007%20-%20Europe%202020%20-%20EN%20version.pdf, accessed December 20, 2015.
29 www.epha.org/a/3968, accessed December 20, 2015.
30 European Parliament (2016), *Poverty in the European Union, The Crisis and Its Aftermath*, www.europarl.europa.eu/RegData/etudes/IDAN/2016/579099/EPRS_IDA(2016)579099_EN.pdf, accessed April 29, 2016; European Parliamentary Research Service: Marie Lecerf Members' Research Service March 2016 – PE 579.099, accessed April 29, 2016.
31 OECD (2013), *Taxing Wages 2013*, OECD.
32 OECD (2009), *Employment Outlook, Tackling the Jobs Crisis*, OECD; OECD (2008), *Growing Unequal? Income Distribution and Poverty in OECD Countries*, OECD: Table 4.7; OECD (2009), *Factbook 2009: Economic, Environmental and Social Statistics*, OECD, p. 283.
33 Koji Fukuda, "The Global Economic Crisis," p. 330.
34 OECD Forum (2015), *Income Inequality in Figures*, www.oecd.org/forum/issues/oecd-forum-2015-income-inequality-in-figures.htm, accessed April 29, 2016.
35 OECD Stat (2015), http://stats.oecd.org/index.aspx?queryid=66670, accessed December 20, 2015.
36 www.mhlw.go.jp/toukei/saikin/hw/k-tyosa/k-tyosa13/dl/03.pdf, accessed December 20, 2015.
37 Ministry of Health, Labour and Welfare Japan (2014), *The Comprehensive Reform of Social Security and Tax*, www.mhlw.go.jp/english, accessed December 20, 2015.
38 OECD (2016), *Taxing Wages 2016*, OECD; OCED Forum, *Income Inequality in Figures*, poverty rates (2013 or latest), Japan: 16.0 percent.
39 Ministry of Health, Labour and Welfare Japan, www.mhlw.go.jp/stf/Shingi/2r9852000002k8ag-alt/2r9852000002k8f7.pdf2011, accessed December 20, 2015; Koji Fukuda, "The Global Economic Crisis," p. 330.
40 Government of Japan Cabinet Office (2008), "Summary of the Immediate Policy Package to Safeguard People's Daily Lives," 30 October.
41 Japan Macro Advisors Inc. (2015), *Japan Household Asset*, www.japanmacroadvisors.com/page/category/economic-indicators/finance/japan-household-asset, accessed December 20, 2015.
42 IMF (2009), "Responding to the Financial Crisis and Measuring Systemic Risks," *IMF Global Financial Report*, April 2009.
43 Statistics Japan (2015), www.stat.go.jp/data/sekai/0116.htm#01, accessed December 20, 2015.
44 Economist Intelligence Unit (2009), "A New Ranking of the World's Most Innovative Countries," p. 7.
45 Ministry of Health, Labour and Welfare Japan (2015), www.mhlw.go.jp/stf/seisakunitsuite/bunya/0000046231.html, accessed December 20, 2015.

8 The diversity of the "neoliberal policy regime" and income distribution

Yuji Harada

Introduction

Since the 1970s most advanced capitalist countries have faced various changes in their domestic institutions and in international economic relations. These changes include financialization, globalization, market deregulation, the privatization of state-owned enterprises, and the retrenchment of the welfare state, all of which had the purpose of allowing market mechanisms to function as freely as possible.

That these changes would significantly affect economic dynamics is commonly accepted. Financialization has the tendency to favor shareholders in the income distribution of firms so that the firms would appear attractive to shareholders, which also leads to a reduction in labor's bargaining power. Globalization tends to intensify competition between firms, resulting in a downward pressure on product costs and prices. One could find a similar effect on firms' pricing behavior in the case of product market liberalization. Deregulation of the labor market could enhance competition between workers so that some earn more and others less within a competitive environment. Regarding bargaining between firms and labor, however, labor could lose power and the wage rate may be reduced or, at most, remain the same.

While these changes and their correlation with economic dynamics are critical, more significant is the fact that such changes interact with one another. For example, under financialization and globalization, financial markets develop beyond national borders, producing a huge amount of international capital flow. Intensive global competition could also intensify the pressure to liberalize domestic markets.

The question is therefore whether these changes observed since the 1970s have been correlated with the dynamics of income distribution, and if so, how? Figure 8.1 shows the evolution of wage share in some advanced countries. Note that here we use an adjusted wage share, which is obtained by dividing the wage share by the ratio of the number of employees to that of workers, in order to adjust the influence of income earned by those who are self-employed. Two observations can be made based on this figure: First, the wage share fluctuates counter-cyclically in the short run. When an economy is booming, the level of

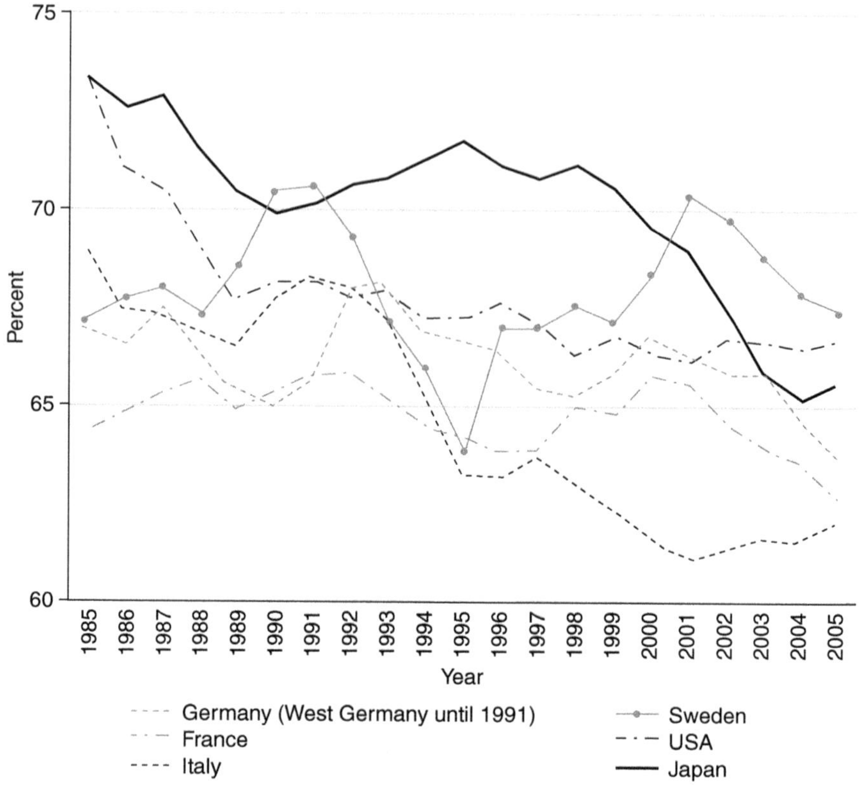

Figure 8.1 The evolution of wage share in some advanced countries.

Source: AMECO database.

wage share in that economy is declining, and vice versa. Such a fluctuation is derived from the fact that the speed of adjustment of employment and/or wage rate is lower than that of demand and supply in product markets.

This chapter focuses on the medium- to long-term evolution of adjusted wage share in order to investigate the effects of institutional changes, which are supposed to change in the medium to long term, on income distribution, although the short-term change of adjusted wage share is significant in itself.

Second, one can recognize the downward trend in wage share common to most advanced countries since the 1980s. Nevertheless, the extent of the decline depends largely on each country. For example, the wage share in France, Italy, and Japan experienced a significant decline, whereas the one in the USA remained relatively stable (see Table 8.1).

How can one explain the compatibility between the divergent movements of income distribution across countries and market-oriented, or neoliberal, institutional changes commonly observed in advanced countries? This chapter investigates the

Table 8.1 Change in adjusted wage share (1985–2005) (% points)

Germany	*France*	*Italy*	*Sweden*	*USA*	*Japan*
–3.17	–6.70	–6.84	0.20	–1.76	–7.83

Source: AMECO database.

Note
* Regarding Germany, the value in West Germany is used as that in 1985.

diversity of change in institutional configurations in advanced countries from the 1980s to the 2000s and its relationship with the evolution of income distribution in each country.

The remainder of this chapter is organized as follows. Section 1 provides an overview of preceding studies. We investigate the determinants of change in income distribution, in particular, that of wage share. We also discuss the differences and similarities in institutional changes across countries, introducing the concept of "policy regime." Section 2 illustrates the diversity of institutional change among advanced countries since the 1980s using multivariate analysis. Based on the results of the previous section, Section 3 provides an econometric analysis to examine the correlation between the diversity of institutional change and the evolution of wage share. Section 4 concludes this study.

1 Preceding studies

1.1 Determinants of the evolution of wage share

Many studies have focused on the determinants of the evolution of wage share.

The first factor is biased technological change, which can be drawn from the logic of neoclassical economics. This logic supposes the existence of the production function, which relates physical outputs from a production process to physical inputs or factors of production and that factors of production such as labor and capital should be remunerated for their contributions to production. Therefore, capital-augmenting technological change leading to an increase in the ratio of capital to labor results in a reduction in labor compensation. In other words, biased technological change raises the remuneration for a specific factor of production by augmenting its contribution to production, but it might also reduce the remuneration for other factors (Bentolila and Saint-Paul 2003).

Second, globalization has been thought to have negative effects on wage share. This argument is based on the Stolper–Samuelson theorem, which predicts that trade increases the returns on relatively abundant factors in a country (Stolper and Samuelson 1941). According to this theorem, income distribution is likely to favor capital in advanced countries where capital is relatively abundant. This argument has been developed both theoretically and empirically. Some theoretical approaches classify labor as high- and low-skilled workers and apply the same logic (European Commission 2007; Guscina 2006; Harrison, 2002;

IMF 2007). As trade increases, high-skilled workers as well as capital in advanced countries are thought to be abundant so that they are better remunerated, although the remuneration for low-skilled workers worsens. In developing countries, where low-skilled workers are abundant, the situation is the opposite. Some empirical studies have verified such a prediction. However, Stockhammer (2012) partially rejects the Stolper–Samuelson theorem from an empirical standpoint by indicating decreases in wage share even in developing countries where labor is abundant.

Third, financialization has also been seen to have a negative impact on wage share. The development of capital markets and the rise in capital flow across the globe lead firms to depend increasingly on capital markets for financing. This causes an increase in shareholder value orientation, resulting from rising claims from shareholders to increase their returns. In other words, it conversely undermines labor's bargaining power. Recent empirical studies have addressed this topic (Dünhaupt 2013; ILO 2011; Stockhammer 2009, 2012). In particular, Stockhammer (2012) finds financialization to be the most significant factor explaining the decline in wage share since the 1990s. Furthermore, Dünhaupt (2012) investigates the differences in the effects of financialization on income distribution between the USA and Germany.

Fourth, the role of product and labor market regulation is emphasized. In a world of imperfect competition, unlike the model generally assumed by neoclassical economics, there are some extra rents in the product market. The relative bargaining strength of firms and workers determines how these rents are distributed among the participating agents in a labor market. In this situation, the liberalization of the product market and the labor market has a double-sided effect: It weakens the market power of firms in the product market and increases the bargaining power of firms relative to labor in the labor market (Blanchard and Giavazzi 2003).

In contrast, the liberalization of the labor market weakens the relative bargaining power of labor, which leads to a reduction in wage share. Much research has attempted to empirically verify this effect by using a variable of trade union density as a proxy of labor's bargaining power. Some found that it has a significant positive effect (Kristal 2010; Stockhammer 2009), whereas others found no significant effects (IMF 2007). Although the bargaining power of labor has been alternatively represented as unionization, strike activity, and government spending, no significant effect of any of these variables is found (Stockhammer 2012).

Lastly, the generosity of the welfare state is examined. Regarding the relative bargaining power of firms and labor, generous social security or government spending is likely to raise the wage level indirectly. Therefore, the generosity of the welfare state, which is represented in empirical literature as the amount (ratio) of government spending, is predicted to increase the bargaining power of labor. Furthermore, social security institutions are known to be associated with labor market institutions; therefore, we should consider the joint effects of different institutions on wage share.

These factors have been observed in parallel in advanced countries since the 1970s. Stockhammer (2012) investigated how each of these factors affects income distribution in advanced and developing countries. More specifically, he considered changes in different institutional domains such as financialization (financial reforms), globalization, welfare state retrenchment, and labor market institution reforms. By conducting a comprehensive econometric analysis of the extent to which each institutional change affects wage share, he found financialization to be the main factor causing the decline in wage share. Although he also found globalization and the retrenchment of the welfare state to have significant negative effects on wage share, he did not verify any statistically significant effects of labor market institutions such as trade union density.

1.2 Institutional complementarity and complex effect of institutional changes

Why previous studies failed to confirm robust results for institutional effects on income distribution may stem from each institution's mode of existence and function. Most of these studies focus on the effects of a single institutional domain such as financialization, market liberalization, or international trade. Although it is important to specify the signs and scale of these effects empirically, we must also note that institutions do not function independently but rather depend on each other. From the viewpoint of comparative institutional economics literature, this approach has been termed "institutional complementarities" (Amable 2003; Aoki 2001; Hall and Soskice 2001) or "institutional hierarchy" (Amable 2003; Boyer 2004).

Regarding the former, coexistence between an institution in one domain and another institution in another domain could reinforce the presence of both (Amable 2003) or improve their economic performances (Aoki 2001; Hall and Soskice 2001). The latter was proposed by the French *régulation* school. In fact, it is argued that the wage–labor nexus was the dominant institutional form during the Fordist era of the 1950s–1960s. However, other institutional forms such as the financial system, competition, and international regimes came to replace the wage–labor nexus as the dominant institutional form after the 1970s (Boyer 2015).

An institutional configuration (or institutional structure) is composed of interdependent institutions from different domains. Amable (2003) suggests that individual institutional change can lead to changes in institutional configuration through the effects of institutional complementarity and hierarchy. In fact, using the concept of political-economic equilibrium, he illustrated how an institutional structure could evolve. According to his argument, an institutional change in one domain can induce institutional change in another domain based on how these two institutions relate to one another in terms of institutional complementarity and hierarchy. In other words, an institutional change would likely result in the deterioration of economic performance and/or the instability of the relevant economic system if it does not induce another change, despite the complementarity between the two (Amable 2003: 58–73). This may be why empirical studies of the effects of institutions on income distribution did not necessarily produce any robust or significant results. Therefore, investigating the composite effects of different institutions rather than the isolated influences of individual institutions is necessary.

Furthermore, considering the diversity and the variability of institutions within time and space, one can observe an institutional configuration inherent in each country and period. The *régulation* school insists that the inherency of institutional configuration is connected to a proper growth regime and a stable pattern of income distribution (Boyer 2015). This is also what Nicholas Kaldor argued. While Kaldor (1958) identified the long-term stability of income distribution as one of the "stylized facts" of the process of economic dynamics, it presupposes a society and/or period in which economic dynamics (e.g., investment coefficient) remain constant. Considering these arguments, we can see that changes in the pattern of income distribution in a country may derive from significant changes in institutional configuration in that country rather than from institutional changes in individual domains such as the financial market, labor market, and so on.

1.3 Policy regime: a common trend of institutional changes

The previous section showed that institutions and/or institutional changes have joint effects on economic dynamics. Thus, the question remains whether any similarities can be found among the various changes observed in advanced countries since the 1970s and, if so, what kinds of changes these were. As already mentioned, financialization, market liberalization, and globalization have affected many countries. These changes share a common trend of market orientation. An interesting concept proposed in the field of political science to explain why and how such a trend has been generated is that of policy regime, proposed by Przeworski (2001, 2014). This concept allows us to recognize different policies or institutional changes as a bundle that has common trends of change and effects on socioeconomic systems.

Przeworski (2001) defines policy regimes as "situations in which major parties, regardless of their partisan stripes, propose and implement similar policies" (Przeworski 2001: 324). Thus, the successful outcome of a particular policy in a particular time and country can lead not only to the adoption of similar policies in different domains within that country, but also to the diffusion of similar policies in other countries. Executing policies can, of course, result in institutional changes in the relevant domains of economic systems.

Focusing on the era of neoliberalism since the 1970s, Przeworski (2001) refers to the policy regime under that era as the "neoliberal policy regime" and attributed to it three characteristics: First, the forms of ownership have changed from nationalization to privatization, with the sales of publicly owned assets to the private sector. This trend is associated with financialization and globalization. Under financialization, dealing with public assets requires the development of financial markets, whereas globalization could be enhanced by the entry of newly created companies into both the domestic and international markets. These changes generally lead to changes in the modes of corporate governance, which could alter the relative positions of firms and workers in their bargaining power.

The second aspect concerns instruments for coping with unemployment. Although the so-called Keynesian policy aiming at full employment was executed in the "golden age of capitalism," it was then almost abandoned because demand stimulation resulting from the policy did not have an adequate effect on employment but instead pushed up inflation. This is associated with changes in the institutional domains of the labor market and social protection.[1]

The third aspect regards international economic arrangements. Trade and exchange-rate arrangements have drastically changed since the 1970s, and this has caused rapid globalization.

The underlying idea of these characteristics of the neoliberal policy regime is that "well-designed market institutions spontaneously maximize the welfare of society, with only a minimal policy intervention" (Przeworski 2001: 327).

The argument of policy regime insists on the similarity between implemented policies, regardless of the political stripes of major parties in different countries. In fact, since the 1970s one can observe market mechanism enhancing changes in different institutional domains in most advanced countries. However, to what extent various policies resulting from the policy regime change can cause institutional changes in a particular country should be constrained by the existing institutional configuration of that country. Furthermore, much research from an institutionalist viewpoint such as varieties of capitalism (VoC) or those stemming from the *régulation* school and comparative institutional analysis have revealed the diversity of institutional configurations (see, for example, Amable 2003; Aoki 2001; Boyer 2004; Hall and Soskice 2001; Harada and Tohyama 2012). Hence, one can observe the diversity of institutional configurations or institutional changes even if the neoliberal policy regime persistently demands similar institutions enhancing market mechanisms in all countries.

Based on these arguments, we can establish the problems to be examined. The first problem is to reveal whether diversity of institutional changes or change in institutional configuration exists under the pressure of the neoliberal policy regime. If it does exist, we then investigate the factors that determine such diversity. The second problem concerns the relationship between institutions (institutional changes) and income distribution. More precisely, we examine whether and to what extent institutional changes related to the neoliberal policy regime affect wage share at the macro level in advanced countries. Furthermore, we also analyze how the diversity of the "neoliberal policy regime" has been correlated with the regime on income distribution.

2 Diversity of the neoliberal policy regime: multivariate analysis

2.1 Variables and data

In order to answer the first question proposed in the previous section, we conduct multivariate analyses using quantified institutional data. To begin with the definition of the neoliberal policy regime from a quantitative perspective, we single out five types of change since the 1980s: globalization, financialization, liberalization of the labor market institution, liberalization of the product market institution, and welfare state reform. We quantify these changes by using institutional data provided by various international organizations such as the OECD, World Bank, ILO, and IMF. The data we use are based principally on those used by Stockhammer (2012).

Furthermore, we include data on product market regulation provided by the OECD (Koske *et al.* 2014).[2] A detailed list of variables is available in the Appendix. Focusing on advanced countries in Europe and Asia, as well as advanced Anglo-Saxon countries,[3] our analysis targets the period 1985 to 2005 in order to investigate the development and the diversity of the neoliberal policy regime. However, the values of some variables for specific countries in our analysis are missing. Although a method that is often used for treating missing values is list-wise deletion, in which subjects with missing values are deleted from the sample, when the subjects consist of many variables, the application of this method can limit the sample significantly and thus impede unbiased estimations. There are many methods for eliminating distortion from estimations and imputing missing values. Among them, we use the method of multiple imputation for the treatment of missing values (Little and Rubin 2002).[4]

We divide the total period into sub-periods of decades and average the data in each sub-period in order to obtain a rough trend, gage the diversity of institutional changes, and gain the stationarity of data that is generally required for multivariate analyses such as principal component analysis (PCA) (Edrem and Tsatsaronis 2013).

2.2 Methods

Each economy is characterized by its institutional configuration, which consists of institutions found in different domains. Regarding the spread of neoliberalism, one can imagine that the neoliberal policy regime would cause institutional changes in some domains, and in turn lead to the transformation of institutional configuration of the economy under investigation. From that perspective, using statistical analysis, we reveal the diversity of trajectories of institutional configurations under the influence of the neoliberal policy regime. More concretely, we investigate what factors determine the diversity and how economies can be classified into groups.

To achieve this goal, we apply two types of multivariate analyses: multiple factor analysis (MFA) and cluster analysis. MFA is a lesser known, extended version of PCA that analyzes the variance of observations described by several sets of variables (Abdi and Valentin 2007; Escofier and Pagès 1998). Here, observation and variable correspond to economies and institutions (or economic performance), respectively. Institutions are grouped into domains. First, we perform the MFA. Next, we conduct the cluster analysis based on the results of the MFA in order to classify the economies into groups.

2.3 Transformation of institutional configuration and the diversity of the neoliberal policy regime

Generally speaking, multivariate analyses such as PCA and MFA are applied to identify factors determining the variance of subjects in a specific point in time (or a specific period). However, what we want to investigate here is the trend and diversity of institutional changes. Hence, we must investigate how the variance of subjects changes. This implies that we must analyze how the diversity of institutional configurations between countries evolves in time.

We conduct the MFA for the period 1985–2005 by dividing the period into sub-periods of 1980s, 1990s, and 2000s, and averaging the data for each sub-period. The result of the MFA throughout the three decades is shown in Figure 8.2.[5] The aim of the MFA is to derive factors determining the variance of countries by making linear combinations of initial variables. The first two factors resulting from the MFA explain 39.73 percent of the variance of countries.

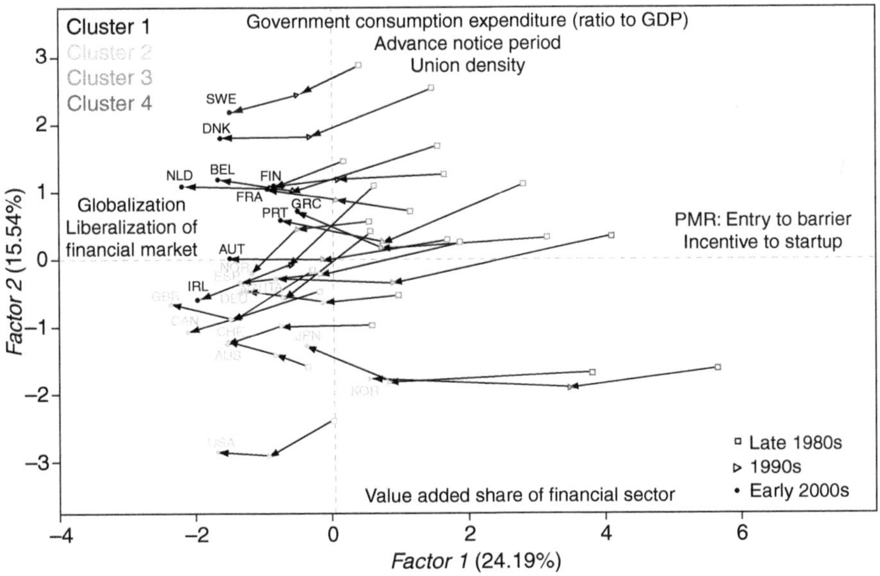

Figure 8.2 Transition of countries from mid-1980s to mid-2000s.

Source: author's calculation.

These two factors have the power to determine variance of more than one variable (whose eigenvalue is more than 1).

The first factor (presented as the horizontal axis in the figure) is correlated with both the intensity of product market regulations, especially the degree of the entry barrier to network sectors, and the ratio of public expenditure to GDP on start-up incentives for the unemployed on the positive side. The same axis is also affected by globalization-related variables, such as information flow and external trade constraints, and variables regarding financial market liberalization, which includes banking supervision, international capital flow, and security markets, on the negative side. This factor as a whole determines 24.19 percent of the variance of targeted countries and may be termed as *the contrast between government involvement in the product market and the globalization and liberalization of the financial market*. The second factor explains 15.54 percent of the variance. We can interpret the vertical axis as representing *the contrast between the generosity of social security, or the protection of workers' rights, and the scale of the financial sector*. Variables such as the ratio of government consumption to GDP, advance notice period, and union density principally determine the second factor on the positive side. In contrast, the negative side of the vertical axis is correlated only with the value-added share of the financial sector, and its coefficient of correlation is lower than those of variables determining the positive side.[6]

Applying cluster analysis to the results of the MFA, we can identify four clusters, which are gray scaled in Figure 8.2.[7] Furthermore, we identify the trajectory of institutional configuration in each country by tracing the points of countries in each period in the figure.

To begin with, we elucidate the characteristics of each cluster. Cluster 1, located in the upper-left portion of the figure, consists of Nordic countries such as Denmark and Sweden starting in the 1990s, continental European countries like Belgium and Netherlands, and countries in Southern Europe such as Greece and Portugal in the 2000s. Its characteristics include a maintained scale of social security, continuation of employment protection, and regulated financial and product markets even under the development of globalization and financialization.

Cluster 2 is located in the lower-left portion of the figure. The number of countries belonging to this cluster increases by period: Anglo-Saxon countries such as Australia, Canada, the UK, and the USA throughout all periods, Germany, Switzerland, and Japan since the 1990s, and Italy, Korea, and Norway in the 2000s. This cluster shares the characteristic of progress in the liberalization of different markets.

Cluster 3 is located mainly in the upper-right portion of the figure. Many European countries in the 1980s or until the 1990s belong to this cluster. They share the characteristics of regulated markets, substantial social security, and employment or worker protection. However, with time, all of the countries in this cluster shifted to cluster 1 or 2 as a result of the introduction of market mechanism enhancing institutions. The same holds for cluster 4, which is situated on the right-hand side of the figure, below cluster 3. Italy and Japan in the 1980s and Korea until the 1990s belong to this cluster, which is characterized by strict regulation of the product market, less liberalized financial markets, and/or more constraints on external trade, compared to the other clusters.

It is apparent that all of the countries shifted left in the figure throughout all the periods, which implies that the dissemination of the neoliberal policy regime, consisting of the progress of globalization and liberalization of different markets, is inevitably taking place among the countries. Nonetheless, this shift does not necessarily indicate that advanced capitalist countries converge to a single model. Observing institutions concerning social security and the labor market presented as the vertical axis in the figure, one can verify two distinct clusters in the 2000s. Thus, the diversity of institutional configurations in advanced countries can be said to persist even with the spread of the neoliberal policy regime.

While it is obvious from the above explanation which various institutional domains mainly influence the formation of the first two factors, we should confirm the effect of each institutional domain on the determination of the first and second factors. Figure 8.3 shows how institutional domains represented as several sets of variables contribute to the first two factors respectively. From this

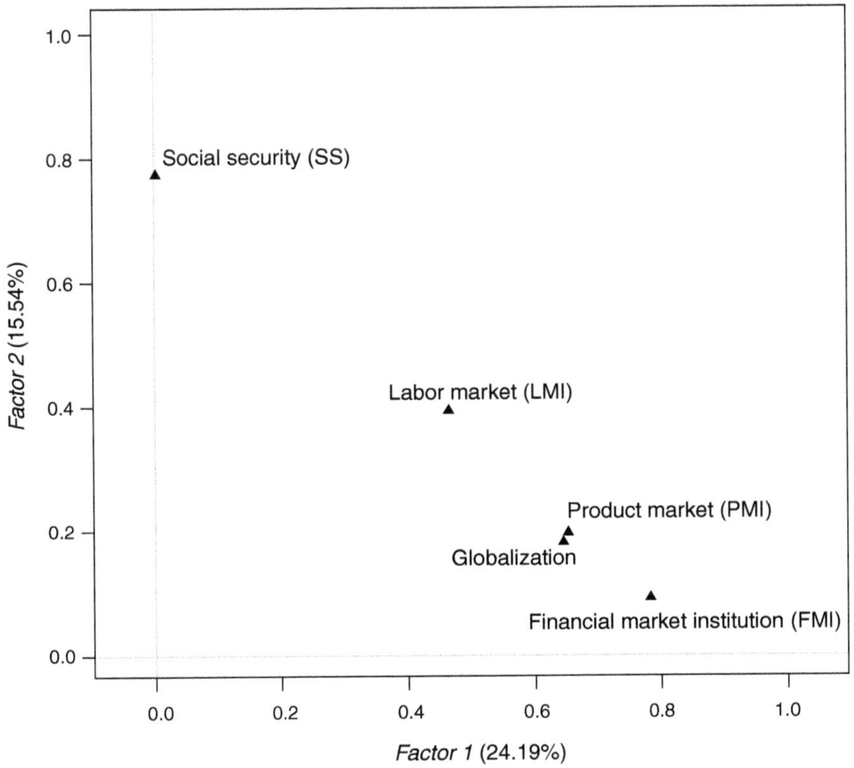

Figure 8.3 Effects of different institutional domains on the factorial plane.

Source: author's calculation.

figure, we can see that the effects of different institutional domains on the factors are diverse. For instance, financial market institutions (FMIs) primarily define the first factor but hardly affect the second, whereas the opposite is the case for social security (SS).

3 The relationship between the "neoliberal policy regime" and income distribution

Now, we investigate whether and to what extent the neoliberal policy regime, regarded as a bundle of policies or institutional changes in different domains, is correlated with functional income distribution. The idea applied in this chapter is the diversity of the regime, which is defined as variations in the combination between *factor 1* (*the contrast between government involvement in the product market and the globalization and liberalization of the financial market*) and *factor 2* (*the contrast between the generosity of social security or the protection of workers' rights, security or the protection of workers' rights, and the scale of the financial sector*) resulting from the MFA in the previous section. In other words, we suppose that the correlation between the regime and wage share could vary according to the clusters or the trajectories of institutional configurations, which are presented as connected arrows, shown in Figure 8.2.

However, the problem we encounter here is that some countries may not necessarily correspond to a particular cluster in time because they may be transitioning from one cluster to another. Therefore, it is difficult to examine the hypothesis mentioned above. To address this problem, we reclassify countries into groups, based on clusters and transition between clusters. The econometric analysis conducted below uses the annual data, whereas the clusters presented here are based on the MFA of decades.[8] The results of the reclassification are as follows:

Group 1: Cluster 2 throughout the whole period (Australia, Canada, UK, USA)
Group 2: Transition from Cluster 3 to 1 (Austria, Belgium, Denmark, Finland, France, Greece, Ireland, Netherlands, Portugal, Sweden)
Group 3: Transition from Cluster 3 to 2 (Germany, New Zealand, Norway, Spain, Switzerland)
Group 4: Transition from Cluster 4 to 2 (Italy, Japan, South Korea)

We examine whether and how the effect that institutional changes have on the evolution of wage share varies according to group.

3.1 Data, variables, and method

What we want to use as a dependent variable in this chapter is the functional income distribution in each country. We use the wage share as its proxy. More precisely, we adopt the measure of adjusted wage share obtained from the AMECO database. Our selection of independent variables is simple. For control variables, which are intended to grasp the effects of fluctuation, we introduce the capital–labor ratio and labor productivity (log scaled). The former concerns biased technological change mentioned in Section 2.1. It is supposed to have a negative effect on wage share. However, note that the installation of a new machine that would lead to changes in capital–labor ratio requires time in order to produce any effect on economic dynamics because a process of adjustment is needed to adapt to a new situation. Concerning the latter, one can expect its negative effect on wage share by the definition of wage share *ceteris paribus*. In fact, many studies point out the counter-cyclical effect of labor productivity on wage share (see Schor 1985). The variables that we should chiefly examine are *factor 1* (*the contrast between government involvement in the product market and the globalization and liberalization of the financial market*) and *factor 2* (*the contrast between the generosity of social security or the protection of workers' rights and the scale of the financial sector*). According to the results of preceding studies, one can anticipate the signs of the effects of these factors to some extent, which are composite indicators of different domains of institutions: Considering the effects of variables that contribute mainly to the factors, we determine that *factor 1* is basically expected to be positively correlated with wage share, whereas the effect of product market regulation is ambiguous. Note that although financialization and globalization should be negatively correlated with wage share, variables related to them determine the negative side of the factor so that *factor 1* is consequently expected to have a positive effect. Regarding *factor 2*, we can find two main parts. The generosity of social security or the protection of workers' rights determining the positive side of the factor should have a positive effect, whereas the scale of the financial sector, regarded as a part of financialization, determines the negative side of the factor, or rather, is expected to be negatively correlated with wage share. Therefore, *factor 2* is expected to have a positive overall effect.

This analysis attempts to determine not only whether the diversity of institutional configurations is correlated with wage share but also whether the correlation between diversity of institutional changes and the evolution of wage share varies according to group; therefore it is necessary to estimate the group-level model.

To accomplish this task, we need to apply a specific econometric method that differs from the ordinal one. The multilevel analysis performed in this chapter, in fact, enables us to conduct such an analysis. The data used in this analysis is hierarchically nested. Individual countries are actually nested within the groups defined in this chapter. Using multilevel analysis, we can estimate econometric models at both the whole-sample and group levels.

3.2 Specification of the model

3.2.1 Theoretical specification

We specify the estimation model according to the manner of multilevel analysis. Theoretically, although one can set up any number of levels of hierarchy, here we construct a two-level model which can be specified in stages by identifying the difference between the ordinary linear regression model and the multilevel one. Our model can be defined with the following simple linear regression:

$$adjWS_{ijt} = \beta_1 + \beta_2 \ln prod_{ijt} + \beta_3 \ln prod_{ij(t-1)} + \beta_4 \ln prod_{ij(t-2)} + \beta_5 caplab_{ijt} + \beta_6 caplab_{ij(t-1)} + \beta_7 caplab_{ij(t-2)} + \beta_8 factor1_{ijt} + \beta_9 factor2_{ijt} + \varepsilon_{ijt} \quad (8.1)$$

where $adjWS_{ijt}$, $\ln prod_{ijt}$, $caplab_{ijt}$, $factor1_{ijt}$, and $factor2_{ijt}$ stand for adjusted wage share, logarithm of labor productivity, capital–labor ratio, and first and second factors of the MFA, respectively. β indicates the average coefficient for the whole sample under investigation. The subscripts i, j, and t represent country, group, and time, respectively. We also consider time lags for labor productivity and capital–labor ratio. Equation (8.1) identifies an intercept and slopes for variables common to all of the countries under investigation. However, we want to show whether and to what extent the effect of the two factors on wage share varies among groups; therefore, we also assume group-specific parameters for the intercept and slopes:

$$\beta_1 = \beta_{1,0} + \zeta_{1,j}, \beta_8 = \beta_{8,0} + \zeta_{8j}, \beta_9 = \beta_{9,0} + \zeta_{9j}$$

where ζ_j represents group-specific effect (random effect), and β_j stands for the fixed effect that is common to all of the countries. Substituting the above equations for (8.1),

$$adjWS_{ijt} = (\beta_{1,0} + \zeta_{1j}) + \beta_2 \ln prod_{ijt} + \beta_3 \ln prod_{ij(t-1)} + \beta_4 \ln prod_{ij(t-2)} + \beta_5 caplab_{ijt} + \beta_6 caplab_{ij(t-1)} + \beta_7 caplab_{ij(t-2)} + (\beta_{8,0} + \zeta_{8j}) factor1_{ijt} + (\beta_{9,0} + \zeta_{9j}) factor2_{ijt} + \varepsilon_{ijt} \quad (8.2)$$

we can identify group-specific effects as well as fixed effects by estimating equation (8.2). Technically, this is a two-level mixed model that includes both fixed and random effects.

3.2.2 Empirical verification and specification of lag structure

Let us verify the relevance of our theoretical specification by comparing it with other possible specifications. As a preliminary step, we show the results of the OLS estimations with different combinations of variables and different lag structures in order to specify the relevant fixed part of the model and its lag structure (Table 8.2). Note that for simplicity we use only a case of the imputed data discussed earlier.

Based on the adjusted coefficient of determination and information criteria such as AIC and BIC, we can select model 11 with a two-year lag for both the variables ln *prod* and *caplab*.

Table 8.3 shows results of the application of the above result to the multilevel analysis.[9] We adopt the restricted maximum likelihood (REML) as an estimation

Table 8.2 Specification of lag structure in the model with OLS

	Model 1	*Model 2*	*Model 3*	*Model 4*	*Model 5*	*Model 6*	*Model 7*	*Model 8*	*Model 9*	*Model 10*	*Model 11*	*Model 12*	*Model 13*	*Model 14*
ln *prod*	0.763***	−3.662	−7.369	0.547***	0.498***	0.504***	−1.956	−12.086	−19.544	−9.363	−14.654	−16.378	−13.497	−15.568
	[0.144]	[14.166]	[9.241]	[0.153]	[0.160]	[0.160]	[15.047]	[13.924]	[14.492]	[9.001]	[9.081]	[14.879]	[9.363]	[14.972]
caplab	4.367**	4.321**	3.978**	153.927***	92.237***	127.649***	3.974**	157.189***	96.626***	162.841***	96.064***	96.387***	116.637***	117.456***
	[1.694]	[1.767]	[1.853]	[31.716]	[18.036]	[43.395]	[1.854]	[31.926]	[18.293]	[32.690]	[18.142]	[18.298]	[43.950]	[44.245]
ln $prod_{(t-1)}$		4.458					−10.689	12.648	20.06			3.354		4.075
		[14.190]					[23.432]	[13.941]	[14.504]			[22.911]		[22.973]
ln $prod_{(t-2)}$			8.185				13.461			9.937	15.191*	13.560	14.035	12.029
			[9.273]				[14.830]			[9.030]	[9.103]	[14.394]	[9.385]	[14.701]
$caplab_{(t-1)}$				−147.611***		−70.168		−151.114***		−157.006***			−41.341	−42.200
				[31.270]		[78.204]		[31.514]		[32.259]			[80.429]	[80.671]
$caplab_{(t-2)}$					−85.887***	−51.064			−90.640***		−90.347***	−90.663***	−69.490	−69.441
					[17.547]	[42.596]			[17.861]		[17.712]	[17.864]	[44.279]	[44.333]
factor 1	1.305***	1.338***	1.419***	1.138***	1.133***	1.133***	1.418***	1.152***	1.152***	1.188***	1.167***	1.166***	1.164***	1.163***
	[0.164]	[0.176]	[0.189]	[0.175]	[0.190]	[0.190]	[0.190]	[0.176]	[0.190]	[0.190]	[0.190]	[0.191]	[0.191]	[0.191]
factor 2	0.084	0.091	0.077	0.193	0.190	0.189	0.075	0.202	0.208	0.185	0.208	0.209	0.207	0.208
	[0.181]	[0.188]	[0.194]	[0.184]	[0.190]	[0.191]	[0.195]	[0.184]	[0.191]	[0.190]	[0.190]	[0.191]	[0.191]	[0.191]
Intercept	34.760***	34.701***	36.492***	25.729***	25.870***	25.451***	36.501***	26.989***	27.824***	28.186***	29.178***	29.150***	28.679***	28.634***
	[8.908]	[9.288]	[9.734]	[9.090]	[9.367]	[9.381]	[9.744]	[9.197]	[9.463]	[9.625]	[9.555]	[9.568]	[9.612]	[9.627]
N	449	430	410	430	410	410	410	430	410	410	410	410	410	410
adj. R^2	0.204	0.205	0.21	0.245	0.253	0.252	0.208	0.244	0.254	0.252	0.256	0.254	0.255	0.253
AIC	2,670.382	2,564.505	2,452.488	2,542.58	2,429.659	2,430.841	2,454.276	2,543.744	2,429.718	2,431.07	2,428.835	2,430.814	2,430.566	2,432.534
BIC	2,690.918	2,588.888	2,476.585	2,566.962	2,453.756	2,458.954	2,482.389	2,572.19	2,457.831	2,459.183	2,456.948	2,462.943	2,462.695	2,468.679

Source: author's calculation.

Notes
Standard errors in brackets.
* $p<0.1$;
** $p<0.05$;
*** $p<0.01$.

Table 8.3 Specification of the model in multilevel analysis

	Model 15	*Model 16*	*Model 17*	*Model 18*	*Model 19*	*Model 20*
Fixed effect						
ln *prod*		0.805***	–26.511**	–32.960***	–17.318*	–19.623**
		[0.172]	[9.138]	[8.677]	[7.609]	[7.471]
ln $prod_{(t-2)}$			27.193**	33.837***	16.992*	19.328**
			[9.166]	[8.706]	[7.640]	[7.495]
caplab		–0.032	107.366***	88.690***	73.853***	71.138***
		[1.630]	[17.436]	[16.830]	[14.629]	[14.476]
$caplab_{(t-2)}$			–105.298***	–83.308***	–63.401***	–60.713***
			[16.885]	[16.387]	[14.327]	[14.199]
factor 1				1.456***	1.619**	1.571**
				[0.203]	[0.583]	[0.534]
factor 2				0.116	–1.701	–1.617
				[0.273]	[2.419]	[2.356]
Intercept	66.687***	57.132***	46.299***	27.516**	12.761	12.657
	[1.606]	[9.027]	[9.849]	[9.695]	[9.004]	[8.835]

Random effect						
factor 1					1.569***	1.543***
					[0.418]	[0.419]
factor 2					1.490***	1.514***
					[0.429]	[0.430]
Intercept	1.155**	0.887*	0.798	0.909*	0.085	0.000
	[0.421]	[0.430]	[0.431]	[0.428]	[0.495]	[0.532]
cov (intercept and *factor 1*)						–1.467
						[0.792]
cov (intercept and *factor 2*)						–1.798
						[1.412]
cov (*factor 1* and *factor 2*)						1.395*
						[0.612]
Residual	1.561***	1.541***	1.510***	1.451***	1.271***	1.272***
	[0.034]	[0.034]	[0.035]	[0.035]	[0.036]	[0.036]
AIC	2,693.5394	2,675.2263	2,406.1594	2,363.3767	2,245.8572	2,242.9797
BIC	2,705.8605	2,695.7614	2,434.2725	2,399.5221	2,290.035	2,299.2059
N	449	449	410	410	410	410

Source: author's calculation.

Notes
Standard errors in brackets.
* $p<0.1$;
** $p<0.05$;
*** $p<0.01$.

method because the estimation would be unbiased with few groups in our model (see Gelman and Hill 2007). Table 8.3 shows a comparison of the estimations. Model 15 is an empty model for reference. A comparison of model 16 and model 17 reveals the introduction of a lag structure for labor productivity and capital–labor ratio. Model 18 indicates the random intercept model. Models 19 and 20 are random-slope models. The difference between these two models is associated with the random-effects covariance matrix. The former assumes an independent structure where all covariances among variables and intercepts are supposed to be zero. As for the latter, the covariance matrix is assumed to be unstructured, where distinct variances and covariances between all random effects covariates are allowed. Comparing the AIC and BIC statistics, that is, smaller-is-better, in Table 8.3, the mixed model or random-slope model (model 19 and model 20) is preferable to the others. Regarding the covariance matrix, we are unable to definitively decide the best fitted model because there is a gap between the values indicated by AIC and BIC, respectively. However, we further investigate model 20 with an unstructured random effects covariance matrix because there is no theoretical reason to suppose that no correlations exist among covariates in our model.

3.3 Results and discussion

The detailed results of the estimation of model 20 are presented in Table 8.4. That is derived from an estimation using ten out of 20 sets of imputed data based on the method of multiple imputation.

The intra-class correlations coefficient is calculated as follows: var(const.)/(var(const.)+var(Residual))=4.652/(4.652+3.585)=0.565, which indicates that the variance between groups is larger than that within a group. Hence, we can confirm that the application of the multilevel analysis is valid.

Let us check the detailed result of an estimation of the model. First, regarding the part of fixed effect, each coefficient of labor productivity (logarithm) and the capital–labor ratio is significant. The estimates of the former correspond to the expectation that labor productivity relates counter-cyclically to wage share (Schor 1985). More interestingly, the negative effect of labor productivity without lag is almost offset by the positive effect of the same variable with a two-year lag. This implies that our model can capture the cyclical correlation between labor productivity and wage share. The same can be said for capital–labor ratio. Here, we can verify that the effect is consistent with the hypothesis of negative correlation with wage share in terms of the variable with a two-year lag. This should result from the fact that an increase in capital–labor ratio, for instance, the installation of new machines, does not necessarily cause an increase in production.

Now, we move on to the fixed effect of factors determining the diversity of transformation in institutional configurations (left-hand side of Table 8.4). The first factor (*the contrast between government involvement in the product market and the globalization and liberalization of the financial market*) is positively correlated

Table 8.4 Detailed results of a mixed model estimation

Part of fixed effect		*Part of random effect: group level*	
Covariate	*Coefficient*		*estimate*
ln *prod*	–20.770***	var(*factor 1*)	0.923
	[7.490]	var(*factor 2*)	4.743
ln $prod_{(t-2)}$	20.426***	var(const.)	4.652
	[7.512]	cov(*factor 1*, *factor 2*)	–0.923
caplabor	70.916***	cov(*factor 1*, const.)	–0.996
	[14.476]	cov(*factor 2*, const.)	0.895
$caplabor_{(t-2)}$	–60.473***	var(Residual)	3.585
	[14.174]		
factor 1	1.537***		N=410
	[0.498]		Number of groups=4
factor 2	–1.609		Observations per group: min=53, average=102.5, max=190
	[2.391]		DF adjustment: Large sample DF: min=45886.23
const.	13.154		Model F test: Equal FMI F(6,80389.6)=14.85
	[8.891]		Prob >F=0.0000

Source: author's calculation.

Notes
Standard errors in brackets.
* $p<0.1$;
** $p<0.05$;
*** $p<0.01$.

with wage share at a significant level, which is consistent with the theoretical expectation discussed earlier. In contrast, the coefficient of the second factor (*the contrast between the generosity of social security or the protection of workers' rights, and the scale of the financial sector*) is negative, which is contrary to our expectation, and not statistically significant. However, it can be compatible with the fact that the dispersion of countries in the mid-2000s (Figure 8.2)[10] is larger in the vertical axis (*factor 2*) than in the horizontal axis (*factor 1*).

With regard to the random effect of the model (right-hand side of Table 8.4), we can point out the following: First, the variances of the factors ("estimates" in the table) are considerably larger than the square of their standard errors (values within square brackets on the part of fixed effect) respectively, so that the magnitude of the effect of each factor on wage share should depend fairly on the group. Second, the variance of *factor 1* is considerably smaller than that of *factor 2*. This implies that the correlation between social security and the protection of workers, and wage share should depend largely on the institutional configuration of each country, even though the distributional effect of the globalization and liberalization of markets could be relatively uniform. It is interesting to compare this implication with the results of the MFA in the previous section. The MFA generates composite factors that can explain the variance of subjects as much as possible. The first and second factors are in order of the power of explanation for the variance. In contrast, concerning the effect of factors on wage share, the second factor has more diverse effects than does the first factor. Such a paradox should be because the subjects in our analysis include countries in different periods. Figure 8.2 shows that the countries are basically similar in their direction and scale of change in *factor 1*, which is globalization and liberalization. This should give rise to robust estimation results. On the contrary, the diverse trajectories of *factor 2*, compared to *factor 1*, should be associated with insignificant estimation results.

After grasping the general features in terms of random effect, we further investigate properties of group-specific effect by calculating the coefficients according to groups. Table 8.5 displays estimates of group-specific parameters. The upper two lines of the table show group-specific effects of the factors on wage share, and the lower two lines show the composite effect of group-specific and fixed effects. The first factor effect in most of the groups is positive for both group-specific (ζ) and fixed effects (β). Note that almost all of the countries

Table 8.5 Group-specific effects of the factors on wage share

	Group 1	*Group 2*	*Group 3*	*Group 4*
$\zeta_{8\ \text{factor1}}$	−1.24	−0.30	0.72	0.82
$\zeta_{9\ \text{factor2}}$	4.12	3.81	−3.19	−4.74
$\beta_8+\zeta_8$	0.33	1.27	2.29	2.39
$\beta_9+\zeta_9$	2.50	2.19	−4.80	−6.36

Source: author's calculation.

move left throughout the periods in Figure 8.2, so that *factor 1* should exert a downward pressure on wage share. On the other hand, for *factor 2*, some countries move upwards, whereas others downwards in the figure. Furthermore, how the transformation of institutional configuration affects the evolution of wage share depends on the group.

When examined more closely, the following observations can be made: First, as for countries that continue to belong to the same cluster during the entire period (Group 1), the scale of the whole effect ($\beta+\zeta$) is relatively small because group-specific effects (ζ) lessen the fixed effect (β). In fact, simulations based on the estimates plot stable fluctuations in the wage share. This is fairly consistent with the actual change in wage share (Figure 8.4).[11]

While the countries categorized in Group 2 experience a transition between clusters, they belong to a cluster other than that in which the countries of Group 1 are included even after the transition. The sign of group-specific effect of their institutional configuration on income distribution is the same as that in Group 1, and its scale is smaller than in Group 1. Hence, the whole effect on wage share in Group 2 is supposed to be larger than the one in Group 1. In particular, its group-specific effect of *factor 1* ($\beta_8+\zeta_8$) is larger than in Group 1 ($1.27>0.33$), which would lead to the downward effect of *factor 1* in Group 2.

Countries in Group 3 and Group 4 commonly move to cluster 2. These two groups share similar group-specific effects in terms of sign and scale. Concerning *factor 1*, their positive group-specific effect (ζ) enforces the downward pressure on wage share by complementing the fixed effect (β). Their sign of the effect of *factor 2* is negative in contrast to that in Groups 1 and 2. A stronger downward pressure on wage share in Groups 3 and 4 than in Groups 1 and 2 can be expected. In fact, the estimated values of wage share decreases over time in Group 4 (upper side of Figure 8.5), which is largely consistent with actual values of wage share (lower side of Figure 8.5).

In sum, what we have shown is the following: First, the wage share in the group that includes countries not transitioning between clusters is relatively stable. Second, one can observe some degree of decline in wage share in the group that consists of countries moving to cluster 1. Third, a distinct decline in wage share in the groups in which countries experience a transition to cluster 2 is confirmed.

Two implications can be drawn from these results. First, the transition of a country or a group between clusters implies a considerable transformation in institutional configuration in that country or group. It is not guaranteed that institutions in any domain change to the same degree in that country. If institutions change to different degrees, it is possible that institutional complementarity or compatibility, which may have been observed in that country, would be lost (see Amable 2003: 68–73). Such institutional changes could result in changes in a hitherto stable mode of income distribution. It also implies the likelihood that wage share would decline in a country where institutional changes occurred to such an extent as to cause a shift from one cluster to another under the dissemination of the neoliberal policy regime. Conversely, if neoliberal institutional

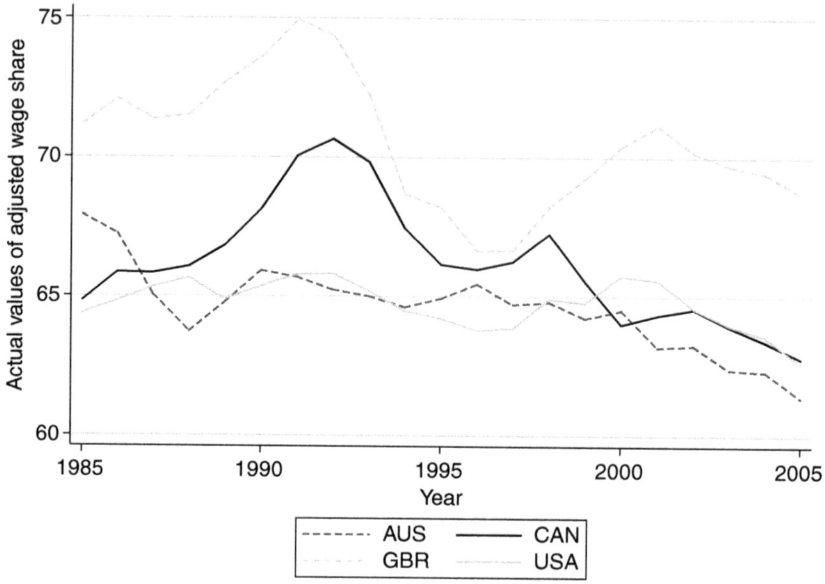

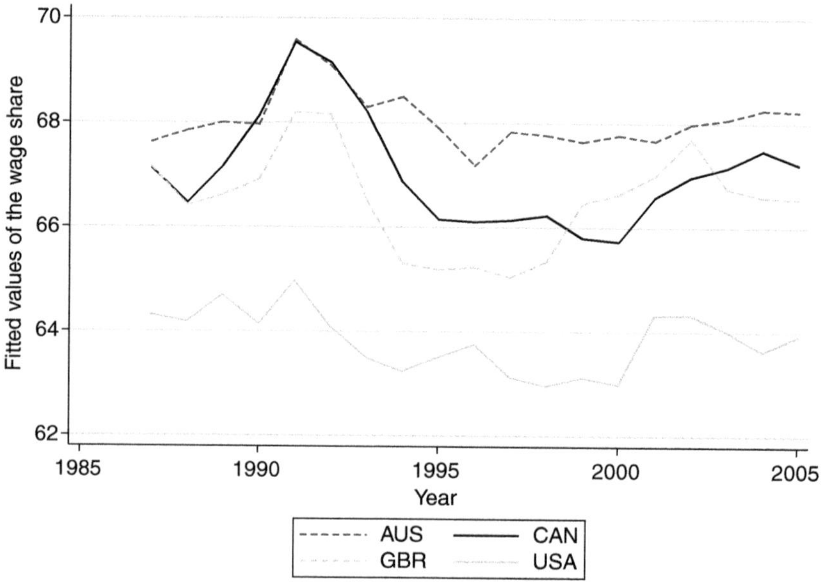

Figure 8.4 Evolution of adjusted wage share: actual and fitted values (Group 1).

Source: author's calculation.

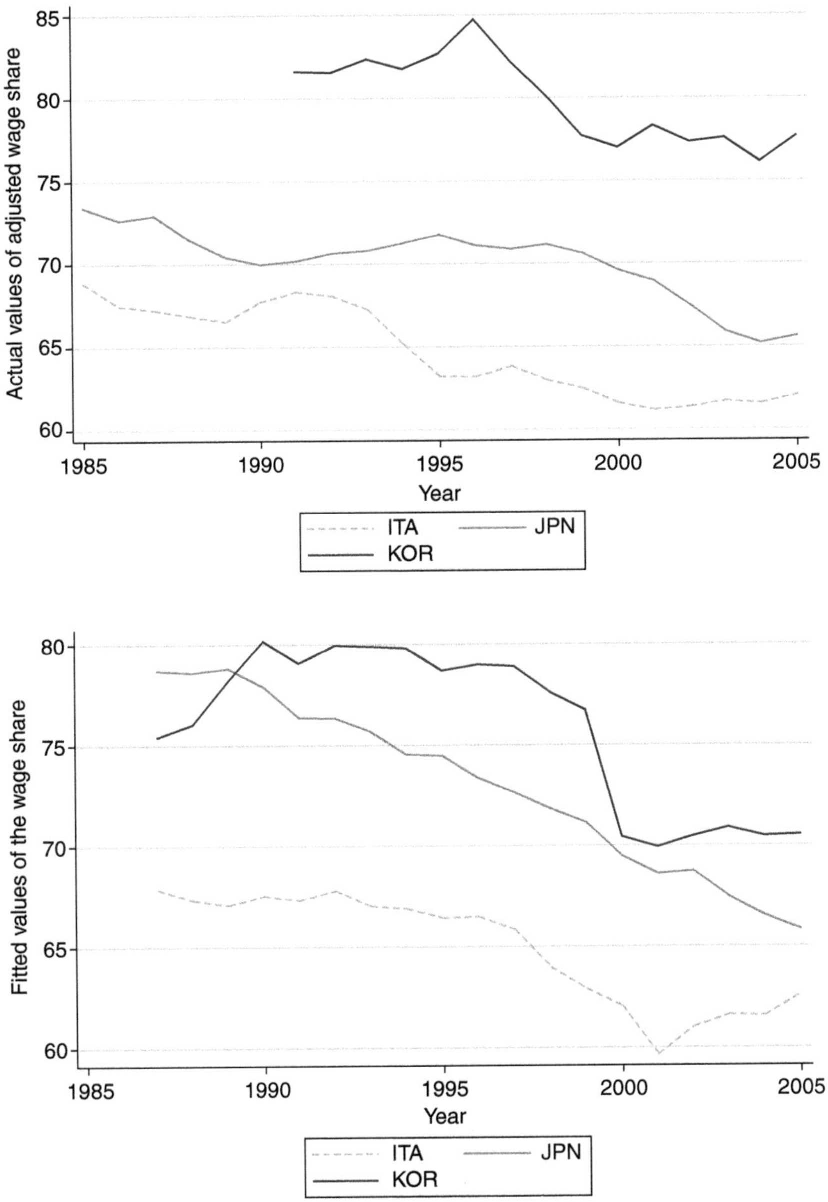

Figure 8.5 Evolution of adjusted wage share: actual and fitted values (Group 4).

Source: author's calculation.

changes do not cause the collapse of the existing coherent structure of institutions in a country, then the stability of income distribution should be maintained in that country, as argued by Kaldor (1958).

Second, even in those countries where institutional configurations change enough to cause a shift from one cluster to another, the extent to which wage share changes depends on the cluster to which the country moves. The countries shifting to cluster 2, including the Anglo-Saxon countries, which have salient globalization and liberalization of markets, experienced a sharper decline in wage share compared to those in cluster 1, which consists of European countries with relatively maintained generosity of social security and protection of workers' rights. This implies that institutional forms in terms of social security and the wage–labor nexus are still important factors determining the mode of functional income distribution even with the progress of neoliberalism.

4 Concluding remarks

We sum up the arguments in this chapter as follows: First, by conducting a statistical analysis of changes in institutional configurations in advanced countries since the 1980s, we identified the diversity of trajectories of institutional configurations among countries even in the progress of the globalization and liberalization of markets. Second, we exhibited factors to determine the diversity of institutional configurations. The first determining factor reflects the degree of development in the globalization and liberalization of markets in reverse order. The second one is *the contrast between the generosity of social security or the protection of workers' rights, and the scale of the financial sector*. The countries with diverse institutional configurations can be classified into four clusters. Furthermore, we categorized countries into four groups by considering their patterns of transition between clusters.

Third, using multilevel analysis to determine how the diversity of institutional configurations derived from the above analysis is correlated with aggregate wage share, we obtained the following results: First, *factor 1*, which is the globalization and liberalization of markets, is positively correlated with wage share at a statistically significant level for the entire sample. Regarding *factor 2*, the generosity of social security and the protection of workers' rights as well as the scale of the financial sector have a negative but statistically insignificant correlation. Calculating the group-specific effects, we see that the influence of both factors varies considerably according to group. We also found a remarkable difference between groups that transition between clusters throughout the period and the group that does not. While the latter has a relatively stable fluctuation in wage share due to the small effect of both factors, the former experiences a decline in wage share. Regarding groups that transition between clusters, those that transition to a cluster consisting of countries with a strong market orientation, such as the Anglo-Saxon countries, are likely to face more intense downward pressure on wage share than those countries that transition to other clusters.

The implications of these results differ from those of previous studies in the relationship between institutions and income distribution. Previous studies indicated that individual institutions affect income distribution regardless of the group to which a country belongs. In contrast, the analysis in this chapter comprehensively outlines a series of institutional changes and phenomena and shows that patterns of income distribution have a relationship with changes in institutional configurations composed of institutions in different domains.

However, it should be noted that the analysis in this chapter is still provisional. Regarding the diversity of institutional configurations, the types of policies and institutional changes that would induce the trajectory of each country should be further investigated. As for the relationship between institutional configurations and income distribution, we should refine both the model and the method of estimation in order to make the estimation results more robust.

Appendix

Appendix Variable list for the diversity of institutional configurations

	Variables	*Source*
Labor market institution	Density of trade union	OECD
	Employment protection legislation	
	Strikes and lockouts	ILO
	Impact of labor market institutions (LMIs)	Schindler and Aleksynska (2011)
	Minimum wage to mean wage	
	Gross replacement rate	
	Unemployment benefits coverage	
	Advance notice period after four years	
	Severance pay after four years	
	LMP public expenditure (%GDP)	OECD
	PES and administration	
	Training	
	Employment incentives	
	Sheltered and supported employment and rehabilitation	
	Direct job creation	
	Start-up incentives	
	Out-of-work income maintenance and support	
	Early retirement	
Financialization	External assets plus external liabilities as a share of GDP	Lane and Milesi-Ferretti (2007)
	Value-added share of financial sector to GDP	EU-KLEM
	Impact of financial reforms	Abiad, Detragiache, and Tressel (2008)
	Measures for credit controls	
	Directed credit/reserve requirements	
	Aggregate credit ceilings	

continued

Appendix Continued

	Variables	*Source*
	Interest rate controls	
	Entry barriers/pro-competition measures	
	Banking supervision	
	Privatization	
	International capital flows	
	Security markets	
Globalization	Trade openness (as imports plus exports as a share of GDP)	World Bank WDI
	Ratio of exports to GDP	
	Terms of trade	AMECO database
	Goods	
	Services	
	Inward FDI/GDP stock	Lane and Milesi-Ferretti (2007)
	Outward FDI/GDP stock	
	KOF economic globalization index	Dreher (2006)
	Actual flow	
	Restrictions	
	KOF social globalization	
	Personal contact	
	Information flows	
	Cultural proximity	
	KOF political globalization	
Welfare state	Government consumption as a percentage of GDP	Penn World Tables
Product market regulation	Electricity (E), gas (G), telecom (T), post (P), rail transport (rail), air transport overall (A), and road transport (road)	OECD
	Entry regulation (E, G, T, P, rail, A, road)	
	Public ownership (E, G, T, P, rail, A)	
	Vertical integration (E, G, rail)	
	Market structure (E, G, T, P, rail)	
	Price control (road)	

Notes

1 Przeworski (2001) insists on the differences rather than the similarities between welfare policies. He points out that "[t]he social protection net was built gradually and through varied paths" (Przeworski 2001: 327).

2 This database consists of indicators of product market regulation in non-manufacturing sectors, including, in particular, seven network sectors (telecommunication, electricity, gas, post, rail, air passenger transport, and road freight) and five service sectors (retail distribution, accounting, legal, engineering, and architectural). We use the indicators of former sectors because they are available for the annual data from 1975 to 2013.

3 Countries examined in this chapter are: Australia (AUS), Austria (AUT), Belgium (BEL), Canada (CAN), Denmark (DNK), Finland (FIN), France (FRA), Germany (DEU), Greece (GRC), Ireland (IRL), Italy (ITA), Japan (JPN), South Korea (KOR), Netherlands (NLD), New Zealand (NZL), Norway (NOR), Portugal (PRT), Spain (ESP), Sweden (SWE), Switzerland (CHE), United Kingdom (GBR), and United States (USA).

4 While various methods of multiple imputation exist, the method employed in this chapter is the Amelia II program, which is provided as part of the statistical analysis package R (Honaker and King 2010; Honaker *et al.* 2012). In general, the imputation of data is based on a particular stochastic distribution. The program's advantage is its ability to consider the possible influence of serial correlation in time-series data on the imputation. However, it also has problems based on just normal distributions for the imputation. Actually, observed values of the variables that we picked up do not necessarily fit normal distributions. Thus, the imputed data may have errors.

5 The result shown here is based on one of the multiple imputed data. The method of multiple imputation generates plural numbers of imputation so as to avoid biased estimations. We conduct the definite analysis using all the imputed data. We show only one of the results in a simple way because any results do not have considerable distortion in our analysis.

6 When the analysis is conducted based on each decade, the variables making up these principal factors are not so different from those shown here, although the composition and the order of relevant variables change slightly. For instance, the generosity of social protection and labor market policies are the most influential in the 1990s, but these elements determine the second factor over the entire period.

7 We apply the Ward method. Calculating values of the aggregation index at each level of the hierarchy, we decide the number of clusters, cutting off the cluster tree at a certain level that makes a particular number of classes, according to the distance between values of the aggregation index at each level. A longer distance from the *s* classes to the *s-1* classes implies that the s classes are firmer (Lebart *et al.* 2002: 180). Moreover, it is also important that cutoff at a certain level has a convincing implication in reality.

8 Although the result of the MFA based on each year is not reported, the resulting factors are highly similar to those of the analysis based on decades. We use the result from the decade analysis to illustrate the rough trend of change in institutional configurations.

9 Here, we make one of 20 sets of data created by multiple imputation. While not shown here, the results of the estimation using all sets of imputed data are almost the same as those shown here. Therefore, we can regard the results in Table 8.3 as a representation of the estimations.

10 The positions of countries in the mid-2000s are marked by filled circles in the figure.

11 However, the wage shares in this group actually declined in the 2000s, whereas the simulations exhibit stable fluctuations (Figure 8.4). This implies that our model does not successfully explain the evolution since the 2000s. Such an inconsistency is also observed for the other groups, which may be due to structural change around the year 2000.

References

Abdi, H. and D. Valentin (2007) "Multiple Factor Analysis (MFA)," in N.J. Salkind (ed.) *Encyclopedia of Measurement and Statistics*, Thousand Oaks, CA: Sage.

Abiad, A., E. Detragiache, and T. Tressel (2008) "A New Database of Financial Reforms," IMF Working Paper, WP/08/26.

Amable, B. (2003) *The Diversity of Modern Capitalism*, Oxford: Oxford University Press.

Aoki, M. (2001) *Towards a Comparative Institutional Analysis*, Cambridge, MA: MIT Press.

Bentolila, S. and G. Saint-Paul (2003) "Explaining Movements in the Labor Share," *The B.E. Journal of Macroeconomics* 3(1), 1–33.

Blanchard, O. and F. Giavazzi (2003) "Macroeconomic Effects of Regulation and Deregulation in Goods and Labor Markets," *The Quarterly Journal of Economics* 118(3), 879–907.

Boyer, B. (2004) *Une théorie de capitalisme est-elle possible?*, Paris: Odile Jacob.

Boyer, R. (2015) *Économie politique des capitalismes: Théorie de la régulation et des crises*, Paris: La Découverte.

Dreher, Axel (2006) "Does Globalization Affect Growth? Evidence from a New Index of Globalization," *Applied Economics* 38(10), 1091–1110.

Dünhaupt, P. (2012) "Financialization and the Rentier Income Share: Evidence from the USA and Germany," *International Review of Applied Economics* 26(4), 465–487.

Dünhaupt, P. (2013) "Determinants of Functional Income Distribution: Theory and Empirical Evidence," Global Labor University Working Paper, No. 18.

Edrem, M. and K. Tsatsaronis (2013) "Financial Conditions and Economic Activity: A Statistical Approach," *BIS Quarterly Review*, March: 37–51.

Escofier, B. and J. Pagès (1998) *Analyzes factorielles simples et multiples*, Paris: Dunod.

European Commission (2007) "The Labor Income Share in the European Union," in *Employment in Europe*, Luxembourg: Office for Official Publications of the European Communities.

Gelman, A. and J. Hill (2007) *Data Analysis Using Regression and Multilevel/Hierarchical Models*, Cambridge: Cambridge University Press.

Guscina, A. (2006) "Effects of Globalization on Labor's Share in National Income," IMF Working Paper, 06/294.

Hall, P. and D. Soskice (eds.) (2001) *Varieties of Capitalism: The Institutional Foundations of Comparative Advantage*, Oxford: Oxford University Press.

Harada, Y. and H. Tohyama (2012) "Asian Capitalisms: Institutional Configuration and Firm Heterogeneity," in Boyer, R., H. Uemura, and A. Isogai (eds.), *Diversity and Transformations of Asian Capitalisms*, Oxford: Routledge.

Harrison, A. (2002) "Has Globalization Eroded Labor's Share? Some Cross-Country Evidence," mimeo, UC Berkeley.

Honaker, J. and G. King (2010) "What to do About Missing Values in Time Series Cross-Section Data," *American Journal of Political Science* 54(2), 561–581.

Honaker, James, Gary King, and Matthew Blackwell (2012) Amelia II: A Program for Missing Data Version 1.6.1. http://cran.r-project.org/web/packages/Amelia/vignettes/amelia.pdf.

ILO (2011) *World of Work Report 2011: Making Markets Work for Jobs*, Geneva: ILO.

IMF (2007) "The Globalization of Labor," *World Economics Outlook*, Washington, DC: IMF.

Kaldor, N. (1958) "Capital Accumulation and Economic Growth," in *Further Essays on Economic Theory*, New York: Holmes & Meier Publishers.

Koske, I., I. Wanner, R. Bitetti, and O. Barbiero (2014) "The 2013 Update of the OECD Product Market Regulation Indicators: Policy Insights for OECD and non-OECD Countries," OECD Economics Department Working Papers.

Kristal, T. (2010) "Good Times, Bad Times: Postwar Labor's Share of National Income in Capitalist Democracies," *American Sociological Review* 75(5), 729–763.

Lane, P.R. and G.M. Milesi-Ferretti (2007) "The External Wealth of Nations Mark II: Revised and Extended Estimates of Foreign Assets and Liabilities, 1970–2004," *Journal of International Economics* 73, 223–250.

Lebart, L., A. Morineau, and M. Piron (2002) *Statistique exploratoire multidimensionnelle*. 3rd edn., Paris: Dunod.

Little, R.J.A. and D.B. Rubin (2002) *Statistical Analysis with Missing Data*, 2nd edn. Upper Saddle River, NJ: Wiley.

Przeworski, A. (2001) "How Many Ways Can be Third?" in Glyn, A. (ed.) *Social Democracy in Neoliberal Times*, Oxford: Oxford University Press.

Przeworski, A. (2014) "Choices and Echoes: Stability and Change of Policy Regimes," in H. Magara (ed.) *Economic Crises and Policy Regimes: The Dynamics of Policy Innovation and Paradigmatic Change*, Cheltenham, Edward Elgar.

Schindler, M. and M. Aleksynska (2011) "Labor Market Regulations in Low-, Middle- and High-Income Countries: A New Panel Database," IMF Working Papers 11/154.

Schor, J. (1985) "Changes in the Cyclical Pattern of Real Wages: Evidence from Nine Countries, 1955–80," *Economic Journal* 95, 452–468.

Stockhammer, E. (2009) "Determinants of Functional Income Distribution in OECD Countries," IMK Studies, no. 5/2009.

Stockhammer, E. (2012) "Why Have Wage Shares Fallen? A Panel Analysis of the Determinants of Functional Income Distribution," Conditions of Work and Employment series, No. 35.

Stolper, W.F. and P.A. Samuelson (1941) "Protection and Real Wages," *Review of Economic Studies* 9(1), 58–73.

Part IV

Regime competition in international rivalry and cooperation

9 Using neo-functionalism to understand the disintegration of Europe

Philippe C. Schmitter and Zoe Lefkofridi

1 Neo-functionalism and disintegration[1]

The European Union's (EU) future has been put into question in practice as well as in theory (Lefkofridi and Schmitter 2015; Schmitter 2012; Vollard 2008). In a purely probabilistic sense, the fact that the EU shows signs of disintegration is hardly surprising since most of the many efforts at transnational regional integration since World War II have exhibited similar symptoms. Either they failed to fulfill their initial commitments, withdrew from tasks already assigned to them or simply collapsed altogether. That so many observers of the EU regarded it as exceptional and, hence, immune to disintegration perhaps explains the apparent surprise among observers. Of course, so far all that has been observed are "morbidity symptoms," not some definitive diminution or demise.

Nevertheless, the events and processes triggered by the dual crises of the euro and the EU do require some re-thinking about the theories (and their presumptions) that have been used to explain the heretofore relative success of regional integration in Europe (for a critical discussion, see Vollard 2008). Prominent among these has been the neo-functionalist approach. The temptation, therefore, would seem to be to call into question its basic assumption, namely the predominant role played by a diversity of self-interested actors competing with each other for the functional distribution of public goods provided by regional institutions. This could then be replaced by another approach, probably some version of inter-governmentalism in which the only relevant actors are states promoting their self-regarding national interests and protecting their citizens from foreign intromission into their affairs and values.[2] In this chapter it is our purpose not to reject but to exploit neo-functionalism as a conceptual and theoretical instrument that helps understand the current crisis and its future consequences. It does not deny that the formal institutions and informal practices of the EU are threatened or that previously unobserved tendencies have emerged, but seeks to interpret them in ways that are consistent with its basic assumptions.

As an approach to understanding transnational regional integration, neo-functionalism has been frequently criticized for its alleged bias in favor of such a process – despite explicit protestations to the contrary by one of its practitioners (Schmitter 2004). The confusion seems due to the fact that the conditions present in Western Europe were unusually favorable to the generation/cultivation of spill-overs from one functional arena to another and from lower to higher levels of common authority. When the approach was applied elsewhere to efforts at regional integration in less favorable settings, it (correctly) predicted failure even to meet the objectives proclaimed in their founding treaties (Haas and Schmitter 1964; Schmitter 1970).

The normal expectation with regard to the performance of such regional or global efforts at functional cooperation/integration is that they should "self-encapsulate," i.e., at best they should perform the initial tasks bestowed upon them by member states (MSs) by international agreement and then persist as stable institutionalized components of the interstate order. Only in exceptional circumstances or conditions should actors within such arrangements be expected to agree to a redefinition of their functional tasks or an upgrading of their authoritative status.

Given the current and concurrent crises of the EU and the euro, it would seem appropriate to explore the hypotheses and presumptions that neo-functionalism might employ to predict "spill-backs" rather than "spill-overs." A spill-back is when MSs no longer wish to deal with a policy at the supra-national level, e.g., the collapse of the euro or MS exits from the eurozone or even the EU – be they coerced (e.g., Grexit) or voluntary (e.g., Brexit). Such "spill-backs" are fervently advocated by parties on the radical Left and Right (albeit for different reasons) in both debtor and creditor states (e.g., *Freiheitliche Partei Österreichs*, *French Front National*, *Communist Party of Greece*). In this piece we apply neo-functionalist theory in an effort to understand the causal logic of disintegration, and its likely point of departure.

When and why should one expect that a given set of institutions of regional integration would agree (or be forced) to withdraw their competence to make policy in an arena previously subject to its transnational "governance"? Or, more dramatically, under what condition might it collapse altogether? The EU is not likely to break as long as it successfully fulfills key functions for the Union's economy and society as a whole; but it *can* and *will* break if it does not. In what follows, we first articulate explicit (and implicit) neo-functionalist suppositions and hypotheses. Next, we try to identify whether and to what extent disintegration is indeed a possibility in the empirical world. To this end, we examine different pieces of empirical evidence in favor or against neo-functionalist expectations; we either employ official databases (e.g., Eurostat, Eurobarometer) or rely on existing analyses. Instead of conclusion, we close with the most recent development, the Greek referendum of July 2015, when politicization and conflict reached its zenith.

2 Neo-functionalist suppositions and hypotheses

As is the case with any theory, neo-functionalism has suppositions that are explicit (some of which may be exclusive to it) and others that are implicit (and usually shared with other theories). These, in turn, produce hypotheses that can be tested against empirical data – quantitative or qualitative. All the explicit ones are ultimately derived from the core assumption of neo-functionalism, namely, that the process of regional integration (in the contemporary setting) depends on the realization of mutual gains from cooperation in policy arenas characterized by high levels of functional interdependence.

I Explicit (and sometimes exclusive) suppositions and hypotheses

1 *Economic integration and interdependence.* The removal of barriers to trade, investment and human mobility (negative integration) and the creation of common, market-regulating rules (positive integration) will produce a continuous increase in the interdependence of MSs. This increase will not only be absolute and general for the transnational regional organization (TRO) as a whole, but it will also be the case for all of its MSs. The distribution of this increase will not accrue primarily to a single MS or a set of "hegemonic" MSs within the TRO. The increase will be distinctively regional, i.e., greater among MSs than between them and non-MSs.

2 *Benefits and public perceptions.* The net benefits from this increase in regional interdependence will be positive, both for the economy as a whole and for the population at large. These benefits will be recognized and appreciated by those affected, and they will be (more or less) evenly distributed and shared across MSs. Therefore, mass publics will tend to support positively the existing TRO and expansions of its *compétences* in the future. This support may take the form of passive consent or active assent, depending on the visibility of threats and the magnitude of benefits.

3 *Security.* The primary expected benefit from regional integration should be greater security, both against predation by outsiders and in favor of material benefits from insiders. In the course of the integration process, actors may shift their perception of expected benefits, especially after some of them have been satisfied. But this will not involve a major shift toward the satisfaction or provision of non-material benefits such as the protection of national identity, the fulfillment of traditional values or the desire for a sense of affective belonging – at least, not until the integration process is sufficiently advanced to have produced a stable political equilibrium.

4 *Role of experts.* Neo-functionalism assigns a major role to experts, both those in the TRO and those in the respective national bureaucracies. They are presumed to be anxious to expand their role in policy making and, therefore, to introduce new initiatives when the opportunity arises (usually as a result of crisis, see supposition I.8 below). They are also supposed to be wary of "premature" politicization and, therefore, to internalize emerging conflicts and resolve them without including outsiders, especially those with a wider political agenda. Experts are presumed to form something approximating an "epistemic community" based on a high level of agreement concerning the nature of the problem and the means for resolving it. Moreover, this shared scientific paradigm is also supposed to be predisposed to favor an increase in intervention by public authority, in this case, by the TRO.

5 *Respect for EU decisions.* The policies of the TRO should be largely self-enforcing, given the presumption of net benefits. MSs will respect their commitments to implementing the policies of the TRO (*pacta sunt servanta*) and do so voluntarily and effectively, even when they have not approved the decisions taken. The TRO will not be obliged to acquire a monopoly on the use of legitimate violence within its territory (i.e., to become a state) in order to ensure compliance because this property can be reliably left to its MSs. The TRO will, however, have to rely increasingly on its capacity for adjudicating disputes ("legal integration") about the distribution of benefits, but especially concerning the honest and reliable implementation of its decisions by MSs.

6 *Convergence.* Increased interdependence of MSs, plus the shared and (more or less) equal distribution of benefits, will lead to a convergence among MSs in economic performance and social protection. Under most favorable conditions, this will mean an "upward" convergence in which the initially less well-endowed and performing MSs will come closer to attaining the levels of performance of the better endowed and better performing ones. In the absence of such a convergence, the TRO should be prepared to compensate the relative losers via some mixture of greater leniency (negative integration) or material redistribution (positive integration).

7 *Incremental positive and negative integration.* The process of regional integration will be incremental, involving a sequence of interrelated decisions. The process does not include major "threshold effects" or decisions that are so much more consequential or controversial that they require a radically different mode of decision making or conflict resolution. This incremental continuity will not be interrupted when (and if) the TRO switches from cooperation among MSs to cooperation of MSs in their relations with outside, non-member states. Nor will this relative continuity be significantly affected when the TRO is compelled to shift its attention from initially easier issues to resolve to more difficult ones whose rewards are less visible and delayed in effect. Nor will it be significantly affected when it shifts from the task of removing barriers to exchange (negative integration) to the task of regulating these exchanges and compensating for their potential perverse effects (positive integration).

8 *Conflict and politicization.* The process of regional integration inevitably generates conflict among MSs, especially given the novelty of the effort and, hence, the impossibility of calculating accurately all the potential consequences of collective decisions. The most significant sources of conflict among MSs and between their constituent interests are endogenous, i.e., produced by the integration process itself, and these are easier to resolve "in house." The usual process for resolving these conflicts is to reach a compromise involving some mixture of increased authority for regional institutions ("build-up") or an extension of their policy scope ("spill-around") or both ("spill-overs"). To the extent this prevails, the result will be an expansion of the role of those TRO institutions most

capable of exercising supra-national authority in relative independence from the authority and sovereignty of MSs. The emergence of greater conflict with regard to the TRO, its policies, and its increased autonomy will unavoidably result in "politicization," i.e., the mobilization of wider and wider publics paying attention to the integration process and expressing a greater diversity of opinions about it. According to supposition I.2 above, this mobilization on balance should be favorable based on the net distribution of benefits to the economy and population.

II Implicit (and not unique) suppositions and hypotheses

1 *Democracy.* The MSs of the TRO must have regimes that are both democratic and liberal. They have regular and reliable mechanisms for holding their rulers accountable to citizens and they are committed to respecting the rule of law and human rights, and tolerant of their citizens engaging in political activities.[3] The type of democracy need not be the same and may even become less so over time, but citizens must be free to form various types of collective political organizations – parties, associations and movements – and to do so across national borders. The regimes of MSs allow their citizens to both support and criticize the policies of the TRO. The political institutions of MSs provide regular and predictable access to representatives of national and international interests, passions and convictions. The governments of MSs do not systematically discriminate in providing information to their citizens – and allow TRO authorities to directly address these citizens. Needless to say, these conditions are not only present at the time of becoming a member, but persist throughout the country's membership.

2 *Consequences of enlargement.* The enlargement of the TRO to incorporate more members does not fundamentally alter the previously established processes or institutions of regional integration. Even if it is highly likely that the new entrants will have different economic and social endowments at the time of entry, existing TRO formal institutions and informal practices will be able to adjust to them. The sheer number of accession states may also make the decision-making process slower and more difficult – and the more that enter at the same time, the greater the impact will be – but it will not result in stalemate, provided that negotiations persist and compromises can be reached.

3 *Pluralistic conflicts.* The pattern of conflicts mentioned above in supposition I.7 will be pluralistic, i.e., it will not result in the formation of a distinctive subset of MSs that are regular and systematic losers across a range of issues. Such a polarization of conflicting actors – whether at the national or subnational level – can be avoided if the distribution of benefits from integration is both proportional and convergent. It can also be avoided if the underlying pattern of social and economic cleavages is cross-cutting, e.g., some small states are rich and others are poor; some centrally located states have more and others less state capacity; some historically dominant powers are willing and others less willing to accept a subordinate position.

4 *La finalité?* All theories of regional integration – explicitly or implicitly – presume that it will eventually end in an enduring and stable set of institutions. Neo-functionalism has been notoriously reluctant to predict what this "la finalité politique" might be (not to mention when it might come about), but it does presume that the TRO will evolve institutionally as a function of the benefits it distributes and conflicts it resolves. As we have seen in supposition I.5, neo-functionalism seemed to presume that it would not be necessary for the TRO (or the EU in this case) to fulfill all of the requisites historically associated with the emergence of a sovereign national state. But what was not imagined was that, instead of forming a distinct hierarchy of institutions concentrated in a single location (Brussels) according to the model set by most previous patterns of national political integration, the EU resulted in a very dispersed set of institutions at different locations with different internal structures and even with different memberships. When the euro crisis hit, the EU possessed no coherent and re-endowed set of institutions to deal with it. The result was a chaotic, competitive and redundant effort to respond to this "mother of all crises" that might otherwise have produced a definitive breakthrough in the path to political integration.

5 *Exogenous shocks*. Any TRO is inserted in a wider variety of international contexts and subject to unforeseen external events. These exogenous shocks and pressures are likely to have a differential impact upon MSs and to be a source of internal conflict, quite independent of the usual presumed endogenous ones. Their timing is also more unpredictable and unlikely to be coordinated with the status or cyclical properties of endogenous conflicts. Moreover, they may be more difficult to resolve since the TRO is less likely to have the installed capacity to do so. And it is highly likely that in doing so the MSs and their regional institutions will have to rely on the cooperation of non-MSs. Especially threatening to neo-functionalism is the possibility that in response to such changes in the broader international context, actors within the TRO will find themselves having to deal with the "high" politics of national identity and security – for which they have no mandate or experience.

6 *Fairness*. Finally, the entire process of regional integration should be perceived by a substantial proportion of its victims as "fair." Some of this will be ensured by the suppositions discussed in I.2 with regard to the evenly shared distribution of benefits and actor perception of this, but fairness is a more elusive property in political relations, especially among states and populations that have had previous histories of unfair treatment by each other. The criteria for judging fairness (or justice) are highly subjective, but it is a definite advantage for any given TRO if these criteria are relatively similar – or at least commensurate – across MSs.

If any one of these hypotheses is proven wrong when applied to the EU, then there are grounds for questioning the validity of that aspect of neo-functionalism – unless, of course, this unexpected variation can be "explained away" by mitigating factors. These disproven results also suggest that there might be some corresponding increase in the likelihood that the EU could disintegrate. If substantial chunks of them are not confirmed, that likelihood should increase exponentially. Needless to say, if all of them are falsified, neo-functionalism should be abandoned in favor of some other theory of regional integration (or the effort at theorizing should be abandoned altogether on the grounds that the EU experience is so *sui generis* that no theory can be based on it). In the next section, we thus attempt a first empirical exploration of the aforementioned suppositions and hypotheses.

3 Empirical evidence: toward disintegration?

In this section we review empirical evidence that could (dis)confirm the above outlined suppositions and hypotheses. Due to lack of space, we limit ourselves to the exploration of the explicit ones;[4] to this end, we rely on a variety of indicators and data sources, which we summarize in Table 9.1. Two caveats: First, the data we use for exploring these suppositions and hypotheses refer to a variable universe of MSs because the union has grown larger with successive enlargements. Second, because we are exploring many expectations simultaneously, we focus on national and EU averages, rather than going into detail, e.g., how specific socioeconomic groups benefit from and/or perceive integration. We structure the empirical discussion as follows: First, we examine degrees of interdependence; second we assess the resulting benefits and how these are perceived by the publics; third, we discuss the role played by experts in this regard; fourth, we review evidence regarding the incremental character of integration and the respect of EU decisions and finally, we discuss conflict and politicization – which were intensified with the economic (2009–) and refugee crises (2015–).

4 Interdependence and hegemony? The case of trade

To explore supposition I.1 we begin by looking at trends in trade, which was the primary initial objective of economic integration and can help us assess the degree of interdependence among EU MSs. To recall, neo-functionalism assumes an increase in interdependence for all Union members equally, and for all members of the Union compared to third countries. The situations where extra-EU trade is more important than intra-EU trade, or when one or a few members become "hegemons" contradict our hypotheses and may also be signaling a higher likelihood of disintegration.

Surprisingly, empirical research on the relationship between economic integration and trade began only in the 2000s. The few studies on the topic suggest a positive relationship between integration and trade: As economic integration deepened within the EC/EU, so did the reciprocal trade among EU members (Agur *et al.* 2007; Rose 2000, 2001, 2004). While the data show a slow but steady rise of intra-EU trade, they also manifest that EU members become more and more open to trade in general, including an increase of external trade (e.g. Agur *et al.* 2007). Although intra-EU trade has been traditionally higher than

Table 9.1 Explicit hypotheses: indicators and data sources

1 The removal of barriers to trade, investment and human mobility (negative integration) and the creation of common, market-regulating rules (positive integration) will produce a continuous increase in the *interdependence of MSs.*	
Indicators	Intra-EU trade and Extra-EU trade in the EU28 in 2013; trends of individual MSs' imports from within and outside the EU (2000–2010).
Sources	Eurostat/Knoema, O'Neill and Terzi (2014), Sadeh (2014)
2 The net *benefits* from this increase in regional interdependence will be *positive*, both for the economy as a whole and for the population at large.	
Indicators	Public attitudes to disintegration of the Union (i.e., how would you feel what if the EU had been scrapped?) (1973–2004); personal meanings of the EU (1997 and 2001); perceived benefits of own country's EU membership (2007 and 2011); Okun's Misery Index; unemployment rates; growth rates.
Sources	Eurobarometer; Lechman (2009); Eurostat/Knoema
3 The primary expected benefit from regional integration should be greater *security*, both against predation by outsiders and in favor of material benefits from insiders.	
Indicators	Public opinion regarding appropriate level of government for security defense in 2000 and in 2010; evolution of prospective perception of (exclusively national) identity (1989–1995).
Sources	Eurobarometer
4 Neo-functionalism assigns a major role to *experts*, both those in the TRO and those in the respective national bureaucracies.	
Indicators	Composition of expert groups that consult the European Commission; role of epistemic communities in the crisis and their conflicts.
Sources	Chwieroth (2007); Gornitzka and Sverdrup (2011); Rosenhek (2013)
5 *Respect* of EU decisions	
Indicators	Total number of cases before the ECJ (1970–2010); new actions for failure of a MS to fulfill its obligations (1952–2010).
Sources	European Court of Justice (2010)
6 Economic *convergence*	
Indicators	Growth rates
Sources	Balcerowicz *et al.* (2013)
7 *Incremental* positive and negative *integration*	
Indicators	Amount of EU legislation; activity of the court
Sources	Miller (2010); European Court of Justice (2010)
8 *Conflict* and *politicization*	
Indicators	Anti-EU party success, social movements
Sources	Accornero and Pinto (2015); Brack (2015); Della Porta (2012); Beichelt *et al.* (2014)

Source: Eurostat.

extra-EU trade, there is variation across MSs; also, Eurostat has observed a change in recent years: intra-EU trade is decreasing.[5] Figure 9.1 shows the difference between EU internal and external trade for the 28 MSs in 2013. Overall, for the EU28, intra-EU trade is much higher than extra-EU trade, though there is

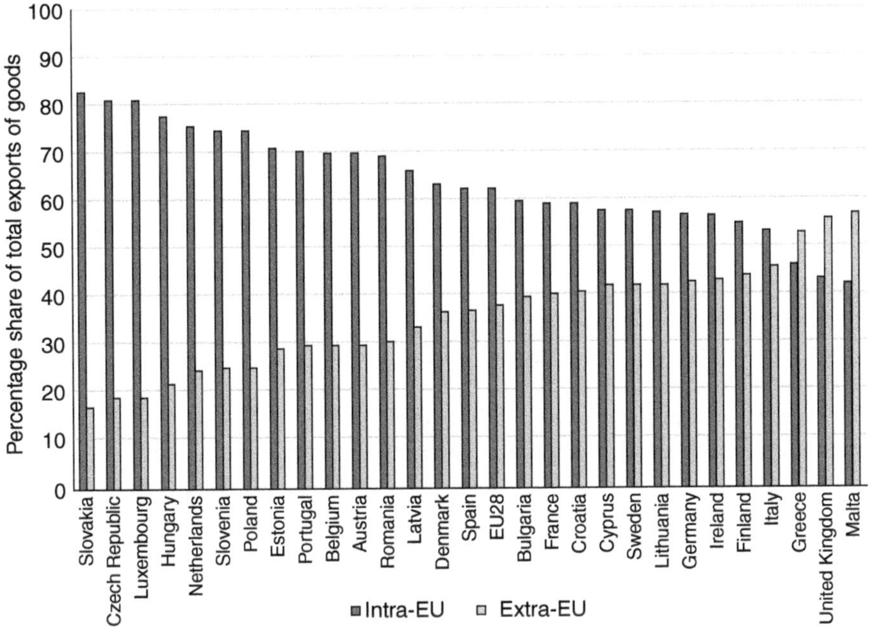

Figure 9.1 Intra-EU and extra-EU trade in the EU28 in 2013.

Source: Eurostat.

variation among MSs. Three EU MSs – Greece, Malta and the UK – engaged more in external than in internal trade in 2013.

In a recent paper O'Neill and Terzi (2014) analyze changes in world GDP and trade and extrapolate what the world trade situation will look like by 2020 if the current trend continues. According to their study, by 2020 the three key EU economies of Germany, France and Italy will be focusing their trade relationships with countries outside the euro area (China; developing/emerging markets) more than within it. Their analysis also suggests that the euro may not have the expected beneficial effects on trade (O'Neill and Terzi 2014).

However, recent research that focuses specifically on the effect of the common currency on trade shows that it has benefited intra-EU trade (Sadeh 2014). Sadeh's (2014) analysis of the euro's impact by type of MS in the period 1999–2006 also produces the interesting finding that trade increased more among peripheral states of the eurozone (Greece, Italy, Ireland, Portugal and Spain) than among its core member states (Austria, Belgium, Finland, France, Germany and the Netherlands). During the same period, an increase in trade was observed between the periphery and the core of the eurozone, albeit less than that observed among the peripheral states. This study thus concludes that at the micro-economic level the euro works despite its macroeconomic difficulties, and also suggests that, in the long run, the euro is especially helpful to peripheral countries.

When we look at trends of individual MSs in imports and exports of goods within and outside the EU, we find great variation, and there is a single MS that performs much better than all others. Figure 9.2 shows longitudinal trends of imports from within (top graph) and outside (bottom graph) the EU. Based on the graph on the left, which concerns imports with the EU, we can see that only a few countries stand out. Germany is the leading importer inside the EU (top line), followed by France, the UK, Italy, Belgium, the Netherlands and Spain; all other countries crowd at the bottom, with Austria and Sweden leading this group. The graph on the right shows imports from outside the EU: here again Germany represents the top line on the graph, followed by the UK, the Netherlands, Italy, France, Spain, Belgium, Austria and Sweden; all the other countries are located at the very bottom.

Figure 9.3 demonstrates the trends in exports within the EU (top graph) and outside it (bottom graph). Regarding exports within the EU, a few among the many EU members stand out. Germany once again has the lead, although in this case its "distance" from other MSs is much larger than in the case of imports. Germany is followed by the Netherlands, France, Belgium, Italy, UK; Spain leads the laggard group, followed by Austria, Sweden, Ireland and Portugal. When it comes to exports beyond the EU market (bottom graph), Germany has by far the best performance, followed by France, the UK, Italy; among the countries in the bottom of the graph the best performers are the Netherlands, Belgium, Spain, Sweden and Ireland.

To summarize, economic integration seems to have benefited trade among MSs of the EU. At the same time, there are clear indications of German hegemony, which consistently outperforms all other MSs (always top) across indicators. When comparing internal to external trade in the case of the EU's best performer, it seems that, to date, internal EU trade has brought more gains than external trade: in 2012 Germany exported more products to other EU MSs than to countries outside the Union (Figure 9.3, top and bottom graphs). That said, we observe a pronounced rise of Germany's exports *outside the EU* since the crisis, which may suggest that the EU's market hegemon is becoming more outward – rather than inward – looking in its search for trading partners.

5 Benefits for the economy and society

The benefits of interdependence for the economy and society are assumed to be positive and recognized by the public. To examine suppositions I.2 and I.3, we combine related data on public opinion with data on citizens' economic discomfort in each MS and trends of MSs' economic growth. We examine public attitudes toward disintegration, the benefits of EU membership, the EU's positive and negative connotations, the appropriate level of government for security and defense, and the evolution of national identity over time. Besides the aforementioned "subjective" evaluations of the benefits of integration, we review data on

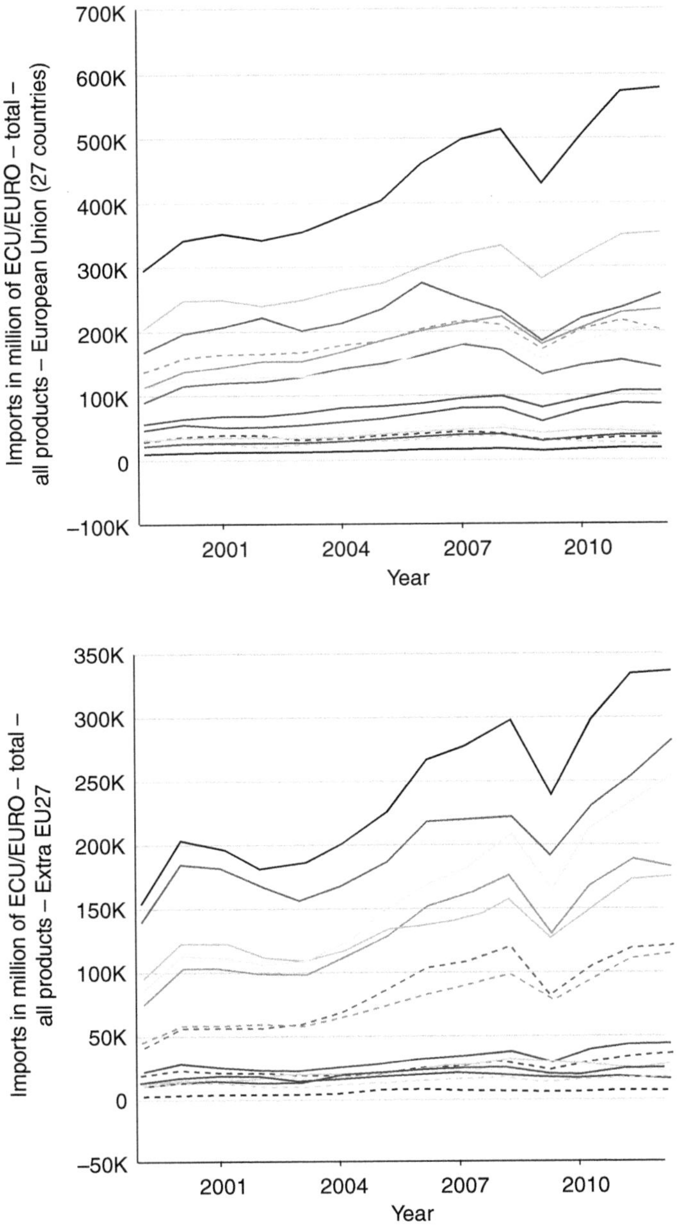

Figure 9.2 Trends of imports from within (top) and outside (bottom) the EU27 (2000–2013).

Source: Eurostat/Knoema.

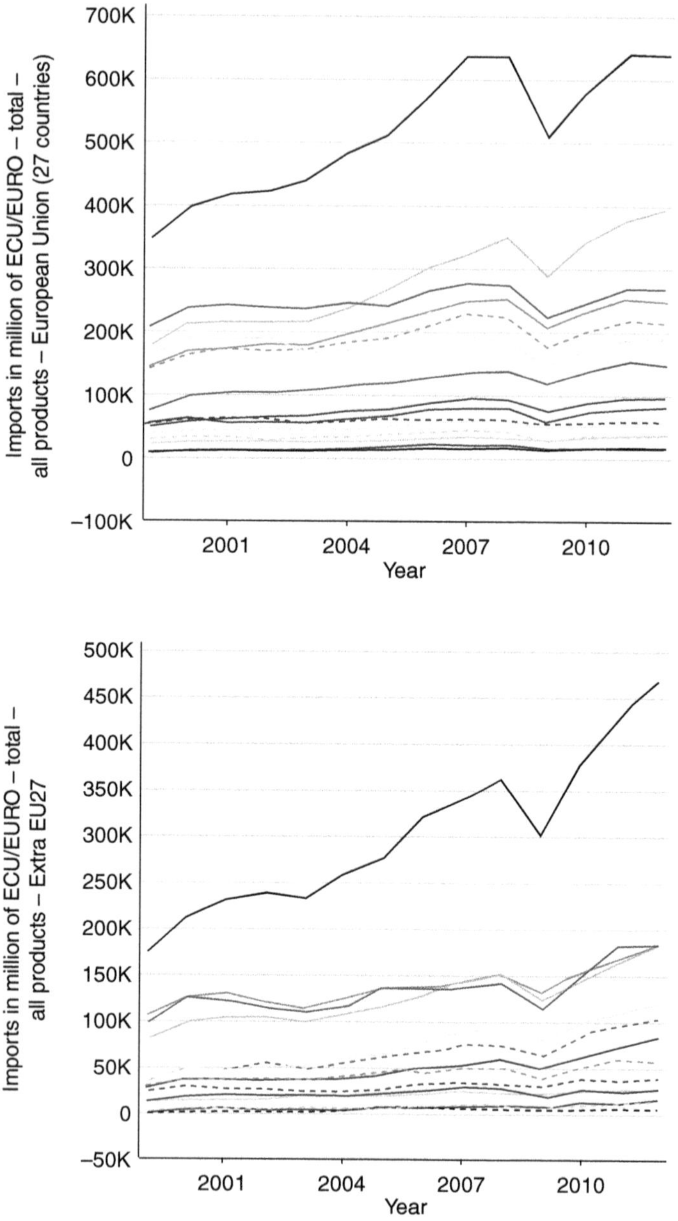

Figure 9.3 Trends of exports within (top) and outside (bottom) the EU27 (2000–2013).
Source: Eurostat/Knoema.

economic discomfort, which constitute "objective" evaluations of the benefits for society, as well as data on growth, which constitute indicators for the benefit experienced by a MS's economy as a whole.

5.1 Public perceptions of European integration

How do general publics perceive integration? How much one appreciates something is reflected in how much one would care about losing it. Fortunately, the Eurobarometer used to contain a question that allows us to measure attitudes of EU citizens to disintegration of the Union. More specifically, EU citizens were asked: "*If you were told tomorrow that the European Community (Common Market) – European Union – had been scrapped, would you be very sorry about it, indifferent or very relieved?*" Unfortunately, we cannot see the impact of the crisis on such attitudes – which has without doubt affected how much citizens appreciate the EU – because the data stop in 2004. Although this question was not asked after this point, it is nonetheless useful to see how Europeans felt about the possibility of disintegration *prior* to the crisis – when "things were going well" at the EU level. Indeed, the data we examine here cover the period from the 1970s until 2004, when important steps toward further economic integration were made, such as the Maastricht and Amsterdam Treaties (in 1992 and 1997 respectively) and the circulation of euro coins (in 2002). Indeed, if citizens perceived integration as beneficial, there should be a sizable amount of them that would indeed feel sorry for the collapse of the Union.

Figure 9.4 shows that, until a decade ago, while a considerable amount of citizens within the EU would be very sorry to hear that the EU collapsed, an equally large amount would be indifferent to disintegration. We also observe that since the 1990s indifference started rising above 40 percent while the percentage of citizens that would feel very sorry if the Union would disintegrate started declining below 40 percent. In the mid-1990s the trends reversed; interestingly, the decline of those who would mourn the end of the Union is parallel to important integration steps, such as the Maastricht (1992) and Amsterdam (1997) treaties; around the introduction of the common currency (2002) we do observe an upward trend. At the same time, it seems that when the data collection stopped both indifference and sadness were experiencing a parallel increase. Over time, we observe a small increase in the percentage of citizens that would even be relieved if the Union disintegrated, while those that do not know how to answer this question remain relatively stable over time, around 10 percent.

Citizens' attitudes to disintegration are related to their perception of the country's membership in the EU, but also to their own, personal perception of the EU's role in their life, and the expectations that are bound to this. First, recognition and appreciation of integration by the citizens can be understood by additionally examining the percentages of citizens that have a positive perception of their country's membership. If these percentages decline over time, it is evident citizens who support integration become fewer and fewer. Figure 9.5 shows

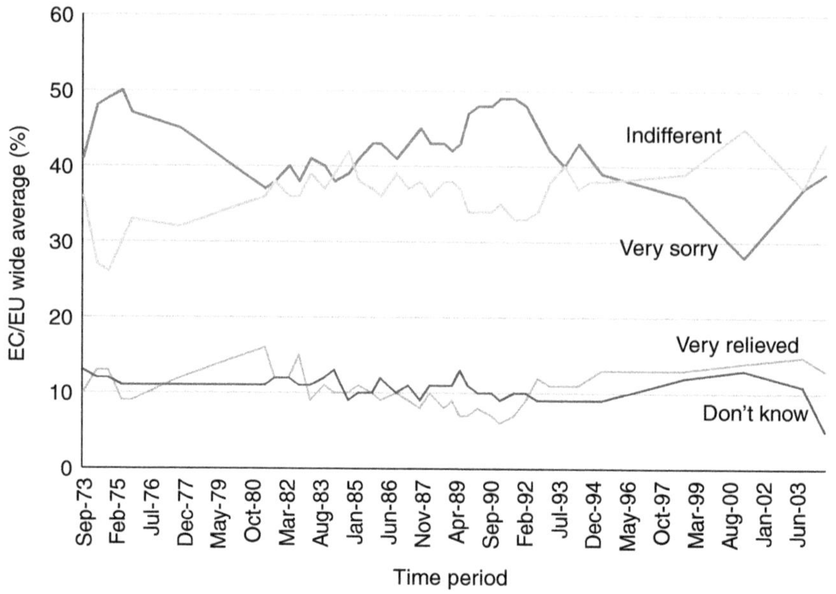

Figure 9.4 Attitudes to the disintegration of the European Community/Union during 1973–2004.

Source: Eurobarometer.

national averages of EU citizens who think that their country has benefited from EU membership both prior to (2007) and during the crisis (2011).

Figure 9.5 demonstrates a clear decline in the proportion of citizens with a positive perception of EU membership before and after the crisis. With the exception of Finland (the most Euro-skeptic MS), where we observe a slight increase in the percentage of Finns that view EU membership positively, all other MSs experienced decline during the crisis years. Again, we do not know how this trend evolved after 2011 because we lack more recent data, so we can only speculate that the trend continues downward, given the developments in the Union and its incapacity to solve the crisis until this moment. Recent analyses of trust in the EU (Armingeon and Ceka 2013), which is a different indicator of the EU's relationship with the citizens it is supposed to serve, also portray a worrisome picture.

Second, we also examine how Europeans perceive the (expected) benefits from integration from a personal perspective. Do citizens associate the EU with positive or negative expectations? To answer this question we examine what the EU means to them personally based on data from 1997 and 2001. Figure 9.6 shows percentages of EU citizens for whom the EU has positive and negative connotations.[6] First, we see that for the majority of respondents the meaning of the EU was linked to positive expectations: The EU meant facilitating travel, a

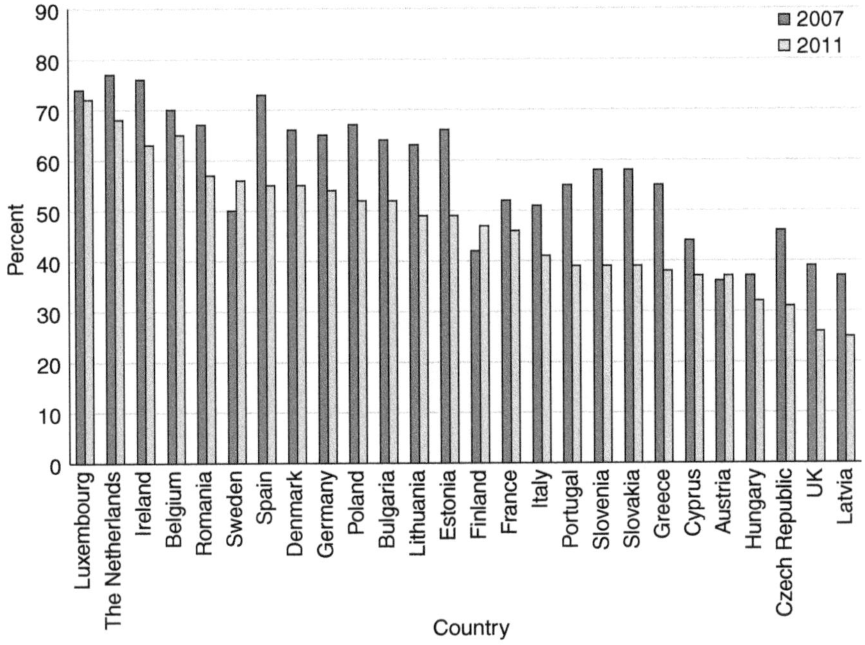

Figure 9.5 Perceived (own country's) benefit from EU membership across the EU in 2007 and in 2011.

Source: Eurobarometer.

European government, improving the economic situation in Europe; creating a better future for young people and providing jobs; ensuring peace and protecting citizens' rights. In sum, the EU meant a lot more than a peace project. For some Europeans, however, the EU presented a risk of losing cultural diversity, while for others it represented bureaucracy, waste of time and money or just an illusory utopia.

When we compare the data from 1997 to that of 2001 we do not see stark differences. Nonetheless, the percentage of those Europeans for whom the EU signified a better future for youths, the creation of jobs and economic improvement, as well as the warranty of lasting peace, declined. At the same time, the percentages of those who identified the EU with easy travel, a European government and the protection of citizens' rights increased slightly. Those for whom the EU had a negative meaning decreased slightly.

As we lack more recent data we cannot present an accurate picture of the EU's current reputation. Yet, we suspect that the picture sketched by Figure 9.6 has changed radically. First, Euro-skeptic parties that oppose the EU out of fear of cultural but also economic losses (e.g., Lefkofridi and Michel 2014) are on the rise. Second, the economic crisis generated massive unemployment and

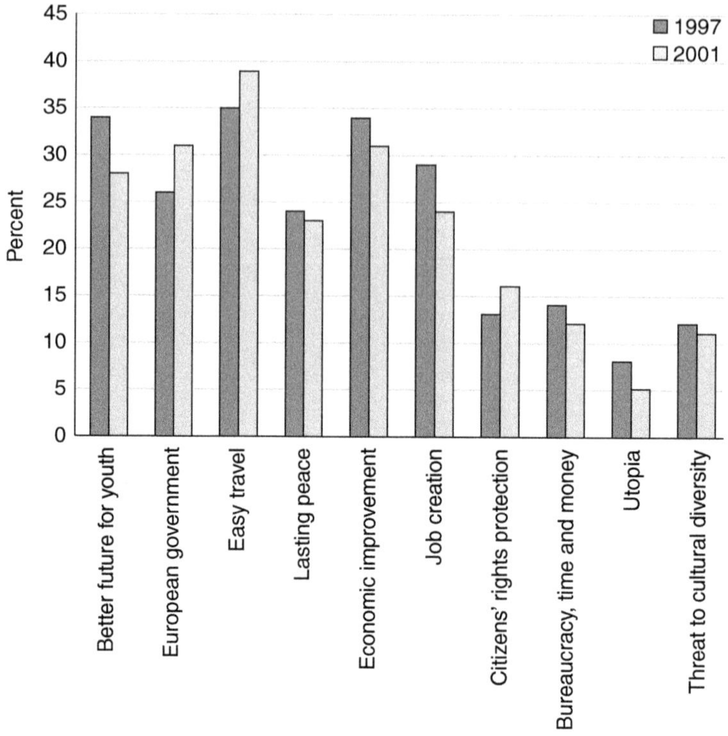

Figure 9.6 Personal meanings of the EU in 1997 and in 2001.

Source: Eurobarometer.

hindered growth, which in turn hurt the image of the EU as an economic solution, or the creator of jobs and of a better future for the young. Third, the refugee crisis in the summer of 2015 led to the partial and erratic suspension of the Schengen Agreement and the reestablishment of border controls between EU MSs, the absence of which had facilitated travel.

Furthermore, neo-functionalism specifically assumed that the primary benefit would be greater security. We take a close look at public preferences regarding the appropriate level of government for security and defense. Though the only data available concern the period 1989–1995, it is worth examining because this was a crucial period for integration. Key treaties – the Single European Act (1987), the Maastricht Treaty (1992) and the Amsterdam Treaty (1997) – which were signed right before, during and after the period covered by these data were milestones for European integration. Therefore, these data give us a hint about whether mass publics during that decisive period tended to support positively the expansions of its *compétences* in very "sensitive" policy areas: If European integration fails to create a feeling of security, the public will be more inclined to believe that security and defense should be dealt with at the national level, without any interference from the EU. On the contrary, if integration makes Europeans feel safer among themselves, the public will be more likely to think that their national government should decide on security and defense matters together with their EU partners. Figure 9.7 shows that European public opinion is divided on this question: about half of the respondents think that security and defense matters should be decided at the national level (by their own country's government exclusively), while the other half thinks that security and defense should be decided jointly with the EU. While there are small fluctuations over time, it is remarkable that both views are equally strong. Also interesting is the fact that while initially (1989–1990) no respondents claimed not to know how to answer this question, the amount of "don't know" responses rises and stabilizes around 5 percent.

An interrelated question is the extent to which integration impacted on Europeans' identity. Since integration was conceived by its founders as an antidote to nationalism, one would expect that the proportion of EU citizens who perceive themselves as exclusively "national" citizens would decline over time. Figure 9.8 shows the percentages of EU15 respondents who see themselves as only national (e.g., Belgian, Italian) in the near future in 2000 and again in 2010. First, we observe that the national averages vary, ranging from around 20 percent

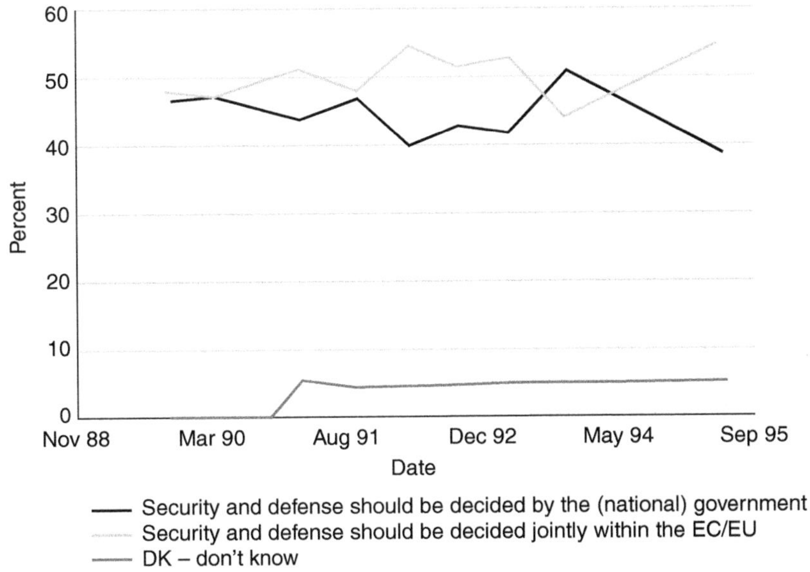

Figure 9.7 Public opinion regarding the appropriate level of government for security and defense during 1989–1995.

Source: Eurobarometer.

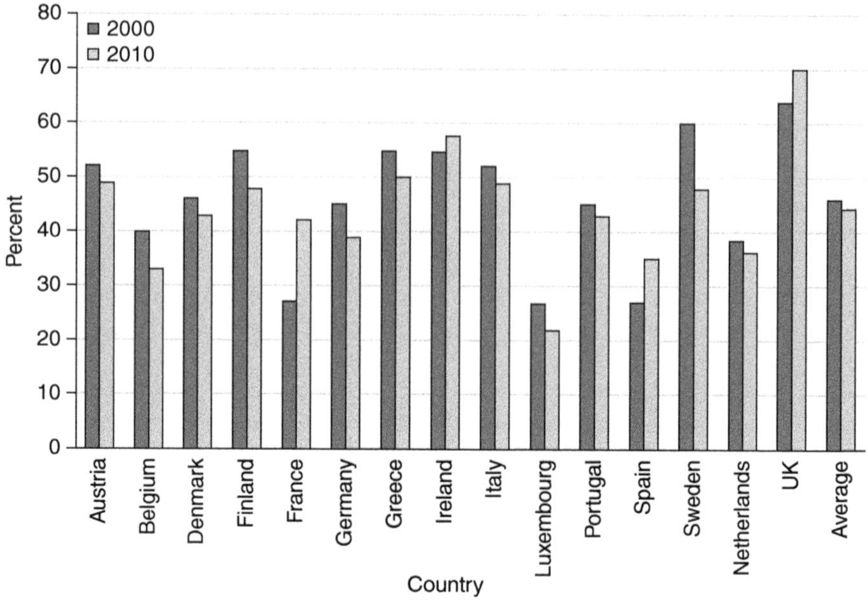

Figure 9.8 Exclusively national perception of identity in 2000 and in 2010.

Source: Eurobarometer.

to 70 percent of citizens who identify exclusively with the nation state (in Luxembourg and the UK respectively). The change during this decade is small, but there is a general trend to decline. Except for France, Ireland, Spain and the UK, in all other MSs the national average of citizens that perceive themselves as exclusively national decreases, albeit slightly. The EU15 average of exclusively national identity remains above 40 percent during a decade of important EU-level developments such as the Treaty of Nice (2001), the European Convention (2002) and the Lisbon Treaty (2009). The above picture of a divided EU public in terms of self-perception as exclusively national (Figure 9.8) combined with a divided public opinion regarding EU involvement in matters of security and defense (Figure 9.7) is telling also for supposition II.5. Of course, one of the reasons why the national self-perception persists may be public ignorance about their rights as "EU citizens." It is hard to play – not to mention like – any game if you do not understand the rules.

Indeed, the development of EU citizenship has faced numerous challenges – mostly due to the difficulties people encounter regarding getting informed about and exercising their rights as EU citizens. This is what a recent study of European citizenship in times of crisis by Closa and Vintila (forthcoming: 29) observes; it concludes that "the social and political panorama in the EU in 2013 is a long way from the initial optimism that accompanied the formal introduction of EU citizenship twenty years ago." Since the EU system is not taught in primary schools (as national political systems are) EU citizens are deprived of information that sets the fundaments of one's belonging to a political community, i.e., knowledge of how the system of governance (rules, institutions, procedures, etc.) that affects their everyday life works.

5.2 Economic prosperity

Economic prosperity has been one of integration's key goals. One way of assessing the distribution of benefits within the Union as well as trends of economic convergence (suppositions I.2 and I.6) is to look at the index of economic discomfort, unofficially known as "Okun's Misery Index." This indicator specifies the level of economic malaise as the unweighted sum of the annual inflation and unemployment rate. Lechman's (2009) calculations of this index in EU MSs (2001–2007) prior to the current crisis revealed mixed variation over time and across states. According to Lechman (2009), discomfort has been lowest in Austria, Denmark and the Netherlands, and highest in Eastern European countries, who were the last to join the Union; that said, since these countries joined, their economic discomfort decreased. Interestingly, Germany is the only strong economy whose index approaches the indices of much weaker economies, such as Greece or Portugal. We suspect that this is because Germany has for a long time engaged in wage dumping in order to acquire a competitive advantage vis-à-vis other MSs. Around 30 percent of workers in Germany work for hourly remuneration that is below the poverty level (BBC 2013).

Since we lack data to demonstrate the evolution of misery indices during the crisis, next we consider trends of a key component of this index: unemployment. Figure 9.9 visualizes unemployment rates within the Union and the eurozone over time compared to that of the USA and Japan (top lines) as well as current rates across EU MSs (bottom lines). First, the top graph shows unemployment trends in the EU and the eurozone during 2000–2015, compared to those of the USA and Japan. In detail, we see that, contrary to Japan's stability of low unemployment over time, the USA and the EU experienced a rise in unemployment rates at the beginning of the crisis in 2009. However, the parallel evolution of the USA and EU unemployment rates was very short-lived; since 2010 the US trend is downward, the EU is upward. This very stark divergence is interesting because the EU and the USA chose very different methods to deal with the economic crisis (see also below, where we discuss the role played by experts in this regard).

Second, the bottom graph of Figure 9.9 demonstrates current levels of unemployment (2014–2015) in each of the MSs. Here we see tremendous differences: Unemployment rates range from 4.7 percent in Germany to 22.5 percent in Greece. This sharp rise has, of course, impacted levels of poverty. As mentioned above, we lack data on the Okun Index in the EU for recent years; however, at least for the eurozone members, inflation is regulated by the ECB, not by the MSs. So based on the aforementioned rise of unemployment, it is normal to expect that misery may have become more salient in some MSs today. For

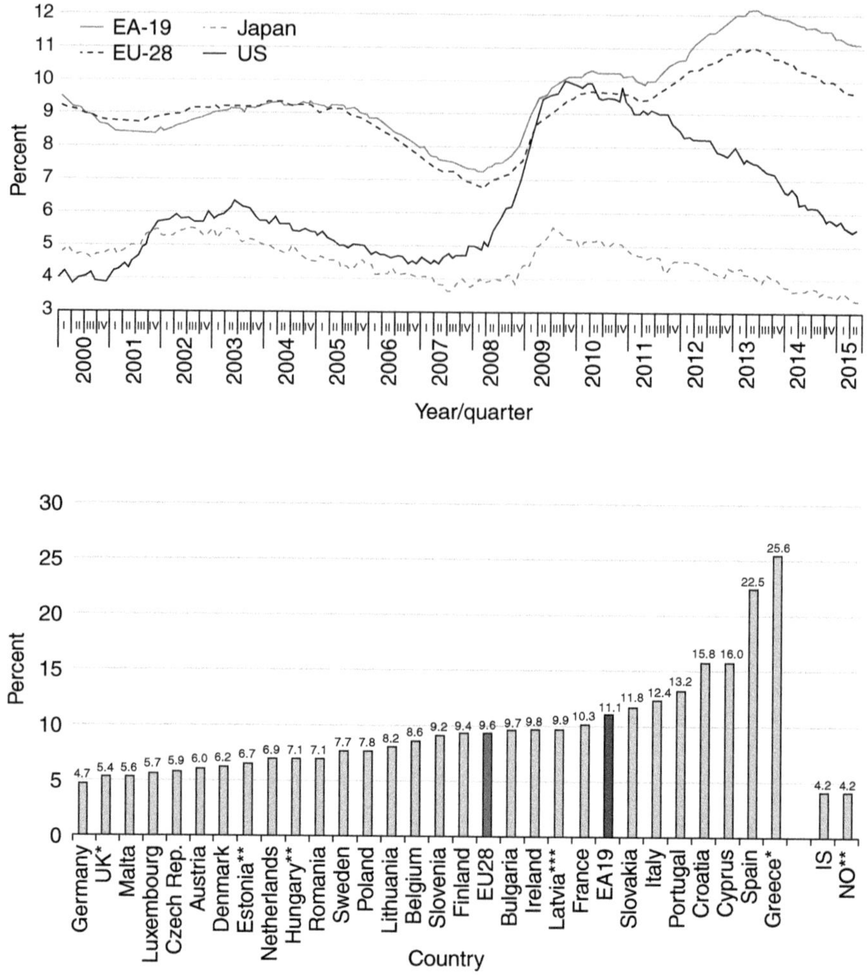

Figure 9.9 Unemployment. *Top graph:* Trends in unemployment over time in the EU and the eurozone (two top lines), Japan (line in the middle) and the USA (bottom line) during 2000–2015. *Bottom graph:* Current unemployment in each of the EU MSs (2014–2015).

Sources: Eurostat/Knoema.

Notes
* March 2014;
** April 2015;
*** Q1 2015.

instance, in the hardest hit MS poverty has seen dramatic increases since the beginning of the crisis. A report by the Director of the National Bank of Greece in 2013 shows that in 2011 (already two years into the crisis) 21.4 percent of the Greek population lived below the poverty line, while 31 percent was at its threshold and, hence, threatened by social exclusion; the amount of people living in households where no one was employed increased by 53.7 percent between 2010–2011 (Bank of Greece 2013: 101–103).

Last but not least, and in relation to supposition I.6, we should note since the onset of the crisis the EU has been performing very poorly in terms of growth, especially when compared to the USA and Japan (Balcerowicz *et al.* 2013). It should be noted, however, that some countries who had experienced decline in growth earlier (Sweden in the mid-1990s, Germany in the 2000s) have witnessed an increase ever since – a trend that continued through the crisis. On the contrary, Italy has had a steady decline in growth since the mid-1990s. Greece, on the other hand, experienced a downward trend until the 2000s, but then boomed until the crisis hit, and growth sharply declined ever since (Balcerowicz *et al.* 2013). Since the beginning of the crisis, the group of "growth leaders" in the EU consists of Germany, Sweden and many countries that joined the EU very recently (Bulgaria, Estonia, Latvia, Lithuania, Malta, Poland and Slovakia).

All the above contradicts neo-functionalist hypotheses that the distribution of benefits would not be skewed, and that MSs would converge in terms of economic performance and social protection. We are currently witnessing exactly the opposite: In the name of increasing competitiveness and making the labor market more flexible, troubled countries' governments have pursued the reduction of wages and pensions. Within the framework of austerity applied to Greece, for instance, the measures implemented in the context of the international loan mechanism (Memoranda of Understanding, MoU) have been combined with violations of trade union and collective bargaining rights (ILO 2012). The situation of labor in Greece after the Troika therapy is entirely different from other MSs, such as France or Austria – so by no means can we speak of convergence of social protection within the EU.

6 The role and conflicts of epistemic communities

Yet, if the Union is performing as badly in terms of growth, unemployment and convergence, the question is raised: What has been the role played by experts? To explore supposition I.4, we review evidence of the behavior of the epistemic community in which the neo-functionalist framework put so much faith.

The role played by experts in EU policy making is well established in the literature (Radaelli 1999), from environmental (Zito 2001) to security issues (David Cross 2007), the creation of the EMU (Verdun 1999) and the convergence of competition policy (Waarden and Drahos 2002). At the same time, a recent empirical study by Gornitzka and Sverdrup (2011) shows that, while the Commission relies on a large expert group system for developing, monitoring and implementing EU policy, the principal actors in this expert group system are officials of national governments. National administrators and national authorities competent on the policy issue of concern constitute 69.8 percent and 34.1 percent, respectively, of experts participating in Commission expert groups, while regional and local administration officials amount to 8.1 percent. At the same time, scientists and business/industry constitute 33.3 percent and 28.5 percent respectively. This study observes a much smaller participation in the Commission's expert group system of NGOs (16.7 percent), practitioners (12.7 percent), social partners/unions (11.8 percent), consumers (8 percent) and international organizations (2.2 percent).

Expertise has been contrasted with politicization (Radaelli 1999) and it seems that, at least for most of the integration process, conflicts were internalized and resolved without reaching the outside, political world.[7] It is very important to note here that, prior to the crisis, a coherent and dedicated group of neoliberal economists came to dominate both regional and global international financial institutions. This global epistemic community has resulted in policy choices becoming increasingly determined by their assumptions, models and policies (Chwieroth 2007). As Rosenhek (2013: 270) explains, the "interpretative plots of the crisis were not offered by outsiders, but rather by established and powerful actors, such as the Fed and the ECB, with recognized expertise and high epistemic authority." Notwithstanding key differences regarding their position in the political economy, their institutional legacy and their definition of the main task of central banks, the diagnoses, notions and themes offered by the Fed and the ECB were very similar (Rosenhek 2013).

During the crisis, the neoliberal epistemic community in Europe by and large internalized its conflicts and has thus had a very consistent approach in favor of austerity. Experts advocated fiscal balance and budgetary austerity with the assumption that this would result in monetary stability and a shift of available investment from public institutions to private firms, which in turn was supposed to have triggered a general expansion of employment, production and prosperity. So much epistemic authority did these experts have that they were even appointed to govern troubled countries (*vide* Monti in Italy and Papademos in Greece). Indeed, the solution of the crisis was thought of as a technocratic issue, as a matter of fiscal consolidation which could only occur under the "objective" rule of technocrats who were not constrained by electoral clienteles. Parties, on the other hand, avoided as much as possible to get their hands dirty with cutting their clienteles' salaries, pensions or even their jobs in order to bring the common household in order. In the case of Greece, for example, the austerity measures lasted for six years although they resulted in GDP shrinking by 25 percent over four years, unemployment rising to 25 percent (and youth unemployment to 50 percent); yet, the epistemic community was insisting that the same kind of medicine be continued.

The neo-functionalism suppositions and hypotheses regarding the role of experts as well as their conflicts (I.4) seem to be confirmed. However, on the issue of whether "austerity was the right medicine," the trans-Atlantic epistemic consensus had been recently challenged. The USA pursued very different policies compared to the EU (e.g., invested money to create jobs and growth) and was much more successful in getting through the crisis and reversing unemployment trends (see Figure 9.9). The rupture between the USA and EU neoliberal economists is also reflected in the fact that the IMF published a report that clearly says that Greek debt is not sustainable (after years of not having expressed a clear position[8]) in an effort to shape political developments during the negotiations of the third Greek bailout in 2015. The timing of the publication was as critical as the content: The IMF management proposed to publish this report on short notice during the meeting of the IMF's board on the Wednesday before the Greek referendum of Sunday July 5, 2015.[9] Among Greece's EU partners, the creditor-countries rightly feared its potential impact on the Sunday vote; but they were heavily outnumbered.

However, the US members of the IMF, who were in favor of its publication, insisted on it becoming public (Reuters 2015a). It is important to note that top economists from the USA have been very critical of the kind of economic mantra Europeans have been following, and vociferously contributed to the debate on the Greek referendum. They even encouraged the Greeks to vote "no" to more austerity (Galbraith 2015; Krugman 2015; Stiglitz 2015), even contrary to the 2015 recommendation by the president of the Commission, Jean-Claude Juncker (and statements by the president of the European Parliament Martin Schulz and the president of the Eurogroup Jeroen Dijsselbloem) in favor of a "yes" vote. In detail, however, while American experts were advising the Greek people to resist further austerity because they assessed it as a *wrong policy direction*, the political leadership of EU institutions (Commission, Parliament and Eurogroup) threatened with Grexit.

7 Incremental integration and *pacta sunt servanta*

Suppositions I.5 and I.7 concern incremental integration and respect for EU decisions respectively. Here we will put special emphasis on the activity of the Court, which relates to both neo-functionalist hypotheses, namely the incremental pace of integration and respect for the legislation that is produced. Taken together, they help us capture integration in terms of both quantity and quality.

To begin with, the incremental trend is reflected by the fact that the EU's policy competences have been ever expanding: Not just more EU policies, but also in more and more policy areas. Throughout time, the EU's *acquis communautaire* – which any country wishing to join the EU must incorporate into its national system of governance – has increased in a number of important policy areas, involving both deregulation (e.g., competition policy) and regulation (e.g., environment). When the number of EU laws peaked in the 1980s (over 14,000 instruments), Commission president Delors even predicted that within ten years "80% of economic legislation, and perhaps also fiscal and social legislation, would be of EC/EU origin" (Miller 2010). Estimating this number is notoriously difficult,[10] and the more integration advances the more difficult it becomes to disentangle EU-induced from nationally induced law. This is also due to sectoral interdependence; integration in one policy sector has led to "technical" pressures pushing for integration in other sectors (Haas 1958; Schmitter 1969).

First, the amount of new cases brought to the European Court of Justice has increased over time, which reflects the production of ever more legislation (European Court of Justice 2011). According to official statistics, the Court has been more and more active over time, although not in a perfectly linear fashion. New cases have been expanding and so have competed and pending cases between 2007 and 2011 (European Court of Justice 2011). Figure 9.10 displays the number of cases and judgments before the ECJ during the period 1970–2010 – and illustrates the increasing trend.

Second, studies of implementation of EU law show that some states comply in most cases, whereas others delay transposition, be it due to domestic political conflict over the content of the policy or due to neglect (Falkner and Treib 2008; Falkner *et al.* 2007). When we examine the bulk of completed cases of failure to fulfill obligations we see that while most MSs have engaged in non-compliance, for some the situation is more pronounced (Court of Justice 2010). Whereas very few MSs do *not* figure on the statistics, more than half had trouble with fulfilling their obligations; the champions of "failure to comply" during 2007–2011 were, in ranked order: Italy, Spain, Greece, Belgium, Luxembourg, Portugal, France, Germany, Ireland, Austria, Sweden, Poland, Czech Republic, the Netherlands, the UK and Finland; all others have negligible percentages but this is primarily because they had transposed most of the *acquis* before joining. Figure 9.11 displays the actions against EU15 MSs during 1952–2010. There is variation across MSs and some perform better than others in implementing EU decisions. Denmark, Sweden and Finland stand out as the least troubling countries, while Italy stands out as the member with the highest number of actions, followed by France, Greece and Belgium. Note that except for Greece, all others in this group of misbehaving members are founding MSs.

Third, often the same violations are treated differently, which could impact the perception of fairness of integration (thus connecting with supposition II.6). At the beginning of the crisis there was much talk about lack of some MSs'

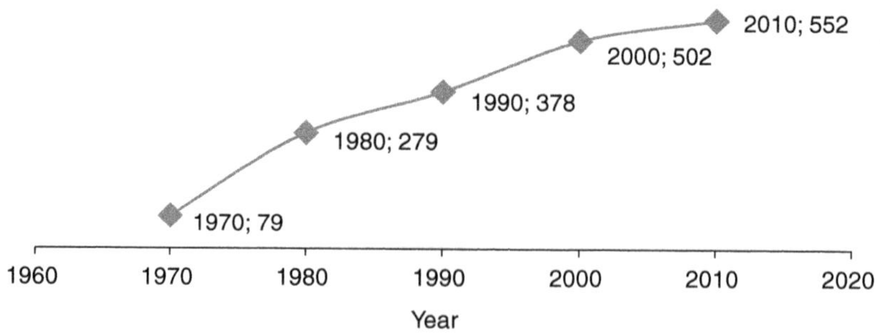

Figure 9.10 Number of cases and judgments before the European Court of Justice.
Source: Court of Justice (1970–2010).

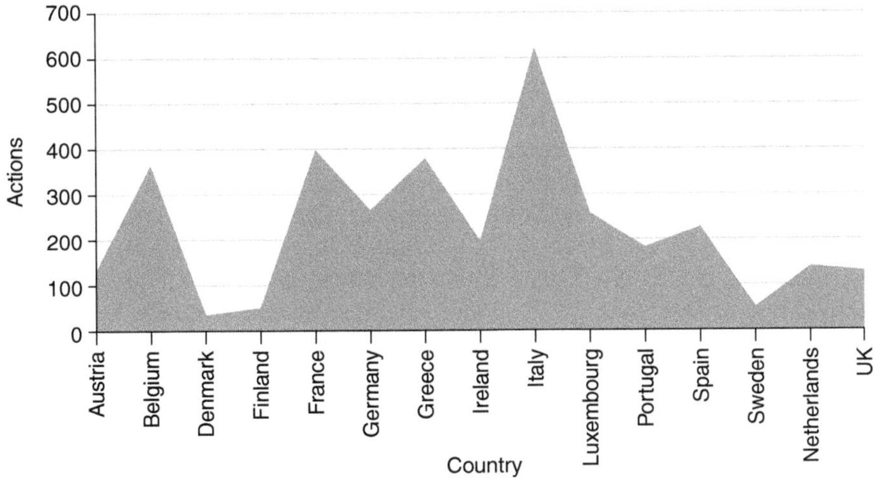

Figure 9.11 Number of actions against an EU member state (1952–2010).
Source: Court of Justice (1970–2010).

respect toward the Stability and Growth Pact (SGP). However, such violations had occurred previously and had been tolerated politically: When Germany and Portugal (2002) and then soon again later (2003) Germany and France were the first to violate the SGP rule[11] the Council of ministers did not resort to punitive measures, *despite* recommendations by the Commission. Violations of the SGP were not admonished, nor were violating members coerced to conform to the rule. Based on an understanding of unfavorable economic conditions, states violating the SGP were given flexibility and time to correct their deficits. As a result, the EU's capacity for legal coercion was substantially weakened.

However, the situation was very different a couple of years later. This time it was not the hegemon but a group of peripheral weaker economies who had breached the rules; and it was not just EU institutions, but also financial markets and international rating agencies who were involved (this, in turn, connects to II.5 on the role played by exogenous factors in causing and solving the crisis; for a discussion, see Lefkofridi and Schmitter 2015). That said, neo-functionalism assumed crises to be endogenous and its solutions as well (see however II.5 on exogenous shocks); in dealing with Greece, a eurozone member, the Council decided voluntarily to involve the IMF in the EU's internal business. The so-called "Troika" composed of the European Commission, the ECB and the IMF was the institution in charge, whose role is to make sure that MoU are honored through constant surveillance and close monitoring, including on-site visits and controls.

8 Conflict and politicization

Throughout the decades, the problem regarding the politicization of Europe was that it was nationally bounded, and controlled by national political parties. In terms of the functions parties are supposed to play in representative democracies they have consistently played a very irresponsible role, either by depoliticizing Europe or by demonizing Brussels (Lefkofridi and Schmitter 2015). Prior to the crisis, only parties at the extreme poles have mobilized around the issue of European integration, albeit for very different reasons. These parties do not politicize integration in order to defend it but to criticize it, and there are nuances and varied degrees of Euro-skepticism within the radical right and left camps. Some Euro-skeptic parties reject the EU altogether, whereas others want to keep it but change either its policies or its polity. Among the mainstream pro-European parties, there has been little or no effort to encourage public debates either about the benefits of European integration or about how to address the EU's problems and deficits. Prior to the crisis, the pro-EU mainstream had thus swept EU affairs under the carpet; when the crisis began this very elite felt threatened by the populist Euro-skeptics and indulged in a kind of rhetoric that had strong nationalist undertones. Five years into the crisis, when European elections were held in 2014, nationalist Euro-skeptic parties thrived. Although their potential for impact on EU-level legislation may be overestimated (Brack 2015), they do affect European developments by influencing the behavior of mainstream, typically pro-EU, parties.

This is true for most EU MSs, even for Germany, which stands out as the country that has benefited the most from economic (and monetary) integration as well as from the Greek crisis (Dany *et al.* 2015; Heinisch 2015). Instead of revealing these facts to the German public, however, the traditionally pro-European CDU/CSU opted for a nationalistic moralizing narrative against the South, when, actually, it is Germany's beggar-thy-neighbor policies that endanger the eurozone and make it impossible to rebalance its balance of payments (Spiecker 2015). Moreover, while German historians reminded their Chancellor that their country has benefited from debt relief many times in its history, the eurozone declared itself ready for a Grexit in July 2015. More specifically, Germany even proposed a "time out" from the eurozone, an exit for an undefined period, an unprecedented spill-back designed exclusively for the case of Greece, but which could prove contagious. This was a highly risky strategy, not least because the UK was preparing for a referendum on Brexit.

At first sight, then, developments seem to contradict some of the expectations outlined in I.8. During the crisis, however, the emergence of greater conflict with regard to European integration, its policies and its increased autonomy did result in ever more politicization, i.e., the mobilization of more and more EU citizens paying attention to the integration process and expressing a greater diversity of opinions about it. We saw an unprecedented mobilization of civil society: Citizens taking to the streets to join demonstrations against austerity and the solutions pursued at the EU and national levels that increased inequality and hurt the middle and lower classes were abundant in the last years (Accornero and Pinto 2015; Beichelt *et al.* 2014; Della Porta 2012). The amount of protest events is enough evidence that many European citizens are concerned with European integration and also that they are not happy with the policies pursued. Europe became even more politicized since the election of the Greek radical Left party SYRIZA in January 2015, whose first half-year in power produced turbulent relations between EU partners and Greece.

Perhaps the most positive of these, admittedly dramatic, developments is that Europeans got thirsty for EU news, about what EU officials and political leaders in other EU countries say or do (Poschardt 2015). Europeans are not as indifferent or ignorant about EU issues as (national) politicians in their (national) parties might have wished for. The days before the Greek referendum even saw thousands of Europeans taking to the streets to express their solidarity with the Greek people, encouraging them to vote "no" in the hope that this would force EU leaders to change policy direction (Reuters 2015b), while prominent academics from all around the world wrote op-eds framing the Greek problem in European terms. They warned that in the case of Grexit the future of the eurozone would be at stake, not because Greece matters much in the EU economy, but because it would set a precedent that would make the EU more vulnerable to global market forces in the future. This could also affect the performance of the strongest economies of the eurozone, given the importance of the currency for trade. However, because national parties feared it could jeopardize their voter optimization strategies, they carefully avoided the discussion about the sustainability of public debt. European solidarity was tested by the economic crisis and found severely wanting.

Unity and solidarity among MSs was tested again during the accommodation of refugees.[12] Germany would this time seek cooperation with all other MSs in dealing with the Syrian war refugees, who arrived *en masse* at the Greek island of Lesbos in the hope of finding shelter in the EU. The issue caused bitter divisions between as well as within the MSs, but also within parties. With national-chauvinism being very prominent in political elites' discourse, large parts of European publics were – at least initially – welcoming of the refugees and of the pursuit of European policy solutions.

9 Conclusion

In this chapter, we have used neo-functionalism as an analytical framework to explore conditions that would favor or hinder disintegration. We outlined a series of suppositions and hypotheses, which we then assessed on the basis of a variety of available data sources and related scholarly research. As this is an exploration of many different expectations simultaneously, we could not go into detail for each and every hypothesis. The empirical picture has been painted with a broad brush, which focused on national and EU averages. Future research should examine these hypotheses by differentiating more between but also within MSs; for instance, what is the exact picture of benefits if we disaggregate

European publics into different socioeconomic groups? Despite its limitations, this study provides a pioneering analysis of (in)fertile conditions for disintegration in Europe. In accordance with neo-functionalism we observe that: Integration has been by and large incremental and that interdependence among MSs did, indeed increase. Significant parts of the public in all MSs recognized the benefits of integration. Experts did play a key (even if not always positive) role and that – with the crisis – integration did become intensely politicized. However, contrary to neo-functionalist hypotheses, the distribution of benefits was skewed; in particular the German economy stands out as the key beneficiary in trade – although the German worker may not really "feel" this success due to decades of low wages. Furthermore, compliance has varied across time and countries – and so have the consequences for violations of the rules. In general, policy outputs at the time of writing (e.g. rising unemployment, lack of convergence) contradict the expectations of both neo-functionalism and EU citizens in terms of economic improvement or a better future for the young. In Southern Europe highly qualified young people are facing massive unemployment. Such results not only go against neo-functionalism, they also suggest that there might be some corresponding increase in the likelihood that the EU could disintegrate. Indeed, the EU is not in a good shape. Even worse, nationalism, chauvinism and racism – all maladies that European integration was supposed to cure – have re-emerged on the European continent. Of course, the EU is a moving target – all the more so in the midst of its most severe crises to date. Whatever one might conclude on the basis of its response so far might well be annulled by future developments.

Notes

1 This chapter is a reprint of Schmitter, P.C. and Lefkofridi, Z. (2016). Neofunctionalism as a theory of disintegration. *Chinese Political Science Review* 1 (1): 1–29.

2 For an extreme version based on the argument that this has always and only been the purpose of regional integration in Europe, see Milward (1992).

3 Both of these became formal obligations for membership in the EU, but were not at the time neo-functionalism was developed as a theory. It was simply presumed as a constant in the case of Europe, but it was a variable in such cases as South American and Central American integration in the 1970s and 1980s.

4 Though the empirics we discuss here do give hints regarding some of the implicit hypotheses, we hope that future research will engage in evaluating these hypotheses in detail.

5 More detailed information is to be found in Eurostat's online publication: http://ec.europa.eu/eurostat/statistics-explained/index.php/Intra-EU_trade_in_goods_recent_trends (accessed June 30, 2015).

6 This figure excludes those citizens who did not know how to answer this question (DK), who amounted to 5 percent in 1997 and 8 percent in 2001, as well as those for whom the EU meant something else (other), who amounted to 1 percent in both years when the question was asked.

7 A notable exception to this rule was the Bolkenstein directive on the liberalization of services, which was criticized by left-wing organizations as a route toward competition among workers, social dumping and income decline.

8 An IMF report issued in summer 2013 discussed the sustainability of the Greek debt

and admitted that the IMF made mistakes in the Greek case (*Wall Street Journal*, 2013); it did not, however, recommend a change in policy direction.

9 The Greek radical Left-led government (SYRIZA-ANEL) was elected in January 2015 with debt relief as its key goal. Although this government, like all others before, conceded (ideological) defeat by accepting *all* creditors' terms about austerity measures in exchange for financial assistance, the creditors also kept on refusing to put the debt issue on the negotiating table. The Greek government thus announced a referendum to be held on July 5, 2015. Greeks, six years under the austerity treatment already, were to accept or reject the creditors' proposal for further austerity measures. The referendum was decisive for Greece but also Europe (see below: politicization and conflict).

10 While there is no "totally accurate, rational or useful way" of calculating the percentage of national laws that are based on or influenced by the EU, related estimates of the proportion vary across members and range from 6.3 percent to 84 percent (Miller 2010).

11 Detailed figures are provided by Morris *et al.* (2006).

12 Though national political leaderships in general have not lived up to the expectations of the kind of integration they themselves pursued with their decisions, among the hardliners against the Greek government and the sharing of the "refugee burden" are the newest and poorest among the eurozone members. The latter wished to join the EU and the eurozone but did so at its most turbulent times.

References

Accornero, G., and Pinto, P. Ramos (2015). "Mild mannered"? Protest and mobilisation in Portugal under austerity, 2010–2013. *West European Politics* 38 (3): 491–515.

Agur, I., Dorrucci, E. and Mongelli, F.P. (2007). How did European institutional integration and intra-European trade interact?. *Economie internationale* 1 (109): 107–146 www.cairn.info/revue-economie-internationale-2007-1-page-107.htm. (accessed June 15, 2015).

Armingeon, K., and Ceka, B. (2013). The loss of trust in the European Union during the great recession since 2007: The role of heuristics from the national political system. *European Union Politics*, doi: 10.1177/1465116513495595.

Balcerowicz, L., Łaszk, A., Rzońca, A. and Kalina, L. (2013). *Economic Growth in the European Union*. Lisbon Council.

Bank of Greece (2013). *Director's Report for 2012*. Athens: Bank of Greece. www.bankofgreece.gr/BogEkdoseis/ekthdkth2012.pdf (accessed March 4, 2014).

Beichelt, T., Hahn, I., Schimmelfennig, F. and Worschech, S. (eds.) (2014). *Civil Society and Democracy Promotion*. Basingstoke: Palgrave Macmillan.

Brack, N. (2015). Populist and radical right parties at the 2014 European Parliament elections: much ado about nothing? In Fasone, C., Fromage, C. and Lefkofridi, Z. (eds.) *Parliaments, Public Opinion and Parliamentary Elections in Europe*, Florence: European University Institute, 92–104.

BBC (2013) Belgium Protests Over German Low Pay in EU Complaint. www.bbc.com/news/world-europe-22080862 (accessed November 1, 2015).

Chwieroth, J. (2007). Neoliberal economists and capital account liberalization in emerging markets, *International Organization* 61: 443–463.

Closa, Carlos, and Vintila, Cristina Daniela (forthcoming). *European citizenship in a time of crisis*.

Dany, G., Gropp, R. and von Schweinitz, G. (2015). Germany's benefit from the Greek crisis. *IWH Online – Leibniz Institut für Wirtschaftsforschung Halle*. www.iwh-halle.de/d/publik/iwhonline/io_2015-07.pdf (accessed September 10, 2015).

Davis Cross, M.A.K. (2007). An EU Homeland Security? Sovereignty vs. supranational order. *European Security* 16 (1): 79–97.

Della Porta, D. (2012). Critical trust: Social movements and democracy in times of crisis. *Cambio* 2 (4): 33–43.

European Court of Justice (2010). *Annual Report – Statistics*. http://curia.europa.eu/jcms/upload/docs/application/pdf/2011-05/ra2010_stat_cour_final_en.pdf (accessed July 1, 2015).

Falkner, G., and Treib, O. (2008). Three worlds of compliance or four? The EU-15 compared to new member states. *JCMS: Journal of Common Market Studies* 46 (2): 293–313.

Falkner, G., Hartlapp, M. and Treib, O. (2007). Worlds of compliance: Why leading approaches to European Union implementation are only "sometimes-true theories." *European Journal of Political Research* 46 (3): 395–416.

Galbraith, J.K. (2015). Only the "no" can save the euro. *Social Europe*, July 4, 2015. www.socialeurope.eu/2015/07/greece-only-the-no-can-save-the-euro (accessed July 4, 2015).

Gornitzka, Å., and Sverdrup, U. (2011). Access of experts: Information and EU decision-making. *West European Politics* 34 (1): 48–70.

Haas, E.B. (1958). *The Uniting of Europe: Political, Social and Economic Forces*. Stanford, CA: Stanford University Press.

Haas, E.B., and Schmitter, P.C. (1964). Economics and differential patterns of political integration: Projections about unity in Latin America. *International Organization* 18 (4): 705–737.

Heinisch, R. (2015). Auf dem Weg zu einem deutschen Europa? Eine internationale Perspektive. In Liebert, U., and Wolff, J. (eds.) *Interdisziplinäre Europastudien: eine Einführung*. Wiesbaden: Springer: 347–368.

ILO (2012). *365th Report of the Committee of Freedom of Association, GB.316/INS/9/1*. Geneva: ILO. www.ilo.org/wcmsp5/groups/public/--ed_norm/--relconf/documents/meetingdocument/wcms_193260.pdf (accessed January 25, 2014).

Juncker, J.-C. (2015). SPEECH/15/5274, June 29, 2015. http://europa.eu/rapid/press-release_SPEECH-15-5274_en.htm?locale=en (accessed July 6, 2015).

Krugman, P. (2015). The conscience of a liberal: Austerity arithmetic. *New York Times*, July 5, 2015. http://krugman.blogs.nytimes.com/2015/07/05/austerity-arithmetic/ (accessed July 7, 2015).

Lechman, E. (2009). Okuns and Barros Misery Index as an alternative poverty assessment tool: Recent estimations for European countries. University Library of Munich, Germany.

Lefkofridi, Z., and Michel, E. (forthcoming). The electoral politics of solidarity. In Banting, K., and Kymlicka, W. (eds.) *The Strains of Commitment: The Political Sources of Solidarity in Diverse Societies*. Oxford: Oxford University Press, Chapter 9.

Lefkofridi, Z., and Schmitter, P.C. (2015). Transcending or descending? European integration in times of crisis. *European Political Science Review* 7 (1): 3–22.

Miller, Vaughne (2010). How much legislation comes from Europe? *Economic Indicators* 7 (10).

Milward, A. (1992). *The European Rescue of the Nation-State*. London: Routledge.

Morris, R., Ongena, H. and Schuknecht, L. (2006). The reform and implementation of the Stability and Growth Pact, Occasional Paper Series No. 47/June 2006. European Central Bank. www.ecb.europa.eu/pub/pdf/scpops/ecbocp47.pdf (accessed July 7, 2015).

O'Neill, J., and Terzi, A. (2014). Changing trade patterns, unchanging European and global governance. Bruegel Working Paper 2014/02.

Poschardt, Ulf (2015). Die Krise macht uns jetzt zu wahrhaften Europäern. *Die Welt*. July 3, 2015. www.welt.de/debatte/kommentare/article143520903/Die-Krise-macht-uns-jetzt-zu-wahrhaften-Europaeern.html (accessed July 7, 2015).

Radaelli, C.M. (1999). The public policy of the European Union: Whither politics of expertise? *Journal of European Public Policy* 6 (5): 757–774.

Reuters (2015a). Exclusive: Europeans tried to block IMF debt report on Greece. Sources. www.reuters.com/article/2015/07/03/us-eurozone-greece-imf-idUSKCN0PD20120150703 (accessed July 3, 2015).

Reuters (2015b). "No more looting": Thousands rally across EU to express solidarity with Greece. http://rt.com/news/271582-europe-greece-rallies-support (accessed July 7, 2015).

Rose, A.K. (2000). One money, one market: The effect of common currencies on trade. *Economic Policy: A European Forum* 30: 7–33.

Rose, A.K. (2001). Currency unions and trade: The effect is large. *Economic Policy: A European Forum* 33: 449–457.

Rose, A.K. (2004). A meta-analysis of the effects of common currencies on international trade, NBER Working Paper 10373.

Rosenhek, Z. (2013). Diagnosing and explaining the global financial crisis: Central banks, epistemic authority, and sense making. *International Journal of Politics, Culture, and Society* 26 (3): 255–272.

Sadeh, T. (2014). The euro's effect on trade. *European Union Politics*. doi: 10.1177/1465116513517013.

Schmitter, P.C. (1969). Three neo-functional hypotheses about international integration. *International Organization* 23 (1): 161–166.

Schmitter, P.C. (1970). Central American integration: spill-over, spill-around or encapsulation? *JCMS: Journal of Common Market Studies* 9 (1): 1–48.

Schmitter, P.C. (2004). Neo-neofunctionalism. In: Wiener, A., and Diez, T. (eds.) *European Integration Theory*. Oxford: Oxford University Press.

Schmitter, P.C. (2012). A way forward? *Journal of Democracy* 23 (4): 39–46.

Spiecker, F. (2015). Konfusion von Links Bis Rechts: Was Soll Griechenland Tun?, *Flassbeck-Economics*, www.flassbeck-economics.de/konfusion-von-links-bis-rechts-was-soll-griechenland-tun (accessed August 7, 2015).

Stiglitz, J. (2015). How I would vote in the Greek referendum. *Guardian*. June 29, 2015. www.theguardian.com/business/2015/jun/29/joseph-stiglitz-how-i-would-vote-in-the-greek-referendum (accessed July 5, 2015).

Verdun, A. (1999). The role of the Delors Committee in the creation of EMU: An epistemic community? *Journal of European Public Policy* 6 (2): 308–328.

Vollard, H. (2008). A theory of European disintegration. Fourth Pan European Conference on EU Politics. September 25–27, 2008, University of Latvia, Riga, Latvia.

Waarden, F.V., and Drahos, M. (2002). Courts and (epistemic) communities in the convergence of competition policies. *Journal of European Public Policy* 9 (6): 913–934.

Wall Street Journal (2013). IMF concedes it made mistakes on Greece. June 5, 2013. www.wsj.com/articles/SB10001424127887324299104578527202781667088 (accessed July 10, 2015).

Zito, A.R. (2001). Epistemic communities, collective entrepreneurship and European integration. *Journal of European Public Policy* 8 (4): 585–603.

10 From the variety of socioeconomic regimes to contemporary international relations

Robert Boyer

Introduction

Régulation theory emerged out of an analysis of the Golden Age growth regime in the USA and it focused upon the structural factors that generated its crisis at the end of the 1960s. At that time, the international relations were hierarchically organized under American hegemony, under the so-called "*Pax Americana.*" The world economy was seen as a process of diffusion of Fordism as an accumulation regime and not only a technological innovation (Mistral 1986). The very success of this diffusion led to a progressive deployment of firms' strategies in the direction of international markets, then the delocalization of production and finally the primacy of financial portfolio management at the world level. In this new context, many scholars have pointed to the inadequate analysis of international relations by *régulation* theory and the absence of any feedback upon the domestic institutional forms (Kebabdjian 1998; Palan 1998). Time has passed and during the last decades the research has developed and shown that Fordism was only one of the accumulation regimes; many others coexist, with quite different features. The present work builds upon the taxonomy of the contemporary socioeconomic regimes in order to understand how they relate with one another and sketches a new configuration at odds with the post-World War II (WWII) Bretton Woods system. Actually most domestic institutional forms are now shaped by the evolution of international relations, and thus the interdependency of national *régulation* modes, without any unchallenged hierarchy, is a key feature of the contemporary world. The converging interests with international political economy are noteworthy (Chavagneux 2010) and this is an invitation to develop the status of international regimes within the theory (Vidal 2002).

The presentation is organized around the following sequence of questions. (1) When quite all the development modes are highly internationalized, what are the requirements over the international configuration? (2) Is it an accident if many crises seem to originate from the surge in natural-resource prices and/or real estate speculation? (3) Do the world crises originate from a single origin and mechanism or are they the outcome of the heterogeneity and interactions between three contrasted sociopolitical regimes? (4) Is the power to influence the evolution of international relations distributed equally among the different nation states? (5) Are not the regions the entities that govern the future and the stability of the world economy, away from the implicit vision associated to the concept of globalization and the quest for a hegemon that would finally replace the USA? (6) Is not the contradiction between more and more economic interdependence and even complementarity on one side and geopolitical rivalry on the other the main threat to the stabilization of international relations? (7) Is not the problematic and difficult emergence of new global commons evidence for the radical uncertainty about the successor to the Bretton Woods system?

1 The extraversion of all development modes

Bretton Woods was a very original international system: Given the huge asymmetry in the distribution of power after WWII, one could have imagined that the USA would use the international organizations for their exclusive benefit. De facto, in order to prevent the repetition of past dramatic episodes and to win the competition with the Soviet bloc, the USA acted as a benevolent hegemon. They helped rebuild the European and Japanese economies according to a largely inward-looking strategy, whereby national policies were largely autonomous in a regime of fixed but adjustable exchange rates, within an international system of payments governed by public authorities. *Pax Americana* allowed thus the coexistence of a series of self-centered growths. This system reached its peak during the mid-1960s, and was theorized as an embedded liberalism (Ruggie 1997). Then the steady process of opening to international competition began and led to the present and totally different configuration (Table 10.1). The emblematic synchronization of mass production and consumption, i.e., Fordism, has now disappeared and has been replaced in the USA by a finance-led regime that attracts capital all over the world and thus allows balancing of the large trade deficit implied by the delocalization of most industrial production of standardized goods. The opening of the world economy is thus a requisite for the viability of this new growth pattern. Trade liberalization has thus opened a space for export growth regimes, typical of German and Japanese contemporary capitalisms. The complete collapse of Soviet-type regimes has led to a large diversity of development models. Russia has been converted into a rentier economy that distributes the income generated by the export of natural resources, in high demand by the old (Germany) and new industrialized countries (China). But China did not have this opportunity given the poor endowment of natural resources: The liberalization of agricultural products launched the industrialization process that continues to be moved by massive investment, both productive and in infrastructures (Boyer 2011b). The excess capacity finds a demand abroad after adhesion to the WTO. Again this regime becomes dependent on the world economy even if the central government maintains strong control over macroeconomic activity and growth via the control of credit and the exchange rate.

The international system has been dramatically transformed. Competition is now the rule, private capital flows have submerged declining public credits, the USA is still the more powerful economy and the supplier of the international

Table 10.1 From inward to outward looking accumulation and production regimes

Golden Age	*Contemporary period*	*Change after 2008*
Fordism synchronization of production and consumption on a domestic basis	Unbalanced finance-led regimes with delocalized production	Still the hope of a credit-led recovery via world financial intermediation (USA, UK)
Innovation-based export-led regime feeding domestic consumption	Still more export-led and disconnection from domestic consumption	The benchmark model for the European Union: export against the domestic market (Germany, Japan)
Soviet types auto-centered investment-led regime	• Collapse in Eastern and Central Europe • Domestic competition led in China with structural trade surplus	• Fragility of a pure rentier regime (Russia) • Obstacle to a domestic needs-led new regime (China)
National resources based rentier regimes	A reversal of secular decline in terms of trade in response to American and Chinese growth	• Volatility and emerging unbalances in most regimes: discrepancy between domestic institutions and integration into the world economy (Venezuela, Brazil)

Source: author.

currency, but the defense of its hegemony is no more in line with the interests of other nation states. Basically the American economy has to cope with the strategy of China and its multinationals have become less linked to the American territory. In a sense, no visible hand is any more organizing international relations. They become the locus where contrasted development modes interact and sometimes clash. The so-called "currency wars" are good examples of this new epoch.

2 Rentier regimes are back and they matter for world dynamics

The reemergence of rentier regimes as necessary components of any relevant analysis of the international system is the second novelty to be stressed upon. In the Golden Age, the productivist industrial model relied upon cheap oil and the low price of natural resources. The legacy of colonialism and political domination played a major role during *Pax Americana.* This is now over after a sequence of converging events. The 1973 and 1979 brutal rise in the price of oil, initially interpreted as an exogenous event, should have been interpreted not only as a reaction to the inflationist bias of monopolist regulation but also as anticipating the limits to growth with natural resources and environmental constraints. Most analysts had difficulties in diagnosing the resurgence of rents as opposed to profit and the role rentier regimes played within the new configuration of the world economy (Table 10.2). In Japan the industrial success of the 1980s was partially converted into urban land rent, exacerbated by the consequence of financial liberalization and the bursting of the bubble that had dramatic consequences for the accumulation regime and the role of Japan in international negotiations. In the USA, too, the dividends of ICT led to a speculative stock market bubble but also the skyrocketing of land and rents in the Silicon Valley. The story has been repeated with the subprime episode: Financial innovation (securitization of low-quality mortgage credit) was supposed to open an unprecedented epoch featuring always-increasing house prices. The *Saving and Loans* crisis was reiterated on a national and extended scale with the dramatic outcome of the near-collapse of the American financial system. After 2008, facing very low short-term interest rates, the financiers have desperately searched for sources with higher rates of return and they found them by speculating on gold, oil, minerals and even agricultural products.

Thus all recent crises are associated with a shift from industrial profit to various types of rents, and the related tensions in relative prices and the purchasing power of wages are the early warning for a reversal of economic activity. Since the rents are unequally distributed across the poles of the international economy, rentier regimes matter for world dynamics. Basically three configurations coexist:

1 Countries with no or few resources had to follow the route of innovation in order to balance their dependency by a surplus in industrial goods; it is especially so for Japan but also for Germany and China in spite of their rich endowment in coal.

Table 10.2 How the various rents have impacted the world economy

Dates	*Event/phenomenon*	*Type of rent*	*Economic impact*	*Political outcomes*
1973 and then 1979	Sharp increase in the price of oil by OPEC decision	Oil rent	Stagflation, recessions and piling of savings outside industrialized economies	• Erroneous diagnosis (a supply shock) • Emergence of an ecological concern
1980s	Expectations of an industrial leadership by Japan	Urban and real estate enhanced by financial liberalization	A short boom and then a long stagnation	Limits of economic policy facing deflation
1990s	New economy technical revolution in the USA	Partial conversion of innovation into land rent in Silicon Valley	Growth and then bursting of the bubble and recession	Long period of low interest rates in response to low inflation and slow growth
2000–2008	Financial deregulation and explosive securitization in the USA	Financial rent by information asymmetry and urban land rent	American financial melting down, systemic economic crisis and its international diffusion	Invention of unorthodox monetary policy
2008–2014	High liquidity of financial capital in search for high rates of return	Speculation over key natural resources and agricultural land at the world level	High volatility and uncertainty for international movements	Growing tensions between emerging and mature industrial economies

Source: compiled by author.

2 In the opposite camp, other countries are so rich in natural resources that their *régulation* mode is governed by the distribution of the income provided by their exports. Saudi Arabia is the typical example, but Russia also has become a rentier economy and the Brazilian trajectory shows how difficult it is to develop a strong industrial basis in a resource-rich country.

3 Some rare continental economies succeed in mixing three sectors: industrial, financial and primary. The recent American boom in shale gas is closely related to the dynamism of innovation applied to natural-resource extraction.

This feature calls for a renewed interest in a more diversified approach to the regimes that have to coexist within a given international system. A significant part of contemporary evolution can be traced back to the rise of rents as opposed to profit and their conversion from one form to another (Figure 10.1). First of all, we should not limit the analysis to Ricardo's analysis of agricultural land rent, since urban rents imply rather different mechanisms, whereas the rents associated with mining deserve another analysis. We dare to extend the concept of rent to two domains quite important in the contemporary world. Whereas conventional theory analyzes innovation in terms of imperfect competition, the long-lasting barriers to entry in some key sectors of information and communication technologies are such that one may use the concept of innovation rents by opposition to profit governed by competition. The second extension relates to the labeling of the income generated by financial innovations, so esoteric that buyers cannot assess the quality and properties of the financial instrument they buy. It seems more relevant to speak about financial rents, frequently sustained by the implicit guarantee of public institutions.

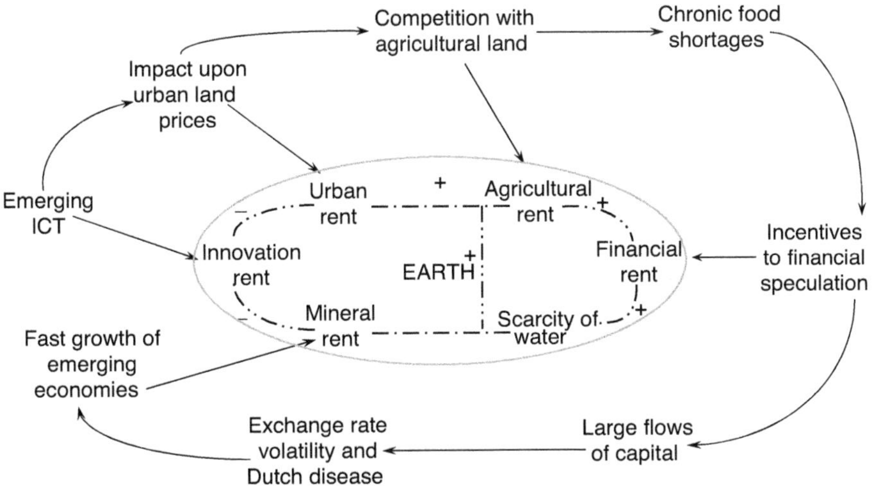

Figure 10.1 The interweaving of the various rents.

Source: author.

A second feature stresses that all these forms are related since they can be converted one into another in line with the transformations of the various accumulation regimes, in such a pattern that it would be illusory to conclude that these rents will finally vanish with more competition. Quite on the contrary, the mobility of capital is constantly searching for new sources of rent to be exploited at the world level. Innovation rents generate high incomes that make some localities especially attractive (Central Tokyo, Silicon Valley, Downtown Manhattan). This feeds land speculation, favored by new financial instruments that warrants to their inventors financial rents (mortgage credit, securitization, swap, options). In turn this growth pattern puts pressure upon agricultural land that may be an incentive to land grabbing and speculation on food in countries with weak subsistence crops. At the end of such a boom, mining rents might become a major concern for investors and speculators as well. Consequently, rents are shaping all accumulation/production regimes and are contributing to the evolution of the world economy.

3 The three socioeconomic regimes that set the world into motion

According to this analysis we can no more rely on obsolete stylizations of international relations. A benevolent hegemon is not diffusing to the rest of the world industrial technological advances: The technological frontier is explored by diverse national production and innovation systems and the issue of property rights protection has become a major source of frictions. Farewell to the post-WWII configuration! Similarly, the period cannot be seen as the equivalent to the transition from the ruling of the British Empire to America's hegemony after 1945. Both the USA and China have definite and specific institutional competitive advantages and for the time being they are rather complementary in stabilizing the world economy in spite of their geopolitical rivalry; for instance in Asia (Boyer 2011b). After Lehman Brothers' collapse, the quick response of China in terms of contra-cyclical public spending in infrastructures has complemented the bailing out of the American financial system. Now the challenge is in the USA: how to retreat from quantitative easing without provoking a new crisis in the developing world?

This chapter is built upon the following hypothesis: The dynamic properties of the contemporary world economy are the unintended outcome of the interaction of three heterogeneous socioeconomic regimes (Figure 10.2):

1. The finance-led capitalisms set the tune for the "animal spirits" of investors via the socialization of expectations about interest rates, exchange rates, rate of returns and growth rates of the different regions/nation states. Capital is moving according to these visions of the next future.
2. The new industrializing capitalisms are leading the international and regional division of labor in the manufacturing sectors. They reap the benefits from the increasing returns to scale associated with standardization and

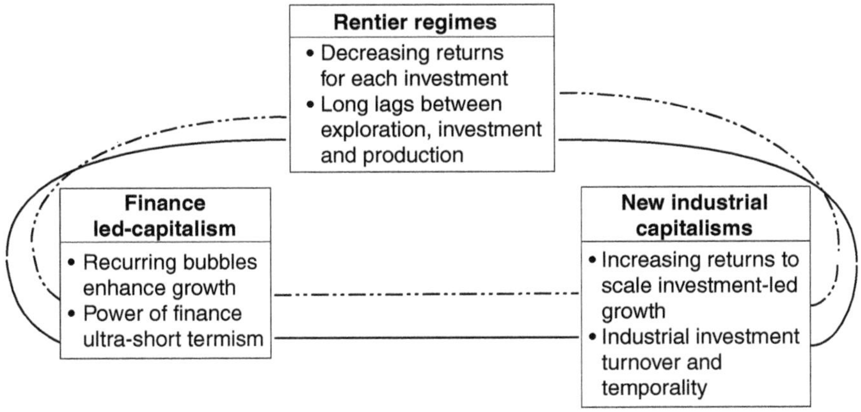

Figure 10.2 A simple representation of the dynamics of the world economy: three logics and temporalities.

Source: author.

modularization for electronic, durable goods that are sold on the world markets, and not only at home. This explains why most of the prices of industrial goods are set in Asia. China is the starting point and key actor of this asymmetric impulse into the international economy.

3 The typical rentier regimes respond to these two impulses – financial and productive – by setting the price of natural resources, since supply is generally quite inelastic in the short run, given the large lag between the evolution of demand and the new investment required to extend capacities. The policy makers rarely exert an active role since rentier regimes follow the dynamics put into motion by the two other regimes. Nevertheless, they have to be put into the picture in order to understand the ups and downs of international trade and domestic macroeconomic junctures.

This heterogeneity is thus the source of unprecedented properties and it is not bound to be eradicated by competition and so-called globalization. On one side, it is difficult to imagine a steady state for the world economy because the increasing returns to scale in manufacturing production are always limited by the decreasing returns in rentier regimes, with the exception of a revolutionary innovation such as the fracture of shale gas. On the other side, the time horizon and time lag of the three regimes are so different: the micro-second for high-frequency trade; the period required between investment decision and the effective extension of productive capacity in manufacturing; and the uncertain lag between exploration, discovery and exploitation in the mining sector.

In the past some authors have proposed a similar theory of the international economy seen as the consequence of the interactions between the industry and the primary sector extracting natural resources (Kaldor 1963). Here, the novelty relates to the resilience of finance-led capitalism (Boyer 2011a). This amplifies the booms via easier access to credit and conversely makes more severe and long the recessions, and in some examples the financial accelerator provokes a cumulative depression (Southern Europe after 2010). Again the prognosis would be an exacerbation of the volatility and instability of the world economy. A definite answer would require a formalization of the interaction described by Figure 10.2. Everything is up to the set of parameters defining these three regimes: a structurally stable configuration or a potentially chaotic dynamic?

4 Leaders and followers: a two-tier world international regime

A third consequence relates to the distribution of power across nations. In theory each nation state has the same voice and power in the deliberations of United Nations organizations and every member state of the eurozone should be part of the deliberation and decisions about the governance of the euro. Many observations suggests that it is not so and the present analysis may explain why. Actually the pace of the world economy is set by the interaction of finance-led regimes and newly industrializing economies submitted to the feedback from resource-based rentier regimes. All other regimes have to adapt with few degrees of freedom (Figure 10.3):

- Before 2008, some regimes were built upon the permanent entry of foreign capital and indebtedness in foreign currency (dollars in Latin America, euro in Europe). If the credit is diverted from productive investment benefiting to the export sector and feeds a real estate speculative bubble or finances current public expenditures, such a development is not sustainable. When international credit is frozen, policy makers have to call for the help of the IMF or EU, with severe conditions attached. Their bargaining power is quite limited and this means the existence of a new international hierarchy.
- The situation is far better for the regimes based upon the role of innovation in promoting high-value exports. They can sell their production to each of the leading poles of the world economy: differentiated and high-quality goods to finance-led regimes, efficient machine tools to newly industrializing capitalism and positional goods in rentier regimes. Given the sharp contraction of trade after 2008 they are severely hit by the crisis but they vigorously bounce back, as shown by the German trajectory until 2015. Nevertheless, it is not among the key players at the geopolitical level, however efficient its productive system. But within the European Union and facing financially dependent economies, the German governments have shown their ability to decide about the strategy to overcome the Euro crisis. This leads to a third tier of international relations: within a regional zone some members are Stackelberg leaders, in the sense that they have the power to impose their strategies on their weaker partners.

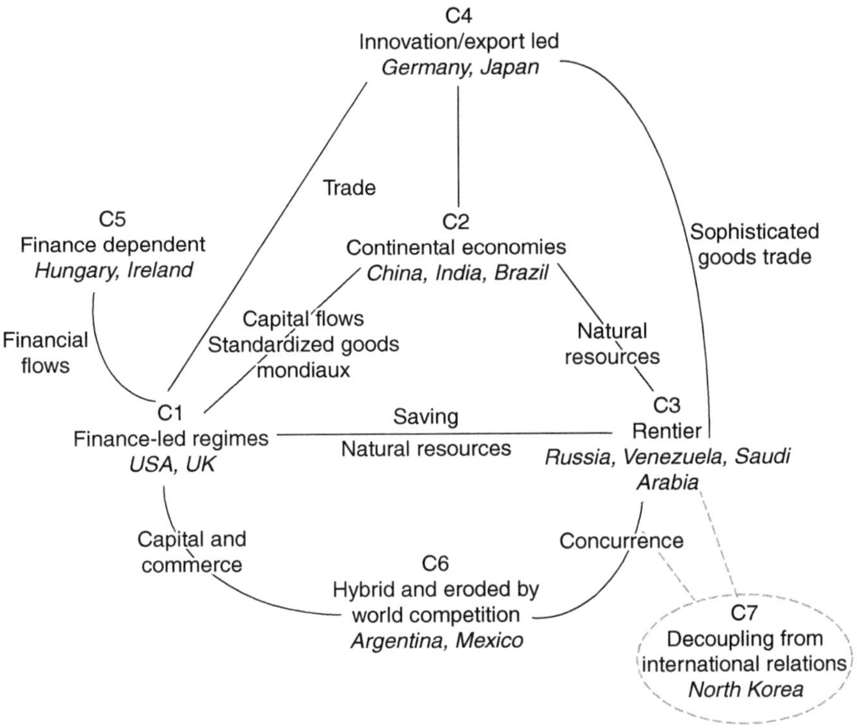

Figure 10.3 How the various configurations interact with the three leading regimes.

Source: author.

- A third kind of domination is associated with various configurations that are eroded or even disarticulated by their integration into the changing international relations and no alternative regime is emerging by lack of relevant political alliances or poor specialization. Argentina since the mid-1970s is an emblematic case, but to some extent Greece is another dramatic example of incompatibility between a national social-economic regime and an incoherent conception of regional integration.
- A last configuration is not a very attractive alternative to globalization acceptance. North Korea is one of the rare examples of decoupling from the world economy.

Thus globalization has generated a new structuring of international relations and promoted regimes that would have appeared as unsustainable in the Bretton Woods system. Finance-led regimes exhibit large and permanent trade deficits that are the mirror image of the trade surplus of the three other regimes. According to this criteria, the innovation/export-led regimes contribute more than expected to the unbalanced finance-led regimes (Figure 10.4).

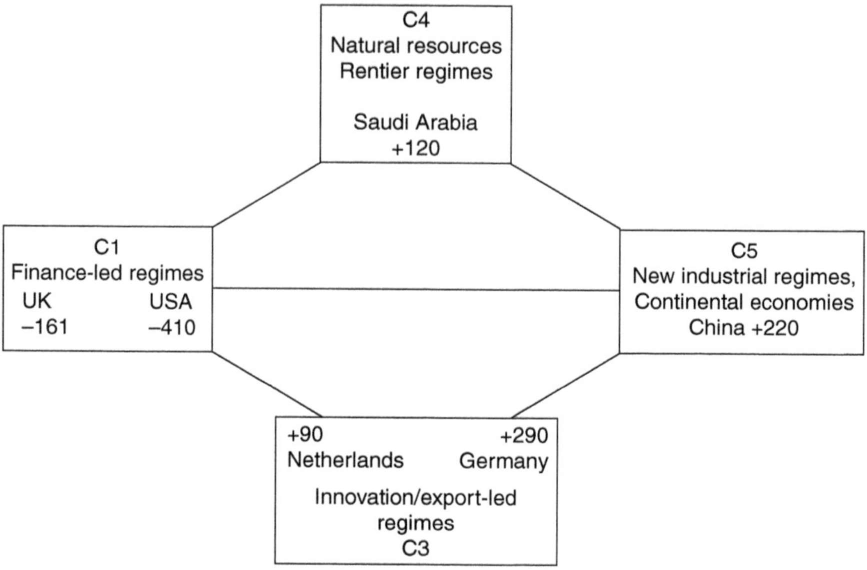

Figure 10.4 Trade surplus and deficits among four regimes.

Source: Haver Analystes, *The Economist*, April 18 and 24, 2015.

5 Growing interdependence among four regions

If there is no single pattern in development modes, how do we explain their persistence? We have progressively shown that they are forming a rather coherent or at least compatible system at the world level (Figure 10.5):

- The finance-led regime and the explosion of higher income in the USA are the mirror of the fast productive modernization in China and the widening of inequality. This is not the only coevolution within the world economy.
- The euro crisis and the threat upon welfare capitalism, built upon an extended welfare system and defense of social solidarity, are the consequence of the joint pressure of China rapidly catching up in most industries and the recurring global financial crises generated by the American victory in promoting liberalization and globalization of trade, capital and finance.
- The Latin American rentier regimes and the recent atypical decline in economic inequality, starting from an extreme social polarization – quite a paradox indeed – are also explained by their specialization in natural resources; that is complementary to that of China and the USA, the ability to learn from the past financial crises and the transition to democracy as providing finally a positive response to demands for social protection.

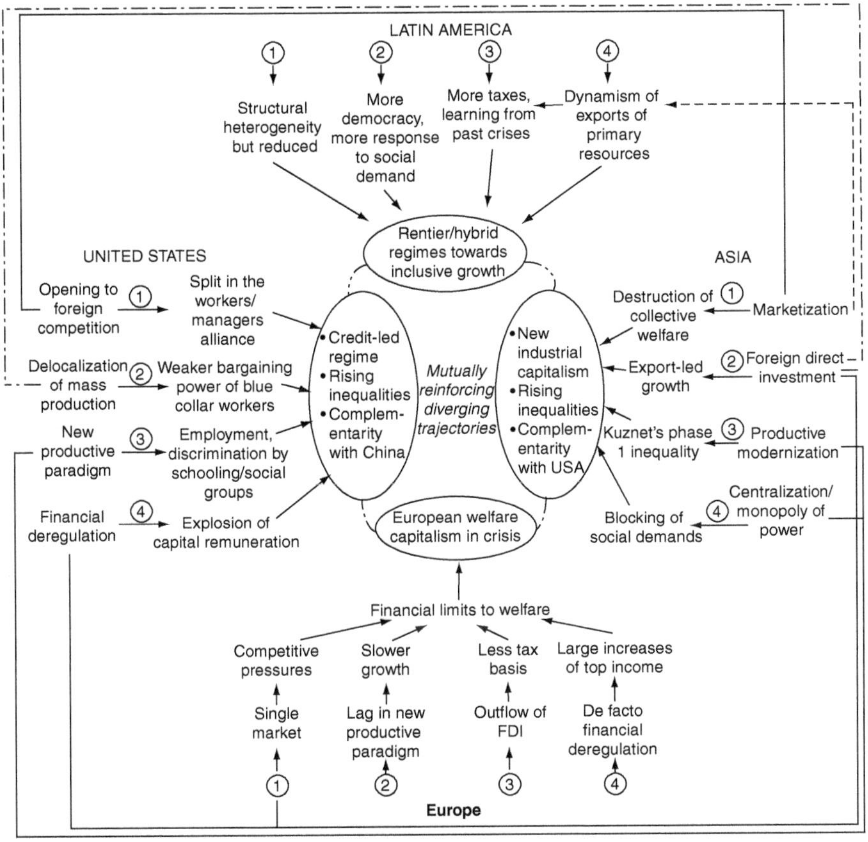

Figure 10.5 How four regions interact and become complementary.

Source: author.

The macroeconomic imbalances, generated by contrasting socioeconomic regimes and the widening of inequality within each domestic economy, are symmetric in the USA and in China. Consequently only the compensating movements in international trade and finance allow the viability of socioeconomic regimes that could not be sustained within closed borders: abundant credit to sustain the American way of living with stagnant average real income in the USA, dramatic industrial overcapacity due to the squeeze of labor share in China; low American household saving rate versus Chinese high savings, partially channeled back to the US financial system.

Thus the internationalization of production, capital and finance makes compatible and viable different inequality regimes, themselves embedded into complementary development modes. Furthermore, this explains the puzzling observation of opposite evolutions concerning inequality: less inequality between nations since globalization allows a variety of growth regimes – credit-led, export-led, innovation-led – but each of these regimes nurtures widening inequalities for individuals within the same nation state, the two major stylized facts identified by the literature.

6 Geopolitical rivalries against economic complementarity

The tipping of the world economy toward Asia made China's economy a reference for many governments, so as to suggest that the Beijing Consensus was substituted for that of Washington in the design of development strategies. Furthermore, the erosion of the American superpower and the uncertainty of its new growth regime leave the field open to a reorientation of international trade flows in favor of China, which became the first partner of a growing number of countries in Latin America, for example Brazil. One can imagine that South–South relations will supplant the old opposition North–South or center–periphery. Finally, this convergence of interests is likely to influence decisively the reconfiguration of an international system marked by the possible abandonment of the dollar as the pivot of international financial relations. Compared with India, China is the origin of most of these changes (Alary and Lafaye de Micheaux 2015).

In fact, the Middle Kingdom is the center of the web of contradictions that operate in the contemporary world: between economic complementarity and geopolitical rivalry in Asia, especially with Japan; between reluctant cooperation and open conflict with the USA; between an alliance for rebuilding international institutions and asymmetrical integration with Latin America and Africa; between the need to maintain with the euro a currency that may compete with the dollar and the pressure in order to turn the yuan into an international currency, so that the autonomy of monetary and exchange-rate policy continues to be the essential tool for governing and controlling the Chinese economy. In this global game, the EU occupies an even less enviable position than Japan: dominated by American finance, open to the winds of Asian competition, Europe is an aggregate of old nations that have given up the exercise of any geopolitical power in the reconfiguring of the coming world and the defense and diffusion of their welfare capitalism (Figure 10.6).

7 A new, shaky and uncertain international system

Can a new international system emerge from the present configuration and deliver more satisfactory outcomes? It is far from evident since the heterogeneity of national regimes, ideologies and interests raises many obstacles, the more so the more policy makers forget the dramatic 2008 near-collapse.

Finance-led capitalisms require complete freedom and mobility of capital to maximize the gains from financial intermediation which, although located on Wall Street and in the City of London, has become global. The emerging industrial capitalisms base their legitimacy on a rapid growth enabling job creation

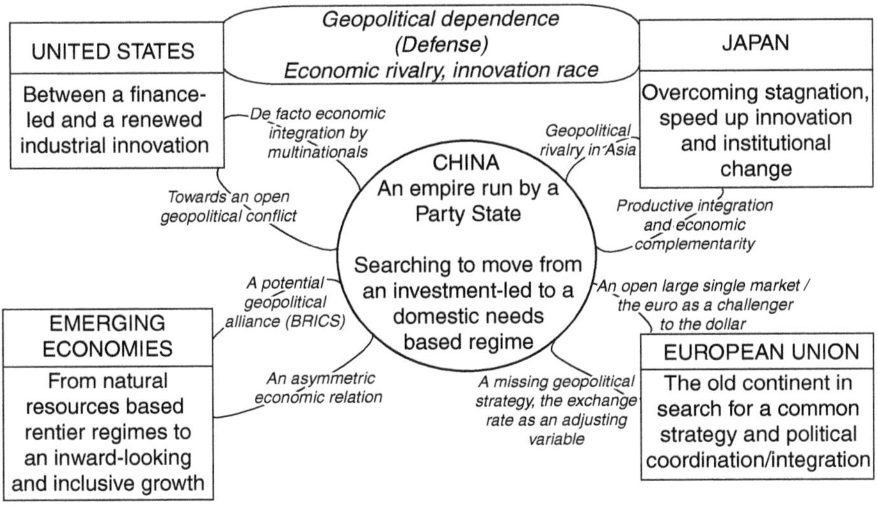

Figure 10.6 The world seen from China: geopolitical rivalry but economic interdependence.

Source: created by author.

and rising living standards. By contrast, in pure rentier regimes the struggles are polarized on rent sharing conflict without great concern for the improvement of domestic production capacity. The capitalisms based on innovation thrive on industrial specialization in products in high demand by the emerging industrial regimes, and they require a full opening of the world economy. The mature industrial capitalisms are torn between strengthening their domestic markets and improving their industrial specialization that would allow them to better integrate into the global economy. Mixed regimes – both rentier and industrial – face a similar dilemma: on the one hand, they push domestic growth in order to promote their domestic production system, potentially self-sufficient, on the other they can also benefit from the redistribution of income associated with the sector exporting raw materials and agricultural products (Table 10.3).

Clearly the pure economic justification does imply political support for institutionalizing such public goods (Hugon 2004). According to another theory a common is a collective resource the commodification of which may cause the crisis of the whole society. But the question remains the same: How do these commons emerge in the international political arena? Finally, can we mobilize the theory of commons? It is not obvious since a community has to agree upon how to implement and manage rules to maintain these commons and it is easier locally than internationally (Ostrom 2010). There is the concern that runs through this present analysis: All institutional arrangements involve political processes and they are especially difficult to build at the international level in the absence of a benevolent hegemon. In order to limit climate change, a new configuration of the

Table 10.3 Each politico-economic regime has different objectives

Politico-economic regime	*Objectives*			
	Domestic growth	*Economic specialization*	*Managing the rent*	*World financial intermediation*
Finance-led capitalism (USA, UK)	**			***
Emerging industrial capitalisms (China, India)	***	**		*
Pure rentier regime (Venezuela, Saudi Arabia)	*		***	*
Capitalism based upon innovation/export (Japan, Germany, South Korea)	*	***		
Mature industrial capitalisms (France, Italy)	**	**		
Mixed rentier/industrial regimes (Brazil, Argentina)	**	*	**	*

Source: author.

Note
The presence and number of asterisks measure the importance of the objective for each regime.

Table 10.4 Conflicting strategies concerning the building of global commons

Politico-economic regime	*Nature of global commons*			
	Financial stability	*An open world economy*	*Fight against climate change*	*International organizations reforms*
Finance-led capitalism (US, UK)	Resistance/reluctance of financiers	***	Weak interest but growing	Resistance to reforms
Emerging industrial capitalisms (China, India)	**	**	Growing interest of public opinion	Strong and recurring demands
Pure rentier regime (Venezuela, Saudi Arabia)	*	*	Variable in relation with geography	Not very present
Capitalism based upon innovation/ export (Japan, Germany, South Korea)	**	**	***	Variable across countries
Mature industrial capitalisms (France, Italy)	***	*	Different from one country to another	Variable
Mixed rentier/industrial regimes (Brazil, Argentina)	**	*		** (for Brazil)

Source: author.

Note
The presence and number of asterisks measure the importance of the objective for each regime.

world economy has to emerge. This is indeed a very uncertain process, open to many unintended outcomes.

8 Conclusion

The present analysis can be summarized by the following findings and hypotheses (Table 10.5), to be explored by a new wave of research:

1 Away from post-WWII inward-looking configurations, internationalization and extraversion define a common trend across all accumulation/production regimes. In the USA the largely self-contained Fordism has been opening to competition and has become an emblematic finance-led regime, living on world financial intermediation. Japan, Germany and South Korea continue to explore an industrial model but they basically rely upon innovation to nurture an export-led accumulation regime. The Soviet regime has been replaced in Russia by a rentier politico-economic regime, totally dependent on external demand for gas, oil and natural resources. None of them is independent from the vagaries of international evolutions and events.

2 All disequilibria generated by each of the leading development modes reverberate across the world with an unprecedented intensity, as shown for instance by the knock-on effects generated by the subprime crisis or the eurozone uncertainty. The name of the game is no more that of the Golden Age, i.e., the diffusion of a canonical industrial model under the aegis of a powerful American hegemon. Instead, the challenge relates to the problematic compatibility of three heterogeneous leading accumulation/production regimes. Finance-led regimes and new dynamic industrial capitalisms set the pace of the world economy but they have to cope with the heterogeneity and specific temporal horizon of resource-based rentier regimes. It is necessary to take seriously these rentier regimes, because they are part in the genesis of most crises since the 1970s and they are involved in the search for a sustainable world system.

3 *Pax Americana* is over, i.e., the bygone epoch when an unchallenged hegemon was organizing its hierarchical domination in all domains of international relations within a set of market economies run by democratic principles, in competition with the Soviet bloc. Nowadays we are living in a two-tier world system. At the core of the present configuration there is a duopoly: the USA and China have first to decide their strategies, taking into account their mutual interests concerning trade, finance, intellectual property rights but also their rivalry in the redesign of power relations in the various zones of the world. In a second step they have to decide how they relate with natural resources supply, i.e., their strategies in the direction of rentier economies: self-sufficiency via innovation (the USA) or long-term contracts with Latin American and African countries (China). Other economies have to adapt to the evolution thus generated by these major players. For instance, Germany is a reluctant hegemon in the European Union but

Table 10.5 From Bretton Woods to the present international configuration

Components	*Golden Age*	*Contemporary world*	*Changes after 2008*
1 Principles of coherence	*Pax Americana* under US hegemony	From a superpower to the challenge by Asia (Japan and then China)	Deepening of previous trends: economic complementarity and geopolitical rivalry in a multipolar world
2 Role of international institutions	Significant via public financing	Decline with ups and downs along with international crises	A modest revival with the European crisis
3 Capital mobility	Very limited	Quasi-complete mobility of private capital	Seeming irreversibility of financial globalization but slow reduction of the exposure to international financial risk
4 Exchange rate regime	Fixed but adjustable	Flexible but changing conceptions of exchange rate regimes	Recurring currency wars and tensions within the eurozone between fixed exchange rate and heterogeneous *régulation* modes
5 Degree of autonomy of national economic policy	Very large	Reduced by capital mobility: monetary policy, tax, public investment	Emerging revolt against the erosion of democratic principles by the power of global finance

Source: created by author.

not a significant geopolitical player. Other nation states have still less autonomy in their integration into the world economy and they have no say about the reform of international institutions.

4 At odds with the frequent confusion that equates globalization with uniformity, the last two decades show two different trends. On one side, regionalization of various zones of the world economy is a striking phenomenon. In Asia, a new division of labor is emerging under the impulse of multinationals, and China is setting the pace of many neighbors' macroeconomic trends, while new socioeconomic regimes prosper (Harada and Tohyama 2012). Clearly the EU explores a specific regional trajectory, since the euro reveals and exacerbates the large heterogeneity between rather competitive Northern member states and lagging Southern ones. On the other side, globalization means an ever-growing interdependency among contrasted and largely complementary politico-economic regimes. The USA continues to rely on a credit-led recovery, China tries to convert its industrial catching up from investment- to consumption-led and Latin America finds how shaky its development based upon high growth and unprecedented prices for their natural resources was. European governments have lost confidence in their welfare capitalism and accept being the weaker region of the world economy. It is difficult to see any long-run convergence of development modes.

5 The surprising resilience of the present disarticulated international relations is difficult to explain. The rise of geopolitical rivalry is impressive and concerns military alliances, open conflicts over the control of some territories, in Asia and Europe, and the future of key international organizations. By chance, an unprecedented interdependency of nation states and zones of the world economy and a new international division of labor are bringing some moderation and until now they have prevented an open conflict among the key players. In this respect, the rise of China has to be analyzed in the light of these two contradictory factors: de facto patient economic strategy of integration into international relations, but open rivalry with the USA and Japan in terms of regional supremacy. The reconfiguration of the world economy is thus especially uncertain since it is not the repetition of the shift from the British Empire to the US hegemony (Kindleberger 1973).

6 The Bretton Woods system was more imposed by the overwhelming American hegemony than negotiated among equal partners. Such an asymmetry no longer exists since the key actors that shape international relations defend quite different objectives, closely related to the requirements of their accumulation or production regimes. Financial stability at the world level should be an important global public good, but the capitalisms that prosper out of financial innovations might be hurt by most of the regulatory systems that would be proposed by old and new industrial capitalisms (Boyer 2011b). Preserving the climate is conceptually a global common but developed and developing nation states have quite different proposals about the distribution

of the implied adjustments to their development regime, and each of them would like tight controls to be applied to all except them. For the first time, a multipolar world has to find rules of the game agreed upon by a multitude of actors.

7 The 2008 crisis will be remembered as a major event, equivalent to the 1929 crisis: It reveals the contradictions of any development mode. Speculative bubbles seem to become the only method for sustaining declining growth trends in finance-led capitalisms. China is experiencing many obstacles in the transition toward an inward-looking regime that is more socially and environmentally sustainable. The Latin American leaders realize how precarious were their inclusive growth strategies, built upon the high prices of their natural resources. Last but not least, European welfare capitalism is at risk, given the heterogeneity of their specialization and ability to cope with acute international competition. In this context, international relations are torn between increasing economic and financial interdependence and the opposition of geopolitical rivalries. If a new world crisis burst out, a major bifurcation may occur: either an unprecedented cooperation generated by urgency allows the negotiation of a multipolar new international system, or a phased withdrawal from world dependency takes place for the continental economies and then regional integration becomes a priority for medium and small economies.

References

Alary, P. and E. Lafaye de Micheaux (2015), *Capitalismes asiatiques et puissance chinoise: Diversité des modèles, hégémonie de la Chine*, Paris, Editions Sciences-Po.

Boyer, R. (2011a), *Les financiers détruiront-ils le capitalisme?*, Paris, Economica.

Boyer, R. (2011b), "A new epoch but still diversity within and between capitalism: China in comparative perspective," in Lane Christel and Geoffrey T. Wood (eds.), *Capitalist Diversity and Diversity within Capitalism*, Routledge, Abingdon, pp. 32–68.

Chavagneux, C. (2010), *Economie politique internationale*, Paris, La Découverte.

Harada, Y. and H. Tohyama (2012), "Asian capitalisms: institutional configuration and firm heterogeneity," in R. Boyer, H. Uemura and A. Isokai (eds.), *Diversity and Transformations of Asian Capitalisms*, London: Routledge, pp. 243–263.

Hugon, P. (2004), "Les biens publics mondiaux et le niveau transnational de la régulation," *La Lettre de la Régulation*, Vol. 48, April.

Kaldor, N. (1963), *Essays on Economic Stability and Growth*, London, G. Duckworth and Co.

Kebabdjian, G. (1998), "La théorie de la régulation face à la problématique des régimes internationaux," *L'Année de la régulation*, Vol. 2, Paris, Editions la Découverte, pp. 107–136.

Kindleberger, C.P. (1973), *The World in Depression, 1929–1939*, Oakland, CA: University of California Press.

Mistral, J. (1986), "Régime international et trajectoires nationales," in Boyer Robert (ed.), *Capitalisme fin de siècle*, Paris, PUF.

Ostrom, E. (2010), *Gouvernance du bien commun: Pour une nouvelle approche des ressources naturelles*, Louvain La Neuve, De Boek.

Palan, R. (1998), "Les fantômes du capitalisme mondial: l'économie politique internationale et l'école française de la régulation," *L'année de la Régulation*, Vol. 2, Paris, Editions la Découverte, pp. 65–90.

Ruggie, J.G. (1997), Globalization and the embedded liberalism compromise: the end of an era, MPIfG Working Paper, 07/1, January.

Vidal, J.-F. (2002), "Les régimes internationaux," in Boyer Robert and Yves Saillard (eds.), *Théorie de la régulation: état des savoirs*, Paris, La Découverte, pp. 171–179.

11 Balance-of-payments constraints, change in income distribution, and economic growth in the era of globalization

Hiroshi Nishi

Introduction

The wave of globalization is one of the most important phenomena in contemporary capitalism. This globalization has been accompanied by a wave of neoliberalism. According to Bresser-Pereira, neoliberalism is the reaction that occurred in the 1980s; in this new ideology, instead of the state the market should coordinate the economy (Bresser-Pereira, 2010: 28). The discourse on neoliberalism also involves the attempt to promote economic growth through market-oriented structural reforms that are based on orthodox macroeconomic theories and policies such as deregulation to enhance market mechanisms. As globalization means the process of achieving market interdependence, it is fair to say that it is encouraged by the neoliberal discourse.

Globalization has had a dual impact on the national economy, as Weiss (2003) indicated. It may be viewed as both a constraint and an enabler of the economic, institutional, and political spheres in national economies. She identified the constraints from capital mobility and international agreement and the enabling face caused by demand from social protection and pressure for innovation, which are mostly political aspects. Economic aspects also matter. Not only has globalization enabled national economies to realize economic growth (stagnation) through the expansion (contraction) of international trade, it has also constrained national economies by way of posing limits on trade deficits and pressure from international financial markets, and involved severe cost price competition in trade. Moreover, capital flight is a more likely outcome when an economy records an external deficit–GDP ratio that is regarded as eventually being unsustainable (e.g. the Asian financial crisis in the late 1990s and the crisis in Argentina). As Andrews' (1994) second image reversed suggests, international capital mobility can be seen as exogenous and as a structural factor that national economies cannot easily control, and which systematically constrains state behaviour by rewarding some actions and punishing others.

These constraints play an important role in establishing the international economic structure and the macroeconomic performance of national economies. For example, deepening international trade with severe competition has made countries more interdependent. Accelerated by financialization that has been led by deregulation in financial markets, the volume of trade and the occurrence of international capital flight have increased rapidly, at least until the financial crisis of 2008. One of the causes of the financial crisis was increasing capital flows that were not compatible with balance-of-payments constraints (BOPC). That is, when an economy reaches an external deficit–GDP ratio that will eventually be unsustainable, financial markets become nervous and international capital flies easily from such an economy to another. Consequently, the value of the currency and the stock price in the economy fluctuate substantially, and the economy goes into panic.

Thus, in the era of globalization, the increasing trade deficit and capital flow are potential factors that may cause an economic crisis in the long run. In other words, an ever-growing deficit is unsustainable because of pressure from the international financial market. This indicates the importance of maintaining the BOPC condition so that an economy will not eventually become involved in a crisis caused by international capital flight. Applying Andrews' (1994) terms, international capital mobility constrains a national economy by rewarding BOPC and punishing an ever-growing deficit.

However, it is not easy for a national economy to constantly maintain the BOPC condition because a trade balance is not automatically achieved by a market adjustment, and various factors affect the dynamics of exports and imports. For instance, the economic activity levels measured by the GDP in a foreign country are one of the determinants of the exports of a domestic country, whereas the home country's GDP is one of the determinants of its imports. The qualities and attractiveness of the commodities that each economy produces also determine the performance of exports and imports. In addition to these non-price factors, the price competitiveness of firms in each economy matters as its determinants, and their role has become more important in the era of globalization.

The trade commodity price, therefore the real exchange rate, does not work to recover the trade balance in a manner that the mainstream economics supposes. Even when there is a trade deficit, it is not always true that the real exchange rate does not change to bring a trade balance. This is because pricing is normally affected by the international competition, wage, productivity, and bargaining for income distribution between labour and capital in national economies. Thus, the distributional factors inevitably concern pricing behaviour in each economy. As a result, they determine the dynamics of the real exchange rate, and consequently, the dynamics of exports and imports are not independent of these factors.

Thus, the performance of the national economy is concerned with many constraints both domestically and internationally (Figure 11.1). It is necessary for an economy to maintain the BOPC so as not to be the target of an international capital attack, but the BOPC is also affected by domestic distributional conditions. In the era of globalization, the international cost price competition also concerns pricing behaviour, and thus severe competition may prevent equitable income distribution between capital and labour in an economy. Finally, sustainable economic growth is a necessary condition for maintaining the employment of labour.

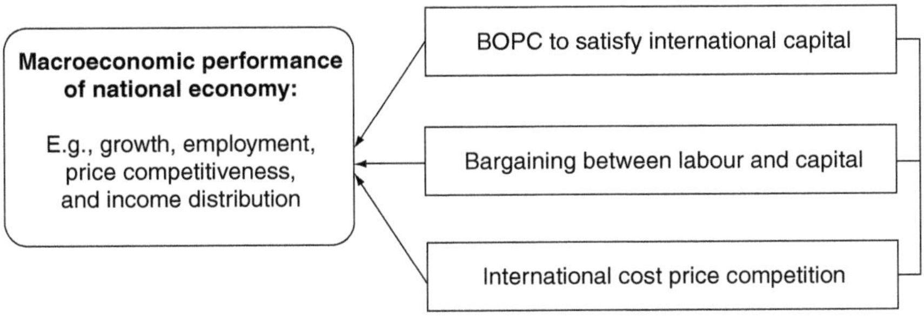

Figure 11.1 Analytical scope of the chapter: macroeconomic performance of a national economy and its structural constraints.

Source: author.

Is it possible to reconcile these conditions simultaneously? More precisely, is it possible to establish an equitable income distribution between labour and capital while maintaining the BOPC and a high economic growth rate?

It is under such a structural environment that we set up the balance-of-payments constrained growth model and explore the dynamic relationship among economic growth, the possibility of equitable income distribution, and the BOPC in this chapter.[1] For this purpose, we use Blecker's (1998) model. Blecker (1998) considered how relative wages (the living standards of workers in two countries) are affected by international environmental factors such as increasing competition and BOPC. One of his contributions is that his structural model shows that it is impossible for a country to simultaneously achieve a high level of economic growth, the BOPC condition, and relatively high wages. In other words, there is a trilemma among these three goals.

His model is suitable for our purpose because it introduces increasing cost price competition into international trade and the BOPC condition, which are structural constraints in the era of globalization. However, his investigation is not sufficient to answer the question of whether the distributional interests of different economic classes can be reconciled while maintaining BOPC under the increasing cost price competition at the global level. This is because his model focuses only on the wage rate and assumes away the wage and profit shares. In order to obtain a sufficient answer to the questions above, it is necessary to introduce a more detailed distributional relationship between labour and capital and to examine the impacts of changes in their shares on macroeconomic performance. For this, we will further extend Blecker's (1998) model by introducing a bargaining process across the income distribution between labour and capital. By doing so, this chapter will theoretically investigate the dynamic relationship among the BOPC condition with severe cost price competition between two countries, the possibility of equitable income distribution, and economic growth of national economies.

This chapter is organized as follows: In Section 1, we consider the relationship between BOPC growth, international competition, and the relative wage rate between two countries, using Blecker's (1998) framework. In Section 2, we newly introduce a bargaining process between capital and labour that includes conflicting claims across the target income distribution shares, and derive some of the implications obtained from the model. An analytical exercise of the model is given in the Appendix. Section 3 concludes.

1 Setup of the model

We consider the international trade of a commodity between two countries, which we call the home country and the foreign country. Our focus is on the determinants of economic growth and income distribution in the home country. In these two economies there exists a single commodity that can be used for exports. This economy contains two social classes, firms (capital) and workers (labour). Firms in both countries produce the same commodity which is substitutable, and the firms in the home country are in competition with the firms in the foreign country over the cost price level of the commodity. Firms produce the commodity by employing workers with fixed-coefficient technology and set the price. Workers supply the labour force to firms and receive wages. The same conditions are also supposed for the foreign country, but in order to focus on the macroeconomic performance of the home country, we assume that the GDP in the foreign country is given.

This study introduces domestic and international constraints into the standard BOPC model. First, by following Blecker (1998), this study introduces the role of increasing international cost price competition between the two countries. Second, in order to explicitly consider the possibility of equitable income distribution, bargaining between labour and capital across the wage, price, and target share of income determination in each country is also introduced.

The BOPC model in this chapter is built on the implicit proposition that there is a limit to the external deficit–GDP ratio. In other words, it supposes that long-run economic growth with an ever-growing deficit is unsustainable because of pressure from the international financial market. As the simplest way to express such a circumstance, the BOPC model in this chapter begins with the condition of a balance-of-payments equilibrium. Thus, the existence of international capital is also supposed; its activities are implicit in this chapter.

1.1 The BOPC condition

The following is a list of the main notations used in this chapter. The subscript H indicates a variable for the home country. Y_H: total output (total income); E_H: employment; q_H: labour productivity; p_H: price of the commodity; X: export demand; w_H: nominal wage rate; e: nominal exchange rate between the two countries; M: import demand; z_H: gross mark-up ratio; π_H: actual profit share. The same variables for the foreign country are expressed by adding the subscript

O to the variable instead of H or by putting a tilde over the variable (for example, the nominal wage rate of the foreign country is denoted by w_O, while the target profit share of foreign firms is given by $\tilde{\pi}_f$).

In this chapter, the BOPC condition is defined by nominal terms at the macroeconomic level. At the aggregate level, the total value of imports and the total value of exports are constrained to be equal. Therefore, the BOPC condition at the aggregate level is given by

$$p_H X = p_O e M, \tag{11.1}$$

where the left-hand side (LHS) represents the total value of exports in the home country and the right-hand side (RHS) represents the total value of imports in the home country at a period.

In order for this BOPC to be maintained over time, it is necessary for the time rate of change in total exports to be equal to that of imports. Therefore,

$$\hat{p}_H + \hat{X} = \hat{p}_O + \hat{M}, \tag{11.2}$$

where we will assume that the rate of change in the nominal exchange rate is zero over time (i.e. $\hat{e}=0$) for simplicity. Equation (11.2) is the BOPC condition in the growth term, where the hat represents the growth rate of each variable.

We assume that the export and import demand functions for each commodity are given by the Cobb–Douglas functional form. First, the export demand (the foreign demand) function for the domestic commodity is given by

$$X = \bar{x}_O \left(\frac{e p_O}{p_H} \right)^{\varepsilon_O} Y_O^{\eta_O}, \tag{11.3}$$

where $\bar{x}_O$ is a constant term, $\varepsilon_O > 0$ is the relative price elasticity, and $\eta_O \geq 0$ is the income elasticity of demand for exports of the domestic commodity. This formalization means that if the real exchange rate appreciates (that is, if there is a fall in ep_O/p_H), exports of the domestic commodity decrease. Equation (11.3) also means that booms in the foreign country induce higher exports of the domestic commodity.

By taking logarithms of equation (11.3) and differentiating them with respect to time, the growth rate of the exports of the domestic commodity is obtained as follows:

$$\hat{X} = \varepsilon_O(\hat{p}_O - \hat{p}_H) + \eta_O \hat{Y}_O. \tag{11.4}$$

This is the dynamic form of the exports of the domestic commodity.

Second, the import demand function for the foreign commodity is given by

$$M = \bar{m}_H \left(\frac{e p_O}{p_H} \right)^{-\varepsilon_H} Y_H^{\eta_H}, \tag{11.5}$$

where $\overline{m}_H$ is a constant term, $\varepsilon_H>0$ is the relative price elasticity, and $\eta_H \geq 0$ is the income elasticity of demand for imports of the foreign commodity. When the real exchange rate appreciates, imports of the foreign commodity increase. Equation (11.5) means that an increase in the home country's income induces higher imports of the foreign commodity.

The dynamic form of the import demand function is derived by the same procedure as above. It yields

$$\hat{M} = -\varepsilon_H(\hat{p}_O - \hat{p}_H) + \eta_H \hat{Y}_H. \tag{11.6}$$

Together with $\varepsilon_O>0$ and $\varepsilon_H>0$, we assume that the Marshall–Lerner condition $\varepsilon_O+\varepsilon_H>1$ holds.

1.2 Cost price competition and the dynamics of the real exchange rate

Using Blecker's (1998) framework, we formalize the relationship between the cost price competition and the dynamics of the real exchange rate (the reciprocal of the terms of trade). Let the price level in the home country be determined by the following mark-up pricing method:

$$p_H = z_H w_H q_H^{-1}, \tag{11.7}$$

where z_H represents the gross mark-up ratio that equals 1 plus the mark-up rate. We assume that labour productivity is constant over time in this section, but it is endogenously determined in the next section. Taking the logarithmic derivatives with respect to time, the domestic commodity price equals the proportional change in the gross mark-up rate plus the rate of change in the nominal wage:

$$\hat{p}_H = \hat{z}_H + \hat{w}_H. \tag{11.8}$$

We further follow Blecker's (1998) formalization and set the dynamics of the gross mark-up ratio to be affected by the 'partial exchange-rate pass-through'. The partial exchange-rate pass-through is also known as pricing to market; it means that the gross mark-up rate changes according to the relative unit labour cost between the two countries in the following manner: When home production becomes more costly relative to foreign production, the gross mark-up rate of the home country is reduced to recover price competitiveness. In contrast, when home production becomes less costly relative to foreign production, the gross mark-up rate of the home country is raised to recover profitability. We formalize this mark-up determination as $z_H=\overline{z}_H(w_H q_H^{-1}/e w_O q_O^{-1})^{-\theta_H}$, where $\overline{z}_H$ is a positive constant. $\theta_H \in [0,1)$ is the elasticity of the mark-up factor with respect to the relative unit labour cost. In terms of the growth rate, the mark-up determination is formalized as follows:

$$\hat{z}_H = -\theta_H(\hat{w}_H - \hat{w}_O), \tag{11.9}$$

where it is assumed that productivity in the foreign country is also constant over time. Using equations (11.8) and (11.9), the commodity price of the home country is determined as follows:

$$\hat{p}_H = (1-\theta_H)\hat{w}_H + \theta_H\hat{w}_O. \tag{11.10}$$

In a similar manner, we formalize the pricing behaviour of firms in the foreign country. The price level in the foreign country is assumed to be determined by the following mark-up pricing method:

$$p_O = z_O w_O q_O^{-1}, \tag{11.11}$$

where z_O represents the gross mark-up ratio of the commodity in the foreign country. Taking the logarithmic derivatives with respect to time, the foreign commodity price is equal to the proportional change in the gross mark-up rate plus the rate of change in the nominal wage:

$$\hat{p}_O = \hat{z}_O + \hat{w}_O. \tag{11.12}$$

The partial exchange-rate pass-through is symmetrically applied to the pricing by foreign firms. Analogously with the home country's case, the mark-up factor is determined by $z_O = \bar{z}_O(w_H q_H^{-1}/ew_O q_O^{-1})^{-\theta_O}$, where $\bar{z}_O$ is a positive constant and $\theta_O \in [0,1)$ is the foreign elasticity of the mark-up factor with respect to the relative unit labour cost. Along with θ_H, we suppose that the restriction $\theta_H + \theta_O < 1$ holds in order to rule out the economically meaningless case in which a rise in relative home unit labour costs could cause extreme profit squeeze behaviour to make home products more price competitive. In addition, we also suppose that these variables are not so large as to realize a negative rate of wage growth and income distribution share.

In terms of the growth rate, the mark-up determination in the foreign country is formalized as follows:

$$\hat{z}_O = \theta_O(\hat{w}_H - \hat{w}_O). \tag{11.13}$$

Using equations (11.12) and (11.13), the commodity price of the foreign country is determined as follows:

$$\hat{p}_O = (1-\theta_O)\hat{w}_O + \theta_O\hat{w}_H. \tag{11.14}$$

Finally, as the real exchange rate is defined by $r = ep_O/p_H$, its rate of change is derived as follows:

$$\hat{r} = -(1-\theta_O-\theta_H)(\hat{w}_H - \hat{w}_O). \tag{11.15}$$

A rise in the home wage rate leads to the appreciation of the home currency (improvement in terms of trade). Thus, it may cause the deterioration of the price competitiveness of the home country unless the wage cost of the foreign country does not change accordingly.

1.3 The BOPC growth rate and the relative wage under international competition

By appropriate substitutions of equations (11.4), (11.6), (11.10), and (11.14) into equation (11.2), the BOPC growth rate that incorporates the existence of international cost price competition is obtained. Let $TB = \hat{p}_H + \hat{X} - \hat{p}_O - \hat{M}$ represent the trade balance over time. Then,

$$TB = (1-\varepsilon_H-\varepsilon_O)(\hat{p}_H-\hat{p}_O)+\eta_O\hat{Y}_O-\eta_H\hat{Y}_H =$$
$$(1-\varepsilon_H-\varepsilon_O)(1-\theta_H-\theta_O)(\hat{w}_H-\hat{w}_O)+\eta_O\hat{Y}_O-\eta_H\hat{Y}_H. \quad (11.16)$$

The BOPC growth rate is obtained when TB is equal to zero. That is,

$$\hat{w}_H-\hat{w}_O = \frac{\eta_H\hat{Y}_H-\eta_O\hat{Y}_O}{(1-\varepsilon_H-\varepsilon_O)(1-\theta_H-\theta_O)}, \quad (11.17)$$

where $1-\varepsilon_H-\varepsilon_O$ is negative because of the assumption of the Marshall–Lerner condition. We suppose that the growth rate of the foreign country, $\hat{Y}_O$, is determined exogenously to focus on the determination of the economic growth rate of the home country.[2]

Figure 11.2 presents the basic characteristics of the Blecker (1998) model. The locus of equation (11.17) is depicted as a downward-sloping line in the $(\hat{Y}_H, \hat{w}_H-\hat{w}_O)$ plane. The points above or to the right of the line represent the trade deficit area (i.e. $TB<0$), whereas the points below or to the left of the line represent the trade surplus area (i.e. $TB>0$).

Equation (11.17) includes the following properties. First, given the elasticities of the imports and exports and those of the mark-up factors, there is one degree of freedom in this equation, and a trade-off exists between the relative wage rate and the economic growth rate of the home country under the BOPC. Second, if the growth rate of the home country is determined, the growth rate of labour demand is also determined since this section assumes that labour productivity is constant over time. As the labour productivity of the home country is $q_H = Y_H/E_H$, the rate of change in labour demand in the home country is equal to the economic growth rate $\hat{E}_H = \hat{Y}_H$. On the basis of this framework, we can understand the relationship among the economic growth rate, unemployment, and relative wages by introducing the growth rate of the labour force into the model. Let n_H represent the growth rate of the labour force in the home country, which is assumed to be an exogenous variable. Then, $n_H - \hat{Y}_H$ approximately represents the rate of change in the unemployment rate. When $n_H > \hat{Y}_H$ because of an insufficient

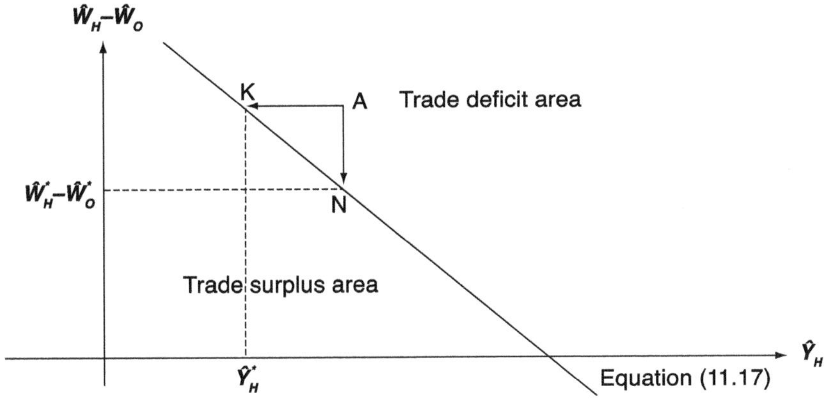

Figure 11.2 BOPC and Keynesian (un)competitiveness and neoclassical (un)competitiveness.

Source: author based on Blecker (1998).

Note
$\hat{w}_H - \hat{w}_O$ represents the relative increase of the home wage and $\hat{Y}_H$ represents the growth rate of the home country. The arrow from A to K indicates the Keynesian uncompetitive case, while that from A to N indicates the neoclassical uncompetitive case.

growth rate, there is growing unemployment in the home country. This means that there is no reason that the BOPC growth rate assures the full employment growth path.

The economic growth rate of the foreign country may be determined independently of the home country's condition, so it is exogenous to the home country and is not controllable domestically. Under such a restriction, changes in the economic growth rate and the relative rate of the home wage increase play an important role. It is also useful and important for the later discussion to explain Blecker's (1998) definition of 'Keynesian and neoclassical (un)competitiveness' and the trade-off that an uncompetitive economy faces. Keynesian (un)competitiveness emphasizes the role of quantitative adjustment, while neoclassical competitiveness emphasizes the role of price adjustment. According to Blecker (1998), if the home country is compelled to reduce its economic growth rate in order to balance its trade at a given rate of change in the relative wage rate, the economy is said to be uncompetitive in the Keynesian sense. For example, as Figure 11.2 shows, if the home country is at point A with the given rate of change in the relative wage rate, it is in a trade deficit situation at this point. In order to recover the trade balance, the home country has to restrain the import demand by reducing the growth rate to $\hat{Y}_H^*$. However, a consequence may be a rise in unemployment over time, especially when the growth rate of the labour force is larger than the economic growth rate. On the other hand, when the home country has to accept a continuous decline in the relative wage rate in order to balance its trade at a given economic growth rate, it is said to be uncompetitive in the neoclassical sense. As Figure 11.2 shows, if the home country is at point A with the given economic growth rate (which is also considered to be determined by the so-called natural rate of growth in the neoclassical framework), it is in a trade deficit situation at this point. In order to recover the BOPC condition, the home country has to accept a reduction to $\hat{w}_H^* - \hat{w}_O^*$ in the relative rate of the home wage increase.

The Blecker (1998) model thus clearly reveals that the trade-off between growth and the relative wage results from structural constraints such as the BOPC condition and international cost price competition. However, the model indicates nothing about how the relative rate of wages between the two countries is determined, as it is given exogenously. Therefore, it is still not clear how changes in the income distribution between capital and labour in both countries affect the relationship among economic growth, the BOPC condition, and the relative rate of wages. In addition, when the relative rate of home wages is positive, the rate of change in the gross mark-up ratio continues to change over time, which consequently leads to the unrealistic result that the profit share of the home country eventually reaches unity, while that of the foreign country reaches zero. This is a theoretical defect to be corrected. Moreover, important issues remain as to what kind of impacts the change in income distribution in one country has on the income distribution in another country and whether it is possible to reconcile the improvement of equitable distribution between capital and labour in a country with its BOPC condition. In order to shed light on these issues, the Blecker model must be further extended. To focus on changes in income distribution, we further introduce the bargaining process across the target income share of each class in both countries by way of the so-called conflicting claim theory (Rowthorn, 1977).

2 Income distribution under international competition and the BOPC growth rate

2.1 Wage–price bargaining and income distribution

We build up the dynamics of wages, prices, and income distribution that change in response to the bargaining power of labour and capital as well as the international cost price competition. In the framework of the conflicting claim model of income distribution, workers and firms have targets for their wage share and profit share, respectively. Workers care about their nominal wage and wage share, but they are also constrained in terms of their relative strength against the firms' bargaining power in claiming their desired nominal wages. Firms set the commodity prices to realize their target profit share, but their price-setting is subject to international cost price competition as well as their relative strength against workers' bargaining power. In a different way from Blecker (1998), we newly introduce the effect of international cost price competition on firms' behaviour that when there is a relative rise in the wage cost in a country, firms in that country attempt to enhance labour productivity so that they can recover their price competitiveness. An increase in wage growth may have a positive effect on productivity growth; for example, firms may react by increasing their productivity-enhancing investment in order to maintain competitiveness or by improving workers' contributions to the production process. Several works have empirically confirmed the positive effect of a wage increase on productivity growth, which is called a wage-led productivity regime (Lavoie and Stockhammer, 2013; Storm and Naastepad, 2012, 2013).

First, we formalize the income distribution shares and the wage rate of the home country. Workers set the nominal wages and firms set prices and enhance productivity, respectively, according to the following reaction functions:

$$\hat{p}_H = \beta(\pi_f - \pi_H), \tag{11.19}$$

$$\hat{w}_H = (1-\beta)(\pi_H - \pi_w), \tag{11.20}$$

$$\hat{q}_H = \varphi_H(\hat{w}_H - \hat{w}_O). \tag{11.21}$$

Equation (11.19) means that firms raise the commodity price when the actual profit share π_H is less than their target profit share π_f. Similarly, equation (11.20) means that workers demand a higher wage rate when the actual wage share $1-\pi_H$ is less than their target wage share $1-\pi_w$. Subscripts f and w represent the variables for capital and labour, respectively. The relative bargaining strength is represented by $\beta \in (0,1)$, and a rise in this value means that bargaining power of capital increases while that of labour decreases. We assume that the target shares are exogenous variables and that $\pi_f > \pi_w$. This is reasonable because firms attempt to set their target profit share as high as possible and workers attempt to set their targets as low as possible. Equation (11.21) means that firms attempt to increase labour productivity when there is a relative rise in the wage of the home country. $\varphi_H \in [0,1)$ represents the elasticity of change in labour productivity to the relative rise in the wage rate. The value of φ_H may depend on many factors, including not only competitive pressure in international trade but also technological conditions. However, this part focuses on the competitive pressure on firms' pricing, and thus regards a large value as meaning that firms are more exposed to severe cost price competition. Firms then try to reduce the commodity price by increasing productivity when there is a relative rise in the wage cost.

We suppose a symmetric situation with the home country and the foreign country. In an analogous manner, we derive the income distribution between capital and labour and the wage rate of the foreign country. Workers set nominal wages and firms set prices and enhance productivity, respectively, according to the following reaction functions:

$$\hat{p}_O = \tilde{\beta}(\tilde{\pi}_f - \pi_O), \tag{11.22}$$

$$\hat{w}_O = (1-\tilde{\beta})(\pi_O - \tilde{\pi}_w), \tag{11.23}$$

$$\hat{q}_O = \varphi_O(\hat{w}_O - \hat{w}_H). \tag{11.24}$$

Equations (11.22), (11.23), and (11.24) incorporate similar implications to those of equations (11.19), (11.20), and (11.21). The relative bargaining strength in the foreign country is represented by $\tilde{\beta} \in (0,1)$, and a rise in this value means the bargaining power of firms increases while that of workers decreases. We also assume that the target wage share and the profit share in the foreign country are both exogenous variables and that $\tilde{\pi}_f > \tilde{\pi}_w$. $\varphi_O \in [0,1)$ represents the elasticity of the change in labour productivity to the relative rise in the wage rate in the foreign country. Similar to the above case, a large value means that foreign firms are exposed to more severe cost price competition.

The dynamics of the actual profit share in each country are obtained from the definition of the profit share as follows:

$$\frac{\dot{\pi}_H}{1-\pi_H} = \hat{p}_H - \hat{w}_H + \hat{q}_H, \tag{11.25}$$

$$\frac{\dot{\pi}_O}{1-\pi_O} = \hat{p}_O - \hat{w}_O + \hat{q}_O, \tag{11.26}$$

where the dot notation indicates the derivatives of the variables with respect to time. In addition, we consider a case in which the actual profit share remains constant over time. In this case, we obtain the prices of the home and foreign countries, $\hat{p}_H = \hat{w}_H - \hat{q}_H$ and $\hat{p}_O = \hat{w}_O - \hat{q}_O$, respectively. Including these two equations, there are six equations, (11.19), (11.20), (11.21), (11.22), (11.23), and (11.24), and eight unknown variables, π_O, π_H, $\hat{p}_O$, $\hat{p}_H$, $\hat{w}_O$, $\hat{w}_H$, $\hat{q}_O$, and $\hat{q}_H$, in this system. Therefore, this simultaneous equation system is complete and we can obtain the solution for these variables. By manipulating these equations, the actual profit share in the home country is determined as follows:

$$\pi_H = \frac{\beta(\pi_f - \pi_w)}{1-\varphi_H(1-\beta)} + \pi_w - \varphi_H \hat{w}_O. \tag{11.27}$$

By substituting this into equation (11.20), the actual wage rate in the home country is obtained as follows:

$$\hat{w}_H = (1-\beta)\left[\frac{\beta(\pi_f - \pi_w)}{1-\varphi_H(1-\beta)} - \varphi_H \hat{w}_O\right]. \tag{11.28}$$

It should be noted that equations (11.27) and (11.28) include not only the bargaining parameter of the home country, but also the rate of change in the foreign wage. This is because the pricing is also affected by the international cost price competition through the change in labour productivity.

Similarly, the actual profit share in the foreign country is determined as follows:

$$\pi_O = \frac{\tilde{\beta}(\tilde{\pi}_f - \tilde{\pi}_w)}{1-\varphi_O(1-\tilde{\beta})} + \tilde{\pi}_w - \varphi_O \hat{w}_H. \tag{11.29}$$

By substituting this into equation (11.23), the actual wage rate in the foreign country is obtained as follows:

$$\hat{w}_O = (1-\tilde{\beta})\left[\frac{\tilde{\beta}(\tilde{\pi}_f - \tilde{\pi}_w)}{1-\varphi_O(1-\tilde{\beta})} - \varphi_O \hat{w}_H\right]. \tag{11.30}$$

Because the pricing of foreign firms is also affected by the international competition, the behaviour of the rate of change in the wage rate of the home country concerns the actual profit share and the wage rate in the foreign country.

By solving the simultaneous equations above, the rate of change of the actual wage rate in both countries is obtained as follows:

$$\hat{w}_H^* = \frac{(1-\beta)}{1-\varphi_H\varphi_O(1-\beta)(1-\tilde{\beta})}\left[\frac{\beta(\pi_f - \pi_w)}{1-\varphi_H(1-\beta)} - \frac{\varphi_H\tilde{\beta}(1-\tilde{\beta})(\tilde{\pi}_f - \tilde{\pi}_w)}{1-\varphi_O(1-\tilde{\beta})}\right], \tag{11.31}$$

$$\hat{w}_O^* = \frac{(1-\tilde{\beta})}{1-\varphi_H\varphi_O(1-\beta)(1-\tilde{\beta})}\left[\frac{\tilde{\beta}(\tilde{\pi}_f - \tilde{\pi}_w)}{1-\varphi_O(1-\tilde{\beta})} - \frac{\varphi_O\beta(1-\beta)(\pi_f - \pi_w)}{1-\varphi_H(1-\beta)}\right], \tag{11.32}$$

where the asterisk indicates the obtained value as a solution. It is also assumed that $1-\varphi_H(1-\beta)>0$ and $1-\varphi_O(1-\tilde{\beta})>0$. These are necessary conditions for the stable behaviour of the actual profit share in both countries. From these two equations, the relative rate of the home wage increase is obtained as follows:

$$\hat{w}_H^* - \hat{w}_O^* = \frac{1}{1-\varphi_H\varphi_O(1-\beta)(1-\tilde{\beta})}\left[\begin{array}{l}\frac{\beta(1-\beta)(\pi_f - \pi_w)}{1-\varphi_H(1-\beta)}(1-\varphi_O+\tilde{\beta}\varphi_O) - \\ \frac{\tilde{\beta}(1-\tilde{\beta})(\tilde{\pi}_f - \tilde{\pi}_w)}{1-\varphi_O(1-\tilde{\beta})}(1-\varphi_H+\beta\varphi_H)\end{array}\right], \tag{11.33}$$

which also determines the dynamics of labour productivity in each country in equations (11.21) and (11.24). As a result, the actual profit shares in both countries are obtained as follows:

$$\pi_H^* = \frac{\beta(\pi_f - \pi_w)}{1-\varphi_H(1-\beta)} + \pi_w - \frac{\varphi_H(1-\tilde{\beta})}{1-\varphi_H\varphi_O(1-\beta)(1-\tilde{\beta})}\left[\frac{\tilde{\beta}(\tilde{\pi}_f - \tilde{\pi}_w)}{1-\varphi_O(1-\tilde{\beta})} - \frac{\varphi_O\beta(1-\beta)(\pi_f - \pi_w)}{1-\varphi_H(1-\beta)}\right], \tag{11.34}$$

$$\pi_O^* = \frac{\tilde{\beta}(\tilde{\pi}_f - \tilde{\pi}_w)}{1-\varphi_O(1-\tilde{\beta})} + \tilde{\pi}_w - \frac{\varphi_O(1-\beta)}{1-\varphi_H\varphi_O(1-\beta)(1-\tilde{\beta})}\left[\frac{\beta(\pi_f - \pi_w)}{1-\varphi_H(1-\beta)} - \frac{\varphi_H\tilde{\beta}(1-\tilde{\beta})(\tilde{\pi}_f - \tilde{\pi}_w)}{1-\varphi_O(1-\tilde{\beta})}\right]. \tag{11.35}$$

It should be noted that a change in the target income distribution share in one country affects the distributional conditions in the other country. This is because under the international cost price competition, a change in the target share of income distribution alters the international cost price competitiveness between two countries. If the pricing by firms in the home country is independent of the international cost price competition (i.e. if $\varphi_H=0$ and $\varphi_O=0$), the wage rate and the actual profit share are $\hat{w}^*_H=(1-\beta)\beta(\pi_f-\pi_w)$ and $\tilde{\pi}^*_H=\beta\pi_f+(1-\beta)\pi_w$, respectively. Thus, only the domestic bargaining conditions determine these variables. However, the foreign bargaining conditions also concern these variables when the domestic firms consider the cost price competition. The same is true for the price and distribution in the foreign country.

Under these circumstances, how do changes in the target distributional share in each class in each economy affect the economic growth rate of the home country? Is a high economic growth rate compatible with equitable distribution among different classes while the BOPC condition is maintained? By focusing on the changes in π^*_O, π^*_H, $\hat{w}^*_O$, and $\hat{w}^*_H$ and the economic growth rate, we will analytically examine these questions.

2.2 Determination of the BOPC economic growth rate and comparative statics analysis

The price dynamics in the home and foreign countries are determined by $\hat{p}_H=(1-\varphi_H)\hat{w}^*_H+\varphi_H\hat{w}^*_O$ and $\hat{p}_O=(1-\varphi_O)\hat{w}^*_O+\varphi_O\hat{w}^*_H$, respectively. By substituting these into equation (11.2), the BOPC growth rate is obtained as follows:

$$\hat{w}^*_H-\hat{w}^*_O=\frac{\eta_H\hat{Y}_H-\eta_O\hat{Y}_O}{(1-\varepsilon_H-\varepsilon_O)(1-\varphi_H-\varphi_O)}. \tag{11.36}$$

In this equation, the values of $\hat{w}^*_O$ and $\hat{w}^*_H$ are now endogenously determined by conflicting claims for the target income distribution share between capital and labour in equations (11.31) and (11.32). As a result, the economic growth rate of the home country must accommodate the changes in these variables. By using comparative static analysis, we will reveal who benefits from changes in the target share of income distribution in each class in both countries, their impacts on economic growth, and via what mechanism it is possible.

Comparative static analysis is mechanical, and thus the calculations are given in the Appendix. In this section we summarize the results of the comparative static analysis and consider some political and economic implications. Table 11.1 gives the results of the impacts of changes in the distributional target share in each class on the wage growth rate and the actual profit share in both countries and the economic growth rate of the home country. International price competitiveness can be measured by the change in the real exchange rate, and the relative rate of the home wage increase is its main determinant. While an increase in the home wage rate implies improvement in living standards of employed workers, *ceteris paribus*, it also leads to a deterioration of the price competitiveness of the home country.

Table 11.1 The results of the comparative static analysis

Change in target share	*Wage rate in home country* $\hat{w}_H^*$	*Wage rate in foreign country* $\hat{w}_O^*$	*Cost price competitiveness* $\hat{w}_H^* - \hat{w}_O^*$	*Profit share in home country* π_H	*Profit share in foreign country* π_O	*Economic growth rate of home country* $\hat{Y}_H$
(1) A rise in π_f	+	−	+	±	−	−
(2) A fall in π_w	+	−	+	±	−	−
(3) A rise in $\tilde{\pi}_f$	−	+	−	−	+	+
(4) A fall in $\tilde{\pi}_w$	−	+	−	−	±	+

Source: author.

The basic interest of capital in each country is to increase its target profit share (i.e. to raise π_f and $\widetilde{\pi}_f$), whereas that of labour is to reduce its target share of the profit share and thus to increase its target wage share (i.e. to reduce π_w and $\widetilde{\pi}_w$). Such changes in the distributional target lead to the following results. (1) A rise in firms' target profit share in the home country leads to rises in the wage rate and the actual profit share there, but it leads to falls in the wage rate and the actual profit share in the foreign country. As there is a rise in the relative rate of increase of the home wage (i.e. a deterioration in the price competitiveness), the economic growth rate of the home country falls. (2) A reduction in the target profit share of domestic workers also leads to a rise in the wage rate, but its impact on the actual profit share in the home country is ambiguous. This impact also leads to falls in the wage rate and the actual profit share in the foreign country. Given a rise in the relative rate of increase of the home wage, the price competitiveness of the home country deteriorates and the economic growth rate of the home country falls. (3) A rise in the target profit share by foreign firms decreases the wage rate and the actual profit share in the home country. In contrast, a rise in this target share leads to rises in the wage rate and the actual profit share in the foreign country. Consequently, the price competitiveness of the home country improves and the economic growth rate of the home country rises. (4) Lastly, a reduction in the target profit share of foreign workers also leads to a fall in the wage rate and the actual profit share in the home country. As this change raises the rate of change in the foreign wage, the price competitiveness of the home country improves. Consequently, the economic growth rate of the home country rises. On the other hand, its impact on the actual profit share in the foreign country is ambiguous.

2.3 The political implications of changes in income distribution and BOPC growth

It should be noted that the income distribution share is defined by the profit and wage shares, and that if one of them rises, the other necessarily falls. Therefore, the profit share necessarily conflicts with the wage share. Hence, we will measure the conflicts and cooperation of income distribution between capital and labour by the rates of change in the wage rate and the profit share.[3] Here, the cooperative income distribution is said to be realized when both the wage growth rate and the profit share increase simultaneously in a country. In other words, there is an equitable (win–win) income distribution relationship between labour and capital. In contrast, the conflictive income distribution is said to be realized when the wage growth rate and the profit share move in opposite directions; this means that when an economic agent or class in a country achieves an increase in its income, others lose such an opportunity. In other words, there is an inequitable (win–lose) income distribution relationship between labour and capital.

On the basis of the results obtained in Table 11.1 (1)–(4), we attempt to present the political implications for economic growth, employment, and conflict–cooperation across income distribution in the two countries. First, focusing on the wage rates of the two countries, the results in (1)–(4) reveal that there are structural conflicts in the labour class in both countries. It is not possible to simultaneously realize rises in the wage rate in both countries when there is a shock on the target share of income distribution. A rise in the target share of the distribution in both countries that contributes to a rise in the wage rate in one country decreases the wage rate in the other country. For example, a rise in the target share of firms in the home country increases the rate of change in the home wage rate, whereas it decreases this distributional variable in the foreign country. Such an impossibility originates from international competition over cost and price reduction between the two countries through the adjustment in labour productivity. As equations (11.31), (11.32), (11.34), and (11.35) indicate, the profit shares and wage rates in the two countries are affected by φ_H and φ_O. If these values are zero, the distributional conditions are determined by internal factors only, and the firms in each country do not have to take international cost differences into account in their pricing. However, if firms' pricing behaviour concerns international cost differences and thus competitive pressure, the dynamics of the wage also depend on the trade partner's distributional conditions.

Second, when there is a rise in the target share of firms in each country, the rate of change in the wage rate and the actual profit share simultaneously increase (cases 1 and 3). Even though there is the possibility of domestic cooperation across income distribution, it cannot be compatible with improvement in the price competitiveness of each economy. Consequently, cooperation in the national economy cannot be compatible with a high economic growth rate either. If a country attempts to achieve cooperation for income distribution, it has to accept increased unemployment over time. Figure 11.3 illustrates such a

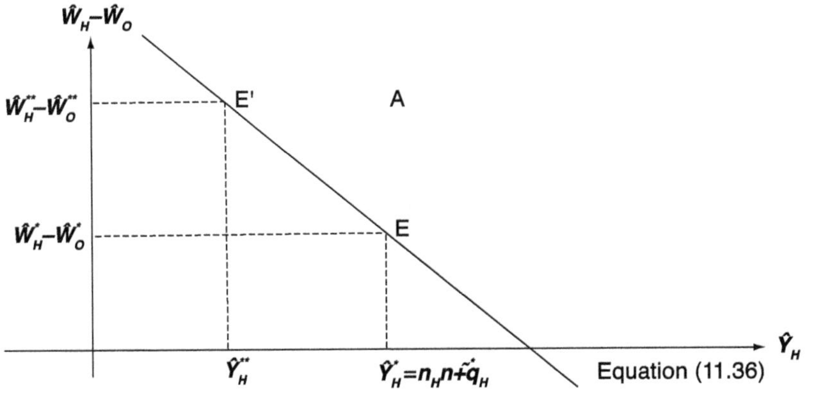

Figure 11.3 Incompatibility of a high economic growth rate and cooperation for income distribution.

Source: author.

Note
If the relative home wage increases by bargaining, the economic growth rate of the home country must be reduced to maintain the BOPC. Consequently, unemployment increases over time according to the difference between $\hat{Y}_H^{**}-\hat{q}_H^{**}$ and n_H.

case. Suppose the home country is initially at point E, where at a given relative wage growth rate, the economic growth rate is sufficient to support full employment over time (i.e. $\hat{Y}^*_H - \hat{q}^*_H = n_H$). A rise in the target profit share by domestic firms simultaneously increases the wage rate and the actual profit share in the home country ((1) in Table 11.1), and it leads to a relative increase in the commodity price of the home country; this, in turn, leads to the appreciation of the domestic currency, which causes a decrease in net exports. At a given rate of economic growth, the home country falls into balance-of-payment deficits over time (point A). However, such a circumstance is not sustainable in the long run because international capital regards such economic growth with an ever-growing deficit as unsustainable. Therefore, the home country is forced to maintain the BOPC over time.

The relationship between the relative wage rate and the economic growth rate has to move from point E to point E′ as long as the economy maintains the BOPC. Recall that firms attempt to cope with a rise in the relative rate of the home wage by enhancing labour productivity so that they can recover price competitiveness. Therefore, there is a rise in $\hat{q}^*_H$, which also reduces the growth rate of labour demand. Consequently, given a growth rate of the labour supply, the economy has to experience unemployment over time as the cost of achieving cooperation for income distribution in the national economy.

Even if economic growth is sustainable at point E′ in terms of BOPC, such a circumstance involves new conflicts. The shift from E to E′ by a change in the income distribution target creates unemployment over time, while the capital and employed labour in the home country continue to benefit from this change in the income distribution. That is, capital can enjoy a rise in the profit share and employed labour can receive an increased nominal wage. However, some workers may lose their jobs because of a decrease in the economic growth rate in the home country, and they do not benefit from the wage rate increase. Therefore, new conflicts between employed and unemployed workers may arise.

Finally, as a natural extension of Blecker's model, the current model also shows the existence of a trilemma among high economic growth, cooperative income distribution in the national economy, and the BOPC. As cases (1) and (2) in Table 11.1 show, whenever there are rises in both the wage rate and the profit share in the home country, economic growth will stagnate because of the relative rise in the domestic commodity price. If the economy attempts to keep the economic growth rate at an initial rate with increased relative wages, it inevitably falls into a trade deficit over time. When faced with a trade deficit, to reduce it either the economic growth rate or the relative wage rate of the home country must be reduced. Then, to maintain the economic growth rate at an initial rate, the relative wage rate in the home country must be reduced, which means that bargaining between capital and labour must be abandoned. Therefore, a high economic growth rate, cooperative income distribution in the national economy, and the BOPC are not simultaneously compatible: only two can be realized at once. The choice by a country is a political problem because the choice has various impacts on the different classes of the economy. An economy pursuing an egalitarian state falls into low growth and high unemployment, whereas an economy that allows inequalities may realize high growth, although its policy may tend to be a neoliberal one that sacrifices wage increases to maintain cost price competitiveness.

The trilemma among high economic growth, cooperative income distribution in the national economy, and the BOPC is depicted in Figure 11.4. When there is a trade deficit caused by a shock: (1) If the BOPC is abandoned, actors in the international financial market will eventually become nervous, and the economy may be jeopardized through their sell-out of the currency, whereas domestic capital and employed workers cooperatively benefit from increases in the profit share and the wage rate, respectively. (2) If bargaining between domestic capital and labour is abandoned, although the economy can satisfy the BOPC condition and maintain the economic growth rate, the domestic capital and employed labour must accept the neoclassical-like adjusted level of income distribution. (3) If a high economic growth rate is abandoned, the BOPC condition can be satisfied, and domestic capital and employed labour cooperatively benefit from increases in the profit share and the wage rate, respectively, by way of bargaining. However, the economy will stagnate and will experience unemployment over time. Consequently, unemployed workers do not benefit from the wage rate increase, which may lead to a new intra-class conflict between employed and unemployed workers.

2.4 New growth models against trilemma: possibility and limit

The theoretical model implies that in the age of globalization, it is difficult to establish the so-called corporatism model. Or, even if a corporatism is established, the severe price competition between countries and constraints of balance of payments in international trade will lead to intra-class conflict among workers in a national economy. That is, the political and economic configuration is completely different between the age of 1980s corporatism and the age of recent globalization.

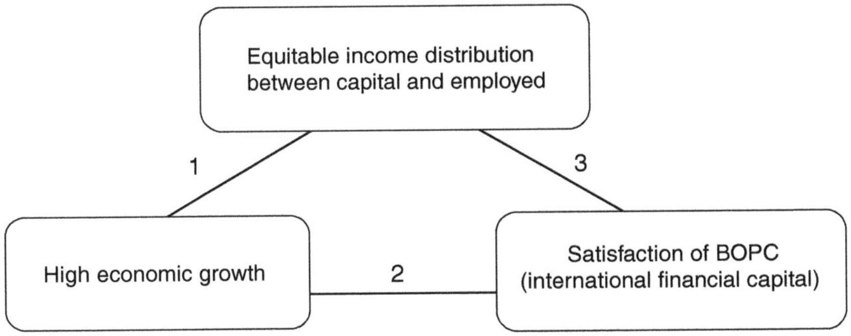

Figure 11.4 Summary of the trilemma.

Source: author.

It is such an emerging structure of the global economy that is a cause of such inter- and intra-class conflict for income distribution and employment in the domestic economy. However, is it possible to reconcile such a situation like Figure 11.1? In other words, is there a way to overcome the trilemma particular to such a situation? Although a part of discussion below may be beyond the results of the model, some suggestion for a new growth model can be presented.

First is to expand the world trade volume and depend on the foreign countries' economic growth. Equation (11.36) implies that a rise in the growth rate of the foreign country increases the exports and brings room for a rise in the relative wages. Thus, an economic boom in foreign countries has an effect to mitigate the trilemma. This growth model is an export-led growth of the foreign-dependent type, and therefore it has its own fragility. As long as the foreign countries are in economic boom, the domestic economy is sustained by it. However, once the foreign countries turn into depression, the exports of the domestic economy shrink accordingly and the constraints of the trilemma work more severely.

Taking the fragility of the foreign country-dependent growth model into consideration, instead we have to think about the possibility of a new growth model based on domestic economy. The second and third suggestions are related to the domestic strategy.

The second is to promote innovation that creates new effective demand. The mechanism is concerned with the values of income elasticities for exports and imports. These values are given as exogenous in the current model, but post-Keynesian thought argues that a demand-creative innovation in a national economy raises the elasticities of demand for exports (Thirlwall, 2012). That is, a large value of income elasticities for exports reflects the attractiveness of export goods produced by domestic firms. With a large value of income elasticities, a rise in foreign countries' income induces a large increase in exports, which accommodates conflicts originating from the trilemma. As equation (11.36) indicates, a rise in the elasticities of demand for exports increases the value of the RHS, which shifts the BOPC line rightward in Figure 11.3.

The third is to promote industrial structural change. It is known that changes in the composition of the structure of export and import goods production also stimulates the economic growth of a domestic economy. Such a mechanism is explained by the multi-sectoral version of the BOPC model (Araujo and Lima, 2007; Setterfield, 2012). In the current aggregate model, a domestic country's growth rate will rise only when the growth rate of the foreign country rises. However, the multi-sectoral BOPC model shows that a domestic country can still raise its growth rate without the foreign country's economic growth if it can change the industrial structure of the economy. To be more precise, the multi-sectoral BOPC model reveals that a country can grow faster by shifting resources to sectors with higher income elasticities for exports and away from sectors with a high income elasticity of demand for imports. This strategy overcomes the first and second suggestions mentioned above. Even if the speed of innovation that raises the elasticities of demand for exports slows down, industrial structural change that alters the sectoral composition of exports and imports still enhances economic growth. Traditional policies of sector-specific import substitution and/or export promotion designed to boost growth may be a possible strategy (Setterfield, 2012).

All these effects of new growth models will lead to rightward shift of the BOPC frontier depicted by equation (11.36), which moderates the degree of the trilemma. It is possible to realize equitable income distribution, satisfaction of the BOPC, and high economic growth as long as the new growth model is effective. However, once the validity of the new growth model reaches the limit, the trilemma will appear once again. In this sense, the above growth models are only temporarily effective. The trilemma is concerned with structural characteristics that are not solved easily.

3 Conclusion

National economies face many constraints in the era of globalization. A national economy must maintain the BOPC to defend itself from international capital attack, but trade performance depends on other factors, such as the degree of international competition, GDP in the foreign country, and cost price competitiveness. The cost price competitiveness of a national economy is affected by domestic distributional conditions. Moreover, the income distribution is stipulated by the bargaining process, which includes a conflicting claim between capital and labour, which is also affected by the degree of international cost price competition.

The current chapter reveals that there is still a macroeconomic trilemma among a high economic growth rate, equitable income distribution for capital and labour in the national economy, and satisfying the BOPC. This result has implications for the difficulty of the reconciliation of inter- and intra-class coalitions between labour and capital and economic growth. If the political goal is to increase both the wage rate and the profit share in the home country, a higher commodity price than that of the other country necessarily results. Thus, the net exports decrease, as does the economic growth rate of the home country under the BOPC condition. Thus, the BOPC is one of the obstacles for an economy seeking to realize wage-led growth through cooperation between capital and labour.[4]

Inversely, establishing an equitable distributional condition is an obstacle for satisfactorily playing games of trade in the globalized economy. Both employed capital and labour can benefit from such a change in income distribution, although its realization comes at the cost of a decrease in employment over time. Even though such a distributional change may contribute to establishing a class coalition between capital and labour, there may also arise new intra-class conflicts between employed and unemployed workers. This is because while the former can enjoy an increased wage and maintain their employment, the latter lose their jobs and cannot benefit from the wage rate increase. That is, cooperation among labour is also difficult. Lastly, if the home country puts a priority on high economic growth, it has to abandon the class coalition between capital and labour. This is because in order to maintain a high rate of economic growth, the economy must maintain price competitiveness, but it is not possible to achieve both an equitable distribution through bargaining and an improvement in price competitiveness.

Section 2.4 considered the effect of three new growth models that may conquer this trilemma. However, the effect of new growth models is valid only in the short term. When its validity reaches the limit, a trilemma soon shows. It is a knife-edge principle to simultaneously coordinate political-economic issues related to international trade relations and power relations between labour and capital within each economy.

Appendix: the calculation of the comparative static analysis

The impacts of a rise in the target profit share of domestic firms on the rates of change in the wage and actual profit shares in both countries are obtained by differentiating equations (11.31), (11.32), (11.34), and (11.35) with respect to π_f:

$$\frac{\partial \hat{w}_H^*}{\partial \pi_f} = \frac{\beta(1-\beta)}{1-\varphi_H\varphi_O(1-\beta)(1-\tilde{\beta})}\left[\frac{1}{1-\varphi_H(1-\beta)}\right] > 0, \tag{11.A1}$$

$$\frac{\partial \hat{w}_O^*}{\partial \pi_f} = \frac{-(1-\tilde{\beta})\varphi_O}{1-\varphi_H\varphi_O(1-\beta)(1-\tilde{\beta})}\left[\frac{\beta(1-\beta)}{1-\varphi_H(1-\beta)}\right] < 0, \tag{11.A2}$$

$$\frac{\partial \pi_H^*}{\partial \pi_f} = \frac{\beta}{1-\varphi_H(1-\beta)} + \frac{\varphi_H(1-\tilde{\beta})}{1-\varphi_H\varphi_O(1-\beta)(1-\tilde{\beta})}\left[\frac{\varphi_O\beta(1-\beta)}{1-\varphi_H(1-\beta)}\right] > 0, \tag{11.A3}$$

and

$$\frac{\partial \pi_O^*}{\partial \pi_f} = -\frac{\varphi_O(1-\beta)}{1-\varphi_H\varphi_O(1-\beta)(1-\tilde{\beta})}\left[\frac{\beta}{1-\varphi_H(1-\beta)}\right] < 0. \tag{11.A4}$$

The impacts of a reduction in the target profit share of domestic workers on the rates of change in the wage and actual profit shares in both countries are obtained by differentiating the above equations with respect to π_w:

$$\frac{\partial \hat{w}_H^*}{\partial \pi_w} = \frac{-\beta(1-\beta)}{1-\varphi_H\varphi_O(1-\beta)(1-\tilde{\beta})}\left[\frac{1}{1-\varphi_H(1-\beta)}\right] < 0, \tag{11.A5}$$

$$\frac{\partial \hat{w}_O^*}{\partial \pi_w} = \frac{(1-\tilde{\beta})}{1-\varphi_H\varphi_O(1-\beta)(1-\tilde{\beta})}\left[\frac{\varphi_O\beta(1-\beta)}{1-\varphi_H(1-\beta)}\right] > 0, \tag{11.A6}$$

$$\frac{\partial \pi_H^*}{\partial \pi_w} = \underbrace{\frac{(1-\beta)(1-\varphi_H)}{1-\varphi_H(1-\beta)}}_{+} - \underbrace{\frac{\varphi_H(1-\tilde{\beta})}{1-\varphi_H\varphi_O(1-\beta)(1-\tilde{\beta})}\left[\frac{\varphi_O\beta(1-\beta)}{1-\varphi_H(1-\beta)}\right]}_{+}, \tag{11.A7}$$

and

$$\frac{\partial \pi_O^*}{\partial \pi_w} = \frac{\varphi_O(1-\beta)}{1-\varphi_H\varphi_O(1-\beta)(1-\tilde{\beta})}\left[\frac{\beta}{1-\varphi_H(1-\beta)}\right] > 0. \tag{11.A8}$$

The impacts of a rise in the target profit share of foreign firms on the rates of change in the wage and actual profit shares in both countries are obtained by differentiating equations (11.31), (11.32), (11.34), and (11.35) with respect to $\tilde{\pi}_f$:

$$\frac{\partial \hat{w}_H^*}{\partial \tilde{\pi}_f} = -\frac{(1-\beta)}{1-\varphi_H\varphi_O(1-\beta)(1-\tilde{\beta})}\left[\frac{\varphi_H\tilde{\beta}(1-\tilde{\beta})}{1-\varphi_O(1-\tilde{\beta})}\right] < 0, \tag{11.A9}$$

$$\frac{\partial \hat{w}_O^*}{\partial \tilde{\pi}_f} = \frac{(1-\tilde{\beta})}{1-\varphi_H\varphi_O(1-\beta)(1-\tilde{\beta})}\left[\frac{\tilde{\beta}}{1-\varphi_O(1-\tilde{\beta})}\right] > 0, \tag{11.A10}$$

$$\frac{\partial \pi_H^*}{\partial \tilde{\pi}_f} = -\frac{\varphi_O(1-\tilde{\beta})}{1-\varphi_H\varphi_O(1-\beta)(1-\tilde{\beta})}\left[\frac{\tilde{\beta}}{1-\varphi_O(1-\tilde{\beta})}\right] < 0, \tag{11.A11}$$

and

$$\frac{\partial \pi_O^*}{\partial \tilde{\pi}_f} = \frac{\tilde{\beta}}{1-\varphi_O(1-\tilde{\beta})} + \frac{\varphi_O(1-\beta)}{1-\varphi_H\varphi_O(1-\beta)(1-\tilde{\beta})}\left[\frac{\varphi_H\tilde{\beta}(1-\tilde{\beta})}{1-\varphi_O(1-\tilde{\beta})}\right] > 0. \tag{11.A12}$$

The impacts of a reduction in the target profit share of foreign workers on the rates of change in the wage and actual profit shares in both countries are obtained by differentiating equations (11.31), (11.32), (11.34), and (11.35) with respect to $\tilde{\pi}_w$:

$$\frac{\partial \hat{w}_H^*}{\partial \tilde{\pi}_w} = \frac{(1-\beta)}{1-\varphi_H\varphi_O(1-\beta)(1-\tilde{\beta})}\left[\frac{\varphi_H\tilde{\beta}(1-\tilde{\beta})}{1-\varphi_O(1-\tilde{\beta})}\right] > 0, \tag{11.A13}$$

$$\frac{\partial \hat{w}_O^*}{\partial \tilde{\pi}_w} = -\frac{(1-\tilde{\beta})}{1-\varphi_H\varphi_O(1-\beta)(1-\tilde{\beta})}\left[\frac{\tilde{\beta}}{1-\varphi_O(1-\tilde{\beta})}\right] < 0, \tag{11.A14}$$

$$\frac{\partial \pi_H^*}{\partial \tilde{\pi}_w} = \frac{\varphi_H(1-\tilde{\beta})}{1-\varphi_H\varphi_O(1-\beta)(1-\tilde{\beta})}\left[\frac{\tilde{\beta}}{1-\varphi_O(1-\tilde{\beta})}\right] > 0, \tag{11.A15}$$

and

$$\frac{\partial \pi_O^*}{\partial \tilde{\pi}_w} = \underbrace{\frac{(1-\varphi_O)(1-\tilde{\beta})}{1-\varphi_O(1-\tilde{\beta})}}_{+} - \underbrace{\frac{\varphi_O(1-\beta)}{1-\varphi_H\varphi_O(1-\beta)(1-\tilde{\beta})}\left[\frac{\varphi_H\tilde{\beta}(1-\tilde{\beta})}{1-\varphi_O(1-\tilde{\beta})}\right]}_{+} \quad (11.\text{A16})$$

Notes

1 The BOPC model is a post-Keynesian economic growth model that attributes the role of the BOPC as the determinant of the economic growth model. The BOPC model has been theoretically developed since the seminal paper by Thirlwall (1979), and its empirical validity has been tested econometrically. Soukiazis and Cerqueira (2012) offer a useful overview of recent developments in BOPC modelling.

2 If the rates of change in the nominal wage in both countries are equal, the growth rate of the home country is equal to

$$\hat{Y}_H^* = \frac{\eta_O}{\eta_H}\hat{Y}_O \quad (11.18)$$

and the so-called 'Thirlwall's law' holds (Thirlwall, 1979).

3 In addition, as we suppose the fixed-coefficient type of production function, the rate of change in the profit rate that the capital is concerned with is also zero when the profit share becomes constant. Therefore, it is not possible to compare the distributional relationship between capital and labour based on the rate of change in the nominal wage and the profit rates.

4 Wage-led growth is usually explained by focusing on the dual functions of the wage in a capitalist economy. The wage plays the roles of the source of demand and the cost of production. The model of Bhaduri and Marglin (1990) is representative in this regard. However, the argument in the current study (as well as in standard BOPC models) is based on the role of the wage as the production cost only, and does not focus on its role as the source of demand.

References

Andrews, D.M. (1994), 'Capital mobility and state autonomy: towards a structural theory of international monetary relations', *International Studies Quarterly*, 38, 193–218.

Araujo, R. and G. Lima (2007), 'A structural economic dynamic approach to balance of payment constrained growth', *Cambridge Journal of Economics*, 31 (5), 755–774.

Bhaduri, A. and S.A. Marglin (1990), 'Unemployment and the real wage: the economic basis for contesting political ideologies', *Cambridge Journal of Economics*, 14 (4), 375–393.

Blecker, R.A. (1998), 'International competitiveness, relative wages, and the balance-of-payments constraint', *Journal of Post Keynesian Economics*, 20 (4), 495–526.

Bresser-Pereira, L.C. (2010), *Globalization and Competition: Why some Emergent Countries Succeed While Others Fall Behind*, New York: Cambridge University Press.

Lavoie, M. and E. Stockhammer (2013), *Wage-led Growth: An Equitable Strategy for Economic Recovery*, New York: Palgrave Macmillan.

Rowthorn, R. (1977), 'Conflict, inflation and money', *Cambridge Journal of Economics*, 1 (3), 215–239.

Setterfield, M. (2012), 'The remarkable durability of Thirlwall's law', in Soukiazis, E. and P.A. Cerqueira (eds), *Models of Balance of Payments Constrained Growth*, Basingstoke: Palgrave Macmillan, pp. 83–110.

Storm, S. and C.W.M. Naastepad (2012), *Macroeconomics beyond the NAIRU*, Cambridge, MA: Harvard University Press.

Storm, S. and C.W.M. Naastepad (2013), 'Wage-led or profit-led supply: wages, productivity and investment', in Lavoie, M. and E. Stockhammer (eds), *Wage-led Growth: An Equitable Strategy for Economic Recovery*, New York: Palgrave Macmillan, pp. 100–124.

Soukiazis, E. and P.A. Cerqueira (eds) (2012), *Models of Balance of Payments Constrained Growth*, Basingstoke: Palgrave Macmillan.

Thirlwall, A.P. (1979), 'The balance-of-payments-constraints as an explanation of international growth differences', *Banca Nationale del Lavaro Quarterly Review*, 128, 45–53.

Thirlwall, A.P. (2012), 'Balance of payments constrained growth models: history and overview', in Soukiazis, E. and P.A. Cerqueira (eds), *Models of Balance of Payments Constrained Growth*, Basingstoke: Palgrave Macmillan, pp. 11–49.

Weiss, L. (2003), 'Introduction: bringing domestic institutions back in', in Weiss, L. (ed.), *States in the Global Economy: Bringing Domestic Institutions Back In*, New York: Cambridge University Press.

Index

Page numbers in *italics* denote tables, those in **bold** denote figures.

A/AP (*Arbeiderpartiet:* Labour Party), Norway 55
Abe administration, Japan 128, 130; Abenomics 122, 128–31, 133
abrupt institutional change 74, 75
acquis communautaire 193
actors, and institutional change 79–80
AfD (*Alternativ für Deutschland:* Alternative for Germany), Germany 42, 48
Africa 214
ageing population 81, 124; Europe 23; Japan 124, 132, 135
agriculture: agricultural land rent 207, **207**, 208; international comparative analysis of de-industrialization *99*, *102*, *103*, *104*, *105*, *106*, *107*, *108*, *109*, 110
Amable, Bruno 61, *71*, 72, 95, 123–4, 143–4
Amsterdam Treaty, 1997 126, 183, 186
Andrews, D. M. 223, 224
application (institutional structure) *78*, 78–9
Argentina 36, 211
Asia 95, 97, 112, 123–4, 220; and geopolitics 214; interdependence **213**
'at-risk-of-poverty' rate 127
Atkinson, A. B. 127
austerity policies 22, 37–8, 192
Australia: income distribution 150, **160**; institutional characteristics **147**, 148
Austria: economic discomfort 189; and the European Court of Justice 194; income distribution 150; labour market performance 9, *9*; New Right parties 48, 50, 60; trade patterns 180, **181**, **182**
Autopartei (Auto Party), Switzerland 50, 56
balanced budget policies 36, 37
bank bailouts 129
Bartolini, Stefano 52
Baumol, W. A. 94
Beijing Consensus 214
Belgium: and the European Court of Justice 194; income distribution 150; institutional characteristics **147**, 148; New Right parties 50, 56, 62; trade patterns 180, **181**, **182**
Bell, Daniel 28–9
benefits, of EU (European Union) 173, *178*, 180, 183–9, **184**, **185**, **186**, **187**, **188**, **190**, 191
Betz, Hans-Georg 50, 55, 56, 58, 59, 60
Beyme, Klaus von 49
Bharatiya Janata Party, India 58
biased technological change 141
big events *75*, 76–7, 79
Blecker, R.A. 225, 226, 228, 230, 231, 232, 240
'*bloc bourgeois*' coalition 13
BOPC (balance of payments constraints) 223–6, *225*, 243–6; comparative statistical analysis 236, *237*, 238, 244–6; and income distribution 232–6, *237*, 238–43, **239**, **241**; model of 226–32, **231**; political implications 238–41, **239**
Boyer, Robert *71*, 72, 122, 123, 202–22
'bracket creep' 29
Brazil 207, 214
'breakdown and replacement' (institutional change) 74
Bresser-Pereira, L. C. 223
Bretton Woods 30, 202, 203, 211, 220
Britain *see* UK

Buchanan, Pat 58
budget surplus 34–5, 36
'build-up' 174
Bulgaria 191
Bundesbank 38
business-related services: international comparative analysis of de-industrialization 11, 99, *99*, **100**, 101, *102*, *103*, *104*, *105*, *106*, *107*, *108*, *109*, 110, 112, 114–15, *115*, 116, 117

Cameron, David 63
Canada: income distribution 150, **160**; institutional characteristics **147**, 148; New Right parties 58
capital flight 223, 224
capital–labour ratio 156
capitalism: emerging industrializing capitalisms 208–9, **209**, **212**, 214–15, *216*, *217*, 218; finance-led capitalisms 208, **209**, 210, 211, 212, **212**, 214, *216*, *217*, 218, 221; innovation led capitalism 210, 211, **211**, **212**; mature industrial capitalisms 215, *216*, *217*; rentier regimes 205, *206*, **207**, 207–8, 209, **209**, 210, 212, **212**, 215, *216*, *217*, 218; tripartite structure 11–12, *12*; types of 95, 118n4, 123–4
capitalist democracy, models of 12–13
capitalist property rights 35
CDU (*Christlich Demokratische Union Deutschlands:* Christian Democratic Union), Germany 53, 196
center–periphery cleavage 53
central banks, and debt states 37, **38**
Centrumpartij (Centre Party), Netherlands 50
charismatic leaders 13
Charter of Fundamental Rights of the European Union 126
China 220, 221; continental mixed capitalism 118n4; as creditor of USA 42n5; geopolitics 214, **215**; import and export dependency **134**; industrialization 81, 203; innovation-led capitalism 205; interdependence 213
Christian parties 53
citizenship, EU (European Union) 188–9
city capitalism 118n4
civic property rights 35
civil society, in the EU (European Union) 196–7
cleavages 51–5, 59–60, 62, *63*, 67
climate change 215, 218, 220–1
Clinton, Bill 31
Closa, Carlos 188
cluster analysis 146, 147, **147**, 148–50, **149**
Cobb–Douglas functional form 227
commons 215, *217*, 220–1
communist parties: Italy 54–5
comparative statistical analysis 236, *237*, 238, 244–6
compétences (EU) 20, 23, 26
conflict: and the EU (European Union) 174, 175, *178*, 196–7; and income distribution 240, 242, 243
conflicting claim model of income distribution 232
conflictive income distribution 238
Conservative Party, UK 54
conservative welfare states 123
consolidation state 27, 31–7, **33**, *36*; European 37–42
consumer services: international comparative analysis of de-industrialization 99, *99*, **100**, 101, *102*, *103*, *104*, *105*, *106*, *107*, *108*, *109*, 110, 111, 115, *115*, 116, 117
consumption, and investment 93
continental European capitalism 95, 97, 100, 101, 110, 123
continental mixed capitalism 118n4
convergence, and the EU (European Union) 174, *178*
conversion 77, 78, *78*, 79
cooperative income distribution 238, 240–1
coordinated market economies 123
corporate value 125
corporatism 4, 5, 241
cost of democracy 47–51, 52, 56, 59, 62, 64–5, 66
'cost disease' of the service sector 28
cost price competition 225, 226, 243
covariance matrix 156
crises: and policy regime change 11–12, *12*
critical junctures 72, 73, **73**, 77
Crouch, Colin 83
CSU party 196
Curtis, Gerald L. 54
cut points 76
Czech Republic 194

DC (*Democrazia Cristiana:* Christian Democracy), Italy 53
'de-commodification' 123

de-industrialization 80–1, 82, 91; four types of 95, *96*; France 110; Germany 101; and the growth regime **92**, 92–5; international comparative analysis 95, **97**, 97–101, **98**, *99*, **100**, 101–17, *102–9*, *115*; by the shift of final demand to the service sector 95, *96*, 116; theoretical framework **92**, 92–5; through manufacturing–service linkages 95, *96*, 116
debt state 27–37, **28**, **31**, **33**, *36*
defence spending, NATO countries 43n11
'deflation gap' 135
Delors, Jacques 26, 125–6, 193
demand formation 92–3
demand growth 93–4
demand regime 93, 116
democracy: ambivalence of 36; cost of 47–51, 52, 56, 59, 62, 64–5, 66; and the EU (European Union) 19, 23–5, 175, *178*; and fiscal consolidation 42; models of 12–13; and neoliberalism 3, 83–4; tripartite structure 11–12, *12*
Denmark: economic discomfort 189; income distribution 150; institutional characteristics **147**, 148; New Right parties 48, 50, 60, 66
DF (*Dansk Folkeparti:* Danish Peoples Party), Denmark 48, 66
Dijsselbloem, Jeroen 193
displacement 77–8, *78*, 79
domestic final demand 93
drift 77, 78, *78*, 79
Dünhaupt, P. 142
DVU (*Deutsche Volksunion:* German People's Union), Germany 50

EC (European Community) 19–20; *see also* EU (European Union)
ECB (European Central Bank) 21, 22, 23, 26, 195; and debt states 37, 38, 39, 40
economic discomfort, index of 189, 190
economic growth: and BOPC (balance of payments constraints) 224, **225**, 236, *237*, 238–43, **239**, **241**, 243–4; and poverty levels 121
economic integration 177; and interdependence 173, *178*; *see also* TROs (transnational regional organization)
economic performance, constraints on 224, **225**
economic prosperity, and the EU (European Union) 189, **190**, 191
ECSC (European Coal and Steel Community) 19–20; *see also* EU (European Union)
education division 123
EEC (European Economic Community) 19–20; *see also* EU (European Union)
elites: and policy regime change 11; technocratic rational democracy 13
embedded liberalism 203
emerging industrializing capitalisms 208–9, **209**, **212**, 214–15, *216*, *217*, 218
Emmenegger, P. 113
employment: and de-industrialization 94; Europe/Japan comparison 6–7; life-time 7; *see also* unemployment
employment growth 94
employment regimes 124
EMU (European Monetary Union): consolidation state 27, 37–42
endogenous causes of institutional change 75, *75*, 77
endometabolism **73**, *75*, 75–6, 77, 78, 79
enlargement, of EU (European Union) 127, 175, *178*
environment (institutional structure) *78*, 78–9
EPAs (economic partnership agreements), Japan 131
epistemic communities *see* experts, role of in the EU (European Union)
EPP (Group of the European Peoples Party) 51, 66
Ersson, Svante O. 52
Esping-Andersen, Gosta 123
Estonia 191
ethnic parties 53
EU (European Union) 11, 36; 'la finalité politique' 176, *178*; ageing population 124; austerity policies 22, 192; benefits of 173, *178*, 180, 183–9, **184**, **185**, **186**, **187**, **188**, **190**, 191; citizenship 188–9; conflict in 174–5, *178*, 196–7; and convergence 174, *178*; crisis 19, 21, 23–4, 26, 171, 172; and democracy 19, 23–5, 175, *178*; disintegration, and neo-functionalism 171–2, 177–98; economic integration 173, *178*; economic prosperity 189, **190**, 191; enlargement 127, 175, *178*; EPA (economic partnership agreement) with Japan 131; Europe 2020 strategy 127–8; European social model 126; exogenous shocks 176, *178*; and fairness 176, *178*; geopolitics 214, **215**; growth strategies

122, 124; identity 187–8, **188**; incremental integration 193–5, **194**; interdependence 173, *178*; Market Integration Plan, 1985 125–6; neoliberalism 122; pluralistic conflicts in 175, *178*; politicization in 174–5, *178*, 192, 196–7; positive and negative integration 174, *178*; public attitudes towards 21, 173, *178*, 180, 183–9, **184**, **185**, **186**, **187**, **188**; respect for decisions of 174, *178*, 193–5, **194**; role of experts in 173, *178*, 191–3; security 173, *178*, 186–7, **187**; social inclusion strategies 125–8; trade patterns 177–80, **179**, **181**, **182**; unemployment 189, **190**, 191
euro crisis 19, 20, 21–3, 50, 100, 101, 171, 172, 196–7, 210, 212
euro-bonds 26
Euro-skepticism 48, 51, 184, 185, 196
Euroland, consolidation state 37–42
Europe: consolidation state 37–42; contemporary crises in 19–26; democratic crisis 19, 24–5; economic growth and income inequality 121; employment 6–7; EU crisis 19, 21, 23–4, 26; and the euro crisis 19, 20, 21–3; income distribution/redistribution 7–8; interdependence **213**; labour market 130; labour incentive 6–7; labour market performance 8–11, *9*; social contract 22–3; social security regime 124; *see also* EU (European Union)
Europe 2020 strategy 127–8
European Commission 21–2, 23, 24, 26, 43n19, 195; and debt states 38, 39, 40; and the OMC (Open Method of Coordination) 127
European Convention, 2002 188
European Council 26, 40, 126, 128
European Court of Justice 22, 26, 194, **194**
European Investment Bank 26
European Model of Society 26
European Parliament 24; 2014 elections 48, 51, 66, 196; and New Right parties 48, 64
European social model 126
eurozone crisis *see* euro crisis
exogenous causes of institutional change 75, *75*, 76–7
exogenous shocks, and the EU (European Union) 176, *178*
experts, role of in the EU (European Union) 173, *178*, 191–3
explicit public debt 35
export core manufacturing: international comparative analysis of de-industrialization 99, *99*, *100*, 101, *102*, *103*, *104*, *105*, *106*, *107*, *108*, *109*, 110, 111, 112, 114, *115*, 116, 117
'export-led growth' 93
export, as element of final demand 93
extreme right *see* New Right parties

fairness, and the EU (European Union) 176, *178*
families: changing structure in Japan 129–30; role of in welfare states 123
FDI (foreign direct investment), and de-industrialization 94–5
final demand 93
finance-led capitalisms 208, **209**, 210, 211, 212, **212**, 214, *216*, *217*, 218, 221
finance-led growth regime *71*, 72
financial intermediation division 123
financial rent 207, **207**, 208
'financial repression' 34
financial services 30; international comparative analysis of de-industrialization 99, *99*, **100**, *102*, *103*, *104*, *105*, *106*, *107*, *108*, *109*, 110, 111–12, 114, *115*, 116, 117
financialization 30–1, 32, 81, 82, 116, 139, 144–5, 223–4; and income distribution 142, 143, 146, 148, **149**, 150, 151, 156, 158, 162, 163–4
Finland: ethnic parties 53; and the European Court of Justice 194; income distribution 150; New Right parties 48; public attitudes towards EU 184; trade patterns 179, **179**
Fiscal Compact 40, 42
fiscal crisis of the state 27–30, **28**, **29**
FN (*Front National*/National Front), France 48, 50, 60, 64, 66
FN (National Front) 50
Fordism 15, 71, 75, 81, 84n5, 85n8, 91, 92, 93, 116, 123, 143, 144, 202; Fordist policy regime 76, 80, 82
foreign trade *see* trade
formal rules 77
FPÖ (*Freiheits Parti Österreich:* Austrian Liberal Party) 48, 50, 60
fragmentation, and de-industrialization 114–16
France: de-industrialization 91, 95, **98**, 99, 100, **100**, *102*, *105*, *107*, 110, 115, *115*, 116; and the EU 23, 41, 42; and the European Court of Justice 194;

France *continued*
growth rates of real output **97**; identity 188, **188**; import and export dependency **134**; income distribution *115*, 140, **140**, *141*, 150; industrial structural changes **98**; New Right parties 48, 49, 50, 60; and the SGP (Stability and Growth Pact) 195; socialist parties 55; trade patterns 179, **179**, 180, **181**, **182**; unemployment rate **97**
Franke, R. 91, 93, 99, 101
Freiheits Partei der Schweiz 56
Fremskridtpartiet, Denmark 50, 60, 66
Fremskrittspartiet (Progressive Party), Norway 50–1, 60, 64, 66
FTAs (free trade agreements), Japan 131
Fukuda, Koji 121–38

gender: and family roles in welfare states 123; and family structure in Japan 129–30
Germany 218; as an EU hegemon 218, 220; Bundesbank 38; de-industrialization 91, 95, **98**, 99, 100, **100**, 101, *102*, *104*, *107*, 110, 113, 115, *115*, 116; economic discomfort 189; economic growth 53, 191; and the EU 23, 26, 41, 42, 196; and the European Court of Justice 194; growth rates of real output **97**; import and export dependency **134**; income distribution *115*, **140**, *141*, 150; industrial structural changes **98**; innovation-led capitalism 205; institutional characteristics **147**, 148; New Right parties 48, 50; and the SGP (Stability and Growth Pact) 195; socialist parties 55; trade patterns 179, **179**, 180, **181**, **182**; unemployment rate **97**, 189, **190**
Gilstrop, Mogens 50
Gini coefficient, Japan 130
global commons 215, *217*, 220–1
global financial crisis, 2008 32, **33**, 50, 70, 100, 101, 121, 221
'global revolution' 56
globalization 58–9, 80, 81, 82, 139, 144, 145; impact on national economies 223; and income distribution 141–2, 143, 146, **149**, 151, 158, 164; and New Right parties 51, 56; and taxation 30
Glyn, A. 113
Golden Age *204*, 205, 218, *219*
Gornitzka, Å. 191–2
gradual institutional change 74, 75; and political elements 77–80, *78*

Great Britain *see* UK
Great East Japan Earthquake, 2011 101
Greece 211; austerity policies 192; economic crisis 192, 193; economic discomfort 189; economic growth 191; and the EU 22, 40, 197; and the European Court of Justice 194; income distribution 150; institutional characteristics **147**, 148; public debt 39; trade patterns 179, **179**; unemployment rate 189, **190**, **191**
Green parties 55
growth rates of real output **97**
growth regime *71*, 71–2; and de-industrialization 91, **92**, 92–5

Hagen, Carl I. 51
Hall, Peter *71*, 72
Harada, Yuji 139–67
Hashimoto, Toru 49, 60, 62, 64, 128
Häusermann, S. 114
hegemony: and EU (European Union) trade patterns 177–80, **179**, **181**, **182**; of USA 202, 203–4, 218, 220
high-tech, low-employment economic pattern 5
historical institutionalism 72–4
Hollande, François 13, 42
Hong Kong 118n4
Høyre (Conservative Party), Norway 54
hybridization *75*, 76, 77, 78, 79

identity, and the EU (European Union) 187–8, **188**
ILO (International Labour Organization) 146
IMF (International Monetary Fund) 11, 31, 36, 40, 146, 193, 195
immigration: anti-immigration parties 48, 50, 51
implicit public debt 35
import, as element of final demand 93
'inactive full employment' 7
income distribution 121, 150; and BOPC (balance of payments constraints) 225–6, 238–44, **239**, **241**; and conflict 240, 242, 243; and de-industrialization 114–16, *115*, 117; and diversity of the neoliberal policy regime 139–43, **140**, *141*, 146–52, **147**, **149**, *153–5*, 156, *157*, *158*, 158–9, **160–1**, 162–4; Europe/Japan comparison 7–8; and institutional change 143–4, 145; Japan 7–8, *115*, 121, 130, 140, **140**, *141*, 150, **161**;

political implications of changes in 238–41, **239**; and wage–price bargaining 232–6; *see also* wage share, distribution of
incremental integration, EU (European Union) 193–5, **194**
India 58
Indonesia 118n4
Industrial Competitiveness Council, Japan 131
industrialization 80
inequality, increasing 36–7, 83, 213–14; and de-industrialization 114
inflation 41
informal constraints 77
Inglehart, Ronald 55
innovation 94, 242–3; global ranking *135*, 135–6
innovation led capitalism 211, **211**, **212**
innovation rent 207, **207**, 208
innovation-led capitalism 112, 118n4, 210
input coefficient matrix 93
input–output analysis 93; WIOD statistics *102–9*
institution (institutional structure) *78*, 78–9
institutional change: historical institutionalism 72–4; and income distribution 143–4, 145; models of **73**; and policy regimes 144–5; types of 74–7
'institutional complementarity' 143
'institutional hierarchy' 143
institutional structure *78*, 78–9
insular semi-agrarian capitalism 118n4
interdependence: and economic integration 173, *178*; and EU (European Union) trade patterns 177–80, **179**, **181**, **182**; and international relations 202, 212–14, **213**, 220
intergenerational poverty 121
intermediate demand 93
internal corporate welfare economic pattern 5
internal rate of return 125
international competition, and BOPC (balance of payments constraints) 226, 230–2, **231**
international relations 202–3, 218, *219*, 220–1; emerging industrializing capitalisms 208–9, **209**, **212**, 214–15, *216*, *217*, 218; finance-led capitalisms 208, **209**, 210, 211, 212, **212**, 214, *216*, *217*, 218, 221; and geopolitical rivalries 214; innovation-led capitalism 210; innovation/export-led regimes 210, 211, **211**, **212**; and interdependence 202, 212–14, **213**, 220; mature industrial capitalisms 215, *216*, *217*; new international system 214–15, **215**, *216–17*, 218; rentier regimes 205, *206*, **207**, 207–8, 209, **209**, 210, 212, **212**, 215, *216*, *217*, 218; two-tier world international regime 210–11, **211**, **212**; US hegemony 203, *204*, 205
international system, tripartite structure 11–12, *12*
international trade *see* trade
internationalization 4, 5, 58–9; and New Right parties 51, 56
investment 93–4; and consumption 93
Ireland: and the European Court of Justice 194; and identity 188, **188**; income distribution 150; public debt 39; trade patterns 179, **179**, 180, **182**
Ishihara, Shintaro 59–600
issue voting 55
Italy: austerity policies 192; Christian parties 53; communist parties 54–5; de-industrialization 91, 97, **98**, **100**, 99, 100, *103*, *104*, *108*, 110–11, 115, *115*, 116–17; economic growth 191; and the EU 40, 41, 42; and the European Court of Justice 194; growth rates of real output **97**; income distribution *115*, 140, **140**, *141*, 150, **161**; industrial structural changes **98**; institutional characteristics **147**, 148, 149; New Right parties 48, 49, 50, 56, 62; public debt 39; socialist parties 55; trade patterns 179, **179**, 180, **181**, **182**; unemployment rate **97**

Japan: 2015 Osaka Referendum 63–4; ageing population 124, 132, 135; changing family structures 129–30; cleavages 52–3; company welfare systems 7–8; as a consolidation state 35; and the cost of democracy 49; de-industrialization 91, 97, **98**, 99, 100, **100**, *103–4*, *106*, *109*, 112–13, 114, 115, *115*, 116, 117; debt 133, **133**, 134; domestic demand 132, 135; economic growth and income inequality 121; employment 6–7, 124; geopolitics 214, **215**; growth rates of real output **97**; growth strategies 124, 128–32; home-makers 133; import and export dependency **134**, 134–5, *135*; income distribution 7–8, *115*, 121, 130, 140,

Japan *continued*
140, *141*, 150, **161**; industrial structural changes **98**; innovation-led capitalism 112, 118n4, 205; institutional characteristics **147**, 148, 149; labour market 130; labour incentive 6–7; labour market performance 8–11, *9*; life-time employment 7; neoliberalism 122, 128–32; New Right parties 51, 60, 62, 63, 64, 66; policy transfer 66; political change 61; post-Abenomics strategy 132–6, **133**, *134*, **134**, *135*; poverty 130, 132; production regime 124; rents 205; rise of 6; social security regime 124; socialist parties 55; total income **133**, 133–4; unemployment rate **97**, 189, **190**
Japan Innovation Party 51, 60, 62, 63, 64, 66
Japan Renaissance Party 63, 64
Japan Restoration Party 49, 51, 60, 62
Japanese management style 6
'Japanization' 6
JSP (Japan Socialist Party) 55
Juncker, Jean-Claude 193

Kaldor, Nicholas 144
Kaldor–Verdoorn Law 94
Kalmbach, P. 91, 93, 99, 101
Kawamura, Takashi 60, 62
Keidanren 53
'Keynesian coalition' 81
Keynesian policy regime 71, *71*, 80, 82
Keynesian (un)competitiveness **231**, 231–2
Keynesianism 145
Kitschelt, Herbert P. 50, 55, 58, 60
Koizumi administration, Japan 128, 131
Komei Party, Japan 53
Korea: import and export dependency **134**, 135; income distribution **161**; innovation-led capitalism 118n4; institutional characteristics **147**, 148, 149; *see also* North Korea; South Korea
KrF (*Kristelig Folkeparti:* Christian People's Party), Norway 53
Kuhn, Thomas 13

labour incentives, Europe/Japan comparison 6–7
labour markets: Europe/Japan comparison 8–11, *9*; regulation, and income distribution 139, 142, 143, 146, **149**, 163
labour movement: decline of 4, 6, 10, 28, 81; and the social-democratic policy regime 4, 6–7
Labour Party, UK 54
labour productivity *153*, 156
Laeken indicators 126–7
land-industry cleavage 53, 54
Lane, Jan-Erik 52
Lange, Anders 50
Latin America 220, 221; and geopolitics 214; rentier regimes 212, **213**
Latvia 191
layering 77, 78, *78*
LDP (Liberal Democratic Party), Japan 52–3, 54, 62
leaders, charismatic 13
Lechman, E. 189
Lefkofridi, Zoe 171–201
'left-libertarian' parties 55
Lega Nord (Northern League), Italy 50, 56, 62
Lehman Brothers bankruptcy 50, 70, 76, 122, 208; *see also* global financial crisis 2008
liberal capitalism 124
liberal democracy 12–13; contemporary European crisis 19, 24–6
Liberal Democrat Party, UK 54
Liberal Democratic Party, Russia 58
liberal market economies 123
Liberal Party, UK 54
liberal welfare states 123
linear regression 152
Lipset, Seymour M. 52, 59–60
Lisbon Strategy, EU 126, 127
Lisbon Treaty, 2009 188
Lithuania 191
Lordon, Frédéric 84n5
low-paid employment 6, 9
low-wage service economy economic pattern 6
Luxembourg 194

M5S (*MoVimento 5 Stelle:* 5 Star Movement), Italy 48
Maastricht Treaty 1992 22, 32, 183, 186
Magara, Hideko 3–16
Mair, Peter 52
Malaysia 118n4
Malta 179, **179**, 191
Manning, Preston 58
manufacturing sector 92, **92**, 93; other manufacturing, international comparative analysis of de-industrialization *99*, *102*, *103*, *104*,

105, *106*, *107*, *108*, *109*, 110, 111, 112, 116; *see also* export core manufacturing; other manufacturing
Market Integration Plan (EU), 1985 125–6
market-based capitalism 95, 97, 111, 116
Marktvolk (creditor constituencies of the debt state) 35, *36*, 40
Marshall–Lerner condition 228, 230
Marx, Karl 54
mature industrial capitalisms 215, *216*, *217*
Mediterranean capitalism 95, 97, 100, 110, 123
MFA (multiple factor analysis) 146–50, **147**, **149**, 150, 158
mining rent 207, **207**, 208
multilevel analysis 151–2, *153–5*, 156, 162
multinational companies 81, 82

Nakasone, Yasuhito 56, 128
nation building, four phases of 59–60
negative de-industrialization 95, *96*, 99, 116; Germany 101; Italy 111, 117; Japan 112; UK 111, 112, 117
neo-functionalism: and EU disintegration 171–2, 177–99; suppositions and hypotheses 172–7
neoclassical (un)competitiveness **231**, 231–2
neoliberal coalition 82–3
neoliberal parties 61
neoliberal policy regime 3, 71, *71*, 144–5; crisis of 70; diversity of, and income distribution 139–43, **140**, *141*, 146–52, **147**, **149**, *153–5*, 156, *157*, *158*, 158–9, **160–1**, 162–4; and Japan 61–2; and New Right parties 47, 55–6, *57*, 58, 60–1
neoliberalism 37, 83–4, 122, 124–5, 223; and democracy 3, 83–4; economic backgrounds and political powers of 80–3; and the EU 22; and fiscal consolidation 32
Netherlands: economic discomfort 189; and the European Court of Justice 194; income distribution 150; institutional characteristics **147**, 148; New Right parties 48, 50; trade patterns 179, **179**, 180, **181**, **182**
'new individualism' 10
New Left parties 55, *57*, 58
New Right parties 47–51, 56, *57*, 58–9, 66–7; global perspective on 59–65, *65*; global phenomenon of 51–2
New Zealand 150
newly-industrialized countries 81
Nishi, Hiroshi 223–47
Nixon shock 76, 77
Nokyo 53
'non-free full employment' 7
North Korea 211
North, Douglass C. 77
Northern member states of EU 23, 25, 39, 41
Norway: Christian parties 53; conservative and liberal parties 54; income distribution 150; institutional characteristics **147**, 148; New Right parties 50–1, 60, 64, 66; socialist parties 55
Ny Demokrati (New Democracy), Sweden 50

Obama, Barack 13
Obuchi administration, Japan 128
O'Connor, James 28
OECD 31, 146
'Okun's Misery Index' 189, 190
Old Right parties 65
oligarchy 11
OMC (Open Method of Coordination) 127
O'Neill, J. 179
opportunity, and policy regime change 11–12, *12*
Osaka Referendum, 2015, Japan 63–4
Osaka Restoration Association, Japan 60, 62, 64
other industry, international comparative analysis of de-industrialization *99*, *102*, *103*, *104*, *105*, *106*, *107*, *108*, *109*, 111, 112
other manufacturing, international comparative analysis of de-industrialization *99*, *102*, *103*, *104*, *105*, *106*, *107*, *108*, *109*, 110, 111, 112, 116
output growth 92, **92**, 94
'outside of politics' 14
owner–worker cleavage 53, 54–5

paid labour relations systems 123
paradigm shifts 13
part-time employment 10–11
Party for Future Generation, Japan 60
party freezing era 49, 52, 53, 55, *57*, 67
path dependence 72–4, **73**, 77
Pax Americana 202, 203, 205, 218
PCA (principal component analysis) 146, 147

PCd'I (*Partito Comunista Italiano:* Communist Party of Italy) 54–5
PDS (*Partito Democratico della Sinistra:* Democratic Party of the Left), Italy 55
peace dividend 31
pension funds 81
Perot, Ross 58
Philippines 118n4
Piketty, Thomas 121
Plaid Cymru 53
pluralistic conflicts, and the EU (European Union) 175, *178*
Poland 191, 194
policy regimes 3–4, 11–14, 70–1, *71*, 72; and institutional change 144–5
policy transfer 66
'political coalitions' 79–80
political parties, and policy regimes 70–1
political power, and neoliberalism 82–3
political–economic equilibrium 143
politicization, and the EU (European Union) 174, *178*, 192, 196–7
populism: and New Right parties 50–1; populist parties in Europe 25
Portugal: economic discomfort 189; and the European Court of Justice 194; income distribution 150; institutional characteristics **147**, 148; and the SGP (Stability and Growth Pact) 195; trade patterns 180, **182**
positive de-industrialization 95, *96*, 116; France 110; Germany 101; Japan 112, 114; UK 111
post-Fordist transformation 10
poverty 121, 127; EU policy 127, 128; Japan 130, 132
privatization: Japan 128–9; 'privatized Keynesianism' 32
product market regulation, and income distribution 139, 142, 146, 148, **148**, 156, 164
product market systems 123
production, dispersal of 6
production function 141
production regimes 122–3
productivity growth 92, **92**, 93–4
productivity regime 94, 116
professionals, non-manufacturing employment 10–11
'profit-led growth' 93
Progressive Party (*Fremskridtspartiet*), Denmark 48
protest movements in the EU (European Union) 196–7
Przeworski, Adam 70–1, 72, 144–5
PS (*Parti socialiste:* Socialist Party), France 55
PS (*Perussuomalaiset:* True Finns) 48
public attitudes towards EU (European Union) 21, 173, **178**, 180, 183–9, **184**, **185**, **186**, **187**, **188**
'public choice' school 27
public debt *see* debt state
public expenditure cuts 31, 34, 35; *see also* austerity policies
public goods 215
public perceptions of EU (European Union) 21, 173, *178*, 180, 183–9, **184**, **185**, **186**, **187**, **188**
public services, international comparative analysis of de-industrialization 11, 99, *99*, **100**, 101, *102*, *103*, *104*, *105*, *106*, *107*, *108*, *109*, 110, 112, 113, 115, *115*, 117
PVV (*Partij voor de Vrijheid:* Liberal Party), Netherlands 48

QI (quantitative easing) 208
quasi-collectivist capitalism 123

radical institutional change 75, *75*, *78*
radical right *see* New Right parties
radical right wing populism *see* New Right parties
random-slope models 156
Reagan, Ronald 56, 65
real output, growth rates of **97**
Reform Party, Canada 58
refugee crisis 186, 197
regime: concepts of 70–2, *71*; definition 70
regime changes 72
regime crisis, and path dependence 72–4, **73**
regional parties 53
régulation theory 15, 71, 75, 84n5, 85n8, 91, 92, 93, 116, 123, 143, 144, 202
Reich, Robert B. 83
relative deprivation 125
REML (restricted maximum likelihood) 152, 156
rentier regimes 205, *206*, *207*, 207–8, 209, **209**, 210, 212, **212**, 215, *216*, *217*, 218
'reproduction by adaptation' (institutional change) 74
Republikaner (Republicans), Germany 50
research and development 125
Ricardo, D. 207
right wing extremism *see* New Right parties

right wing parties: Europe 20–1; *see also* New Right parties
right wing populist parties *see* New Right parties
RKP (*Suomen ruotsalainen kansanpuolue:* Swedish Peoples' Party), Finland 53
ROE (return on equity) 125
Rokkan, Stein 51–2, 59–60, 65
Rose, Richard 52
Rosenhuk, Z. 192
Rowthorn, Bob 9, *9*, 94, 95, 113
Russia: import and export dependency **134**; New Right parties 58; as a rentier economy 203, 207, 218

S&D (Group of the Progressive Alliance of Socialists and Democrats in the European Parliament) 51, 66
Salamon, Lester 123
SAP (*Sveriges socialdemokratiska arbetaparti:* Swedish Social Democratic Party), Sweden 55
Saudi Arabia 207
Schengen Agreement 186
Schmitter, Philippe C. 19–26, 171–201
Schulz, Martin 193
Schwander, H. 114
Scotland 53
Scottish National Party 53, 62
SD (*Sverigedemocraterna:* Swedish Democratic Party) 48
SDJP (Social Democratic Party of Japan) 61
security, and the EU 173, *178*, 186–7, **187**
seikaisaihen, Japan 61
Senterpartiet (Center Party), Norway 54
service sector 5, 81; 'cost disease' of 28; and de-industrialization 94; *see also* business-related services; consumer services; financial services; public services
SFP *(Svenska folkpartiet i Finland)* 53
SGP (Stability and Growth Pact) 195
shale gas 207, 209
Shiratori, Hiroshi 47–69
Singapore 118n4
Single European Act 1986 22
Single European Act 1987 186
single-person households, Japan 129
Six-pack 40
Slovakia 191
Social Charter: Community Charter of Fundamental Social Rights for Workers 126
'social coalitions' 80
social contract, rupture of 22–3
social dumping 125
'social Europe' 128
social exclusion 125; EU policy 126, 127
social security *see* welfare state
social-democratic capitalism 95, 124
social-democratic policy regime *57*; decline of 9–10; limits of 3, 4–11
social-democratic welfare states 123
Soskice, David *71*, 72, 122–3
South Korea 218; *see also* Korea
Southern member states of EU 23, 25, 39
sovereign debt, EU member states 20
sovereignty, national, and the EU 22, 24
Spain: and the European Court of Justice 194; identity 188, **188**; income distribution 150; public debt 39; trade patterns 180, **181**, **182**
SPD (*Sozialdemokratische Partei Deutschlands:* Social Democratic Party of Germany), Germany 55
'spill-around' 174
'spill-backs' 172
'spill-overs' 172, 174
Staatsvolk (citizen constituencies of the debt state) 35, *36*, 40
Stackelberg leaders 210
state capitalism 123
state–church cleavage 53
Stiglitz, J. E. 122
stock prices, increases in 125
Stockhammer, E. 142, 143
Stopler–Samuelson theorem 141–2
Streek, Wolfgang 27–46, 77–8
sub-culture-based politics 51–2
subject *vs.* dominant culture cleavage 62
super-rich, and neoliberalism 82
'supra-national governance' 24
'survival and return' (institutional change) 74
Sverdrup, U. 191–2
Sweden: economic growth 191; and the European Court of Justice 194; fiscal crises 31; income distribution **140**, *141*, 150; institutional characteristics **147**, 148; New Right parties 48, 50; socialist parties 55; as a technocratic rational democracy 13; trade patterns 180, **181**, **182**
Switzerland: income distribution 150; institutional characteristics **147**, 148; New Right parties 50, 56

Tahara, Shinji 91–120, 93, 99
Taiwan 118n4
Takenaka, Heizō 131
Tax Reduction Japan 51, 60, 62, 66
tax state (*Steuerstaat*) 27
'tax wedge' 131
taxation: and the 'fiscal crisis of the state' **29**, 29–30; Europe 23; tax revenue as a percentage of GDP **29**
Tea Party movement 35
technocratic rational democracy 12, 13
Terzi, A. 179
Thailand 118n4
Thatcher, Margaret 56, 65
Thelen, Kathleen 74–5, 77–8
Thirlwall's law 246n2
'threshold effects' **73**, *75*, 76, 77, 174
tipping points 76, 77, 79
TPP (Trans-Pacific Partnership) 131
trade: and de-industrialization 94–5; EU (European Union) patterns 177–80, **179**, **181**, **182**; and neoliberal policy regime 145
trade-led industrializing capitalism 118n4
'transfer union' 41, 42
Treaty of Nice, 2001 126, 188
trickle-down effect 121, 124
trilemma **241**, 241–3
tripartite structure 11–12, *12*
Troika 195
TROs (transnational regional organization) 171–2; *see also* EU (European Union)
TTIP (Transatlantic Trade and Investment Partnership) 131

Uemura, Hiroyasu 91–120
UK: 2015 General Election 62, 63; de-industrialization 91, 97, *98*, 99, *100*, *103*, *105–6*, *108*, 111–12, 114, 115, *115*, 116, 117; and the EU 22; and the European Court of Justice 194; financial services industry 30; growth rates of real output **97**; identity 188, **188**; import and export dependency **134**; income distribution *115*, 150, **160**; industrial structural changes **98**; institutional characteristics **147**, 148; New Right parties 48, 50; regional parties 53; trade patterns 179, **179**; unemployment rate **97**
UKIP (UK Independence Party), UK 48, 63, 64–5
unemployment 8–9; and the debt state 29; EU (European Union) 189, **190**, 191, 198; Europe/Japan comparison 6–7; international comparison of rates **97**; and neoliberal policy regime 145; and the social-democratic policy regime 7; *see also* employment
unions: decline of 4, 6, 10, 28, 81; and labour market regulation 142; and the social-democratic policy regime 4, 6–7
upper classes, and neoliberalism 82
urban rent 207, **207**, 208
Urwin, Derek W. 52
USA: balanced budget policies **31**, 31–2; as a consolidation state 35; de-industrialization **98**, 99, 100, **100**; economic growth and income inequality 121; economic policies 192–3; financial crisis, 2008 205, 208; financial services industry 30; financialization 30; fiscal consolidation 32; geopolitics **215**; growth rates of real output **97**; hegemony 202, 203–4, 218, 220; import and export dependency **134**; income distribution 140, **140**, *141*, 150, **160**; institutional characteristics **147**, 148; interdependence **213**; New Right parties 58; peace dividend 31; public debt 30; QI (quantitative easing) 208; shale gas 207, 209; unemployment rate **97**, 189, **190**

Venstre (Liberal Party), Norway 54
Vintila, Cristina Daniela 188
Vlaams Blok (Flemish Block), Belgium 50, 56, 62
VoC (varieties of capitalism) 145
voter behaviour in Europe 25

wage dumping 189
wage share, distribution of 139–41, **140**, *141*, 162–4; effect of institutional changes on 150–2, *153–5*, 156, *157*, 158, 158–9, **160–1**, 162; multivariate analysis **146–50**, 149, **147**; preceding studies 141–5
'wage-led growth' 93
wage–price bargaining 232–6
Wales 53
Wallonia 50
Washington Consensus 214
Watanabe, Yoshimi 60
Weberian political entrepreneurship 12, 13
Weiss, L. 223
welfare states 47, 52, 123, 221; crisis in 4; Europe 8, 221; and income distribution

142, 143, 146, 148, **149**, 150, 151, 158, 162, 164; and New Right parties 59–60; social security regime 124; social-democratic 123; types of 123
welfare, company provision of in Japan 7–8
Wells, J. 95
Western Europe: labour movement 4; social-democratic policy regime 3–4; welfare state 8
women: employment 10–11; and family roles in welfare states 123; and family structure in Japan 129–30
working poor 9; Japan 130
World Bank 36, 146

Yamada, Toshio 70–87
Your Party, Japan 60, 62

Zhirinovsky, Vladimir 58

For Product Safety Concerns and Information please contact our EU
representative GPSR@taylorandfrancis.com
Taylor & Francis Verlag GmbH, Kaufingerstraße 24, 80331 München, Germany

www.ingramcontent.com/pod-product-compliance
Ingram Content Group UK Ltd.
Pitfield, Milton Keynes, MK11 3LW, UK
UKHW022037061126
477531UK00008B/382
* 9 7 8 1 1 3 8 3 6 5 9 9 5 *